2018

JANUARY
M	T	W	T	F	S	S
1	2	3	4	5	6	7
8	9	10	11	12	13	14
15	16	17	18	19	20	21
22	23	24	25	26	27	28
29	30	31				

FEBRUARY
M	T	W	T	F	S	S
			1	2	3	4
5	6	7	8	9	10	11
12	13	14	15	16	17	18
19	20	21	22	23	24	25
26	27	28				

MARCH
M	T	W	T	F	S	S
			1	2	3	4
5	6	7	8	9	10	11
12	13	14	15	16	17	18
19	20	21	22	23	24	25
26	27	28	29	30	31	

APRIL
M	T	W	T	F	S	S
						1
2	3	4	5	6	7	8
9	10	11	12	13	14	15
16	17	18	19	20	21	22
23	24	25	26	27	28	29
30						

MAY
M	T	W	T	F	S	S
	1	2	3	4	5	6
7	8	9	10	11	12	13
14	15	16	17	18	19	20
21	22	23	24	25	26	27
28	29	30	31			

JUNE
M	T	W	T	F	S	S
				1	2	3
4	5	6	7	8	9	10
11	12	13	14	15	16	17
18	19	20	21	22	23	24
25	26	27	28	29	30	

JULY
M	T	W	T	F	S	S
						1
2	3	4	5	6	7	8
9	10	11	12	13	14	15
16	17	18	19	20	21	22
23	24	25	26	27	28	29
30	31					

AUGUST
M	T	W	T	F	S	S
		1	2	3	4	5
6	7	8	9	10	11	12
13	14	15	16	17	18	19
20	21	22	23	24	25	26
27	28	29	30	31		

SEPTEMBER
M	T	W	T	F	S	S
					1	2
3	4	5	6	7	8	9
10	11	12	13	14	15	16
17	18	19	20	21	22	23
24	25	26	27	28	29	30

OCTOBER
M	T	W	T	F	S	S
1	2	3	4	5	6	7
8	9	10	11	12	13	14
15	16	17	18	19	20	21
22	23	24	25	26	27	28
29	30	31				

NOVEMBER
M	T	W	T	F	S	S
			1	2	3	4
5	6	7	8	9	10	11
12	13	14	15	16	17	18
19	20	21	22	23	24	25
26	27	28	29	30		

DECEMBER
M	T	W	T	F	S	S
					1	2
3	4	5	6	7	8	9
10	11	12	13	14	15	16
17	18	19	20	21	22	23
24	25	26	27	28	29	30
31						

2019

JANUARY
M	T	W	T	F	S	S
	1	2	3	4	5	6
7	8	9	10	11	12	13
14	15	16	17	18	19	20
21	22	23	24	25	26	27
28	29	30	31			

FEBRUARY
M	T	W	T	F	S	S
				1	2	3
4	5	6	7	8	9	10
11	12	13	14	15	16	17
18	19	20	21	22	23	24
25	26	27	28			

MARCH
M	T	W	T	F	S	S
				1	2	3
4	5	6	7	8	9	10
11	12	13	14	15	16	17
18	19	20	21	22	23	24
25	26	27	28	29	30	31

APRIL
M	T	W	T	F	S	S
1	2	3	4	5	6	7
8	9	10	11	12	13	14
15	16	17	18	19	20	21
22	23	24	25	26	27	28
29	30					

MAY
M	T	W	T	F	S	S
		1	2	3	4	5
6	7	8	9	10	11	12
13	14	15	16	17	18	19
20	21	22	23	24	25	26
27	28	29	30	31		

JUNE
M	T	W	T	F	S	S
					1	2
3	4	5	6	7	8	9
10	11	12	13	14	15	16
17	18	19	20	21	22	23
24	25	26	27	28	29	30

JULY
M	T	W	T	F	S	S
1	2	3	4	5	6	7
8	9	10	11	12	13	14
15	16	17	18	19	20	21
22	23	24	25	26	27	28
29	30	31				

AUGUST
M	T	W	T	F	S	S
			1	2	3	4
5	6	7	8	9	10	11
12	13	14	15	16	17	18
19	20	21	22	23	24	25
26	27	28	29	30	31	

SEPTEMBER
M	T	W	T	F	S	S
						1
2	3	4	5	6	7	8
9	10	11	12	13	14	15
16	17	18	19	20	21	22
23	24	25	26	27	28	29
30						

OCTOBER
M	T	W	T	F	S	S
	1	2	3	4	5	6
7	8	9	10	11	12	13
14	15	16	17	18	19	20
21	22	23	24	25	26	27
28	29	30	31			

NOVEMBER
M	T	W	T	F	S	S
				1	2	3
4	5	6	7	8	9	10
11	12	13	14	15	16	17
18	19	20	21	22	23	24
25	26	27	28	29	30	

DECEMBER
M	T	W	T	F	S	S
						1
2	3	4	5	6	7	8
9	10	11	12	13	14	15
16	17	18	19	20	21	22
23	24	25	26	27	28	29
30	31					

GW01325900

Court of Protection Practice 2018

THE QUARKXPRESS HANDBOOK
Windows Edition

The QuarkXPress Handbook
Windows Edition

Diane Burns
Sharyn Venit

BANTAM BOOKS
NEW YORK • TORONTO • LONDON • SYDNEY • AUCKLAND

THE QUARKXPRESS HANDBOOK
Windows Edition
A Bantam Book
November 1992

QuarkXPress and QuarkXTension
are registered trademarks of Quark, Inc.

*Throughout the book, the trade names and trademarks of some companies
and products have been used, and no such uses are intended to convey
endorsement of or other affiliations with the book or software.*

All rights reserved.
Copyright © 1990, 1992 by Diane Burns and Sharyn Venit
No part of this book may be reproduced or transmitted in any form or
by any means, electronic or mechanical, including photocopying,
recording, or by any information storage and retrieval system, without
permission in writing from the publisher.
For information address: Bantam Books.

ISBN 0-553-37007-3

Published simultaneously in the United States and Canada

Bantam Books are published by Bantam Books, a division of Bantam
Doubleday Dell Publishing Group, Inc. Its trademark, consisting of the
words "Bantam Books" and the portrayal of a rooster, is Registered in
U.S. Patent and Trademark Office and in other countries. Marca
Registrada, Bantam Books, 666 Fifth Avenue, New York, New York 10103

PRINTED IN THE UNITED STATES OF AMERICA

0 9 8 7 6 5 4 3 2 1

Foreword

From the time Quark released the first version of QuarkXPress for the Macintosh in 1987, our company has been committed to professionalism in the publishing world. We are proud to observe that QuarkXPress has earned high praises from professional designers and publishers. Now users of IBM PCs and compatibles can also benefit by the extensive advantage of QuarkXPress over other products in this category.

A commitment to professionalism in publishing means a commitment to the principle of the free press. Publishing technology is too important to be placed in the hands of a few. Small publishers need as much access to affordable quality tools as large publishers do. Our users include nonprofit organizations helping to make this a better world, educational institutions working with our youth, small businesses concerned with profit margin, and special interest groups with information to share.

At the same time, it is critical that publishing solutions include the full complement of features from layout to design to color separation. The list of professional publishers who use QuarkXPress stands as testimony that QuarkXPress is truly an "industrial-strength" tool: Time, Inc., Tribune Media Services, Mattel Toys, CBS Records, Landor Associates, and others.

We are very pleased to have been involved in this Bantam book project with two writers I have known and respected for many years. I sought them out years ago as industry experts and experienced users of publishing tools to show them early versions of QuarkXPress, and collect their praises and criticisms.

The real value of this book is that it incorporates the practical experiences and knowledge of the authors and other QuarkXPress experts, readily serving as your own "off the shelf" consultants.

—*Fred Ebrahimi, President, Quark, Inc.*

Preface

The *QuarkXPress Handbook, Windows Edition* is a complete reference designed to answer your questions about all QuarkXPress commands, tools, and techniques. The book is an invaluable tool for professionals who use the program every day, and will be useful to anyone seeking professional results. It can also be used as a training manual for beginning QuarkXPress users, or as a reference for professional designers who need to know the capabilities of QuarkXPress for Windows.

The book includes expert advice about all QuarkXPress features, tips about increasing speed and productivity, and specific techniques used to create special effects or solve particular problems. The beginning user will quickly learn how to use QuarkXPress tools and commands. The intermediate user will learn new and valuable techniques for producing complicated documents. The advanced user will receive expert tips on how to use QuarkXPress more effectively, and gain insight into how experienced publishers solve complex problems with QuarkXPress.

How This Book Is Organized

We have organized this book into two parts which follow a brief introductory chapter that describes QuarkXPress and the production process.

Part I: Using QuarkXPress

The first eight chapters provide an overview of the tools, commands, and features available in QuarkXPress for Windows. In Chapter 1 you will find an introduction to basic Windows operations and an overview of the screen display in QuarkXPress including the Document window, and the various palettes. This chapter defines the basic terminology that is particular to Windows and QuarkXPress.

Chapter 2 goes through the preliminary steps in starting a new document and positioning elements on a page. Chapter 3 continues the page layout process in adding pages to a document, creating multiple master pages, editing items on a page, and changing QuarkXPress *defaults*. Chapters 4 and 5 give detailed descriptions of the commands used to handle text. Chapter 6 describes how graphics and imported pictures can be handled. Chapter 7 covers how to create and apply colors, as well as how to set up documents for color separation. Chapter 8 discusses all of the issues related to printing a document.

Part II: Advanced Techniques

The next seven chapters describe some of the more advanced techniques and procedures that can be used to save time or solve difficult problems. Chapter 9 describes how to set up a template system, with some design tips included. Chapter 10 is full of tips for minimizing the time and trouble involved in laying out pages. Chapter 11 offers more tips specific to handling text created on a mainframe computer or in a database, and Chapter 12 offers tips specific to typography. Chapter 13 includes some special tips on handling graphics. Chapter 14 offers ideas about project management and file organization methods for large projects or workgroup environments.

The impact of desktop publishing on designers, professional publishing companies, corporate publications departments, and self-publishing associations and individuals is best seen through the experiences of those who have made the transition from traditional methods to electronic publishing over the past few years. Chapter 15 of this book offers four case studies of professional publications that were once produced using traditional methods and are now produced using QuarkXPress. For each example you will find descriptions of how the publisher organized the project and/or handled tricky page elements.

The appendix lists some of the QuarkXPress shortcuts we use most frequently.

Conventions Used in This Book

We have included icons or **symbols throughout** this book to make it easy to find topics or interpret **terms that apply to** icons you will see on the screen while working in QuarkXPress. Most of the symbols embedded in the text are self-explanatory in that they look like the element they are intended to represent.

Borrowing the convention used in the QuarkXPress manuals, we have used a special arrow symbol (➛) **as a shorthand** method of referencing commands and their menus. **Instead of saying** "...choose the Cut command from the Edit menu..." **we say simply** "...choose Edit ➛ Cut..."

We have added two icons in the **left margin** as reference aids:

A tip icon appears next to **paragraphs that** describe the fastest method to accomplish a specific **task, or that describe tricks** that can make production more efficient.

The alert icon appears next to **paragraphs that** mention things you should not or cannot do in QuarkXPress, **or things** that might happen if you change something on a page. In most cases these are simply things you need to be aware of in **making decisions.**

Acknowledgments

The QuarkXPress Handbook, Windows Edition was made possible thanks to the cooperation and participation of a large number of people, only some of whom could be named here.

We first thank the contributors to the case studies in Chapter 15 for their time and efforts in supplying examples of documents they have created using QuarkXPress.

For contributions to Chapter 15 we acknowledge Gary Ferguson and Wendy Croft at Landor Associates, Bob Clifford, Wade Lapan of Tribune Media Services, Rick Young, Rand Worrel, and Luis Solorzano from Mattel Toys, Tamura Westmark, Christine Homan and Michael Grossman of *Entertainment Weekly*, Diane Croce and Barry DeJaynes from Croce Advertising, Amy Jordan of Rocky Mountain News, Rick Boyde, and all the support staff who helped assemble sample disks and pages.

The people at Quark, Inc., were extremely helpful in supplying names of QuarkXPress users, Beta copies of the software, and early drafts of their manuals for the product—this in the midst of their own heavy production schedule for meeting their own release deadlines. We especially thank Dee Buchanan for her assistance throughout the project; John Cruise, Jeff Gregory, Eric Fife and Paula Budzak for reviewing the manuscript; Johanna McLaverty (IRL QSS Ireland) for providing information on International Versions; and Mark Niemann-Ross for providing information on QuarkXTensions. We especially thank Fred Ebrahimi for his enthusiasm and interest in this project.

The production group at TechArt (San Francisco) was consistently calm and courteous in meeting the last-minute deadlines that always result when the writers keep writing and the editors keep editing up to the last minute. In particular we thank Kim Nogay and Glen Shannon who were responsible for the layout of the book.

Acknowledgments

Finally, we would like to thank a group that is not often mentioned in book acknowledgments—the people at Bantam Electronic Publishing and their freelance editors, especially Michael Roney who (as the primary editor and project manager) was a great support throughout the project.

We would have liked to include every individual who helped on this book by name, however in some cases the help came anonymously through the companies we contacted, and some companies prefer to be listed by company name only rather than credit individuals who were assigned the task of helping us. If you helped in any way with this book, please know that we are very appreciative.

Book Overview

Introduction   3

PART I   USING QUARKXPRESS

1   *Basic Concepts and Terminology*   23
2   *Creating One Page*   55
3   *Expanding the Document*   109
4   *Word Processing*   147
5   *Typography*   195
6   *Graphics*   227
7   *Color*   261
8   *Printing*   289

PART II   ADVANCED TECHNIQUES

9   *Templates and Design*   329
10   *Advanced Page Layout*   351
11   *Working with Text from Databases and XPress Tags*   379
12   *Tips on Typography*   401
13   *Special Graphic Techniques*   423
14   *Managing Documents*   445
15   *Case Studies*   461

Appendix: Summary of Keyboard Shortcuts   477

Index   483

Contents

Forward v

Preface vii

    How This Book Is Organized vii

        Part I: Using QuarkXPress vii Part II: Advanced Techniques viii

    Conventions Used in This Book ix

Acknowledgments xi

Introduction 3

    Desktop Publishing: A Brief History 3

    System Requirements 4

    Anatomy of a QuarkXPress Document 4

    Desktop vs. Traditional Publishing 6

        Design Traditions 6 Typesetting Traditions 7 Printing Traditions 7 Computer Traditions 8

    Overview of Publishing with QuarkXPress 8

        Design Pages and Typography 9 Collect Text 10 Collect Illustrations 11 Build the Pages in QuarkXPress 11 Final Reproduction, Binding, and Distribution 13

Desktop Publishing Systems 14
QuarkXPress and Other Software 14
Equipment Configurations 15

Summary 19

PART I USING QUARKXPRESS

1 *Basic Concepts and Terminology* 23

Microsoft Windows Basics 24
Using Drop-Down Menus 24   Controlling a Window 26
Making Entries in a Dialog Box 28   The Control Menu 30
Using the Cut, Copy, and Paste Commands 30   Using Paste
Special, Paste Link, and Links Commands 31

QuarkXPress Basics 32
Installing the Program 32   Starting QuarkXPress 32

Examining a QuarkXPress Document 33
Master Pages and Document Pages 34   Lines, Text Boxes, and
Picture Boxes 35   Relationships between Items 36
Guides 36   Style Sheets 37   Templates and Documents 38

Examining QuarkXPress Windows and Palettes 39
Examining the Document Window 40   Examining the Tool
Palette 40   Examining the Measurements Palette 43
Examining the Document Layout Palette 45   Examining the
Style Sheets Palette 46   Examining the Colors Palette 46
Examining the Trap Information Palette 47   Examining the
Pasteboard 48   Examining the Menus 48

Summary 54

2 *Creating One Page* 55

Setting Up a New Document 56
Organizing Your Disk Files 56   Creating a New Document 57
Building a New Document from an Existing Document 64

Viewing Pages on the Screen 65
Using the Scroll Bars, Grabber Hand, and Keyboard
Equivalents 65   Using the View Menu Commands and
Keyboard Shortcuts 66   Using the View Percent Area 67
Using the Zoom Tool 68   Hiding and Displaying Nonprinting
Elements 69   Hiding and Displaying Palettes 70

Creating Text Boxes, Picture Boxes, and Lines   71
   Creating a Box 71   Creating a Line 72

Selecting Items   72
   Selecting One Item 72   Selecting Multiple Items 73   Using the Select All Command 74

Moving and Resizing Items   74
   Using the Mouse 75   Using the Measurements Palette 75   Using the Item → Modify Command 76

Rotating Items   78

Changing the Appearance of Items   80
   Applying Color and Shade to Items 80   Adding a Frame to a Box 81

Importing Text and Pictures   83
   Importing Text 83   Importing Pictures 85

Deleting Items   86
   Deleting Lines or Boxes 86   Deleting Text or Graphics from Within a Box 87   Undoing Your Most Recent Action 87

Using Rulers to Position Items on a Page   88
   Ruler Guides 89   Using the Snap-to Effect 90

Controlling Text Runaround   91

Duplicating Items   92
   Using the Duplicate Command 93   Using the Step and Repeat Command 93

Arranging Items in Layers   94
   Clicking through Layers 94   Using the Send to Back/Bring to Front Commands 94

Aligning Items   95

Creating Relationships between Items   95
   Linking Text Boxes 96   Anchoring Text and Graphics 99   Grouping Items 101   Constraining Items within a Box 103   Locking Items 104

Saving Your Work   104
   Saving a Document or Template 104   Saving with a Changed Name, Format, or Drive/Directory Location 106   Reverting to

the Most Recently Saved Version 106   Closing a Document Window 107   Quitting QuarkXPress 107

Summary 107

3 Expanding the Document 109

Working with Master Pages 109

Creating a New Master Page 111   Naming a Master Page 112   Viewing and Editing a Master Page 113   Adding Text and Graphic Elements to a Master Page 114   Applying a Master Page to a Document Page 117

Adding, Deleting, and Moving Pages 120

Adding Pages 120   Deleting Pages 123   Moving Pages 123   Copying Pages from One Document to Another 125   Viewing Different Pages 125

Numbering Pages and Sectioning a Document 127

Assigning Page Numbers 127   Dividing a Document into Sections 128   Referencing Page Numbers 129

Using the QuarkXPress Library 130

Library Labels 131

Changing Preferences 132

Setting Application Preferences 133   Setting General Preferences 137   Setting Typographic Preferences 143   Setting Tool Preferences 144

Summary 145

4 Word Processing 147

Setting Up a Text Box 148

Setting Columns 148   Gutter Width 149   Text Inset 149

Sources of Text 149

Typing Text 149   Importing Text 153   Text from a Library 157   Pasting Text from the Clipboard 158   Using Object Linking and Embedding with Text 158

Selecting and Editing Text 158

Basic Windows Techniques for Selecting Text 159
QuarkXPress Techniques for Selecting Text 160

Character Formatting 160
    Font 162   Size 163   Type Style 164   Color 166
    Shade 167

Paragraph Formatting 167
    Alignment 168   Indents 169   Space Before/Space After
    Paragraphs 171   Keep with Next Paragraph 172   Keep Lines
    Together 172   Tabs 172   Paragraph Formatting Characters
    175

Working with Style Sheets 177
    Creating and Editing Style Sheets 178   Applying Style Sheets
    180   Deleting Style Sheets 181   Duplicating Style Sheet
    Specifications 182   Appending Style Sheets from Other
    Documents 182

Finding and Changing Text 183
    Find or Change Text 185   Find or Change Character
    Attributes 186

Checking Spelling 188
    Customizing Your Own Dictionaries 191

Exporting Text to Other Programs 192

Summary 193

5 *Typography* 195

Setting Global Conditions 195
    Loading Screen Fonts 196   Typographic Preferences 197

Special Typographic Characters 202

Working with Leading 203
    Setting the First Baseline 204   Lock to Baseline Grid 206
    Vertical Alignment 207   Baseline Shift 207

Hyphenation and Justification 208
    Creating and Editing H&Js 209   Applying H&Js to Text 212
    Deleting H&Js 213   Duplicating H&J Specifications 213
    Appending H&Js from Other Documents 213   Suggested
    Hyphenation 214   Discretionary Hyphens 214
    Hyphenation Exceptions 215

Kerning and Tracking Text   215
    Editing Tracking Values 218   Global Kerning Adjustments 219   Editing Kerning Tables 220

Special Effects   222
    Horizontal Scale 222   Drop Caps 223   Applying Rules to Text 224

Summary   226

6 Graphics   227

Working with QuarkXPress Drawing Tools   228
    A Review of Modifying Picture Boxes 229   Changing the Shape of Picture Boxes 231   Reshaping Polygons 232   Modifying Lines 233

Importing Graphics from Other Sources   238
    Types of Graphics 239   Importing Graphics 244   Using OLE 247

Manipulating Imported Graphics   248
    Scaling Imported Graphics 249   Moving a Picture Within a Box 250   Rotating a Picture Within a Box 251   Skewing a Picture Within a Box 251

Applying Color and Contrast to Pictures   251
    Applying Color and Shade to a Picture 253   Applying Contrast to a Picture 254

Defining Halftone Screens   257
    Applying Predefined Screen Setting 257   Applying Custom Screens 259

Summary   260

7 Color   261

General Considerations   262
    Color Calibration 262   Spot Color vs. Process Color 263   Screen Angles 264

Creating Colors   266
    The Edit Color Dialog Box 267   Appending Colors 273   The Edit Trap Dialog Box 274

Applying Color   274
    Applying Color to Text, Rules, and Pictures 275   Applying Color to Lines and Box Backgrounds 277   Applying Two-color Blends 278   Applying Registration "Color" 279

Working with Trapping   280
    Setting Automatic Trapping 280   Trapping Colors 281   Trapping Items 283   Separating Graphics Created in Other Programs 285

Summary   287

8 Printing   289

Differences Between Printers   290
    Resolution 290   Printer Fonts 291   Paper Size and Type 291   Color 292

Printing from QuarkXPress   293
    Choosing the Target Printer 293   Printer Setup 296   The Print Command 300

Making a PostScript File Version of a Document   306

Special Considerations in Printing   307
    Printing Master Pages 307   Font Management 307   Working with Large Picture Files 312   Changing Systems and Using Service Bureaus 314   Oversize Documents 314   Document Setup 316

Diagnosing Problems in Printing   317
    Diagnosing Mechanical Problems 317   Solving the Problem of Limited Disk Space 318   Diagnosing Problems with Graphics in the Document 319   Diagnosing Problems in Printing Colors 320   Diagnosing Problems in Printing Fonts 321   Using the Windows Error Handler 325   If All Else Fails 325

Summary   325

PART II   ADVANCED TECHNIQUES

9   Templates and Design   329

Creating Design Alternatives 330
   Create a Grid System 332

What Is a Template? 334

Benefits of Using Templates 336
   Templates Save Repeated Setup Steps 337   Templates Help You to Think Ahead! 337   Templates Let You Create Different "Default" Preferences 337   Templates Embody Design 338   Templates Help Enforce Consistency 338

Creating a Template Document 338
   Define the Page Size, Margins, and Columns 339   Select a Unit of Measure and Display Rulers 341   Set Up the Master Pages 341   Set Up Style Sheets 345   Identify Common Text and Graphic Elements 345   Design Specifications for Graphics Programs 348   Instructions for Working with the Template 349   Test the Design and Template 350   Template File Management 350

Summary 350

10 Advanced Page Layout 351

Storing Commonly Used Items 351
   Using a Library 351   Using the Pasteboard 352   Using the Clipboard for Repeated Copies 352

Tips on Aligning Items 354
   Using Commands for Aligning Text 354   Using the Snap to Guides 354   Using Column Guides as Spacing Guides 355   Using the Space/Align Command 356

Creating Relationships between Boxes 357
   Linking Boxes That Are Already Filled with Text 358   Linking Text Boxes on Nonconsecutive Pages 360   Working with Anchored Boxes 362   Working with Constrained Boxes 364

Tricky Page Designs 364
   Double-Sided Documents 364   Creating Spreads 368   Bleeding Text or Graphics 369   Controlling Text Runaround 370   Creating Forms 373

Summary 377

11 Working with Text from Databases and XPress Tags 379

Finding and Changing Special Characters 380

Eliminating Unwanted Paragraph Breaks 380   Converting Data Files to Tabular Format 382   Converting Data Files to Nontabular Formats 385   Embedding Format Codes in Data Files 389   Using Wild Cards in Searches 394

Inserting XPress Tags in ASCII Text 395

Character Attributes 395   Paragraph Attributes 396   Page Number Characters 399   Insert Special Characters 399

Summary 400

12 Tips on Typography 401

Designing Type Specifications 401

Match the Type Specifications to the System Capabilities 402   Use Only One or Two Typefaces 403   Use Larger Point Sizes for Longer Text Line Lengths 403   Don't Use Underscores 403   Use All Caps Judiciously 403   Differentiate Figure Captions from Body Text 404

Tips on Using Style Sheets 404

Benefits of Using Style Sheets 404   Tips for Creating and Applying Style Sheets 406   Formatting Headings with a Style Sheet 409

Adjusting Text Spacing 410

Adjusting the Leading (Line Spacing) 410   Hyphenation and Justification 411   Adjusting Word and Character Spacing 412

Special Typographic Effects 414

Making Drop Caps and Variations 414   Creating Shadow Type 417   Reversing Type on a Black Background 418   Rotating Text Boxes in a Symmetrical Circular Pattern 419   Text Inside a Shape 421

Summary 422

13 Special Graphic Techniques 423

Working with Graphics 423

Using Two Sets of Defaults for Picture Boxes 424   Creating Drop Shadows 425   Layering Lines for Special Effects 427

Drawing Polygons 428   Drawing Cartoon Balloons and Other Special Shapes 431

Creating Business Graphics with QuarkXPress 433

Creating Bar Charts 433   Using the Space/Align Command 438   Organization Charts 440

Summary 443

14 Managing Documents 445

Organizing Your Disk Files 445

The QuarkXPress Program Directory 446   The Windows Directory 448   The Publication Directory 450   Moving Files 452   Backup Procedures 452   Optimum File Size 452   Organizing Libraries 453

Workgroup Scenario 453

The File Server 454   Individual Workstations 455

Memory and System Resource Management 456

The Program Manager at Startup 457   Open Applications 458   Reboot to Recover Memory 459

Summary 459

15 Case Studies 461

Magazine: *Entertainment Weekly* 462

Description 463   Production Steps and Tricks 464

Brochure by Croce Advertising 467

Description 468   Production Steps and Tricks 469

Packaging by Mattel Toys 470

Description 471   Production Steps and Tricks 471

Corporate Identity Manual by Landor Associates 473

Description 474   Production Steps and Tricks 475

Summary 476

Appendix: Summary of Keyboard Shortcuts 477

Index 483

THE QUARKXPRESS HANDBOOK
Windows Edition

Introduction

QuarkXPress for Windows is a powerful new tool for publication design and production on DOS-based personal computers. Its progenitor, Quark XPress for the Macintosh, has already taken that market by storm, becoming the standard composition software for scores of national magazines, newspapers, books, directories, brochures, and other commercial publications. In fact, it is one of the most successful products of the "desktop publishing" revolution.

QuarkXPress greatly improves upon functions once served by the layout artist's tools and resources: pens, pressure-sensitive tapes, knives, wax, blue-line boards, and acetate overlays. It lets you compose complete documents—including text and graphics—and view full pages on the screen before printing them out to a high-resolution printer or typesetter. You can incorporate text and graphics that were created in other applications, or you can create finished pages using QuarkXPress alone.

Desktop Publishing: A Brief History

The ability to merge text and graphics on a screen is not unique to desktop publishing systems. Professional page-composition systems have been doing this for years. *Time* magazine, for example, started composing its pages on a mainframe computer over 20 years ago. (Recently, *Time* announced that two years of research had yielded a new publishing system for the magazine. The new system uses personal computers running QuarkXPress.)

Merging text and graphics using personal computers began in 1985 with the introduction of low-cost laser printers, the PostScript page description language, and WYSIWYG (What You See Is What You Get) software, which could accurately display typefaces, layouts, and graphics on the computer's display. These combined technologies made it possible to produce and manipulate type and graphics with an efficiency and convenience never before available. Since then, the combination of capabilities encompassed by the term "desktop publishing" has had a tremendous impact on designers, typesetters, professional publishers, corporate publications departments, and small businesses, as well as on those of us who dream of producing our own great novels.

The primary benefit of using QuarkXPress and the personal computer for publishing is that it affords more control than traditional methods—control over every phase of the process of publishing—at a lower cost, and with greater quality and flexibility than ever before. The benefits are not solely economic. Designers can experiment more freely, editors find that they have more control over content and format, and the time spent preparing documents for printing has been reduced significantly.

This introduction presents an overview of the features of QuarkXPress by first analyzing the anatomy of a page produced using the software, then by stepping you through production of a typical document. (The steps in the production cycle are keyed to later chapters in this book.) It also suggests why you might want to invest in a more expanded system (more memory) to run QuarkXPress, and learn what other software and hardware peripherals can be useful in creating and producing documents.

System Requirements

This book shows you how to use QuarkXPress under Microsoft Windows 3.1, with a mouse, on an MS-DOS personal computer. The minimum system requirements include an 80386 processor (or higher), MS-DOS® version 3.1 or later, Microsoft Windows version 3.0 or later, 4MB of memory and 6MB free space on a hard disk drive. You need a VGA (or better) graphics card for good screen display, and a mouse that is supported by Windows.

If you are already familiar with QuarkXPress (under Windows or on a Macintosh), you can skip this introduction and go to Chapter 1 for more specific descriptions of some of the interface features specific to QuarkXPress under Windows 3.1.

Anatomy of a QuarkXPress Document

A QuarkXPress document might be composed of text and graphics created in QuarkXPress as well as text and graphics brought in from other programs. Figure I-1 shows a typical page created using QuarkXPress.

Figure I-1 Anatomy of a page created using QuarkXPress.

The body copy (text) was typed in a word processing program, then imported into QuarkXPress. The kimono graphic was created in an illustration program, then sized and cropped in QuarkXPress. Some of the short text elements such as the rotated banner across the left side of the page were typed directly into QuarkXPress. Hairline rules and boxes were added using QuarkXPress' graphics tools. Footers and automatic page numbering were set up on the document's *master pages*—special pages that contain elements that will appear on *every* page of the document. (Master pages are discussed in more detail in Chapter 3.) In Chapter 2 we present a more detailed description of how a page is created in QuarkXPress.

Desktop vs. Traditional Publishing

Desktop publishing with QuarkXPress merges traditions from four different disciplines—typesetting, graphic design, printing, and computing—each with its own set of technical terms and standards. Professionals from each of these fields are finding that they need to add a few terms to their vocabulary in order to "speak" desktop publishing. They are gradually discovering that terms like *leading* and *line spacing* mean the same thing and that each area of experience has something to teach the other.

Design Traditions

Designers take a lot of pride in their ability to interpret a client's tastes and ideas and translate them into beautiful finished products. The process of putting design ideas down on paper using traditional methods can be painstaking, time-consuming, and expensive.

QuarkXPress makes it possible to rough out design ideas quickly and deliver finished-looking layouts rather than the traditional penciled sketches that are commonly used to present ideas in the preliminary design stages. In many cases, the efforts that go into producing a design idea with a computer are not lost—the same files can be fine-tuned for the final production. Furthermore, the same files can be duplicated and modified for other documents in the same series, or similar documents in another series.

The fact that even amateurs can produce nice-looking designs with a computer program seems a bit frightening to professionals, but good design will always require some of the knowledge and skills that are part and parcel of the trade. You'll learn some of these principles in this book, as well as the production methods that will help you blend the designer's tradition of excellence with the business community's demand for expedience.

Typesetting Traditions

One advantage of QuarkXPress over its competitors is precision in typographic controls. It lets you set the spacing between lines and letters in finer increments than are possible with most other page-composition packages, for instance. Furthermore, with QuarkXPress you can set the width or depth of text precisely—in numbers—rather than using the less precise visual alignment of an on-screen ruler. Traditional typesetters, therefore, need simply to learn how to apply their traditional measures using QuarkXPress commands. Meanwhile, desktop publishers who are already familiar with QuarkXPress can learn something from the traditions of typesetting. You'll learn some of the special terminology and functions related to typesetting later in this book.

Printing Traditions

Laser printers make it possible to print the entire image of the page—including halftones—directly on whatever color paper you choose. Instead of reproducing your master copy using xerographic or offset printing equipment, you can print out hundreds of "originals" on a laser printer, ready for immediate distribution. The production of hundreds of originals is not desktop publishing's primary benefit, however, since in most cases the direct output from QuarkXPress is camera-ready page layouts, on paper or film, to be reproduced by an offset printer.

Whether you use camera-ready mechanicals and an offset printer or a master copy and xerographic equipment, the final result depends on the condition of the original page. Good pasteup artists have the skill of surgeons in meticulously trimming typeset galleys and photostats of line art, painstakingly aligning them (horizontally on the page, vertically with the margins, precise distances from each other), and burnishing down the waxed pieces so they will not fall out of alignment during all the handling on the way to the camera. This, then, is a primary feature and a revolutionary contribution of desktop publishing to the history of publishing: the ability to produce clean, camera-ready master pages, including text and graphics, without the marks and hazards of physically pasted-up boards.

Desktop publishing does not always preclude the need for pasteup, nor does it guarantee perfect reproduction under some conditions. You will find—as designers, typesetters, artists, and printers well know—that the camera (used in making plates for offset printing) does not see the image the same way you do. Black text on a gray background might be easy for your eye to read on the laser-printed master, but the camera that produces the negatives might have trouble keeping the gray tone without overexposing the text.

You'll learn how to prepare your QuarkXPress files for output for offset printing, as well as some of the vocabulary you will need to communicate with your printer.

Computer Traditions

The final elements in our "melting pot" of desktop publishing are derived directly from the computer industry. Pixels and screen fonts, ports and baud rates, icons and menus are all terms that you will quickly become familiar with as you move into the realm of desktop publishing.

Throughout this book you will find that we draw clear analogies between the various terms used by different industries to describe the basic concepts underlying desktop publishing: the assembly of finished pages of text and graphics.

Overview of Publishing with QuarkXPress

QuarkXPress can assist in the total publishing process: formulating an idea, creating the document, editing and formatting it, and printing it out. QuarkXPress brings together many functions that were once divided among different people at different locations.

For example, before desktop publishing, a designer would have created comprehensives (samples) with pens and markers, a typist might have typed in the text of a newsletter and sent the file—either on paper or on disk—to the typesetter for formatting and typesetting as per the designer's specifications. Meanwhile, the graphics department used a computer or just pens and ink to create the graphic images, and sent them to an outside service to be photostatted to the size needed. Eventually, the galleys of type and the photostats of the figures landed on a drafting table where the layout artist used X-ACTO knives and wax to trim the paper and paste it down on boards to create final, camera-ready boards.

Now, the same person might type in the text, draw the graphics, and compose the pages directly on the screen using QuarkXPress. The fact that one person is performing the entire sequence of steps does not mean that the steps themselves are much different. The one person responsible for the entire production is likely to be strong in some areas, weak in others. For this reason, many desktop publishing departments still divide the tasks of desktop publishing among different people. Nevertheless, when the production team is small (as is common in desktop environments),

Introduction   9

there can be weak spots in the production cycle—areas in which no one on the team has experience. This book can help you by providing tips in those areas of expertise that you and your team might lack.

Following is a quick overview of the steps involved in producing a document, from verifying that you have all the necessary disk files, to printing the final copy. Later chapters provide more details and tips on how to execute each step.

The steps for creating a document with QuarkXPress fall into three areas:

- Designing and planning your document.
- Constructing the text and graphics with QuarkXPress or other applications.
- Producing the final page layouts in QuarkXPress.

Once you understand the basic steps in creating a document, you can fit the detailed steps explained in the rest of this book into the overall process.

Whether you are producing a layout from design to final camera-ready mechanicals on your own, or working with a team, an overview of all of the steps involved in a typical production cycle will help you to set up an efficient production schedule. The steps outlined under the next headings do not necessarily occur sequentially or in the order shown. Some steps can take place simultaneously, and some projects will call for a slightly different sequence. A typical production schedule showing the relationships between the steps is shown in Figure I-2.

Figure I-2   A typical production schedule.

The following overview of the steps involved in producing a document includes references to other chapters, which discuss each step in more detail.

Design Pages and Typography

Document design really begins with an idea and an outline, but for our purposes we jump into the process at the point where the editor hands the written manuscript (and, hopefully, the text on disk) to the design department. Here, the designer develops the design specifications, including:

- Typefaces, sizes, and styles for different elements within the text.
- Basic text format. Will the paragraphs have a first-line indent? What will be the space between paragraphs? Will the text be justified? Will headings be flush left or centered?
- Basic page layout or grid, including page size, margins, orientation, number of columns, and positions of other nonprinting guides. This is some of the information required before you create a new QuarkXPress document.
- Final (maximum) size of illustrations, as well as typefaces, type sizes, and type styles to be used within the illustrations and in the captions.
- Final page count, or the range of pages expected to be filled. This will help you decide whether and how to divide a long publication into smaller documents or sections, as well as help you estimate the printing costs.

Designing has traditionally been performed after the text is written, since the design itself may be affected by the content and structure of the text. If the authors know what the design specifications are before they write the text, however, they can participate in the production by setting tabs and other paragraph format requirements as they go along.

Traditionally, design specifications have been handwritten or typed and illustrated as rough pencil sketches with penciled lines indicating text position. However, you can use QuarkXPress as a design tool for developing specifications (see Chapter 9). Before individual page layout begins, the page design can be set up on a master page (see Chapter 2) or in a QuarkXPress template document (Chapter 9), and the type specifications can be captured in a QuarkXPress style sheet (Chapter 4).

Collect Text

You can type text in QuarkXPress much the way you type text using your word processor. Although you can build documents from scratch using QuarkXPress alone, often QuarkXPress documents are composed of text that has been typed in other programs.

For instance, most contemporary authors use a computer to write the text, or someone else who has a word processor is paid to type the manuscript. Even if the word processing was not done on a personal computer running under MS-DOS, any text can be converted or telecommunicated to your MS-DOS machine and then be imported into QuarkXPress.

A design editor usually marks the author's unformatted printed manuscript for formatting according to the design specifications. With

QuarkXPress, you can format text using the style sheet feature (Chapter 4). This simplifies the process of formatting text. The designer can describe in detail each different format only once for entry into a QuarkXPress style sheet. The text can then be marked up with simple style names that can be applied using keyboard shortcuts, a Style palette, or menu commands in QuarkXPress.

Collect Illustrations

You can draw simple shapes—lines, boxes, polygons, and circles—in QuarkXPress, but you can also import more complicated graphics or other graphic formats (including black-and-white halftone images and color illustrations) that were created using other programs.

Since QuarkXPress lets you import files created with other software programs, you can create the illustrations using the graphics program best suited for each (see Chapter 6):

- PostScript-type drawing packages, like Micrografx Designer, CorelDRAW, Arts & Letters, Adobe Illustrator, or Aldus FreeHand, are best suited for line art and technical illustrations.
- Scanners can digitize photographs or line drawings that can be manipulated using software like Aldus' PhotoStyler, Micrografx' Picture Publisher, or Computer Presentations ColorLab. Scanned images can also be traced, creating fine line art using PostScript drawing programs.
- Paint-type programs such as PC PaintBrush and Windows Paint are best suited for working with digitized images and for creating "fine art" illustrations.
- Spreadsheets or charting programs are most efficient for charts that are derived from tables of numbers.
- Some illustrations or graphic elements can be added directly in QuarkXPress.

Build the Pages in QuarkXPress

After the text and graphics have been prepared in other programs, you start QuarkXPress and begin building the document. In this step, you may begin with either a new file or a template file that is already set up with the design specifications (see Chapters 2 and 9).

Define Master Pages

Master pages are nonprinting pages that automatically format document pages. Any item you position on a master page will appear on all other pages in the document associated with that master page. The master pages can include running heads, footers, and any other elements that appear on every page. Master pages also contain the underlying grid—a baseline grid for text plus a matrix of margin guides, column guides, and ruler guides that appear on the screen but are not printed. This grid can be used to align objects consistently on all pages of the document.

Add Text and Pictures

The basic building blocks on any page in QuarkXPress are called *boxes*. You create text boxes to hold text and picture boxes to hold imported graphics. You use the Get Text and Get Picture commands to import text and graphics files created in other programs. You can add other text and graphic elements using QuarkXPress' tools.

With QuarkXPress you can arrange text in columns and jump text from one page to another, including nonsequential pages. You can use the automatic features to wrap text around graphics or anchor specific graphics frames to captions within the text. (See Chapter 3.)

Once the text and graphics are in QuarkXPress, you can easily move them around on the page, change their size and shape to fit the space allowed on individual pages, duplicate them, or delete them. QuarkXPress can also rotate text and graphics. In addition, QuarkXPress can adjust the contrast and line screening for grayscale images (Chapter 6).

Create and Use a Library

Besides importing elements from other applications, you can create libraries of elements collected into QuarkXPress and easily share them among documents through the Library feature. (See Chapter 3.)

Edit Text

You can edit the text using all of the normal edit commands, such as Copy, Cut, and Paste. QuarkXPress also lets you perform functions normally associated with word processing only, such as Find/Change text (global search and replace), Check Spelling, and Add Dictionary Terms to a custom dictionary (Chapter 4). You can also Edit H&J Specifications (the hyphenation and justification specifications) to adjust the appearance of the text.

You can use commands in the Style menu to format text, or create a style sheet to simplify and speed up the process of formatting text (Chapter 4). QuarkXPress offers a wide range of typographic controls that can be applied to text, including customization of kerning and tracking tables (Chapter 5).

Edit Graphics

Besides normal page-layout activities such as positioning, sizing, and cropping pictures, QuarkXPress lets you rotate graphics, adjust the contrast and brightness settings of images, and select from one of several screen patterns for halftone printing (Chapter 6).

Add Color and Edit Colors

You can create colors and apply them to selected text, lines, or box frames or backgrounds, then print color separations for either spot-color printing or process-color printing (Chapter 7).

Print Drafts and Finals

You should expect to print a document many times before you print the final version. Even if you have thoroughly edited the text and graphics before placing them on a page, you still need to print drafts of the QuarkXPress version of the pages to review for format and alignment. QuarkXPress is a WYSIWYG program: "What you see (on the screen) is what you get (on the printed page)." However, there are always minor differences between the screen and the printed page because of the differences in resolution. These minor discrepancies cannot be seen until you print the document.

After each draft printing, there will be the normal rounds of proofing, and many of the steps outlined above will be repeated as the text and graphics are corrected and massaged until the document is perfect.

Lastly, you will print the final camera-ready masters (including color separations). These might be printed on a laser printer at 300–600 dots per inch resolution, or they can be printed at higher resolutions on an imagesetter.

Final Reproduction, Binding, and Distribution

In most cases, the final document will be reproduced from the single final copy printed from QuarkXPress. This master copy might simply be reproduced on a photocopier, or it can be offset printed from camera-ready masters produced by QuarkXPress. You can print QuarkXPress pages out as negatives on film and you can print color separations directly from QuarkXPress, thereby saving steps normally left to the offset print shop. Chapter 8 describes QuarkXPress' printing capabilities.

When the project is finished, copy all of the files related to that document onto one or more floppy disks or removable hard disks for archiving. Chapter 13 offers more tips on archiving and moving files.

Desktop Publishing Systems

One characteristic of desktop publishing is that it is not a single-product application. QuarkXPress is just one part of a complete system that requires additional software, powerful hardware, new input devices, and high-resolution output devices for a total solution.

QuarkXPress and Other Software

The three key application areas in document production are text processing, artwork (illustrations), and page layout. You can handle all of these elements using only QuarkXPress and a scanner, or you can supplement the capabilities of QuarkXPress by adding other specialized applications to create text and graphics that can be imported into a page in QuarkXPress.

Word Processing

QuarkXPress can import text created by most word processing programs on the PC including RTF (Rich Text Format) documents and documents created in Microsoft Word 4.0 for DOS, Microsoft Word for Windows versions 1.0 and 2.0, Microsoft Write, WordPerfect 5.1, WordPerfect for Windows, Ami Pro 2.0, and XyWrite III Plus. You can also import ASCII files from any word processor (including non-PC applications, after transferring the text to a PC disk), data saved in ASCII format from a spreadsheet or database program, and text that has been telecommunicated from another computer.

QuarkXPress' text formatting features offer a wider range of typographic controls than those of most word processors, so you will probably want to do most of the formatting using QuarkXPress commands. However, you can format text before importing it into QuarkXPress by using any supported word processor's formatting commands, or you can format text in any word processor by embedding XPress Tags (ASCII codes) that will be translated into formats when you import the text into QuarkXPress. (See Chapters 4 and 10.)

Paint and Drawing Applications

Graphic applications offer a wider range of drawing tools and commands than QuarkXPress. By working directly with a drawing or painting program you can access sophisticated features such as curved lines, air-brush effects, and pixel-by-pixel image manipulation. You can also use a paint program to clean up images that have been digitized through a scanner.

The types of graphics formats that can be imported into QuarkXPress include bitmap (.BMP, .DIB, .RLE), Compuserve GIF (.GIF), Paintbrush (.PCX), Windows Metafile (.WMF), Computer Graphics Metafile (.CGM), HPGL (.PLT), Macintosh PICT (.PCT), Micrografx Designer (.DRW), Scitex (.CT), TIFF (.TIF), and Encapsulated PostScript (.EPS).

The formats listed here are described in more detail in Chapter 6 on Graphics.

Equipment Configurations

Understanding the uses of and differences between the different software applications used in desktop publishing is one half of the process of outfitting a usable desktop publishing system. The other half of the process is to make sure your equipment meets your needs. The root of a QuarkXPress publishing system is an IBM-compatible personal computer—an expandable machine that offers access to a range of peripherals that can maximize the capabilities of your system. This book addresses IBM PC and compatible systems running MS-DOS and Microsoft Windows 3.1 or later. (QuarkXPress also runs on Apple Macintosh computers, addressed in a separate book by the same authors.)

Along with QuarkXPress, a full desktop publishing system may include a computer, a laser printer for draft or final printouts, a high-resolution imagesetter for final masters, and a scanning device. Other peripherals, such as video digitizers and color printers, add to the flexibility of a desktop publishing system. The following discussion gives you the background you'll need to make wise hardware decisions for desktop publishing.

Computer Models and Memory

Windows requires at least a 286-based system and 2-megabytes (2MB) of memory. You can't run QuarkXPress with this minimum—you need at least a 386 system and 4MB of memory. Adding more memory will make your applications run faster. Some graphics programs that you might be using in your publishing efforts can require more than 4MB of memory in order to run. Aldus PhotoStyler can easily use 8MB of memory or more to process high-resolution color images. The speed of the processor becomes more important the larger the volume of pages and graphics. If you are working with many scanned images, you will appreciate the faster performance of a 486 system with 8MB or more of memory.

Storage

Besides the temporary storage that is built into any computer (such as RAM plus extended memory), you need to save programs and documents on disks for permanent storage or transportation. Because desktop publishing usually involves the use of several different applications (word processing, graphics, and page composition) and the assembly of files from many sources, it is convenient to store all of your applications and your current document files on a hard disk while you are working, and use removable hard disks, optical drives, tape, or floppy disks for backups.

QuarkXPress requires at least 6MB hard disk space if you want to install all of the files that come with the program. Hard disks that are built into the PC usually store 20MB, 40MB, 80MB, or 100MB of information, and you can get hard disks in many other sizes to use as your primary hard disk or to use in combination with your internal hard disk.

You will want to invest in a large hard disk if you are working with high-resolution images. In addition, you might want an extra hard disk system just to handle your archived documents. Removable hard disks can be useful for a backup system, but we do not recommend relying on a removable cartridge system for your active daily work.

Monitors

If you do a lot of publishing, a large-screen monitor can increase your productivity by letting you see a full 8.5-by-11-inch page of work. By eliminating scrolling around the screen, it can boost your productivity by 50 percent. Even larger monitors which display full views of two facing pages or oversized pages are available now.

A color monitor lets you display high-resolution color images. You can take advantage of QuarkXPress' color capabilities even without a color monitor—using PANTONE colors and mixing your own colors by entering percentages that you can look up in a color reference book—but if you intend to work in color, we recommend a color monitor and at least an 8-bit video card.

Scanners

A full-service publications department will also want to add a scanning device for digitizing photographs, logos, and line art that already exist on paper. A scanner or digitizer is an input device that converts a printed image into computer-readable dots. Digitized images can be saved in one of the paint-type formats supported by QuarkXPress such as Tag Image File Format (TIFF).

With a scanner you can incorporate halftones or line art of scanned images into your desktop publishing work as final artwork or as position holders for photographic halftones that will be stripped in later at the print shop. Scanners are a good source of graphics if you are not a fine artist and you have a library of logos, line art, and photographs to which you (or your clients) own the rights.

The software that accompanies scanners can offer many of the features of paint programs, with eraser and pen tools for touching up scanned images. There are a number of packages available for editing high-resolution scanned images—Aldus' PhotoStyler, Micrografx' Picture Publisher, or Computer Presentations ColorLab, for example. With the right combination of scanner, page-layout program, and printer, you can produce high-resolution graphics that look like inked line art or halftone photographs. For good results with color photographs, we recommend using high quality scanners. Most "desktop" color scanners, priced for individual use at under $5,000, are not adequate for high-quality results.

Most black-and-white flatbed scanners accept 8.5-by-11-inch or larger pages; color scanners can digitize images from a variety of sources, including 35mm slides, transparencies, or flat color artwork. You can also use a video camera to convert printed or three-dimensional images into computer-readable images. Any scanner requires software to set up the specifications for the input image size, the finished image size, the degrees of brightness and contrast, and the resolution of the stored image.

Most scanners let you store the image at 300 dpi (dots per inch) or more, and high-resolution images can approach the quality of true halftones when printed on a high-resolution printer. However, a full-page scan can require several megabytes of storage space when saved at high resolutions. You can save scanned images in low-resolution paint formats (usually 72 dpi) but, when printed on a 300 dpi (or higher) printer the image will always appear jagged compared with high-resolution scans (unless the image is composed simply of horizontal and vertical lines).

Text-scanning (OCR, or optical character reader) technology has improved over the last few years, becoming faster and more accurate. The breakthrough of most relevance for desktop publishers is that some scanners can interpret typeset text in various sizes (whereas in the past OCRs could read only special characters and typewritten text).

Printers and Other Output Devices

Desktop publishing, by definition, requires a printer that can produce text in a mixture of different sizes and styles merged with graphics on the same page. QuarkXPress documents can be printed on some dot-matrix printers, but the final printer usually is a laser printer or typesetter. The most widely used page description language (PDL) for desktop publishing is PostScript. PostScript has been implemented in dozens of laser printers and at least three phototypesetters. You can also add a PostScript interpreter on a card that you install in your computer so you can print PostScript to a non-PostScript laser printer. QuarkXPress also supports PCL—the language used by Hewlett-Packard laser printers—as well as other printers supported by Windows.

Besides the PDL built into the printer, the one variable that is directly related to the price of any printer is resolution. *Resolution* is a measure of the sharpness of the edges of printed characters and graphics. It is commonly measured by the number of dots or spots per inch. Laser printers assemble characters and graphics as a pattern of dots, and they use a fine beam of light (a laser beam) to produce the dots in patterns of 300 dpi or more. The laser beam puts electromagnetic charges on a drum which then either picks up powdery charged particles of the toner and lays the toner on paper, or transfers the electromagnetic charges onto photosensitive paper. The resulting text and graphics appear very smooth to the naked eye.

Phototypesetters that use the laser technology to set a page image on photosensitive paper or film are available. Linotype, Varityper, Agfa Compugraphic, and other manufacturers offer PostScript laser typesetters that image at various high resolutions. The resolution can be from 600 to 3,500 dpi, and the output is much crisper, of course, than the output from toner-based laser printers.

Color printers are useful for printing proof copies of color pages, or finished color overhead transparencies or slides.

Modems

Files can be telecommunicated over the phone lines or through a cable from one computer to another. You can also convert files from one application to another type, using communications software that allows you to transfer and translate files. Once the files are transferred, you can edit them using any word processor (if they are ASCII text files), or use the same application that created them to edit them, or import them directly onto a page in QuarkXPress.

Modems can be set to send files at different speeds, measured as baud rates (bits per second). The lowest baud rate is 300; it can take a long time to send a file at this rate, but it ensures a high degree of accuracy in the transmission. A 1200, 2400, or 9600 baud rate is more commonly used to send files over the phone lines. Even higher transmission speeds can be used over direct optical cable connections (rather than over phone lines).

Networks

Desktop publishing in a networked workgroup allows people to share information. This is especially important in a production setting where one person is responsible for writing copy, another for designing graphics, and still another for laying out the page, for example. Network users can share printers, files, and information.

There are several server-based networks available for the PC, including Novelle, NetWare, VINES, and Lan Manager. These high-end networks also allow various brands of computers to be used within one workgroup. At the lower end of the spectrum, you can connect a few PCs together for under $500 with DOS-based networks like LANtastic.

Summary

Electronic publishing systems bring together the features and capabilities that were once dispersed among different professional specialties. The rest of this book will help you identify the different tasks associated with a full publishing project, and also update your current designs and production procedures to take advantage of the capabilities of QuarkXPress under Windows. This book will also help you to understand the basic vocabulary of desktop publishing applications, to distinguish between the different types of programs used in desktop publishing, to identify the possible sources of text and graphics in any document produced using QuarkXPress, and to determine your own software and hardware needs.

The impact of desktop publishing on designers, professional publishing companies, corporate publications departments, and self-publishing associations and individuals is best seen through the experiences of those who have made the transition from traditional methods to electronic publishing over the past few years. Chapter 15 of this book offers several case studies of QuarkXPress users.

PART I

USING QUARKXPRESS

1 Basic Concepts and Terminology

This chapter will help you understand the basic concepts and terms used in the Windows environment and in QuarkXPress procedures. You will learn some basic operations that are common to most Windows applications on the PC—operations that we assume you are familiar with in the rest of this book. You will also learn the concepts and terminology of the page-layout process as applied in QuarkXPress.

If you have never used a Windows application before, you should review this entire chapter carefully. We also recommend that you study the manuals and go through the tutorial included with Microsoft Windows.

If you have used Windows 3.1 but have never used QuarkXPress before, you may opt to skip the Windows Basics sections, but read the sections about QuarkXPress. If you have used earlier versions of Windows, you ought to skim this chapter for a description of new features of Windows 3.1, especially Object Linking and Embedding.

If you have used QuarkXPress 3.1 on a Macintosh computer, read the Windows Basics sections, where you'll learn about how to work with windows, menus, and dialog boxes in the Windows environment. If you have used earlier versions of QuarkXPress, skim the rest of this chapter to learn about some of the new features introduced with version 3.1, such as the Style Sheets palette, Colors palette, and Trap Information palette.

Microsoft Windows Basics

QuarkXPress implements the basic Microsoft Windows interface features and commands common to most Windows applications. Throughout this book we assume that you are familiar with Windows basics and that you know how to work with the Windows Program Manager and File Manager. You should also be familiar with common terms that describe mouse operations, such as *click* and *drag*. Some of the basic procedures are summarized here as they apply to QuarkXPress.

QuarkXPress runs under Microsoft Windows version 3.0 or later. This book specifically describes procedures under Windows 3.1. Beginners may need to refer to the appropriate manuals for MS-DOS and Windows to supplement the information found here.

Using Drop-Down Menus

One of the advantages of Windows on the PC is that you are not forced to enter obscure, hard-to-remember commands through the keyboard. Rather, Windows lets you choose commands from lists on drop-down menus. Menu titles appear along the menu bar at the top of the screen. When you position the mouse pointer (⬧) over a menu title and click the mouse button, the menu drops down to show all commands in that menu (Figure 1-1).

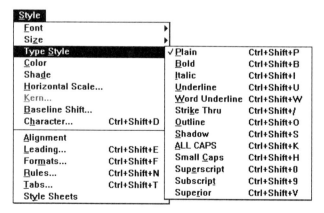

Figure 1-1 A QuarkXPress drop-down menu with a submenu displayed.

You can close the menu without choosing a command by clicking the mouse on the menu title or anywhere else on the screen, or by pressing the Escape (ESC) key (to close the menu but keep the menu bar active and choose another menu from the keyboard), or by pressing ALT or F10 (to close the menu and return to the application window).

You can select a menu command quickly with the mouse by pointing to a menu name, then holding the mouse button down and dragging to the desired command name, releasing the mouse button when the command is highlighted. If the menu is already open on the screen (using any of the techniques described in the previous paragraph), you can select a command by positioning the pointer on the desired command and clicking the mouse button.

A check mark (✓) in front of a command indicates a toggle switch (an on/off option such as Snap to Guides) or the active option in a series of mutually exclusive commands, such as Fit in Window and Actual Size. The feature is on if it is checked; you can turn off the feature by selecting the command. The feature is off if it is not checked; you can activate the feature by selecting the command.

Instead of showing check marks, some commands toggle between Show and Hide. For example, if you choose Show Colors from the View menu, the Colors palette is displayed in a new window on the screen, and the command changes to Hide Colors on the menu.

Ellipses (...) following a command indicate that a dialog box asking you for more information will be displayed when you select the command. The dialog box always offers you a chance to cancel the command without making any changes.

A right-pointing black arrow (▶) on a menu indicates a submenu. When you select a command that is followed by a black arrow, a secondary menu will pop out, and you can click the mouse on the desired selection or type the letter that is underscored in the command name.

Keyboard Shortcuts

Menus make it easy to find a command, but using a menu is usually slower than entering a keyboard command. For this reason, and to support users who do not have a mouse, Windows offers standard keyboard alternatives. You can open a menu by holding the ALT key and typing the first letter of the menu title. For example, pressing ALT+E opens the Edit menu. You can also press either ALT or F10 to activate the menu bar, then use the right and left arrow keys to highlight a menu name, and press ENTER to open the highlighted menu.

You can also select a menu command by typing the letter that is underlined in the command name on the menu. For example, when the Edit menu is open you can choose the Copy command by simply pressing C. You can highlight a command on an open menu by pressing the down arrow key until the command is highlighted, then pressing ENTER to activate the command.

Besides the Windows keyboard commands, most commonly used commands in QuarkXPress have their own keyboard alternatives which do not require you to first open the menu, such as holding down the Control key (CTRL) while pressing another key. These keyboard shortcuts are shown in the menus, next to the command name. For example, the keyboard alternative to File → New is CTRL+N. It is easy to remember the keyboard shortcuts for the commands you use most often. If you have used QuarkXPress on a Macintosh computer, you'll notice that the CTRL key is the PC's equivalent of the Command key (⌘) on the Macintosh.

To execute the command, hold down the CTRL key while you type the letter shown. Command shortcuts can also include the Alternate key (ALT) and the Shift key (SHIFT).

Controlling a Window

Microsoft Windows derives its name from the fact that a document is displayed in a *window* on the screen. When you start Windows, the Program Manager displays programs and groups of related applications as icons in windows on the screen (Figure 1-2). You can open a window through the Windows Program Manager by selecting an icon and choosing the File → Open command or by double-clicking on an icon on the desktop.

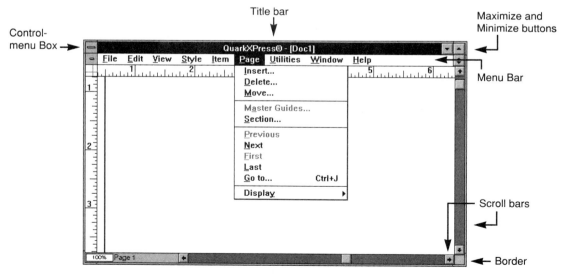

Figure 1-2   Common elements of windows.

You can close a window under the Program Manager by choosing the Close command from the Control menu—opened by clicking on the Control-menu box at the upper left corner of the window—or by double-clicking on the Control-menu box. You can also close a window from within QuarkXPress (and most Windows applications) by choosing the Close command from the File menu.

A window can be moved by dragging the title bar, or by choosing the Move command from the Control menu and using the arrow keys to move the window. Open the Control menu from the keyboard by pressing ALT+SPACEBAR (to open the application window's control menu) or ALT+HYPHEN (to open the document window's Control menu).

You can adjust the size of most windows by positioning the mouse pointer over any border or corner of the window until the pointer changes to show two direction arrows, then holding down the mouse button as you drag the mouse. If you choose the Size command from the Control menu, you can use the arrow keys to change the size of the window.

To enlarge a window so it completely fills the screen, use the Maximize command from the Control menu, or click on the Maximize button that shows an upward pointing arrow in the top left corner of the window, or double-click on the title bar. If a Window has already been Maximized, a Restore button shows up and down arrows at the top right corner of the window—clicking the Restore button returns the window to the size it was before it was maximized. If a window has been maximized, you can also return it to its previous size by double-clicking on the title bar.

To reduce a window to an icon at the bottom of the screen, click the Minimize box at the top right of the window. You can open the window again by double-clicking on the minimized icon that shows the window name. Minimized icons will not be visible if the active window is enlarged to cover the bottom of the screen—you might have to reduce the size of the large window in order to get access to the minimized icons.

Scroll bars can be found in windows and in many dialog boxes that offer lists—whether in QuarkXPress or any other application. To move the view in the window or in the list in small increments, click on an arrow. Click in the gray area of a scroll bar—on either side of the scroll box—to move the view in the window up or down in larger increments. Drag the scroll box to move any distance, or position the mouse pointer over a scroll arrow and hold down the mouse button to continuously scroll. The position of the scroll box on the scroll bar indicates the relative position in a window. For example, if the scroll box is in the center of a scroll bar, you are viewing the center of that window's contents.

If more than one window is open on the screen, you can activate a window by clicking on it. If you cannot see the window—or if you don't want to use the mouse—you can cycle through the different open application windows by pressing ALT+ESC. Cycle through different document windows by pressing CTRL+F6 or CTRL+TAB.

Making Entries in a Dialog Box

Commands that are followed by ellipses (...) usually yield dialog boxes. Dialog boxes might also be displayed with error message, warning messages, or simply information messages in response to some actions you attempt in QuarkXPress or under Windows. Some dialog boxes are like windows in that they can be moved on the screen (by dragging the title bar or by choosing the Move command from the dialog box's Control menu). Dialog boxes that are the result of commands offer a variety of options (Figure 1-3). These options work the same way in most dialog boxes under Windows:

- Click on an option button or its label, or hold the ALT key and type the letter that is underscored in the button label to make a selection from a list of mutually exclusive options. Instead, you can press the TAB key to move through the controls and use the arrow keys to select from a list of options. The selected option shows a black dot in the circular option button.
- Click on a check box or its label, or hold the ALT key and type the letter that is underscored in the label to make one or more selections from a list of options. Instead you can press the TAB key to move through the controls and press the space bar to activate or deactivate a check box when it is highlighted.
- Tab to or click in a text box, or hold the ALT key and type the letter that is underscored in the label, and type a value. When a text box is active, a flashing vertical text insertion point appears in the box, or the current text entry is highlighted.
- Click on a name in a list box to select the name. Scroll bars are available if the list box contains more entries than fit in one view. You can also highlight a name in a list box by pressing the TAB key until you activate the list box, or hold the ALT key and type the letter that is underscored in the field label; then use the arrow keys to highlight an entry.
- Click on a drop-down list indicator to display a drop-down list, then click on the selection you wish to make. Alternatively, you can TAB to the field, or hold the ALT key and type the letter that is underscored in the field label, then use the up and down arrow keys to scroll through the list, viewing choices one by one in the text area.

- Command buttons initiate actions which might close the dialog box or open another one. The currently selected command button is outlined in a darker border than the rest. You can activate any command button by clicking on it, or by pressing the ENTER key to activate the currently selected command button.

  You can also hold the ALT key and type the letter that is underlined in the command button name. For example, type ALT+Y for Yes or type ALT+N for No. Click on Cancel or press ESC to cancel the command and ignore any entries you have made in the dialog box. Or you can use the TAB key to highlight any of the command buttons and press ENTER or the SPACEBAR to activate the highlighted choice.

  A command button that shows a command name followed by ellipses (...) will open another dialog box. A command button that includes greater-than signs (>>) expands the current dialog box. Unavailable command buttons are dimmed.

Figure 1-3 The Print dialog box shows examples of a variety of dialog box controls.

The basic techniques for working with all QuarkXPress dialog boxes are the same. Specific dialog box entries and their meanings are described throughout this book.

The Control Menu

The Control menu, which is always displayed at the top left corner of a window lists the commands that are used to change the size of a window—Restore, Move, Size, Minimize, and Maximize (Figure 1-4).

Figure 1-4   Control Menu.

The Control menu also includes the Switch To command, which allows you to switch between running applications and rearrange windows and icons on the desktop. In addition, the Control menu under applications other than QuarkXPress might list one or more of the following commands: Next, Edit, Settings, and Fonts. All of these commands are explained in your Windows manual.

Using the Cut, Copy, and Paste Commands

The Edit menu contains basic editing commands that are common to all Windows applications, such as Undo, Cut, Copy, Paste, Delete, Select All, and Show Clipboard. They usually have the same keyboard shortcuts across most Windows applications: Undo (CTRL+Z or ALT+BKSPC), Cut (CTRL+X or SHIFT+DELETE), Copy (CTRL+C or CTRL+INSERT), Paste (CTRL+V or SHIFT+INSERT), Select All (CTRL+A), and Delete.

Both Edit → Cut (CTRL+X or SHIFT+DELETE) and Edit → Copy (CTRL+C or CTRL+INSERT) put selected objects in the Clipboard (a temporary storage space in computer memory). The Cut command removes active objects from a page, while the Copy command leaves the objects on the page and puts a copy in the Clipboard. Edit → Paste (CTRL+V or SHIFT+INSERT) positions whatever is in the Clipboard onto the page in QuarkXPress. Using the Paste command does not change the contents of the Clipboard—you can use the Paste command to paste copies of the same thing from the Clipboard onto the page as many times as you like.

You can use the Copy or Cut command in any other application that supports these commands under Windows, then Paste the selection into a QuarkXPress document. However, QuarkXPress' Get Text and Get Picture commands are more commonly used for importing objects from other applications.

Clipboard Versus QuarkXPress Library

The *Clipboard*—a standard Windows feature—is a temporary, memory-resident storage area that is active while you are working. It stores a copy of the most recent selection that you cut or copy, and the contents of the Clipboard remain the same until the next time you use the Cut or Copy command (or until you exit Windows or turn your computer off). The same Clipboard is in effect regardless of what applications you are running. If you draw something using Windows Draw and make a copy of it, for example, then open a QuarkXPress document, you can use the Paste command to pull that graphic from the Clipboard onto the QuarkXPress page. Rather than using the Clipboard, however, it is usually more convenient to use QuarkXPress' File ➤ Get Picture or File ➤ Get Text command to import graphics or text from other applications into QuarkXPress documents.

Once an object is imported into QuarkXPress, you can add it to a QuarkXPress library if you plan on using the same element repeatedly. The QuarkXPress Library is a more permanent, disk-based storage facility that holds any number of separate items that can be accessed through the Library palette, and copied and pasted into a QuarkXPress document.

Using Paste Special, Paste Link, and Links Commands

The Paste Special, Insert Object, Paste, and Paste Link commands are designed to be used under Windows version 3.1 and higher that support Object Linking and Embedding (commonly referred to as OLE—pronounced "oh-lay"). You can link or embed an object (such as an illustration) from another application that supports OLE into a QuarkXPress document. First create the illustration in the other application, then use QuarkXPress' OLE command to import the object.

If the object is embedded, then the illustration remains under control of the original application. The other application is used to create the screen image and to print the object; so if you move the QuarkXPress document to another system, that system needs to have the application that created the embedded object. When you double-click on the object with the Content tool, you automatically open the original application, enabling you to edit the object.

If the object is linked, changes you make through QuarkXPress are made directly to the source file. Also, you can specify whether the object is updated automatically in QuarkXPress if it is changed using the original application when QuarkXPress is not active. You can specify whether the updating is done automatically or only when you request it. You can also update or change your link preferences through the Links command.

See Chapter 6 for more information on embedding and linking graphics using OLE commands.

QuarkXPress Basics

The rest of this chapter describes the basic QuarkXPress installation, windows, palettes, and menus. You will need to be familiar with these elements in order to understand the next two chapters, which detail specific steps you can follow to build a QuarkXPress document.

Installing the Program

QuarkXPress is packaged on several diskettes because the program itself is larger than one floppy diskette. During the installation process, the pieces on these diskettes are assembled into one large program file on your hard disk (along with other files that support QuarkXPress). The manuals that come with QuarkXPress contain complete instructions for installing the program.

Starting QuarkXPress

Once QuarkXPress is installed on your system, there are three ways to start QuarkXPress from Windows.

Figure 1-5   To start QuarkXPress, double-click either the program icon displayed by the Program Manager, or a QuarkXPress document icon that you have set up under the Program Manager.

- The simplest method is to open the QuarkXPress window under the Windows Program Manager and double-click on the program icon (Figure 1-5)—this is the usual shortcut to the alternative of selecting the icon and choosing the File ➤ Open command.

  The QuarkXPress program icon is set up automatically when you install QuarkXPress, or you can create the program icon and document icons in any window under the Program Manager by opening the window, then choosing New from the File menu. A dialog box will ask you to name the icon and give the full path and program name (see your Windows manual for details).

- If the QuarkXPress program icon is not set up under the Program Manager, or if you don't want to bother opening windows on the screen, you can choose File → Run from the Program Manager's or File Manager's File menu. When the Run dialog box is displayed, type the path and program name. The normal path and program name, if you accept all of QuarkXPress' defaults when installing the program, is C:\XPRESS\XPRESS.EXE.

  If you can't remember the full path and program name, you can click the Browse button in the Run dialog box and click through the directory lists until you find the program, then double-click on XPRESS.EXE.

- The third method is by opening the File Manager under Windows, normally found in the Main window under the Program Manager. Use the standard Windows methods of clicking through directories under the File Manager until you find XPRESS.EXE, then double-click on the file name (Figure 1-6). If you want to open a QuarkXPress document or template that your have already created, you can display and double-click on the name of a document.

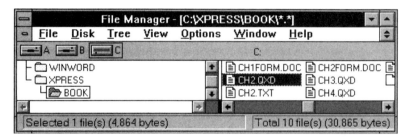

Figure 1-6 Double-click the program name or a QuarkXPress document name displayed through the File Manager.

Examining a QuarkXPress Document

You can learn a lot about the basic principles and terminology of QuarkXPress by first examining a QuarkXPress document. The next sections describe a document that was briefly profiled in the introduction. Here we introduce some of the terms used in the QuarkXPress manuals and throughout this book. (See also Chapter 15 for descriptions of other documents created using QuarkXPress.)

Figure 1-7   *A newsletter page created in QuarkXPress.*

QuarkXPress is well suited for designing and producing a wide variety of printed documents, including books, newspapers, magazines, manuals, reports, directories, brochures, packaging—or any printed communication. All of these items can be created using the same basic set of building blocks and tools used in creating the newsletter page described here (Figure 1-7).

Master Pages and Document Pages

A QuarkXPress document can be composed of up to 2,000 document pages plus up to 127 master pages. Master pages can contain text and graphics that are repeated on multiple document pages. Both document pages and master pages can contain guides (margin guides, column guides, and ruler guides) that help you position items consistently. Document pages are the ones you'll usually be printing, of course, but QuarkXPress allows you to print out master pages as well.

For example, to create our sample newsletter page, we set up a master page with half-inch margins and with the text of the footer that runs at the bottom of every page to which this master page is applied.

You can apply a master page to any document page; if you do so, then all master page elements will automatically change on that document page

(Figure 1–8). You can also delete master pages from a document. In this example the master page is very simple; however, a master page can contain more guides and other text and graphic elements, as described in the next section.

Figure 1-8 Master page elements.

Lines, Text Boxes, and Picture Boxes

The basic building blocks on any page in QuarkXPress—master pages or document pages—are boxes and lines drawn with QuarkXPress tools. These are called *items*; the tools that create them are called *item creation tools*. Boxes drawn using QuarkXPress tools can stand alone as graphic elements, or they can contain text or pictures.

Page 1 of our sample newsletter includes one text box and the footer from the master page. The first page also includes items on the document page—one picture box containing the kimono graphic, and three additional text boxes, containing the newsletter banner, the article title, and the article lead-in (Figure 1-7).

The illustration is an EPS (encapsulated PostScript) graphic created in Adobe Illustrator and imported into a picture box. The banner "Kimono West" was typed directly into a text box and rotated 90°. The title text above the illustration is in a one-column text box that is the width of the three-column article. Below the illustration is a one-column text box. The body of the article starts on this page in a three-column text box. The text box containing the article is from the master page, but it has been modified for the first page of the newsletter. You can easily change master page items on individual document pages.

Relationships between Items

Items (boxes and lines) can stand as separate elements on a page, or they can be associated in several ways: as text chains, as anchored items, or as constrained items. Relationships between items are described briefly here and in more detail in Chapter 3.

The Automatic Text Box and Other Linked Text Chains

Text boxes can be chained to direct the flow of text from one page to another or from one box to another on the same page. This will happen automatically if you set up an *automatic text box* on the master page, or you can use the Linking tool manually to link a series of text boxes and create a chain. The stream of text that flows through a linked chain of text boxes is called a *story*.

Anchored Boxes

Text boxes, picture boxes, and rules can be anchored within a text box. For example, you can create a graphic symbol, import it into a picture box, then paste the picture box into the stream of text. This way, the graphic symbol will move with the flow of text even if the text before it is edited.

Constrained Items

Text or picture boxes and lines can be constrained within a constraining text or picture box. Constrained items cannot be moved beyond the boundaries of the constraining box, but the entire constrained group can be copied, moved, or deleted.

Guides

You can create *guides* on any page in QuarkXPress—document pages or master pages. Guides are nonprinting lines that appear on the screen and have a snap-to effect: If the optional snap-to effect is turned on (under the View menu), the pointer or the edges of items (boxes and lines) will be pulled into alignment with a guide when you move them close to the guide. In QuarkXPress, the distance at which objects will "snap" to guides can be set in units of pixels in the General Preferences dialog box. (See Chapter 3.)

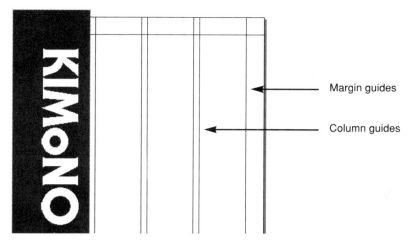

Figure 1-9 Guides used in our sample newsletter.

Nonprinting guides include *margin guides* that are defined on the master page, *column guides* that can be set up on the master page or in any text box, and *ruler guides* that can be dragged onto a page from a ruler. Guides used in our newsletter sample are shown in Figure 1-9.

Style Sheets

QuarkXPress offers a wide variety of tools and commands for editing and formatting text. In our newsletter sample, the process of formatting text was simplified through the use of *style sheets* (Figure 1–10).

Figure 1-10 A style sheet specification.

A style sheet is simply a shortcut for applying type specifications (character attributes and paragraph formats) used throughout a document. It lets you define the character attributes, paragraph format, and ruled lines, or rules, for each type of text element in a document, such as major headings, subheadings, captions, and body text.

Once you set up a style sheet for a document, you can format text by simply using the menu command Style ➤ Style Sheets or keyboard equivalents that you've assigned to a style sheet, instead of using several commands and different dialog boxes to format text. QuarkXPress also lets you apply style sheets using the Style Sheets palette.

Templates and Documents

You can save a QuarkXPress document as a document or as a template. A document is a final product that you print, reproduce, and distribute. A template is usually a partially complete document, containing common elements that may appear in many documents.

Banner on first page

Column guides on master page appear on every page

Mailing label on back page

Figure 1-11 The template used for this newsletter includes master page elements, the banner on page 1, plus a mailing label area on page 4.

For example, the template for this newsletter (Figure 1-11) includes a master page and special items on document pages that appear in every issue, such as the banner on the first page. The template for our newsletter also includes style sheets that are used to format the text consistently. Every issue of the newsletter is started from this template; this saves having to start from scratch every month.

Examining QuarkXPress Windows and Palettes

When you first start QuarkXPress, the screen shows drop-down menu titles on the menu bar of the application window, but no document window is open and most of the commands are gray and cannot be selected.

After you enter the initial specifications in the New dialog box, or when an existing document is open, QuarkXPress displays pages in the document window (Figure 1-12). The screen might also display any one of six palettes: a Tool palette, a Measurements palette, a Document Layout palette, a Style Sheets palette, a Colors palette, or a Trap Information palette, depending on how your screen looked when you last quit QuarkXPress. A quick look at the document *window* and QuarkXPress' palettes gives you an idea of the program's versatility.

Figure 1-12 A new QuarkXPress file displays the upper left-hand corner of the first page of the document.

A document window can be moved and sized on the screen. You can have more than one document *window* open at a time, but the active document window usually displays on top of any other document windows (unless you have arranged them side by side). If you close a document window, you are closing the document.

A *palette*, on the other hand, displays on top of all document windows and is related to the active document only. You can close any palette without closing the active document. Like windows, palettes can be moved anywhere on the screen, and some of the palettes can be resized.

If you are examining the document window for the first time, choose View ➤ Fit in Window (CTRL+0, where 0 is a zero and not the letter O) and follow our descriptions under the next headings.

Examining the Document Window

The document window in QuarkXPress is a standard Windows document window. The mouse pointer shows the current position of the mouse and is used for selecting commands and items on the page or pasteboard. The page image shows the outline of the edges of the paper; nonprinting dotted or color lines on the page indicate margins and columns. The surrounding area serves as a pasteboard for storage of text and graphics while you are working. Optionally, rulers can be displayed at the top and right sides of the document window. The bottom left corner of the screen shows the current page view percentage and the page number (Figure 1-13).

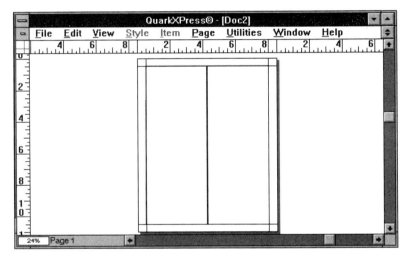

Figure 1-13   The document window.

You can view and work on a display of one page at a time, two facing pages at a time, or spreads consisting of two or more pages in documents that might be folded or include fold-out pages. Facing pages can be set up in the New dialog box, or later in the Document Setup dialog box. Facing pages let you set up master pages with different margins, headers, and footers on left and right pages.

Examining the Tool Palette

QuarkXPress' Tool palette is much like a conventional artist's assortment of drawing tools. Here pens, rulers, protractors, and knives are replaced by icons, which you select to perform the artist's work.

The Tool palette is a separate window on the screen (Figure 1-14). You can drag the palette by its title bar to any position on the screen and close it by double-clicking on the Control-menu box at the top left corner of the palette or by selecting View → Hide Tools. To redisplay the Tool palette after you close the palette, select View → Show Tools.

Figure 1-14 The Tool palette.

Selecting a Tool

To select any tool in the Tool palette, click on the tool. Press CTRL+TAB to select the tool immediately below the currently active tool or CTRL+SHIFT+TAB to select the tool immediately above the currently active tool—or continue pressing CTRL+TAB or CTRL+SHIFT+TAB until the tool you wish to use is selected. The currently active tool determines the appearance of the pointer on the screen.

Some tools remain active until you deselect them by choosing another tool—the Item tool (✥), Content tool (☝), and Zoom tool (🔍) fall into this category. All the other tools revert to the Item tool or the Content tool as soon as they are used once. To keep the same tool active for repeated use, hold the ALT key as you select it.

Double-clicking on a tool brings up the Tool Preferences dialog box (described in Chapter 3, Expanding the Document), which enables you to set the default specifications for the Zoom and Item Creation tools (boxes and lines) in the Tool palette.

Editing Tools

The four icons in the first section of the tool palette are for the Item tool, the Content tool, the Rotation tool, and the Zoom tool. Select the **Item tool** to move boxes or lines on a page. When the Item tool is selected, the pointer becomes an arrow (↖). It changes to a four-pointed arrow, or mover pointer (✣), when you position it over a box or line created with one of QuarkXPress' item creation tools, and it changes to a pointing finger or resizing pointer (☞) when positioned over the handle of an active item.

You need not select the Item tool from the Tool palette in order to move a box or line: With any tool selected, you can hold down the Control key (CTRL) to temporarily activate the Item tool at any time. When you release the CTRL, the previously selected tool becomes active. To move a box, click on it to select it and drag. You can see the outline of the box move if you drag quickly, or pause for half a second before moving a box if you want to see the box contents as you move.

The **Content tool** (☝) must be selected in order to modify the contents of boxes, both text and picture boxes. When this tool is selected and the pointer is positioned in a text box, the pointer changes to an I-beam (I) for inserting and editing text; when positioned in a picture box, the pointer becomes the picture mover pointer (☝).

To select text with the Content tool (☝), position the I-beam beside a character inside an active text box and drag it to the end of the desired selection. Selected text is highlighted or reversed on the screen. Other methods of selecting a range of text are described in Chapter 4, Word Processing.

To select a picture with the Content tool, position the picture mover pointer (☝) inside an active picture box and click once. You can move the picture within the box by dragging the picture mover pointer. To modify the contents of a picture box, including scaling or skewing the picture, you must select the Content tool.

The **Rotation tool** (↻) lets you rotate text boxes, picture boxes, lines, or active groups of boxes and lines, on a page. When this tool is selected, the pointer becomes a target symbol (⊕) at first, and an arrowhead (▶) indicates the direction of the rotation around the target point.

The **Zoom tool** (🔍) lets you change the scale in which you are viewing the page. When this tool is selected, the pointer becomes a magnifying glass with a plus sign inside (🔍) for zooming in, or increasing the page view percentage. By holding down the ALT key, the tool changes to a magnifying glass with a minus sign inside (🔍) to zoom out, or decrease the page view percentage.

Item Creation Tools

The next seven tools on the tool palette are the item creation tools. They include one text box creation tool, four picture box creation tools, and two line creation tools. When any of these tools is selected, the pointer becomes a crosshair (+), called the Item Creation pointer.

Select the **Text Box tool** (△) to create boxes on the page that will contain text. Select the **Rectangle Picture Box tool** (⊠), the **Rounded-Corner Rectangle Picture Box tool** (⊠), and the **Oval Picture Box tool** (⊗) to create boxes with square corners, boxes with rounded corners, and circles or ovals, respectively. The boxes created with these tools may contain graphics imported from other sources. Use the **Polygon Picture Box tool** (⊠) to create boxes with any number of sides that may also contain graphics imported from other sources. Select the **Orthogonal Line tool** (✛) to draw horizontal and vertical lines, and the **Line tool** (◊) to draw lines at any angle.

After selecting any one of these tools, you create an item by dragging the pointer on the page or the pasteboard, as described in Chapter 2, Creating One Page.

Linking Tools

The last two tools are called the **Linking tool** (⊕) and the **Unlinking tool** (⊕). Use these to direct the flow of text from one text box to another, as described in Chapter 2.

Examining the Measurements Palette

The Measurements palette (View → Show Measurements) displays information about the currently active item on a page. This information will change dynamically as you move, scale, or otherwise change an active item. You can also change the specifications by making entries directly through the Measurements palette.

The Measurements palette provides a quick method for modifying many item and content attributes that can also be changed through the menus and dialog boxes; the information can be changed in either area. The Measurements palette is by far the fastest way to view or change values. As a result, you only need to go into a dialog box when you want to change other variables not shown in the Measurements palette or when the Measurements palette is not displayed.

You can move the Measurements palette anywhere on the screen by clicking and dragging on its title bar. The contents of the palette will vary depending on the type of item selected, as shown in Figure 1-15.

Figure 1-15 Measurements palette when a text box (top) and a picture box (bottom) are active.

When the Measurements palette is displayed, you can jump to its first control area by pressing CTRL+ALT+M, or you can activate any control area by simply clicking on it. Once in this palette, as in any dialog box, you can move through the controls by pressing the TAB key, or press SHIFT+TAB to tab in reverse order.

Make entries in the Measurements palette by editing the entry as text, using scrolling arrows to select values, or choosing from drop-down lists. To exit the palette and activate all changes, press the ENTER key, or click the mouse in any other window. Changes made to the information on the left side of the palette (related to items, such as boxes and lines) are not reflected on the page until you exit the palette. Changes you make on the right side of the palette (related to the contents of active items) are implemented when you click on an icon in the Measurements palette or exit a control area.

Entering Measurements

QuarkXPress offers unique flexibility in entering measurements. Regardless of the unit of measure that is currently displayed, you can enter a new value in inches, millimeters, centimeters, picas, points, or ciceros. To enter a measure in units other than the current unit of measure, simply indicate the measurement system using the abbreviations listed in Figure 1-16.

Units	Abbreviation	Example
Inches	"	1"
Millimeters	mm	1mm
Centimeters	cm	1cm
Picas	p	1p
		1p3 (one pica, three points)
Points	pt	1pt
Ciceros	c	1c
		1c3 (one cicero, three points)

Figure 1-16 Measurement units and their abbreviations.

You can enter most measurements in increments as fine as .001 and font sizes from 2 to 720 points. Change an entry by adding or subtracting from the current value displayed in any control area. For example, if the current measure is 4 inches, you can increase it by 1/4 inch by positioning the cursor after the 4 and typing +.25—you need not enter the unit of measure if it is the same as the current default measure. Similarly, you could increase the 4-inch measure by 2 picas and 3 points by typing +2p3 after the 4.

Examining the Document Layout Palette

The Document Layout palette (View → Show Document Layout) shows the document pages or master pages as icons (Figure 1-17). You can move the Document Layout palette around on the screen or enlarge it for a view of more page icons as your document grows.

Figure 1-17   The Document Layout palette.

When you first open the palette, document page icons are displayed in the lower area of the window. The line down the middle of the palette indicates the binding edge of a facing-page document. The gray areas to the left and right of the document page icons represent a visual reminder of the 48-inch width, which is the maximum page width or spread width QuarkXPress allows. Each page icon shows the master page assigned to it, and the absolute page number (i.e., the page sequence within this document—not the user-defined page number) below each page. The active page is shown in bold italic type on the page icon in the Document Layout palette.

The bar above the page icons has two menus. The Document menu is used for inserting new pages, deleting pages, or displaying master page icons. The Apply menu is used for applying different master pages to document pages. You can have up to 127 different master pages in a document.

To display master pages, choose the Show Master Pages command from the Document menu on the palette. When master page icons are displayed, you can add new master pages or delete master pages.

You can double-click on a page icon in the Document Layout palette to display that page in the document window. The Document Layout palette can be used as an alternative to turning to pages by using the keyboard, the scroll bars, or various commands on the Page menu such as Previous, Next, or Go To page.

To rearrange pages, drag the page icons in the Document Layout palette to the new position. This can be used as an alternative to rearranging pages in Thumbnails view. Text links will not be maintained when you rearrange pages this way.

Examining the Style Sheets Palette

The Style Sheets Palette (View ➤ Show Style Sheets) allows you to apply formats to text easily, as an alternative to applying character formats using many commands from the Style menu, or applying styles via the Style ➤ Style Sheets command. To apply a style sheet, select the text you wish to format, then click on the appropriate style sheet name in the Style Sheets palette (Figure 1-18). The Style Sheets palette is not active unless the text I-beam pointer (I) has been clicked in a text box.

Figure 1-18   The Style Sheets palette.

You may also use the Style Sheets palette to edit style sheet specifications. Hold down the Control key (CTRL) and click on a style sheet name in the palette to quickly display the Edit Style Sheet dialog box for that specific style sheet. This is an alternative to selecting the Edit ➤ Style Sheets command, then clicking on the style sheet name to display the Edit Style Sheet dialog box.

Examining the Colors Palette

The Colors palette (View ➤ Show Colors) provides a convenient way of applying color to text, pictures, box backgrounds and frames, and lines

(Figure 1-19). Using the Colors palette is the only way to apply a two-color blend to a box background.

Figure 1-19   The Colors palette when a text box is selected.

To apply colors, choose one of the icons across the top of the palette, then choose a color and shade percentage. The icons across the top of the palette will change depending on what type of item is selected. If a text box is selected, for example, the icons across the top are, from left to right, for applying color to the text box frame, the text, or the text box background. An adjacent drop-down list lets you assign a shade percentage, or you can type in any percentage. The palette lists all the colors created for the document under Edit ➤ Colors.

The Colors palette may also be used to open the Colors dialog box. Hold down the Control key (CTRL) and click on the name of a color in the palette to quickly display the Colors dialog box. This is an alternative to selecting the Edit ➤ Colors command.

Examining the Trap Information Palette

When you print color separations, QuarkXPress slightly expands the edges where two colors meet to prevent white spaces from appearing due to minor registration variance. This is called color *trapping*. The Trap Information palette (View ➤ Show Trap Information) allows you to specify the trapping relationship between adjacent colors on an item-by-item basis (Figure 1-20). Trapping between colors for a document is defined in the Edit Trap dialog box (Edit ➤ Colors), but those relationships may be changed on individual items using the Trap Information palette.

Figure 1-20   The Trap Information palette when a framed text box is selected.

When a box is active, the Trap Information palette shows the trapping values for both the color of the box background and the box contents; if a line is selected, the palette shows the trapping specifications for the color of the line. If a box is framed, trapping may be specified for the way the frame color traps against the background color.

Drop-down lists provide six different options for defining trapping relationships; you can define your own trapping values by choosing Custom and entering a value in the area to the right of the drop-down list.

For more information on trapping, see Chapter 7, "Color."

Examining the Pasteboard

The area surrounding the master page and document page spreads, the pasteboard, is a nonprinting area for storing text and graphics. You can also use the pasteboard as a work area. The "pasteboard" is a metaphor for the traditional graphic artist's table: You can put text and graphics on it that you are not using at the moment, or that you want to work on before placing on your page.

The width of the pasteboard is initially determined by the width of your pages and the width of the spread. The default setting is for the pasteboard to extend the width of a page off each side of a spread. The pasteboard is always ½ inch above and below a page or spread. You can change the width of the pasteboard to less than 100 percent of the spread size if desired. The maximum width of the pasteboard *plus* a full spread is 48 inches.

Examining the Menus

QuarkXPress menus function the same way standard Windows menus function, described earlier in this chapter. They are divided logically into commands that relate to one another. Further, each menu is sectioned by a gray line, separating groups of commands on each menu.

The File Menu

The File menu includes commands that are common to most Windows applications, such as New, Open, Close, Save, Save As, Printer Setup, Print, and Exit (Figure 1-21). QuarkXPress adds a Revert to Saved command that lets you cancel any changes you made to the document since you last saved it.

```
File
  New...              Ctrl+N
  Open...             Ctrl+O
  Close
  Save                Ctrl+S
  Save as...
  Revert to Saved
  Get Text...         Ctrl+E
  Save Text...
  Save Page as EPS...
  Document Setup...
  Printer Setup...
  Print...            Ctrl+P
  Exit                Ctrl+Q
```

Figure 1-21   The File menu.

Other commands on this menu let you import text and graphics from other applications, save text to disk, save an entire page as a color or black-and-white Encapsulated PostScript (EPS) file, and change the document setup (page size).

The Edit Menu

The Edit menu (Figure 1-22) includes commands common to most Windows programs, such as Undo, Cut, Copy, Paste, Delete, Select All, and Show Clipboard. QuarkXPress adds Object Linking and Embedding (OLE) commands, and commands that let you perform global searches and adjust preferences (default settings). You can also define colors, style sheets, and hyphenation and justification rules.

```
Edit
  Can't Undo          Ctrl+Z
  Cut                 Ctrl+X
  Copy                Ctrl+C
  Paste               Ctrl+V
  Paste Special...
  Paste Link
  Delete
  Select All          Ctrl+A
  Links...
  Show Clipboard
  Find/Change         Ctrl+F
  Preferences       ▶
  Style Sheets...
  Colors...
  H&Js...
```

Figure 1-22   The Edit menu.

The View Menu

The View menu (Figure 1-23) changes the size of the page view in the document window and hides or displays other elements on the screen. None of these commands affects how the document looks when it is printed.

Figure 1-23   The View menu.

The Style Menu

The commands listed in the Style menu change depending on what is active when you view the menu (Figure 1-24). Style menu commands affect the content of boxes and line characteristics.

Figure 1-24   Style menu when a text box (left), a picture box with an image (center), or a line (right) is active and the Content tool is selected.

The Item Menu

The Item menu (Figure 1-25) includes commands that let you modify, duplicate, group, and align boxes and lines.

Figure 1-25   The Item menu.

The Page Menu

Commands in the Page menu (Figure 1-26) add, delete, and move pages, set up master guides and page numbers within the document, and change the page view percentage.

Figure 1-26   The Page menu.

The Utilities Menu

The Utilities menu (Figure 1-27) includes commands used in checking spelling and setting up a hyphenation exceptions dictionary. The Library command lets you set up and easily access collections of commonly used text and graphic elements. Font Usage and Picture Usage commands let you view and edit lists of all the fonts used in a document and all the pictures imported into the document. Through this menu you can also edit or create your own tables used for kerning or tracking the space between letters.

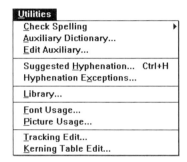

Figure 1-27   The Utilities Menu.

The Windows Menu

The Windows menu (Figure 1-28) offers four commands that are basic Windows options: Tile automatically sizes all the windows so they butt up against each other and fill the screen, Cascade shows windows layered on top of each other, Arrange Icons aligns the icons of document windows that have been minimized and appear at the bottom of the application window, and Close All closes all open documents and windows. In addition, the Windows command lists the names of all open documents, so you can choose a different document from the menu (as an alternative to clicking on the document window).

Figure 1-28   The Windows Menu.

The Help Menu

QuarkXPress offers a list of Help topics that are available if the XPRESS.HLP file is in the directory with the QuarkXPress program. The About QuarkXPress command tells you what version of the program you are using (Figure 1–29).

Figure 1-29   The Help menu and the About QuarkXPress dialog box.

When you choose one of the Help commands, a scroll list of topics shows a tiered help system. A dialog box displays a list of the main topics covered by the command (Figure 1-30). The How to Use Help command explains how to navigate through the topics. Double-click on the Control-menu box to return to the document window—or click the Minimize button to change the Help window to an icon at the bottom of the screen so you can activate it easily and return to the same view of Help topics by double-clicking on the icon. (You might have to change the size of the QuarkXPress windows in order to see minimized icons at the bottom of the screen.)

Figure 1-30   Help information.

The serial number, along with other information, can be found in the QuarkXPress Environment window (Figure 1-31). Hold down the CTRL key and select About QuarkXPress from the Help menu. Knowing the version of your program and your serial number is important if you use Quark's technical support to resolve program problems. This service, available to registered owners, is well worth the subscription fee if you plan to do a great deal of production with QuarkXPress.

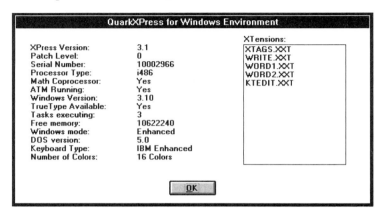

Figure 1-31   The QuarkXPress Environment window.

Summary

You should now be familiar with some of the basic concepts and terminology that you will encounter in learning QuarkXPress. The best way to learn QuarkXPress is to use it. If you have never used QuarkXPress before, go through the tutorial provided with the program to get a quick overview of its features. No matter what your level of experience, you'll find many useful tips throughout this book for using QuarkXPress efficiently.

2 Creating One Page

Before you can master QuarkXPress, it's important to understand the basics. In the introduction we summarized the overall sequence of steps involved in creating a QuarkXPress document. In this chapter we isolate the basic steps in the page-layout process and describe them in more detail: starting a new document, defining the page size and margins, and working with items on a page.

You will learn how to start a new document or open an existing one. Because text boxes and picture boxes, called *items*, are the most basic building blocks of any page in QuarkXPress, we will demonstrate how to use QuarkXPress' *item creation tools* to create boxes and lines. In addition, you'll be introduced to several key procedures that are expanded upon extensively in later chapters: how to type or import text into a QuarkXPress text box, how to draw simple graphics with QuarkXPress tools, and how to import text and pictures from other applications into QuarkXPress. You will learn how to select items and how to resize, rotate, and apply color to them. Finally, we'll take our first look at how to create relationships between items by linking text boxes, anchoring boxes and lines within text, and grouping and constraining items.

This chapter focuses on positioning and determining the appearance of items on a page. Chapter 3 describes commands for adding pages, maneuvering through a document, and changing the page layout. It also describes how to work with master pages and how to use the library feature. Commands for working with the *content* of items—editing text and graphic elements—are described in more detail in Chapters 4 to 6.

We assume that you have already read Chapter 1, which presented an overview of the common procedures for working with menus, dialog boxes, and windows under Microsoft Windows, and introduced some of the basic concepts and terminology related to QuarkXPress. If you encounter a term you are unfamiliar with, please refer to that chapter or to the detailed glossary in the QuarkXPress documentation.

Setting Up a New Document

You can create a new document in QuarkXPress by double-clicking on the QuarkXPress program icon, selecting the File → New (CTRL+N) command, and making entries in the New dialog box. If the document you want to create is similar to other documents that you have already created, you may save time by opening the similar document, modifying it, and saving it under a different name. These two options are described later in this section.

Before you begin any project, it's a good idea to plan what you'll be doing. If the document will include text and graphics created in other programs, organize your disk files before you start to build a QuarkXPress document.

Organizing Your Disk Files

Here is a quick summary of our recommendations about file organization:

- Decide on the conventions you will use in naming all new files created during the project.
- Copy all of your source files onto one hard disk drive.
- Keep a backup version of all files, and back up files regularly.
- Keep all files related to one document in a single directory.

These few steps are worth taking before you begin assembling text and graphics on a page. Spending time on these preliminaries can save you hours over the life of a large project. It's easy to apply these simple steps to small projects as well. Chapter 14 offers more detailed suggestions about organizing large projects and working in networked environments.

Creating a New Document

Once you have organized your files, you can launch QuarkXPress. As described in Chapter 1, there are three methods of starting a program through Windows. The simplest method, however, is to open the QuarkXPress window under the Windows Program Manager and double-click on the program icon.

When you start QuarkXPress, the startup screen displays copyright information and the version number of the program you are using. The screen then changes to display the menu bar. You create a new QuarkXPress document by choosing File → New (CTRL+N). QuarkXPress then displays the New dialog box (Figure 2-1), where you specify the page size, column guides, and margin guides.

Figure 2-1   The New dialog box.

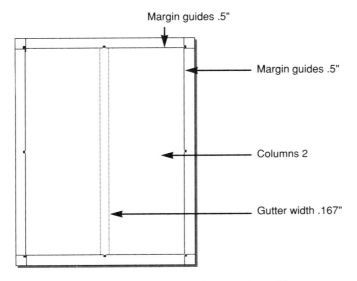

Figure 2-2   How the New dialog box entries affect a page.

The values shown when the New dialog box first opens are the same as those specified the last time you started a new document. In other words, the Page Size, Margin Guides, Facing Pages, Column Guides, and Automatic Text Box entries are maintained as new settings each time you use the New command. Once you close the New dialog box, QuarkXPress displays a blank page 1 for a new document. Figure 2-2 shows how the settings in the New dialog box affect a page.

Entries in the New dialog box are applied automatically to the first document page and the first master page of the document. If you decide to change these settings after you have started the document, you can do so using the File → Document Setup command or, if a master page is displayed, using the Page → Master Guides command. The following sections discuss the effects of these settings.

Page Size

QuarkXPress offers five standard page sizes, or you can enter any size from 1 inch by 1 inch up to 24 inches by 48 inches (if Facing Pages is selected) or 48 inches by 48 inches (for single-sided documents). You can see the five standard page measurements by selecting each one from the Page Size controls and viewing the width and height measurements associated with each.

US Letter	8.5 by 11 inches
US Legal	8.5 by 14 inches
Tabloid	11 by 17 inches
A4	210 by 297 millimeters (8.268 by 11.693 inches)
B5	176 by 250 millimeters (6.929 by 9.843 inches)

US Letter and US Legal are standard American paper sizes; A4 Letter and B5 Letter, usually specified in millimeters, are standards in other countries. Tabloid is a small newspaper size.

The page size is always displayed in inches in the New dialog box, but you can enter values in any unit of measure by using unit of measurement abbreviations, as explained in Chapter 1. You can also change a value by adding or subtracting from the current setting. QuarkXPress will convert and display your entries in inches when you redisplay the dialog box.

The page size you specify in the New dialog box is not necessarily the size of the paper that you will be feeding into a laser printer or imagesetter. The page size determines the measurements of the page defined by the page border on the screen. You may specify Tabloid size, for example, and print the large page out in two pieces on 8.5-by-11-inch sheets of paper, using the Tiling option of the Print command. (See Chapter 8.)

Or you may specify a page size smaller than the sheets of paper you print on. In that case, you can use the Registration Marks option in the Print command's dialog box to print crop marks that indicate where the pages will be trimmed and registration marks used in aligning color separations (Figure 2-3).

Figure 2-3   Page layouts that are smaller than the paper in the printer can be printed with crop marks and registration marks.

If you decide to change the page size after you have started working on a document, use the File ▸ Document Setup command (Figure 2-4).

Figure 2-4   The Document Setup dialog box lets you change page size.

If you increase the page size after starting to build a document, all items will retain their position relative to the top left corner—that is, you will have wider white areas to the right and bottom edges of the page. If you decrease the page size to the point where an item no longer fits on the page, the item will extend onto the pasteboard (Figure 2-5).

Figure 2-5   Items are forced onto the pasteboard when page size is decreased.

   The automatic text box, described later in this chapter, changes size when you change page size. Changing page size will cause the text to reflow on all pages that use the automatic text box.

Columns

QuarkXPress' default setting is 1 column. The number of columns you specify in the New dialog box applies to all pages of the document, unless you change individual master pages. The number of columns you set in the New dialog box will apply to the first master page and also to the automatic text box, if you have specified that option. Column guides on a page serve as aids in positioning items on the page, but they do not affect text. Column guides in an automatic text box define the width of text that is typed, imported, or pasted into the box.

QuarkXPress' default gutter width—the space between columns—is equal to 1 pica, or 0.167 inches. When you enter the number of columns and the amount of space you want between each column, QuarkXPress divides the page into equal columns between margins (Figure 2-6).

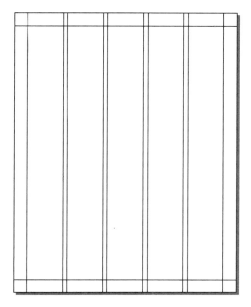

Figure 2-6   QuarkXPress divides a page into columns of equal width.

   QuarkXPress imposes a maximum limit of 30 columns per box, and the gutter width can be set from a minimum of 3 points to a maximum of 288 points (or 4 inches). Therefore, the maximum number of columns allowed on a particular page is limited by the distance between the margins of the page and the space between the columns, and not just the 30-column maximum. In practice, you should rarely exceed this limit.

   On a black-and-white monitor, master column guides are represented as thin black lines. On a color monitor, they display in the default color, blue, unless you change their color by selecting Edit ➤ Preferences ➤ Application. You can set guides to display in front of or behind boxes on the page by using the Edit ➤ Preferences ➤ General command (CTRL+Y), described in Chapter 3.

   You can change column settings for text boxes using the Item ➤ Modify command or the Measurements palette. You can change the number of columns and gutter width for individual master pages using the Page ➤ Master Guides command as described in Chapter 3.

Margin Guides

Like column guides, the margin guide values entered in the New dialog box apply to all pages of a document, unless they are changed for individual master pages by selecting the Page ➤ Master Guides command.

On a black-and-white monitor margin guides, like column guides, are represented as thin black lines; on a color monitor they display in the default color, blue, unless you change their color in the dialog box under Edit → Preferences→ Application.

Margin guides serve as guides only and do not affect the position of text except through their effect on the automatic text box. Margins determine the distance from the edges of the automatic text box to the edges of the page. You normally position running headers and footers (page numbers, for example) outside these margins; you can also position other text or graphics beyond the margins if your design calls for it.

When the Facing Pages option is selected, the inside margin measure is applied to the left margin of odd-numbered pages and to the right margin of even-numbered pages. The inside margin is often set wider than the outside margin, to accommodate binding.

Facing Pages

The Facing Pages option lets you create and view pages that will face each other in double-sided printing. Deselect the Facing Pages option if you want to create a single-sided document. Figure 2-7 illustrates both choices.

Single-sided documents in QuarkXPress are distinguished by two characteristics:

- They let you create only single-sided master pages.
- They let you specify Left and Right margins. The Left Margin is usually set wider than the Right Margin to accommodate binding.

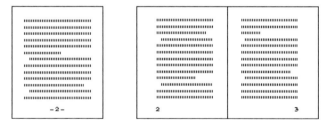

Figure 2-7   Single-sided versus facing-page documents.

If you create a new document as a single-sided document, the first master page will be a single-sided master and will remain so, even if you change to Facing Pages later through the File → Document Setup command. If you do change to Facing Pages, however, you will be able to create single-sided or facing-page masters later.

Facing-page documents in QuarkXPress are distinguished by the following characteristics:

- They let you view two facing pages at once.
- They offer both single-sided and facing-page master pages. Facing-page master pages provide two page masters each: one for left (even-numbered) pages and one for right (odd-numbered) pages.
- They let you have different headers and footers on left and right pages.
- They let you specify inside and outside margins. The Inside Margin measure applies to the right margin of left pages and the left margin of right pages. Inside margins are usually set wider than outside margins to accommodate binding.

Single-sided and facing-page documents both offer the option of creating spreads—adjacent pages that will face each other across a fold in the final publication (Figure 2-8). Two facing pages are also a spread, separated by a bound edge rather than by a fold. You can *bleed* an illustration across pages in a spread.

Figure 2-8 Document Layout palette shows a facing-page document with a fold-out page spread (left) and a single-sided, three-fold brochure set up as a three-page spread (right).

You can use the File → Document Setup command to turn Facing Pages on or off, regardless of the option chosen in the New dialog box. However, to turn Facing Pages off, you must first delete all facing-page masters.

Automatic Text Box

Remember that the *box* is the basic building block in QuarkXPress. Text boxes can be linked to direct the flow of text from one page to another or from one box to another on the same page. This will happen automatically if you set up an *automatic text box*, or you can use the Linking tool manually to link a series of text boxes and create a chain.

If Automatic Text Box is checked in the New dialog box, QuarkXPress will automatically create a text box with margins and columns as specified in the New dialog box. This text box will appear on the first master page and on the first page of a new document. When you type or import text into an automatic text box, a new page will be added automatically as needed to accommodate text overflow, unless you set Auto Page Insertion *off* in the General Preferences dialog box.

If Automatic Text Box is not checked, margin and column guides will be displayed on the pages, but the text box will not be created automatically. An automatic text box can be added later using techniques described in Chapter 3.

Building a New Document from an Existing Document

After you first install QuarkXPress, you will probably be building all of your documents from scratch, starting with a new blank page. If you are learning QuarkXPress for the first time, however, it would be easier to start with a template or document that someone else has already created. You can open any document or template by double-clicking on the document name under the File Manager, or you can launch the QuarkXPress program and use the File → Open command to open an existing QuarkXPress document or template. If you use the File → Open command, a dialog box is displayed that shows the list of QuarkXPress files in the currently open directory on the current drive (Figure 2-9). You can change directories by clicking on the folder icons in the Directories area, and change drives through the Drive drop-down list. The default list shows All QuarkXPress Files, but if the list is too long you can choose to list only Documents (*.QXD) or Templates (*.QXT) from the List Files of Type drop-down list. Chapter 9, lists specific differences between templates and documents.

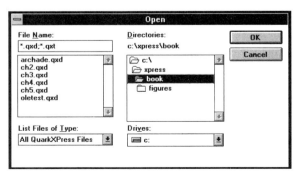

Figure 2-9 The Open dialog box, with drop-down list of higher directory levels.

To open a file, simply double-click on the file name of the document you want to open. This is the shortcut to clicking on the file name to highlight it, then clicking on the OK button. You can also select directories and files by using the Tab and arrow keys, as in any dialog box under Windows, then pressing ENTER when the desired file name is highlighted.

If QuarkXPress displays a warning message about "Nonmatching Preferences" when you open a document, it means that the XPRESS.PRF file has changed since the document was first created. The significance of this for your document is explained in Chapter 14.

When you open a document or a template, QuarkXPress displays the first page of the document in the view scale in which the document was last saved. Once a document is open, you can modify it using all of the techniques described here and in subsequent chapters.

Viewing Pages on the Screen

When you open a QuarkXPress document, often you can see only part of a page or document in the document window. You can change your view of the page on the screen in several ways. You can use the scroll bars in the document window to scroll up or down on a page or up or down from one page to the next. You can use the View menu commands, the Zoom tool (Q), or input a view percentage directly in the View Percent area in the lower left corner of the screen to jump to enlarged views of a particular area or reduce the page image to a smaller size. The View menu also offers commands for hiding certain elements on the screen or on the page view. These techniques are described below.

Using the Scroll Bars, Grabber Hand, and Keyboard Equivalents

You can use the scroll bars at the right and bottom edges of the document window to change your view of the page or to scroll to adjacent pages in the document. These work the same way that scroll bars work in most Windows applications: to move the view in the window in small increments, click on an arrow. Click in the gray area of the scroll bar on either side of the scroll box to move the view in the window up or down in larger increments. Drag the scroll box to move any distance.

If Live Scroll is checked in the Application Preferences dialog box, you can see the page(s) move as you drag the scroll box. Since this can slow the speed of scrolling, you might prefer to work with Live Scroll turned off (as described in Chapter 3), so you don't see the new view until you release the mouse button after dragging the scroll bar. In either case, you can temporarily turn Live Scroll on or off (i.e., reverse the Application Preferences setting) by holding the ALT key as you drag the scroll bar.

The position of the scroll box on the right scroll bar indicates the position of the page in the window relative to the whole document. For example, if the scroll box is at the top of the scroll bar, then you are viewing a page at the beginning of the document. You can jump to the end of the document by dragging the scroll box to the bottom of the right scroll bar.

The scroll box in the bottom scroll bar indicates your view relative to the current spread, including the surrounding pasteboard. If the scroll box is in the center of a scroll bar, you are viewing the center of the spread. You can jump to the pasteboard by dragging the scroll box to either end of the scroll bar.

The scroll bars move the view horizontally or vertically. You can use the Page Grabber Hand (✋) to move the view diagonally, or to move in more controlled increments. To do this, select the Content tool in the Tool palette, then hold the ALT key and the mouse button as you drag the mouse to display the Page Grabber Hand; drag the view in any direction. In order for this to work, Page Grabber Hand must be enabled through Preferences → Application.

If you prefer using the keyboard rather than the mouse, QuarkXPress offers these equivalents:

PAGE UP	Scroll up one screen
PAGE DOWN	Scroll down one screen
CTRL+PAGE UP	Scroll to first page
CTRL+PAGE DOWN	Scroll to last page
SHIFT+PAGE UP	Scroll to top of previous page
SHIFT+PAGE DOWN	Scroll to next page

You can also use keyboard shortcuts to move through a document when the Content tool is selected and the cursor is positioned within a story that extends beyond the current screen view:

CTRL+HOME	Scroll to start of story
CTRL+END	Scroll to end of story

Using the View Menu Commands and Keyboard Shortcuts

The first six commands in the View menu change the size of your view of the page—enlarging or reducing your view of the page on the screen. The currently selected view shows a check mark. The two most commonly used views have their keyboard combination shortcuts shown on the menu—Fit in Window (CTRL+0) and Actual Size (CTRL+1). There are several other shortcuts you will find useful.

You can jump from any view to Actual Size by clicking the right mouse button. If you are already in Actual Size view, the right mouse button jumps to Fit in Window. Therefore, you can use the right mouse button as a shortcut for toggling between Fit in Window and Actual Size views while you are working.

There's a similar synergy between the 200 percent and Actual Size views. You can jump from any view to 200 percent view by holding the CTRL key and clicking the right mouse button on the area you wish to enlarge. If you are already in 200 percent view, CTRL with the right mouse button jumps to Actual Size. Therefore, you can use CTRL and the right mouse button as a shortcut for toggling between 200 percent and Actual Size view.

When no items are active (selected), changing view percentage through the menu or through the View Percent area (described under the next heading) zooms in and out from the center of the current view. If Fit in Window is selected and no items are active, changing view zooms into the displayed page area before you chose Fit in Window.

The Fit in Window command centers the current page on the screen. To center the current *spread* plus the pasteboard area on the screen, hold the CTRL key as you select the command from the menu.

If an item is active, changing view percentage centers the display on the active item(s) *if the screen shows some part of the page containing the active item.* If part of the page is not shown, but any part of the *spread* containing the active item is shown, you can zoom to the active item by holding the CTRL key when you choose the new view.

Fit in Window is a good view for checking and changing the position of objects on the page and for viewing facing pages or multiple-page spreads. Select 50 percent to view the full width of 11-inch-wide formats on a 9-inch screen (or up to 16 inches on a 13-inch screen); 75 percent is ideal for viewing the full width of an 8½-by-11-inch page (without seeing its full length on a normal 9-inch or 13-inch screen). Actual Size is the normal view for editing text and graphics. The 200 percent view is useful for editing small-size text. The Thumbnails view lets you see miniatures of all pages at once, but you cannot edit individual items on a page.

Using the View Percent Area

The percentage of the view scale is shown in the lower left corner of the document window. This area, called the *View Percent* area, is interactive (Figure 2-10). It not only shows what view you are currently in, but also allows you to type in the view percentage you wish to display. At times, this method will be the fastest and most useful way to change the view of a page.

Double-click on the area, and enter the scale view you prefer. Pressing the ENTER key or clicking in the document window causes the display to change to the scale indicated.

View percent field

Figure 2-10   You can type directly in the View Percent area.

 If you want to see many pages of your document at once, type in a small percentage, such as 15 percent. The display is similar to that shown in Thumbnails view, which does not allow editing; but, by using 15 percent view, you can easily move items from one page to another.

Using the Zoom Tool

The quickest way to change the size of your view of the page is with the Zoom tool (Q). Choose the Zoom tool from the Tool palette, position the pointer over the portion of the page you want to enlarge, and click. To reduce the scale, hold down the CTRL key as you click the pointer on the page. The Zoom tool pointer shows a plus sign (⊕) when you are enlarging, a minus sign (⊖) when you are reducing, and is empty (Q) when you are already at the maximum enlargement or minimum reduction. The current view percentage is displayed in the lower left corner of the document window. The Zoom tool does not operate in Thumbnails view.

The View Scale settings in the Edit ➤ Preferences ➤ Tools dialog box determine the range and increment of the view changes when you click with the Zoom tool selected. (See Chapter 3 for information on setting tool preferences.) You can also drag the Zoom tool to outline a rectangular area on a page; the area you select will enlarge to fill the screen. If you select a very small area on the screen, for example, the view percentage will be as high as needed to make the outlined area fill the document window.

The most efficient way to use the Zoom tool is to switch to it at any time by holding down the SHIFT key and clicking or dragging with the right mouse button to enlarge the view. Hold SHIFT+CTRL and click the right mouse button to reduce the view. To toggle between Fit in Window and Actual Size views, simply click the right mouse button.

Hiding and Displaying Nonprinting Elements

Four of the next commands in the View menu—Hide Guides, Hide Baseline Grid, Hide Rulers, and Hide Invisibles—let you hide or display nonprinting elements on the screen. These elements include guides (margin guides, column guides, and ruler guides), the baseline grid, rulers, and invisible characters, such as carriage returns and tabs (Figure 2-11).

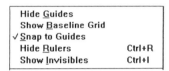

Figure 2-11 View menu commands that affect nonprinting elements on a page.

These commands are toggle commands that change in the menu when selected. If the guides are currently displayed, for example, the command in the menu is Hide Guides. When you choose Hide Guides the command in the menu changes to Show Guides. The same is true for the other commands in this section of the View menu. The exception is the Snap to Guides command, which is also a toggle, but it shows a check mark when selected. (The snap-to effect is described later in this chapter.)

Hide/Show Guides

These elements include margin, column, and ruler guides. To view the page exactly as it will appear when printed, deselect all items by clicking in the margin of the page outside all boxes and choose Hide Guides.

Hide/Show Baseline Grid

The Show Baseline Grid command displays the baseline grid as horizontal lines across the page. The preset default is that the baseline grid is not displayed. The increments of the baseline grid can be defined by selecting the Edit ➤ Preferences ➤ Typographic command, and you can force text to align to the baseline grid. Both of these options are discussed in more detail in Chapter 5.

Hide/Show Rulers

Rulers appear on the left side and top of the document window. The preset default is that rulers are displayed. The measurement system shown on the rulers can be defined by selecting the Edit ➤ Preferences ➤ General command, which is described in Chapter 3.

Hide/Show Invisibles

Invisibles are all of the nonprinting characters, such as spaces, carriage returns, and tabs that can be typed as part of text, using the keyboard. All of QuarkXPress' invisible characters are discussed in detail in Chapter 4. You may find it useful to display these characters, especially when typing directly in QuarkXPress, because it makes it easier to see exactly what you are typing. For example, accidentally typing in a space after a tab character can cause your text to be misaligned; it is difficult to see the extra space unless invisible characters are displayed. The default setting is that invisible characters are not displayed.

Hiding and Displaying Palettes

QuarkXPress offers six palettes that provide various aids to efficient production: the Tools palette, the Measurements palette, the Document Layout palette, the Style Sheets palette, the Colors palette, and the Trap Information palette (Figure 2-12). The function of each of these palettes is discussed in detail in later chapters.

```
Hide Tools
Hide Measurements
Show Document Layout
Show Style Sheets
Show Colors
Show Trap Information
```

Figure 2-12 Commands for displaying or hiding QuarkXPress palettes.

When you first install QuarkXPress, only the Tools and Measurements palettes are displayed. Like the Show/Hide Guides commands, the commands to Show or Hide palettes act as a toggle switch. For example, when the Tools palette is already visible, the command on the menu reads Hide Tools. If the Tool palette is not visible on the screen, the command reads Show Tools.

You can easily close these palettes by double-clicking on the Close Box in the top left corner of the palette. The menu commands are most efficiently used only to Show the palettes when they are not displayed.

Creating Text Boxes, Picture Boxes, and Lines

As we have said, the box is the basic building block for all text and pictures in QuarkXPress documents. Before you can add text or a graphic to a page, you must create a box to contain it. The next sections describe the basic steps for adding text boxes, picture boxes, and lines—all referred to as *items* in QuarkXPress terminology—to a page, and how to modify them. The techniques described in the following sections can be used to add items to document pages or master pages.

You can fill a box with text or an imported picture. Boxes and lines can also stand alone as graphic elements on the page if you assign a visible background or frame. These procedures are described briefly in this chapter, and detailed in Chapters 4 and 6.

Creating a Box

There are two kinds of boxes in QuarkXPress: text boxes and picture boxes. You can let QuarkXPress automatically create a text box on each page if you select the Automatic Text Box setting in the New dialog box, as described earlier in this chapter. You can also create text boxes using the Text Box creation tool (⬜). After drawing the box, select the Content tool (☞), and a blinking text cursor appears in the upper left corner of the box. Then you can type text directly into QuarkXPress or import it from a word processing program. Detailed descriptions of how text is typed or imported, edited, and formatted can be found in Chapters 4 and 5.

Boxes that can contain graphics are drawn using the Rectangle Picture Box tool (⊠), the Rounded-Corner Rectangle Picture Box tool (⊠), the Oval Picture Box tool (⊗), and the Polygon Picture Box tool (⊠). These tools create boxes with square corners, boxes with rounded corners, circles and ovals, or polygons, respectively. These shapes can stand alone as graphic elements on a page or they can contain graphics imported from other sources.

To create a box with any of these tools, select the tool and position the Item Creation pointer (+) on the page. As you drag the pointer on the page, you create a box. The size of a box is displayed in the Measurements palette as you draw, if that palette is open.

The one exception to this technique is the Polygon Picture Box tool [⊠], which is used by clicking on each point of the polygon shape you wish to draw, double-clicking or clicking on the first point to close the polygon. The size of the polygon does not display in the Measurements palette until it is closed.

Hold down the SHIFT key as you draw in order to constrain boxes to square shapes (for text or rectangular graphics boxes) or circles (for oval graphics boxes). When you release the mouse button the box is active, as indicated by its dark border and eight black "handles" (Figure 2-13).

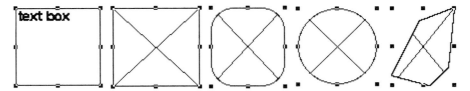

Figure 2-13 Drag the item creation pointer to create a box. When you release the mouse button, the box is active, as indicated by its dark border and eight handles.

Creating a Line

Select the Orthogonal Line tool (+) to draw horizontal and vertical lines, and the diagonal Line tool (\) to draw lines at any angle. The Orthogonal Line tool is simply an alternative to the Line tool, since you can constrain any line drawn with the diagonal Line tool to 0-, 45-, or 90-degree angles by holding down the SHIFT key as you draw. The SHIFT key also constrains lines to these angles when you resize them by dragging one of their handles.

Selecting Items

While you are creating a document in QuarkXPress, you can use the menu commands, tools from the Tool palette, or keyboard shortcuts to edit text or to work with graphics. Most of these commands will affect only the object or objects that are selected or active at the time the command is invoked; if nothing is active at the time the command is used, then nothing happens! This may seem obvious, yet beginners often mistakenly execute a command without first selecting the object for which it is intended. In this section we describe how to select boxes and lines created with QuarkXPress' item creation tools.

Selecting One Item

To select a single text box, picture box, or line with the Item tool (✥), position the pointer over the box or line and click once to select it. Active boxes show small black handles at the corners and midpoints of edges, and lines have one handle at each end (Figure 2-14).

Figure 2-14 Handles on an active line.

You do not have to select the Item tool from the Tools palette; instead, regardless of what tool is active, hold down the Control key (CTRL) to change the pointer to the Item tool pointer temporarily.

If an item is hidden by another, QuarkXPress allows you to activate the hidden item underneath. With the Content tool selected, hold down CTRL+ALT+SHIFT before clicking where the hidden item is located. If several items are stacked on one another, successive clicks of the mouse will activate items from the top to the bottom.

Selecting Multiple Items

In QuarkXPress you can select more than one item at a time. For multiple selection you must select the Item tool from the Tool palette; you cannot use the Control key shortcut to temporarily change the pointer to the Item tool. There are five ways to select multiple items, with the Item tool (✥) selected in the Tool palette:

- Hold down the SHIFT key as you click on several different items—one at a time. You can select more than one item at a time this way, and the items need not be adjacent to each other.
- If the items are adjacent to each other, you can position the Item tool pointer (▶) in an empty area at the top left corner of the area to be selected and drag the pointer to the bottom right corner. A selection rectangle will appear as you drag. Active items will be marked with handles. (Items that are partially encompassed will also be selected.)
- You can use a combination of the preceding two methods: holding down the SHIFT key, clicking to select one item at a time, and dragging to select other groups of items.
- Use Edit → Select All (CTRL+A) to select all of the items on the active page or spread, including the pasteboard.
- Use any of the first four methods to select a group of items, then hold down the SHIFT key and click on an active item to *deselect* it from a group.

The multiple-item select feature enables you to select multiple items and perform actions on all those items at once. For example, when you select multiple items, you can use commands described in this chapter to move, cut, copy, paste, align, duplicate, delete, and lock all items; send all items behind; or bring all items forward. You can also apply the Group command to establish and maintain a group relationship.

The multiple-item select feature works only with the Item tool and only on items within a spread. You cannot select multiple items with the Content tool or select multiple items that are not part of the same spread.

Using the Select All Command

The effect of Edit → Select All (CTRL+A) depends on the current tool selection and pointer position on the screen:

- If the Content tool (🖑) is selected and the cursor is positioned in a text box (by positioning the I-beam pointer [I] in the text box and clicking once to position the blinking text cursor), then the Select All command will select all of the text in the active box *and the text in all boxes linked to the active box*.
- If the Item tool (✥) is selected, then the Select All command will select all text boxes, picture boxes, and lines on the active spread and on the adjacent pasteboard area. If any of the active items are locked, then the pointer will change to a padlock (🔒) when positioned over *any* item (locked or not), and the active group cannot be moved with the mouse unless you unlock all items in it or deselect the locked items.

Whenever multiple items are selected, only those commands that are applicable to *all* types of items in the selection will be available. For example, if the selection includes only text boxes and picture boxes, you can use the Item → Frame command to set a common frame (border) for all the active items. If the selection also includes any lines, however, the Frame command will not be available. Commands that are not available will be gray in the menus, or the system will beep when you try to select one inappropriately.

Moving and Resizing Items

QuarkXPress offers different methods for accomplishing the same task. Items often can be modified by using the mouse, keyboard shortcuts, the Measurements palette, the Colors palette, or commands from the Item menu, especially the Item → Modify command. The next sections describe various techniques for moving (repositioning) and resizing items.

Using the Mouse

Once a box is created, you can change the position of a box on the page by selecting the Item tool (✥), clicking on an item, and dragging the item by any part except its handles to move it. As mentioned in the previous section, a good shortcut to use is to hold down the CTRL key to activate the Item tool temporarily, then move the item. Hold down the shift key to constrain the movement of an item horizontally or vertically as you move it.

If you click on an item and drag it immediately, you will see only an outline of the item as you move it. If you pause one-half second before you move an item, you will see the item and its contents as you move.

If you select an item with the Item tool selected (not the Content tool), you can move the item using the arrow keys on the keyboard. Each time you press a key, the item will move in 1-point increments. Hold down the ALT key and press an arrow key to move in .1-point increments.

With either the Item tool or the Content tool selected, you can change the size of the box by dragging a handle of the box. Drag a corner handle to scale both dimensions (horizontal and vertical) at once. Drag a side handle when you want to scale only one dimension. When resizing a box, you can constrain it to a square or circle by holding down the SHIFT key as you drag a handle.

To change the length of a line using the mouse, drag one of the handles on either end of the line. Hold down the shift key to keep the line straight as you resize it or to constrain it to 45° angles.

Using the Measurements Palette

You can also change the position and size (and other features) of a box or line through the Measurements palette (Figure 2-15) or through the Item → Modify command, described in the next section. The Measurements palette is probably the easiest way to modify items, and we highly recommend that you display and use it.

X: 4p	W: 7p	∠ 0°	
Y: 6p	H: 4p6	Cols:1	

Figure 2-15 You can view or change the location and size of a box through the Measurements palette.

When a box is active, the control areas in the Measurements palette related to size and position include:

- X—the horizontal position of the origin of the box relative to the current zero point on the rulers.
- Y—the vertical position of the origin of the box relative to the current zero point on the rulers. (Note that the origin is the *original* top left corner of the box, which is not necessarily the apparent top left corner if the box has been rotated.)
- W—the width of the box.
- H—the height of the box.

You can change the position or the size of a box by selecting the appropriate control area in the Measurements palette and entering a new value. Press the ENTER key or click on the document window for the new value to take effect. You can also add or subtract values from the current values; QuarkXPress calculates the new value and changes the box accordingly.

The Measurements palette is different when a line is selected (Figure 2-16); the values you enter to reposition or resize a line depend on the orientation you have selected: Endpoints, Left Point, Midpoint, or Right Point.

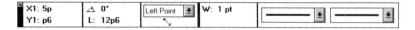

Figure 2-16   The Measurements palette when a line is selected.

Besides the position coordinates and size, additional entries in the Measurements palette will vary depending on whether the active item is a text box, an anchored text box, a picture box, an anchored picture box, or a group. These entries are explained in detail in Chapters 3 through 6.

Using the Item ➤ Modify Command

Commands on the Item menu (Figure 2-17), discussed here and throughout the chapter, affect items themselves, as opposed to the *content* of items. Entries for changing the position and size of items, as displayed on the Measurements palette, are duplicated in the dialog boxes displayed by using the Item ➤ Modify command.

Figure 2-17   The Item menu.

The Item ➤ Modify command is available when a text box, picture box, line, or group is active. You can access this command by choosing it from the menu, using the keyboard shortcut (CTRL+M), or simply double-clicking on an item with the Item tool (✥) selected. Depending on which type of item is active, the Modify command displays one of four dialog boxes: Text Box Specifications, Picture Box Specifications, Line Specifications, or Group Specifications.

The values for position and width entered in these dialog boxes (Figure 2-18) are the same as those displayed in the Measurements palette. Remember that in this or any dialog box, you can enter any unit of measure, or you can change a value by adding or subtracting from the current setting.

Figure 2-18   Text or Picture Box Specifications dialog boxes let you enter values for changing the position and size of boxes.

In the Text Box Specifications and Picture Box Specifications dialog boxes, **Origin Across** and **Origin Down** indicate the numerical position of the origin as measured from the zero point on the rulers. (The *origin* is the *original* top left corner of the box, which is not necessarily the apparent top left corner if the box has been rotated.). **Width** and **Height** are the dimensions of the box. By entering these four values numerically, you can specify precise placement of a text box on a page up to .001 units of any measure.

The minimum text box width and height is 12 points. Text boxes that have no leading (that is, empty ones or ones that contain only one character) can be scaled down to within 10 points (plus the Text Inset value) of the top of the box without causing text to overflow. See Chapter 4 for more information on other modifications that can be made to text boxes and Chapter 6 for more information on picture boxes.

The Line Specifications dialog box also duplicates the position and size values shown in the Measurements palette. And, as in the Measurements palette, values entered for changing the position and length of a line depend on whether Endpoints, Left Point, Midpoint, or Right Point is selected (Figure 2-19).

Figure 2-19   The Line Specifications dialog box showing values for the same 2-inch-long line with Endpoints, Left Point, Midpoint, and Right Point selected.

Rotating Items

You can use the Rotation tool (↻) to rotate an item: First, select the item with the Item tool, then select the Rotation tool. Next, click once on or near the item to position the axis of rotation (the point around which the item will rotate), then drag the pointer away from the axis point in a circular motion to rotate the item. You can see the axis point and a line indicating the rotation angle as well as a "ghost" of the item rotate as you move the pointer (Figure 2-20).

Chapter 2: Creating One Page   79

Figure 2-20   In rotating an item with the Rotate tool, you can see the axis point and a line indicating the rotation angle as well as a "ghost" of the item as you move the pointer.

You can enter angles of rotation numerically in either the Measurements palette or by selecting the Item ➤ Modify command (Figure 2-21). A positive value indicates a counterclockwise rotation, a negative value indicates a clockwise rotation. Boxes are rotated from the center by means of dialog box entries or from first mouse position when rotated with the Rotate tool. If Endpoints mode is selected, lines cannot be rotated using dialog box entries.

Figure 2-21   Specify the angle of rotation of a box numerically in the Measurements palette or in any of the Box Specification dialog boxes (Item ➤ Modify).

Changing the Appearance of Items

There are several ways in which you can modify the appearance of an item, independently of the *content* of the item. For example, you can apply a color to the background of a text box without affecting the text at all. This section looks at the basic steps involved in applying color and shade to an item, and how to add a frame to a box. Reshaping picture boxes is discussed in Chapter 6.

Applying Color and Shade to Items

All boxes drawn in QuarkXPress can have color and shade applied to them, using either the Item → Modify command or the Colors palette (Figure 2-22). The available colors listed include a default set of colors that cannot be deleted, such as black, white, registration, cyan, magenta, and yellow. You can add other colors with the Edit → Colors command (explained in detail in Chapter 7).

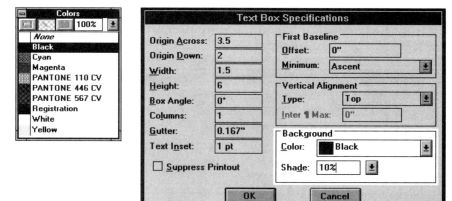

Figure 2-22   Apply a color and shade to the background of a box using the Colors palette or in any of the Box Specification dialog boxes (Item → Modify).

For any box, you can specify a Background of any Color listed in the drop-down list or on the Colors palette. You can indicate any shade from 0 to 100 percent in .1 percent increments, or choose from the 10 percent increments in the drop-down list. Specify a background color of None to make a transparent box. The default setting for the background color of a box when it is first drawn is 0 percent black.

Using the Colors palette, you can apply two-color blends to picture or text box backgrounds. See Chapter 7 for more details on how to create blends.

For any line, you can specify a color and shade using the Measurements palette, the Item → Modify command, or the Style menu.

When a text box, even a transparent one (0 percent shade), is made active and the Content tool () is selected, the box is made temporarily opaque (that is, you cannot see through it) and is brought in front of all other boxes and lines to make editing its text easy.

In specifying screen percentages, be sure to take into account the differences between printers that will be used throughout the production cycle and typesetters that will be used for final camera-ready copy. For example, a 10 percent gray screen will seem darker when printed on a 300 dpi printer than on a 1200 dpi typesetter; at 2400 dpi the screen will nearly disappear. Screens that are below 50 percent gray will tend to print lighter on a high-resolution typesetter than on a low-resolution printer; screens that are above 50 percent gray will tend to print darker on a high-resolution typesetter than on a low-resolution printer.

Adding a Frame to a Box

Use Item → Frame (CTRL+B) to add a decorative frame or border around an active text box or picture box. Using this command, you can frame boxes that contain text or imported graphics, or you can add frames to create framed geometrical items (boxes, ovals, circles) that stand alone as graphics on a page.

Figure 2-23   Frame Specifications dialog box.

The border around the Frame Specifications title in the dialog box reflects the current frame for the active box, and that frame is highlighted in the list of frame styles. You can select from a variety of styles that come with QuarkXPress and customize to some extent by choosing your own width, color, and shade for a frame. (See Figure 2-23.)

Style

The Style scroll window shows all of the frames that come with QuarkXPress. These are mathematically generated frames (consisting of continuous solid or dashed lines) that can be applied to any box, including rounded-corner rectangles, and to ovals and circles.

Width

Frames can be specified to any width from .001 points to 504 points. When you specify a frame for a text box, the distance between the text and the frame is determined by the Item → Modify → Text Inset setting for that box. When you specify a frame for a picture box, the frame may cut off or crop the picture. Remember that in this or any dialog box you can enter any unit of measure, or you can change a value by adding or subtracting from the current setting.

The Edit → Preferences → General command, described in Chapter 3, lets you specify whether new frames will display inside or outside the edges of a box. If the frame is added inside, the dimensions of the box remain the same. If the frame is added outside, the dimensions of the box increase by the frame width. Frame width will be limited under two conditions:

- If there is not enough room between the box edge and the edge of the constraining box in a constrained group or the edge of a pasteboard, and the General Preferences Framing option is set to Outside, and
- If there is not enough room inside the box, and the General Preferences Framing option is set to Inside.

Under these conditions, you can choose a smaller frame or enlarge or move the box. You can remove a frame from a box by choosing 0 as the frame width.

Color and Shade

The Frame Specifications dialog box allows you to select different colors or shades as options. Use the drop-down list to select any color from a list of colors created using the Edit → Colors command. You can also type a number for any shade (in .1 percent increments) or choose from the 10 percent increments in the drop-down list.

Chapter 2: Creating One Page 83

Importing Text and Pictures

Although you can create text and graphics directly using QuarkXPress' tools, it's common to import text and graphics from other sources into a QuarkXPress document, using the File ➤ Get Text and File ➤ Get Picture commands. Many authors use a dedicated word processing application for their text, for example, then hand their disk files over to a production group for final page layout in QuarkXPress. The author or a graphic artist might also choose a dedicated graphics application to develop complex graphics and manipulate scanned images before importing them into QuarkXPress.

Here we assume that you have already prepared the text and graphics that you intend to import into QuarkXPress. The next sections provide a brief overview of how to import text and graphics. For more detail on importing text, see Chapter 4; more information on importing graphics may be found in Chapter 6.

Importing Text

You can import text into an empty text box or into a text box that already contains text. Imported text will come in at the text insertion point—this can be within text that is already in the text box—or it will replace text that is selected. With a text box active and the Content tool (☞) selected, choose File ➤ Get Text to import text. (If the Get Text command is dimmed in the menu, be sure that a text box is active and that you have selected the Content tool.)

Figure 2-24 The Get Text dialog box.

The Get Text dialog box (Figure 2-24) displays a list of text files in the current directory on the current drive. You can change directories by clicking on the folder icons in the Directories area, and change drives through the Drive drop-down list. The default list shows All Text Files, but if the list is too long you can choose to list only one type from the List Files of Type drop-down list.

QuarkXPress lists files it recognizes as word processing files, including ASCII and RTF (Rich Text Format) documents and documents created in Microsoft Word 4.0 for DOS, Microsoft Word for Windows versions 1.0 and 2.0, Microsoft Write, WordPerfect 5.1, WordPerfect for Windows, Ami Pro 2.0, and XyWrite III Plus. If the file you wish to import is not listed, it might have been saved with an unusual extension. You can try listing all files (*.*) or entering the exact name of the file you seek. Some formats require that an import/export filter be present in the QuarkXPress program directory before you launch QuarkXPress. (See Chapter 4 for more detailed information about importing text.)

Check Convert Quotes to convert quotation marks that were typed with the inch (") and foot (') symbols to proper opening and closing quotes that are generally preferred by publishers. (You type proper opening and closing quotes in QuarkXPress and in other applications under Windows by pressing ALT+[, ALT+], SHIFT+ALT+[, and SHIFT+ALT+] to get ', ', ", and ", respectively.)

Check Include Style Sheets if you want QuarkXPress to pick up the styles that were applied in Microsoft Word or as tag codes in ASCII text. Chapter 10 describes QuarkXPress Tags that can be typed in ASCII text files.

Double-click on a text file name to import it into the active text box. As the text is being imported, QuarkXPress displays the percentage of completion in the lower left corner of the document window, to the right of the View Percent area. Text following the insertion point will be reflowed to accommodate the imported text. How to handle text overflow will be described next.

Importing Text within a Stream

To import text into the middle of an existing stream of text, select the Content tool (), click the I-beam to position the cursor at the point in the text where you want the new text inserted, or select a range of text that you want to replace, then choose File → Get Text and follow the procedures just described.

Text Overflow

If you type or import text into an automatic text box, or any chain of two or more boxes, and Auto Page Insertion is on in the General Preferences dialog box (described in Chapter 3), QuarkXPress adds pages at the end of the section for the overflow text, if the text file you import cannot fit in the automatic text box.

When you type or import more text than will fit in a text box that is not linked to another text box, a small square (⊠) appears in the bottom right corner of the box (Figure 2-25). You can see the rest of the text by making the box larger or by linking the text box to another, empty text box. The procedures for linking text from one box to another are described later in this chapter.

Figure 2-25 Symbol in lower right corner indicates text overflow (left) unless text box is enlarged (middle) or linked to another text box (right).

If you find that there is overflow text (as indicated by a ⊠ in the lower right corner of the last text box in a chain) but new pages are not added automatically when you import the text into the first box, then one of three conditions exists: The Auto Page Insertion is disabled in the General Preferences dialog box, the master page specified in Auto Page Insertion has a broken chain icon (⛓) in the upper left corner, or the overflow is from a single text box that is not defined on the master page as the automatic text box.

Importing Pictures

To import a graphic, draw or select the picture box that will contain the graphic, select the Content tool (☝), then choose File → Get Picture. The Get Picture dialog box (Figure 2-26) displays a list of graphic-format files in the current directory on the current drive. To import a file into the active picture box, double-click on a file name.

Figure 2-26 Get Picture dialog box.

QuarkXPress can import any of these formats: bitmap (.BMP, .DIB, .RLE), Compuserve GIF (.GIF), Paintbrush (.PCX), Windows Metafile (.WMF), Computer Graphics Metafile (.CGM), HPGL (.PLT), Macintosh PICT (.PCT), Micrografx Designer (.DRW), Scitex (.CT), TIFF (.TIF), and Encapsulated PostScript (.EPS). If the file you wish to import is not listed, it might have been saved with an unusual extension. You can try listing all files (*.*) or entering the exact name of the file you seek. HPGL, DRW, and CGM formats require that an import/export filter be present in the QuarkXPress program directory before you launch QuarkXPress. (See Chapter 6 for more detailed information about importing graphics.)

The entire unscaled picture that you import is placed in the active picture box, replacing any previous contents of the box. You may need to scale the picture to make it fit the box, using a combination of keyboard and mouse techniques, described in Chapter 6.

Deleting Items

Four alternatives are available for deleting selected items from a page: choosing Edit → Cut (CTRL+X or SHIFT+DELETE), choosing Edit → Delete, pressing the Backspace key, or choosing Item → Delete (CTRL+K). The effects of these commands depend on what *tool* as well as what *items* are selected, as described under the next headings.

Regardless of what tool or element is selected, the Edit → Delete command, the Item → Delete command, and the Backspace key do *not* put the selection into the Clipboard, as the Edit → Cut command does. The selection cannot be retrieved using the Paste command. The only way to retrieve objects after using the Delete command, or the Backspace key is to use the Undo command *immediately*.

Deleting Lines or Boxes

You can delete an *un-Anchored* line or box (including all box contents) by selecting it with the Item tool (✥) and choosing Edit → Cut (CTRL+X or SHIFT+DELETE), choosing Edit → Delete, pressing the Backspace key, or choosing Item → Delete (CTRL+K). The Item → Delete command is a useful alternative to using the Cut command, because it deletes items whether the Item tool (✥) or the Content tool (☝) is selected.

If a deleted text box is linked to any other text boxes, the links are reconnected around the deleted box and the text is reflowed to the other boxes in the chain. If deletion of a linked text box causes text to overflow in the linked chain, one or more new pages will be inserted automatically to handle the overflow if Auto Page Insertion and automatic linking on the master page are both enabled. You can prevent this by using Edit ➤ Preferences ➤ General to turn Auto Page Insertion off before deleting linked text boxes.

Deleting Text or Graphics from Within a Box

To delete text or graphics from within a box without deleting the box itself, you must select the text or picture with the Content tool (☞), then choose Edit ➤ Cut (CTRL+X or SHIFT+DELETE), Edit ➤ Delete, or press the Delete or Backspace key.

The Content tool automatically activates the entire contents of a picture box that contains an imported graphic. In deleting text from a text box, you can select all of the text or only part of it, using text selection methods described in Chapter 4.

If you select contents of a box and choose Item ➤ Delete (CTRL+K), QuarkXPress will delete the entire box. If you first choose the Item tool (✥) to select a box, the Item ➤ Delete (CTRL+K), Edit ➤ Cut (CTRL+X or SHIFT+DELETE), Edit ➤ Delete, or the Backspace key deletes the entire box.

Undoing Your Most Recent Action

The Edit ➤ Undo (CTRL+Z or ALT+BKSPC) reverses the action taken immediately before the command was invoked. For this reason, work cautiously when you are making major changes, such as altering the type specifications or formatting a whole block of text or a whole story. Check the results of each action as you go along. You can reverse your last action if you use the Undo command *immediately* after making a mistake or changing your mind.

When you use the Undo command, the menu changes to Redo until you perform the next action. This command allows you to perform an action, then Undo and Redo as many times as you like, so long as you do not go on to any other actions. The command is handy for reversing mistakes or changing your mind; you can use this command to compare two ideas while designing a page.

Some actions cannot be reversed by the Undo command. QuarkXPress usually displays a dialog box warning you that the action you are about to perform cannot be undone and gives you a chance to cancel the action.

Using Rulers to Position Items on a Page

Use View → Show/Hide Rulers (CTRL+R) to display or hide the horizontal and vertical rulers at the top and left edges of the document window. You can use these rulers to help position ruler guides, text, and graphics on the page, to measure distances, or to draw or scale graphics to fit an area.

To display rulers on the screen, select View → Show Rulers (CTRL+R). This is a toggle command—the menu displays Show Rulers if they are hidden and Hide Rulers if they are displayed.

The position of boxes or lines on the screen is indicated by a dotted marker on each ruler when you initially create the item or when you click, drag, or scale the item with the Mover pointer (✥) (Figure 2-27). This marker can be especially helpful in positioning items visually on the screen. (You can specify an item's position precisely in numerical terms through the Measurements palette or the Item → Modify command.)

The ruler origin is the intersection of the zero points of the two rulers. Normally, the origin is set at the top left corner of the page or spread (depending on the Item Coordinates setting in the General Preferences dialog box), but you can move the zero points by positioning the pointer in the small box where the rulers intersect and dragging the zero point to a new position. Crossed lines appear as you drag the zero point, to help you see where the new location will be when you release the mouse.

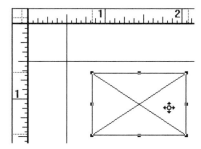

Figure 2-27 Markers on the rulers show the position of items as they are being moved or scaled.

You can position the zero point anywhere on a page. To restore the zero point to the upper left corner of the page, click on the box where the rulers intersect. (One instance in which you change the zero point is when you print with the Manual Tiling option, described in Chapter 8.)

The rulers must be displayed in order to create nonprinting guides on the page, as described below.

Choosing the Unit of Measure

Use Edit ➤ Preferences ➤ General (CTRL+Y) to set the unit of measure displayed on the rulers. You can change the unit of measure at any time without affecting the document itself—only the rulers and other displays that show measurements will change. You may choose to work with one unit of measure throughout the production, or with different measures (using picas for margins and columns, and inches for scaling figures, for example).

The number of increments displayed along the rulers will vary depending on the size in which you are currently viewing the page. Rulers show finer increments of measure in enlarged views, such as 200 percent, than in reduced views.

Ruler Guides

In addition to the margin and column guides, up to 100 vertical and 100 horizontal ruler guides can be dragged from the rulers. You can use ruler guides on any page to help align items horizontally and vertically, as described here. You can also create ruler guides on a master page as a grid for positioning items consistently on document pages. Figure 2-28 illustrates how ruler guides are displayed on color and monochrome monitors.

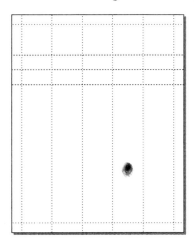

Figure 2-28   Ruler guides are displayed as green lines on color monitors and solid lines on monochrome monitors.

To create a ruler guide on any page, first choose View ➤ Show Rulers to display the rulers at the top and left edges of the document window, then hold down the mouse pointer on the vertical or horizontal ruler and drag a vertical or horizontal guide onto the page. The current position shows as a dotted line on the ruler as you drag and in the Measurements palette. Release the mouse to position the guide. You can reposition the guide at any time by dragging it, or you can delete it by dragging it back to the ruler.

 You can delete all ruler guides at once by holding the ALT key and clicking on each ruler.

Note that in order to move a ruler guide, you should click on it in the margins of the page or some place where it is not positioned on top of anything else on the page. Otherwise, you might move the item instead of the guide.

Ruler guides are useful for positioning items on a page, but they do not directly affect the width of text (as column guides do). Ruler guides that you create on a master page show on all pages created from that master; ruler guides created on a document page show on that page only.

Using the Snap-to Effect

Guides—margin guides, column guides, and ruler guides—have a snap-to effect: They pull the pointer or the edges of a line, a text box, or a picture box into position when you bring the item to within 6 pixels of the guide. The snap-to effect is extremely useful when you want to align items quickly and precisely, especially when you are working in reduced views, such as Fit in Window.

Sometimes you may prefer to work with the snap-to effect turned off—as when you are forcing something into a position outside of the basic grid structure. You can do this by choosing View ➤ Snap to Guides. This is a toggle switch—it is checked in the menu when the effect is on, and it is not checked when the effect is off. Turning snap-to on and off has no effect on text and graphics that have already been positioned on the page.

The margin and column guides that have a snap-to effect are those on the master pages—created by entries in the New dialog box when you first start a document, or by the Page ➤ Master Guides command. Margins and columns within text boxes *do not* have a snap-to effect except in two instances: The margin guides in the automatic text box also have a snap-to effect, and the margins of a constraining box (created with the Item ➤ Constrain command, described later in this chapter) have a snap-to effect on constrained elements within the box.

Controlling Text Runaround

Text *runaround* is text that is forced to flow around a box or a line that falls within the text column. In QuarkXPress, runaround is controlled entirely by the Item → Runaround command.

Use Item → Runaround (CTRL+T) to set the Runaround specifications for an active box (Figure 2-29). You can set Mode to None, Item, Auto Image, or Manual Image. Runaround settings of None or Item can be applied to text or picture box; Auto Image or Manual Image runaround apply to picture boxes only.

Selecting a Mode of None allows text to flow behind the active item. You can force text to flow around any item—including a transparent box or line—by setting Mode to Item.

Figure 2-29   Runaround Specifications dialog box.

Item

If the active item is a text box or picture box and you have selected Item mode, you can specify the distance between the runaround text and the top, left, bottom, and right edges of the box. However, when you flow a single column of text around an item, the text will flow only on the side with the widest text area (between the item and the column edges). To flow text around both sides, you must set up two or more columns.

Auto Image

If the active item is a picture box, you can have text automatically flow around the picture edges by setting Mode to Auto Image. Text will be positioned to follow the contour around the picture edges—whatever the shape—at the distance specified as the Text Outset in the Text Box Specifications dialog box. The shape created by the Auto Image option cannot be edited.

Manual Image

Set Mode to Manual Image and QuarkXPress creates an editable runaround polygon (a many-sided object) around the picture in the active picture box. You can modify a runaround polygon by adding, removing, or repositioning handles and by repositioning segments, as described in Chapter 6. You can specify the Text Outset for Manual Image mode just as you can for Auto Image mode.

When you specify Manual Image for an empty picture box or for a picture box whose picture is out of view, QuarkXPress creates a runaround polygon along the inside edge of the box.

You can also select Invert to run the text inside a picture's manual image polygon. After setting up the polygon, you can delete the picture and the polygon will remain (Figure 2-30).

Figure 2-30   Examples of text runaround (left to right): Mode = Item, Mode = Auto Image, Mode = Auto Image with text set in two columns, Mode = Manual Image with Invert option.

Duplicating Items

You can make copies of boxes and lines in QuarkXPress using the standard Windows Copy and Paste commands, but QuarkXPress also offers two commands—Duplicate and Step and Repeat—that provide more control over the positioning of the duplicated elements.

The difference between these two commands is that Step and Repeat lets you make one or more duplicates at a time and specify new offsets (horizontal and vertical distances that determine where the copies will be positioned relative to the original) through the dialog box, whereas Duplicate makes one duplicate at a time using the previously specified offsets.

Using the Duplicate Command

Use Item ➤ Duplicate (CTRL+D) to make an exact copy of any active box or line, as an alternative to using the Copy and Paste commands from the Edit menu. When you copy and paste, the pasted item is positioned in the center of the view of the active page in the document window. When you use Duplicate, the new copy is positioned relative to the original at the offset distances specified in the Step and Repeat dialog box, described next. If you duplicate again, the next duplicate will appear in the same relative position.

A linked text box or a box containing a linked constrained box cannot be duplicated. The Duplicate command will not position a copy of an item outside its constraining box if it is part of a constrained group; the message "Can't make the duplicate using these offsets" will display if you try to do so.

Using the Step and Repeat Command

Use Item ➤ Step and Repeat (or the keyboard shortcut, CTRL+ALT+D) to specify the offset distance used by the Duplicate command (just described) or as an alternative to the Duplicate command. Step and Repeat lets you make one or more duplicates at a time and specify new offsets through the Step and Repeat dialog box (Figure 2-31).

Figure 2-31   Step and Repeat dialog box.

Repeat Count is the number of duplicate copies to be made. **Horizontal** and **Vertical Offset** determine where the copies will be positioned relative to the original. Positive entries are to the right or below the original, negative entries are to the left or above the original. You can enter measurements in any unit of measure, and you can change a value by adding or subtracting from the current setting (like other dialog boxes).

A quick alternative to using the Step and Repeat command to make multiple duplicates is to use the keyboard shortcut for the Duplicate command—CTRL+D—as many times as needed.

By the way, the Duplicate and Step and Repeat commands do not affect the contents of the Clipboard. Part II provides more tips on using Duplicate and Step and Repeat in creating forms and other special layouts.

Arranging Items in Layers

One feature of QuarkXPress that is characteristic of drawing applications, and that distinguishes it from any word processing program, is that items can be arranged on top of each other in *layers*. Normally, the first item you position on a page establishes the bottom layer, and each item added occupies another layer on top of the last.

An item is concealed when it falls on a layer below any box that contains a graphic or a background color. Text boxes also become temporarily opaque when you edit them, even if they are set to have a transparent background (i.e., background color set to None or 0 percent shade). To find a hidden item, you can click through to items hidden underneath others, or you can use the Send Backward, Send to Back, Bring Forward, and Bring to Front commands to change the order of layered items.

Clicking through Layers

Clicking through layers is an important feature to learn and use frequently. Any time an item is hidden under another, you can select the hidden item easily by holding the SHIFT+ALT+CTRL keys and clicking on the location of the hidden item. Repeated clicks will select items on successive layers. If there are more than two layers, keep clicking until the item you seek is selected. This feature is useful when multiple layers are stacked on top of one another.

Using the Send to Back/Bring to Front Commands

The Send Backward and Send to Back commands are available only if the active item is layered above another item on the page. Send Backward moves items by one layer only, while Send to Back sends the active item to the bottom layer in a series. The Bring Forward and Bring to Front commands are available only if the active item is behind another item. Bring Forward moves items by one layer, and Bring to Front brings an item to the "top" of a stack of items.

If the active item is a constraining box, then it and all of its constrained items will be moved to another layer. If the active item is a constrained item, it will be layered relative to the other constrained items within the same constraining box, but not behind the constraining box.

Aligning Items

Use Item → Space/Align to control the position of active items relative to one another. First select two or more items on a page, using any of the multiple-select methods described earlier in this chapter. Then choose Item → Space Align to display the Space/Align Items dialog box (Figure 2-32).

Figure 2-32   The Space/Align Items dialog box.

Check Horizontal to align the active items horizontally, check Vertical to align the active items vertically, or check both to align the active items along both axes at once. In each case, you can specify the amount of space you want between items. If three or more items are active, you can let QuarkXPress determine the space between items by selecting Distribute Evenly.

You can specify that QuarkXPress measure the horizontal space between items, left edges, centers, or right edges, and measure the vertical space between items, top edges, centers, or bottom edges. See Part II for more tips on when to use this command.

Creating Relationships between Items

There are several ways to create a relationship between items on a page.

- Text boxes can be *linked* in a chain so that the text flow from text box to text box is automatically readjusted in all linked boxes when text is edited.

- Text boxes, picture boxes, or lines can be *anchored* within text, so that the anchored box or line automatically moves whenever the text shifts due to edits.
- Multiple items can be *grouped* so that whenever you select one of the items with the Item tool (✥), you automatically select them all. Individual items within a group can still be moved or edited with the Content tool (☜).
- A group can also be *constrained* so items within it cannot be moved beyond the borders of the constraining box.

Each of these options is described more fully under the next headings.

Linking Text Boxes

You control the flow of text through a document by linking text boxes. In QuarkXPress terminology, any series of linked text boxes is called a *chain*, and the text in a chain is called a *story*. Normally, the primary text chain is linked automatically in any QuarkXPress document. When you import more text than will fit in a text box, QuarkXPress automatically adds pages for the text overflow *if all of the following conditions are true*:

- Auto Page Insertion is enabled, *and*
- The master page specified in Auto Page Insertion has an automatic text chain (as indicated by the intact chain icon {⛓} in the upper left corner of the master page), *and*
- The overflow is from the automatic text box.

Automatically inserted pages will be added at the location specified in the Auto Page Insertion drop-down list in the General Preferences dialog box. Options include End of Section, End of Story, or End of Document, as described in Chapter 3.

You can use the last two tools in the Tool palette—the Linking (⛓) and Unlinking (⛓) tools—manually to direct the flow of text from one text box to another or to sever existing links. Manual linking is useful for creating independent text chains within the document—separate from the automatic text chains (described next).

Also, use these manual linking tools to insert and link a new text box into a chain of linked text boxes. Not only can you link text boxes in any order, but you can also link boxes that are separated by many intervening pages (as is common in newspapers and magazines). You can link or unlink boxes in any view except Thumbnails, but the Fit in Window view makes the process easiest.

Automatic Text Chains

The automatic text box, described earlier in this chapter, creates a chain of linked text boxes as needed for text overflow. A master page can have only one automatic text box. A text box on a master page, however, can result in more than one *chain* in a document. Let's say you flow a story into an automatic text box on page 1, for example, and two additional pages are added automatically. The first three pages are one chain or one story. If you insert a new page 4 based on the same master page that has the automatic text box, any text you type or import to page 4 will start a new chain or a new story (Figure 2-33). There is no linkage between the text on page 3 and the text on page 4.

Figure 2-33   First three pages contain one story, linked in an automatic text chain. A new story—and a new automatic text chain—starts on page 4 and continues to page 5.

You can add or remove boxes in these linked chains manually, as described under the next headings, as well as create additional chains of text boxes—not connected to the automatic text chain.

Creating a New Chain of Linked Text Boxes

To create a new chain of linked text boxes, first draw the text boxes. Either leave all boxes empty or fill only one with text. (You cannot link two boxes that both have text.) Then select the Linking tool (⬛), and click on the first text box in the chain. The box will be surrounded by a marquee (moving dotted line) to indicate that it has been activated by the Linking tool. Then click on the box you want to link to the first, and continue clicking sequentially through all of the text boxes in the order you want them to be linked.

Adding Text to Empty Linked Boxes

To add text to newly linked boxes, select the first empty box in the chain, then type the new text, or choose File ➝ Get Text, or use the Edit ➝ Copy and Edit ➤ Paste commands to copy text from another source. If any box in the newly linked chain already contains text that cannot fit in that box, the overflow text will automatically flow into the next linked text box.

Linking Boxes That Already Contain Text

You can link a box that contains text to subsequent empty text boxes, but you cannot link two boxes that contain text. To link boxes that already contain text, first select and Edit ➤ Cut (CTRL+X or SHIFT+DELETE) the text from the *second* box. Then select the Linking tool and link the two boxes. Finally, use Edit ➤ Paste (CTRL+V or SHIFT+INSERT) to insert the cut text at the end of the linked text.

Viewing the Links between Boxes

To view the links between boxes, select a box on the page, then select the Linking or the Unlinking tool. The page will display existing links as arrows.

Unlinking Boxes

To unlink boxes, first select a box from the chain you want to unlink, then select the Unlinking tool () to display the link arrows. Click on either the head or the tailfeathers of the arrow you want to delete, thereby severing the link. The unlinking tool must be completely within the box. When you unlink two boxes in a chain, the last box before the break in the chain will contain all of the overflow text, and subsequent boxes in the broken chain will appear empty.

Inserting a New Box in the Middle of a Linked Chain

To insert a new box in the middle of a linked chain (and make it part of the chain), first use the Text Box tool () to create the new box. Next select the Linking tool (), and click on the last box in the chain preceding the new box(es), then click on the new, empty box(es). The text will automatically flow through the original chain.

Inserting New Pages within a Linked Chain

To insert a new page within a linked chain (and make it part of the chain), first select either the Item tool () or the Content tool () and activate any text box in the chain. Then choose Page ➤ Insert Pages and, in the Insert Pages dialog box, check Link to Current Text Chain. This option is available only if the master page applied to the last page before the insert shows an intact chain in the upper left corner. Note that the text will flow into the new pages from the *end* of the story, even if the pages are inserted in the middle of the chain.

Anchoring Text and Graphics

You can anchor a text box or a picture box to text so that the anchored box moves when editing causes the text to reflow. This feature is useful for anchoring figures to captions, anchoring graphic drop caps to paragraphs, including graphic symbols in the text, and many other functions. You can also anchor rules to text using QuarkXPress's paragraph formatting specifications (rather than creating and anchoring lines as separate graphic elements) as described in Chapter 5.

Anchoring Boxes in Text

To anchor a box in text, select the Item tool (✥) and activate the box or line you want to anchor, then choose Edit ➤ Cut (CTRL+X or SHIFT+DELETE) or Edit ➤ Copy (CTRL+C or CTRL+INSERT). Next select the Content tool (☝), position the text insertion point in the text where you want the box anchored, and choose Edit ➤ Paste (CTRL+V or SHIFT+INSERT).

If the Item tool (✥) is selected when you paste, the item will be pasted onto the active page but not anchored to the text.

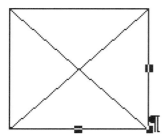

Figure 2-34   An active anchored box displays three handles that you can use to resize the box.

Once anchored, you can select the item and the text around it using the Content tool (☝) and normal text selection techniques. You can cut or copy selected text and paste it elsewhere, along with the anchored item. You can resize an active item by dragging one of the handles (Figure 2-34).

You can apply Style ➤ Baseline Shift to raise or lower the anchored item, and use paragraph alignment commands to align the item (if it is on a line of its own). In addition, you can use Item ➤ Modify to make entries in the

Anchored Text Specifications (Figure 2-35) and Anchored Picture Specifications (Figure 2-36) dialog boxes, or to make entries in the Measurements palette (Figure 2-37), to position an anchored item with its bottom edge aligned with its associated text baseline or with its top edge aligned with the top of the text. In the Measurements palette, click on ▣ to align the anchored item with the text ascent, or on ▣ to align the anchored item with the text baseline.

Figure 2-35   Anchored Text Specifications dialog box.

Figure 2-36   Anchored Picture Specifications dialog box.

Figure 2-37   Anchored Text Measurements palette (top), and Anchored Picture Measurements palette (bottom).

To move an anchored item from its current text location, use the Content tool (☞) to select the item by dragging over it to highlight the box, then use the Cut and Paste commands—you cannot move an anchored item by dragging it with the Item tool (✥). Do not simply click on the box to highlight it, or the Cut command will delete the contents.

Note that you cannot anchor an item to text that is within an anchored box.

Deleting Anchored Items

To delete a box or line that is *anchored within* a text box, you must select the box by dragging over it with the I-beam pointer (I), then choose Edit → Cut, Edit → Delete, or press the Delete or Backspace key. You can also position the text insertion point immediately after the anchored box and press the Backspace key.

Grouping Items

You can select multiple items using the techniques described earlier in this chapter. If you want a group of items always to be associated (and selectable) as a group, you can select them all and choose Item → Group (CTRL+G).

You will notice that whenever you have selected multiple items on a page—whether they are grouped or not—the Measurements palette (Figure 2-38) changes to display only three variables: X (horizontal position of the origin of the group's boundary or bounding box relative to the current zero point), Y (vertical position of the origin of the group's boundary relative to the current zero point), and rotation angle of the group, if it was rotated as a group. (Remember that the origin is the *original* top left corner of the group, which is not necessarily the apparent top left corner if the group has been rotated.)

Figure 2-38   Measurements palette when a group is selected.

These are the only variables from the Measurements palette that can be changed for the group as a whole. You cannot resize a group, for instance, but you can rotate the group as a whole.

Similarly, when multiple items are selected—whether or not they are grouped—the available menu commands and dialog box entries will be limited to only those that can be applied to the group as a whole; this will depend on the composition of the group. Also, you cannot cut or copy a group that contains a text box that is part of a chain.

Items within a group are still separate entities that can be selected, edited, scaled, or repositioned individually. Any item can be selected with the Content tool (🖑) and edited normally or scaled by dragging a handle. To move an item or to use any of the commands that call for selection with the Item tool (✥), first select the Content tool, then hold down the CTRL key as you click on the item and drag. Holding the CTRL key temporarily activates the Item tool, and you can select individual items instead of the whole group with the ✥ pointer.

Group Specifications

When a group of items is selected, the control areas in the Specifications dialog box and in the Measurements palette change to allow only those entries that are appropriate for *all* items in the group. For example, if the entire group is composed of text boxes, the Item ➤ Modify command will display a full Text Box Specifications dialog box with all control areas as described earlier for text boxes. If the group contains both text boxes and picture boxes and lines, the Item ➤ Modify command will display a Group Specifications dialog box with only those control areas that are common to all types of items: Origin Across, Origin Down, Angle, Color, Shade, and Suppress Printout.

Deleting Items from a Group

To delete a box or line that is part of a group (created by selecting several items and using the Item ➤ Group command), you must select the item with the Content tool (🖑), then choose Item ➤ Delete (CTRL+K). Edit ➤ Cut (CTRL+X or SHIFT+DELETE), Edit ➤ Delete, or the Delete or Backspace key is not available when an item within a group is selected—whether or not the group is also constrained.

If you select an item within a group and choose Item ➤ Delete (CTRL+K), QuarkXPress will display a warning that "This will delete an item from a group and cannot be undone. OK to continue?" If you click on OK in the warning box, you will delete the item *and there is no way to reverse that action.*

If you use the Item tool (✥) to try to select an item within a group, you will be selecting the whole group. Item ► Delete (CTRL+K), Edit ► Cut (CTRL+X or SHIFT+DELETE), Edit ► Delete, or the Backspace key will delete the entire group.

Constraining Items within a Box

Normally, you can move items anywhere on a page, regardless of their relationship to other items on a page, because the normal default for the Auto Constrain option in the General Preferences dialog box is off. If you turn this option *on*, any items you create within a box are constrained by that box. You cannot position a constrained item beyond the constraining box's boundaries or scale them to be larger than the constraining box.

In place of Auto Constrain, you can use Item ► Constrain to constrain a group of items to within one box or use the Unconstrain command to reverse a constraint. Item ► Constrain can override the Auto Constrain setting for active items. You can also use Constrain to associate a group of boxes that were not originally set up that way.

Constraining a Box or Line

To constrain a box or line when the Auto Constrain setting is On in the General Preferences dialog box, first draw and select the box that you want to be the constraining box. Then choose the appropriate tool and, starting within the constraining box, draw the box or line that you want to be constrained.

Constraining a Group of Items

To Constrain a group of items, first create the items, including one box that surrounds all of the items and falls on the lowest layer of the group—this box will become the constraining box. Select all of the items and choose Item ► Group; then choose Item ► Constrain. When a group is constrained, items within the bounding box can be moved or changed individually, but they cannot be resized or moved beyond the edges of the constraining box. If you delete the constraining box, all associated constrained items are also deleted.

Removing the Constraint Attribute

To remove the constraint attribute, select the constrained group, then choose Item ► Unconstrain. (The command in the menu changes from Constrain to Unconstrain when a constrained group is active.) The

Unconstrained set is still grouped until you choose the Ungroup command.

See Part II for ideas on how constrained groups can be useful when creating business forms.

Locking Items

Use Item → Lock (CTRL+L) to lock an active box, line, or a group on the page so you cannot inadvertently move or scale it. Locked boxes can still be moved or scaled through the Measurements palette or the Item → Modify command, but they cannot be moved or scaled with the mouse. Locked lines must be unlocked in order to be moved or scaled. Most menu commands can be applied to locked items, including Delete.

The Lock command is a toggle switch: If you select an unlocked item, the command displays as Lock in the Item menu; if you select a locked item, the command displays as Unlock in the Item menu. In either case, the keyboard shortcut is CTRL+L. When you position the Mover pointer over a locked item, the pointer changes to a padlock (🔒).

Saving Your Work

While you are working on a document, the work you do is being stored in the computer's memory (RAM)—a temporary work area that is "erased" whenever the computer is turned off or when you quit an application. If the power fails or something else forces you to restart the computer, anything in the computer's memory is erased; but whatever you have saved on the disk drive is preserved. For this reason, save your document often while you are working. QuarkXPress handles this function like most other Windows applications—with the added advantage of a Revert to Saved command, as described under the next headings.

Saving a Document or Template

Use File → Save (CTRL+S) to save your work onto a disk drive. Each time you use the Save command to save the document, the version that is in memory is copied to the disk drive.

The first time you use the Save command on a new document, a dialog box is displayed in which you can specify the name of the document and the disk drive or directory where you want to store it (Figure 2-39). This dialog box is common to most Windows applications.

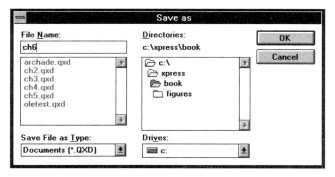

Figure 2-39   The Save dialog box.

In assigning a new document a name, QuarkXPress will add the extension .QXD (for documents) or .QXT (for templates). If you type your own extension as part of the name, QuarkXPress will not override your entry—but it only looks for .QXD and .QXT extensions when you use the Open command unless you tell it exactly what extensions to look for. In other words, you should let QuarkXPress assign the extension unless you want to make your life difficult in the long run. Use the first eight characters of the name to distinguish between chapters or versions of similar documents.

Certain information related to a document's appearance is normally shared by all documents through the XPRESS.PRF file. You can optionally save this information as part of a specific document—but this is an advanced feature that you might never need to use; it is explained in Chapter 14.

You should become accustomed to saving your work at regular intervals—not just at the end of a work session. The keyboard shortcut (CTRL+S) makes saving your document easy.

When to Save a Document

A document should be saved
- When you finish a page—before turning to another page.
- When you finish placing a long text file.
- When you finish placing, sizing, and cropping a graphic.
- As you are working, every five minutes or so.
- Before you print.
- Before you globally change type specs or format.
- After you make any changes to the master pages.
- Before leaving your computer, using the phone, or pausing.
- OFTEN!

You can save a QuarkXPress template to use as the basis for starting other documents. Type the .QXT extension as part of the file name or choose Templates (*.QXT) from the Save File as Type drop-down menu in the Save dialog box. The next time you open the file and save it, QuarkXPress will display the Save dialog box so that you rename the template file as a document.

Saving with a Changed Name, Format, or Drive/Directory Location

Use the File → Save As command to save an existing document under a different name. This feature is useful when you want to create a new document based on one that you have previously created. For example, you could start the February newsletter by opening the file for the January newsletter (called Vol. 1 No. 1, for instance) and saving it under a new name (such as Vol. 1 No. 2). See Chapter 9 for suggestions about creating templates instead of copying complete documents.

You can also use the Save As command to put the document into a different directory or onto a different disk drive. This ability is useful when you want to make an updated version of a document without changing the name or modified date (recorded by the System) of the original version, thereby creating a backup version. For example, you could start the second revision of a heavily edited report by opening the file for the first version (stored on a file server, for instance) and saving it on a different disk drive (your own local hard disk).

You can also use the Save As command to save the document in a different format (template versus document). For example, after finishing the first newsletter in a series, you can save the newsletter as a *document* (to store as an archive), then use Save As to create a *template* (for use in starting subsequent issues).

The Save As dialog box is the same as the Save dialog box (Figure 2-39) and is common to most Windows applications.

Reverting to the Most Recently Saved Version

The Revert to Saved command in the File menu can be used to eliminate all of the edits or changes made since the last time the document was saved. This command is simply a convenient shortcut to an alternative that is available with almost any application: Close the active document without saving changes, then reopen the saved version of the document.

Closing a Document Window

As mentioned earlier, choosing Close from the File menu has the same effect as double-clicking on the Control Box in the active document window, or choosing Close from the Control Box menu. When you close a document that has never been saved or that has been changed since it was last saved, QuarkXPress displays a dialog box asking if you want to save the changes.

Figure 2-40   A warning dialog box is displayed when you close a document without saving changes.

Click Yes, press ENTER, or type ALT+Y to save the changed document or to display the Save As dialog box; click No or type ALT+N to ignore the changes; or click on Cancel to cancel the Close command and keep the document open. You can also use the TAB key to highlight any of the buttons and press ENTER to activate the highlighted choice.

Quitting QuarkXPress

Use the File ➤ Exit command when you want to exit QuarkXPress. If you use this command when a document window is open and the document has not been saved since the last change, QuarkXPress will prompt you to save the document. You'll see the same warning dialog box as is displayed when you close a document window without first saving the changed document (Figure 2-40).

Summary

This chapter presented an overview of how to create a new QuarkXPress document and how to add items to document pages, and described how you can modify text and picture boxes in QuarkXPress and create relationships between them. We provided an overview of how to change the position or appearance of boxes and lines created using QuarkXPress' tools (except the Picture Box Shape and Reshape Polygon commands, which are covered in Chapter 6). Some of the other commands from the Item menu are also reviewed in Chapters 4 to 6, where you learn how to edit *lines* and change the *contents* of boxes (text and graphics).

The next chapter continues the page-layout process by adding, moving, or deleting pages, including master pages. You will also learn how to change the *defaults,* or assumed settings, for QuarkXPress.

3 Expanding the Document

By now you should have a basic understanding of how to work with items—boxes and lines that are the building blocks of QuarkXPress documents. If all of your documents will be simple, one-page designs, you can probably skip this chapter and use the rest of the book simply as a reference, looking up special topics as needed. However, if you intend to create longer documents, you'll need to understand how to work with multiple pages. It's also important to know how to change QuarkXPress' default Preferences settings, so you can customize these settings to make each project run efficiently.

In Chapter 2, you learned how to start a new document, position items on a document page, and create relationships between items. This chapter covers additional aspects of the page layout process, including creating master pages, sectioning a document, and adding, moving, or deleting pages. You will also learn how to create and use a QuarkXPress library and how to change the *defaults,* or assumed settings, for the program using the Edit ➞ Preferences command.

Working with Master Pages

Whenever you start a new document, QuarkXPress displays a blank page. You can begin building a document (as described in Chapter 2), by immediately creating boxes on each page and using the File → Get Text and File → Get Picture commands to bring in text and graphics that you have prepared in other programs, or by using QuarkXPress' built-in graphics and text tools. You can create finished documents without ever knowing that a master page exists (even though every document starts with one).

However, if you are creating a document that is more than one or two pages in length, you can use master pages to establish common elements in the document, thereby saving a lot of time in the production of pages. Any text, graphics, or guides on the master page appear on every page based on that master page. Using master pages, you can fit each page layout to an overall "grid". A master page simply gives you a head start in building a new page in a document. Settings made on master pages can be changed on individual document pages as needed, and you can move or delete master items on document pages.

Figure 3-1 shows items that are normally included on master pages: column guides, running headers and footers, and nonprinting guides that define the basic grid of the document's design.

Figure 3-1 Master page elements usually include column guides, running header and footer, ruler guides, and other text or graphic elements that repeat on every page based on this master.

Every document starts with at least one master page, with the margin guides, column guides, and (optional) automatic text box as specified in the New dialog box, described in Chapter 2. This master page serves as the basis of all document pages, unless you choose to create document pages based on *no* master (described later in this chapter) or to create additional master pages (described next).

Creating a New Master Page

When you open a new document, the document contains one master page, labeled "M1-Master 1". This is represented as a master page icon in the Document Layout palette. To create a new master page, display the Document Layout palette (View ➤ Show Document Layout) and choose Show Master Pages from the Document menu on the palette (Figure 3-2) to display the master pages in the document.

Figure 3-2 Display the master pages in a document by choosing Show Master Pages in the Document Layout palette.

From the Masters menu, use the Insert command to add a Blank Single Master or a Blank Facing Master, or to apply the existing master to a new master page. Note that if you have selected the Facing Pages options in the New or Document Setup command dialog box, you will be able to add both single-sided and facing-page master pages; otherwise, you will be able to create only single-sided master pages.

Once you have chosen the type of master you wish to add, the cursor changes to a small page icon that can be positioned after or in between existing master pages by clicking on the appropriate location on the palette. You can create up to 127 master pages for a single document or you can delete all master pages.

You can position a new master after any existing master page icon, or rearrange the order of the master page icons by dragging them to new positions in the Document Layout palette, but the number assigned to each master will always be based on the sequence in which the master was *created* rather than the sequence in which the masters are *arranged* (Figure 3-3).

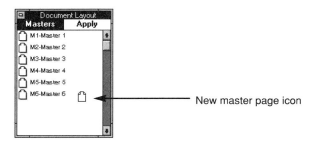

Figure 3-3 Once master pages are displayed in the Document Layout palette, you can add new master pages.

To view the new master page, double-click on the master page icon. Those elements—text, graphics, and lines—that are set up on the right page of a facing-page master page will appear only on odd-numbered pages of facing-page documents. Elements that are set up on the left master page will appear on even-numbered pages of facing-page documents. Single-sided master page elements—such as guides, text boxes, and graphics—will appear on every page to which the master page is applied.

You can replace or overwrite an existing master page by first clicking on the master page icon, then using the Apply menu on the palette to select an existing master page or a new blank master to be applied to the selected master page. QuarkXPress always displays a warning box asking you to confirm that you want to overwrite a master.

Naming a Master Page

QuarkXPress assigns a number preceded by the letter "M" to each master page you create, but you can add a more descriptive name, such as "Chapter Opening Master" or "Contents List Master" by selecting the label and retyping a new one. The label you type will be preceded by the number assigned by QuarkXPress, for example, "M1-Chapter Opening."

Viewing and Editing a Master Page

To activate or turn to a master page, choose Page → Display and select the master page you want to view or edit, or you can turn to a master page by double-clicking on the appropriate master page icon in the Document Layout palette when master pages are displayed.

Changing Master Page Margins and Column Guides

A new master page takes on the margin and column settings that you initially specified in the New dialog box when you first started the document. You can change those settings for any master page through the Master Guides dialog box that is displayed when you use the Page → Master Guides command (Figure 3-4). This command is available only when the active document window displays a master page.

Figure 3-4   Master Guides dialog box.

Once you define the margins and column guides for a master page, those settings will apply automatically to any page in the document based on that master page. The master guides serve two functions: On the master page that includes the automatic text box (defined in Chapter 2), column guides define the number of columns in the automatic text box. On pages that do not have an automatic text box, master guides define the number of guides that appear on the page itself. These guides serve as aids in positioning items on the page, but they do not affect text—the width of text is determined by the columns set up for each text box that you manually create on the master page or on each document page.

If you later change the margin settings for a master page, or if you select a different master page for a document page that you have already started, QuarkXPress automatically resizes the automatic text box on the page (if one has been specified) and resizes any other text box whose four sides exactly meet the margin guides.

If you change the number of columns on a master page that contains an automatic text box, QuarkXPress automatically divides the automatic text box on each document page based on that master page if the text box has not been moved or changed on individual document pages. All other page items remain unchanged when you redefine margins and columns on a master page.

Adding Text and Graphic Elements to a Master Page

You can add text and graphic elements to a master page the same way you add text or graphics to any page in the document, as described in Chapter 2. The next sections describe elements that are commonly used on master pages: the automatic text box, text boxes for headers and footers, and other elements that you want to appear repeatedly on document pages.

The Automatic Text Box

If the Automatic Text Box option is selected in the New dialog box, the first master page (and the first document page) of that document includes an empty text box that has the margins and columns you set up in the New dialog box. The master page shows an intact chain icon (⚭) in the top left corner when the automatic text box is in effect (Figure 3-5).

You can change the margin and column settings through the Page → Master Guides command; changes made to these settings will affect the size and number of columns in the automatic text box. You can also use the Item → Modify and Item → Frame commands (described in Chapter 2) to further change the automatic text box specifications.

Any text formatting that you apply to this text box—character attributes or paragraph formatting—will become the default format when you type text in this box on document pages. Note that you cannot type text in an automatic text box on a master page.

Figure 3-5   Master page with automatic text box shows an intact chain icon in the top left corner.

When you type or import text into an automatic text box on a document page, additional pages are automatically added as needed for text overflow, unless you turn Auto Page Insertion *off* in the General Preferences dialog box (described later in this chapter).

Creating an Automatic Text Box

Documents that were started with the Automatic Text Box option turned *off* in the New dialog box, or those in which the automatic text box is later turned off, have no automatic text box. Pages will not be added automatically for overflow text, even if the Auto Page Insertion option is turned *on* in the General Preferences dialog box (described later in this chapter).

To create an automatic text box in a document without one, first display the master page that you want to hold the box. Select the Text Box creation tool (□) and add a text box to that master page (if it does not have one already). Select the Linking tool (⚭) and click on the broken chain icon (⚭) in the upper left corner on a master page. The broken chain icon will be surrounded by a marquee. Treat this icon as the *previous text box*, and click on the text box that you wish to become the automatic text box. Use this same technique to link text boxes on other master pages to the automatic text box.

Removing the Automatic Text Box

To turn the automatic text chain off on a master page, select the Unlinking tool (⚭) and click on the intact chain icon in the top left corner on the master page. When you break the chain icon, a text box will remain on the master page, and new pages based on this master page will have a text box, but it will not be an automatic text box (Figure 3-6). Therefore, text overflow from new text added to pages based on this master will no longer automatically add pages in the document.

Figure 3-6   A master page without an automatic text box shows a broken chain icon in the top left corner of a master page.

You can delete this text box using the Edit → Cut, Edit → Delete, or Item → Delete commands. Removing the automatic text box will not affect any document pages on which the automatic text box has already been filled with text. Only pages with an empty automatic text box, and any new pages based on the changed master page, will reflect the change.

Headers, Footers, and Page Numbers

Additional text elements that are most commonly added to the master page(s) include a header and/or footer, showing the page number and any other text that you want to appear on every page.

To create a header or footer, first choose the Text Box creation tool (A) and draw a text box at the top or bottom of the page—usually beyond the top or bottom margin defined for the automatic text box (unless that box defines the entire printing area of the page). Then type and format the text that you want to appear on every page.

In the position where you want the page number to appear, type CTRL+3 (Figure 3-7). On the master page(s) the page number appears as the characters <#> (angled brackets around the pound sign or number sign). On document pages the page number will appear as assigned through the Page → Section command, described later in this chapter.

Figure 3-7 Type CTRL+3 to position the page number in a text box in the header or footer on the master page.

Other Text and Graphics Elements

You can add other text boxes, picture boxes, and lines to the master page. If you add blank text boxes to master pages, for example, and any text formatting that you apply to these boxes will become the default formats when you type text in these boxes on document pages. Similarly, you can format a picture box with predefined settings for background, frame, or contrast, for example. Those settings will be the default in that box on every document page based on that master.

Remember, any elements that you add to a master page automatically appear on all pages based on that master—pages that have already been created as well as new pages based on that master. See Chapter 8 for tips on how the master pages can be part of a template document to increase productivity.

Applying a Master Page to a Document Page

You can add a new page to a document and apply a master page to it, thus creating the new document page with all of the guides plus any printing items that are set up for that master.

There are two ways to create a *new* document page based on an existing master page: Use either the Page → Insert command or the Document Layout palette. The Page → Insert command displays the Insert Pages dialog box; choose the master page you wish to apply to newly inserted document pages from the Master Page pull-down menu. (This command is described in more detail later in this chapter.) To apply a master page as you insert new document pages using the Document Layout palette, select the appropriate master from the Document → Insert command on the palette while document pages are displayed. (Figure 3-8). The cursor will change to a page icon that can be inserted anywhere in the document by clicking on the palette.

Figure 3-8   Inserting a new document page based on an existing master page.

To apply a master page to an *existing* document page, use the Document Layout palette (Figure 3-9). With the document page icons displayed, click on the page(s) to which you wish to apply a new master page, then select the appropriate master using the Apply menu on the palette.

Figure 3-9   Applying a different master page to existing document pages.

You can use the procedures described in Chapter 2 to add or change any of the elements on a document page—including changing or deleting elements that are derived from the master page on which a particular document page is based. If you change elements on the master page later, those changes will be reflected in the document pages based on that master, *except* that the master page–based elements you *changed* on the document pages will not be changed. In other words, when you modify master page items, the modifications are *not* applied to the corresponding items on document pages that you have moved or changed in any way.

When you drag a master page icon onto an existing document page, QuarkXPress deletes all previous *unmodified* master page elements from that page and applies the new master page elements. The effect on elements that have been modified is discussed in the next section. Figures 3-10 and 3-11 show how master page changes affect a document page when no elements have been modified on the document page. In these examples note that the text box on Master B has been linked to the automatic text box as described earlier under "Creating an Automatic Text Box." If the text box on Master B had not been linked to the automatic text box, a page would be inserted with no text in the text box.

Figure 3-10   Master page A (left) and a document page based on Master A (right).

Chapter 3: Expanding the Document   119

Figure 3-11   Master page B (left) and the same document page with Master B applied (right).

Keep Changes Versus Delete Changes

Modified items might be kept or deleted when the new master page is applied, depending on the setting for Master Page Items in the General Preferences dialog box (described later in this chapter).

Figure 3-12   Master page A (left) and a document page based on Master A (right), with logo position modified.

Figure 3-13 The same document page with Master A reapplied when Keep Changes (left) or Delete Changes (right) is specified in the General Preferences dialog box.

Modifications include *moving* a master page element on a document page. If you position a logo in the upper right corner of the master page, for example, then move it to the upper left corner on page 1 (Figure 3-12), the logo will remain in the upper left corner when you change the master page or apply a new master to page 1 if Keep Changes is specified in the Master Page Items area of the General Preferences dialog box (Figure 3-13, left). It will be deleted if Delete Changes has been specified in the Master Page Items area (Figure 3-13, right). If you change this setting after working on a document, the new setting will apply only to pages added to the document.

Adding, Deleting, and Moving Pages

QuarkXPress offers several methods for adding, deleting, or moving pages in a document. When you insert, delete, or move pages, QuarkXPress automatically updates the page numbers on all pages that have been set up using automatic page number characters, as described earlier in this chapter.

Adding Pages

As described in Chapter 2, QuarkXPress can automatically add pages for text overflow that occurs when you type or import more text than a text box can display. It performs this function only under the following conditions:

- Auto Page Insertion is enabled (via Edit ➤ Preferences ➤ General); *and*
- the master page specified in Auto Page Insertion has an automatic text chain (as indicated by the intact chain icon [⚭] in the upper left corner of the master page); *and*
- the overflow is from the text box defined on the master page as the Automatic Text Box, or from a chain of at least two text boxes.

You can add a new page based on a particular master page by choosing the Document ➤ Insert command on the Document Layout palette; the cursor changes to a page icon and you can drag it into the desired position on the palette. You can also add a new blank page *not* based on a master page by choosing Blank Single Page or Blank Facing Page from the Document ➤ Insert menu.

While you are dragging the page icon to add it to the document, the pointer changes to indicate how the page will be inserted.

- A right page icon (a page icon with the right corner dog-eared—◱) indicates that the added page will become a right-facing page (that is, right of the spine in a facing-page document) and will not affect the spread placement of existing document pages.
- A left page icon (a page icon with the left corner dog-eared—◲) indicates that the added page will become a left-facing page (that is, left of the spine in a facing-page document) and will not affect the spread placement of existing document pages.
- A left- (↢) or right-pointing (↣) arrow indicates that the page will become part of a spread, forcing one or more pages out from the spine.
- A down-pointing arrow (⤓) indicates that the page will force all subsequent pages down one position but will not affect the spread placement of previous document pages.

To view the new page, double-click on its icon.

Insert Pages Dialog Box

If you want to insert a new page, or more than one page at a time, use the Page ➤ Insert command. QuarkXPress displays the Insert Pages dialog box (Figure 3-14).

Figure 3-14   Insert Pages dialog box.

The Insert Pages dialog box lets you insert up to 100 pages in the active document. This is the limit *per insertion*—not the limit for the document. You can specify whether the pages are to be inserted before or after the active page (or whatever page number you specify), or at the end of the document.

You can enter an actual page number, or you can enter the *absolute* location within the active document by preceding the number with a plus sign. For example, if the active document includes 10 pages beginning with a user-defined page number 11 and you want to insert a new page 13, you can insert after page 12, or you can insert after page +2 (that is, after the second page in the document). An *absolute page sequence* number represents a page's sequential location in a document, regardless of the automatic page numbers.

In specifying a page number, you must include any prefix that has been assigned as part of the page number through the Page → Section command (described later in this chapter).

Choose the master page you want to apply to the inserted pages from the Master Page drop-down list, which lists all of the master pages that have been set up in the active document.

If the automatic text box on a document page is active when you insert pages, you can check Link to Current Text Chain to link the inserted pages automatically to the automatic text chain. The active text box or chain can be anywhere in the document. This option is available only if the intact chain icon (⚐) is in the upper left corner of the master page and the automatic text box or chain is active on a document page.

When you add an odd number of pages to a facing-pages document, subsequent pages are automatically updated to contain the appropriate left- or right-facing master page items.

Deleting Pages

You can delete a page by using the Document ➤ Delete command on the Document Layout palette, or you can use the Delete command from the Page menu.

The Page ➤ Delete command displays the Delete Pages dialog box (Figure 3-15), through which you can delete any number of pages by user-specified page number or by absolute page sequence (which you can enter with a plus sign as described above for inserting pages). In specifying a section page number, you must include any prefix that has been assigned as part of the page number through the Page ➤ Section command.

Figure 3-15   The Delete Pages dialog box.

If the deleted pages contain text that is linked to text boxes on remaining pages, the text is reflowed and anchored items are retained. QuarkXPress automatically replaces the deleted pages with newly inserted pages, using the master page format of the page preceding the first automatically inserted page. It does this if the remaining pages cannot fit all the text from the deleted pages, the Auto Page Insertion is enabled (through the Edit ➤ Preferences ➤ General command), and the master page to be used has the intact chain icon (⛓) in the upper left corner.

If you delete a master page, document pages will lose all items that were derived from that master page if they have not been modified (depending on the setting of Master Page Items in the General Preferences dialog box). These document pages will no longer be based on any master. You cannot delete the only page in a one-page document.

Moving Pages

You can rearrange pages within a document by dragging the page icons in the Document Layout palette or by dragging the thumbnail icons in the document window (when set to View ➤ Thumbnails). Otherwise, use the Move command from the Page menu to rearrange pages. Each of these alternatives is described below.

Moving Pages in the Document Layout Palette

To move a page in the Document Layout palette, choose View → Show Document Layout, then drag any page icon into the desired position and release the mouse button. You can select multiple pages by holding the SHIFT key as you click on different pages.

Moving Pages in Thumbnails View

To move a page in Thumbnails view, choose View → Thumbnails, then drag the thumbnail page image from one position to another and release the mouse button. As in the Document Layout palette, you can select multiple pages by holding the SHIFT key as you click on different pages.

While you are dragging pages in either Thumbnails view or in the Document Layout palette, the pointer changes to indicate how the page will be inserted (see the pointer descriptions under "Adding Pages", earlier in this chapter).

Moving Pages Using the Move Command

You can also use the Page → Move command to get the Move Pages dialog box. The Move Pages dialog box lets you move any number of pages by user-defined page number or by absolute page sequence number, which you can enter with a plus sign, as described above for inserting pages. You can specify whether the pages are to be moved before or after the active page (or whatever page number you specify), or at the end of the document.

In specifying a page number, you must include any prefix that has been assigned as part of the page number through the Page → Section command.

Regardless of which method you use when you move pages, QuarkXPress does not change the links—the order in which text flows between text boxes. For example, a story starts on page 2 and continues on page 3 but, if you move page 2 to follow page 3, then the story will still start on the *moved* page and flow backward (Figure 3-16). You can change the flow by manually changing the links—breaking the links, then relinking the boxes in a new sequence—as described in Chapter 2.

Figure 3-16 Moving Pages does not change the order in which text is linked.

Copying Pages from One Document to Another

To move entire pages from one document to another, open both documents (using File ➤ Open) and select View ➤ Thumbnails for both documents; then drag pages back and forth between the document windows. You can select and move multiple sequential pages by SHIFT+clicking on two or more pages, then dragging the multiple-selected pages. Use CTRL+click to select multiple, nonsequential pages. As you drag the pages into position, the pointer changes as described above, under "Adding Pages".

Links between text boxes on moved pages are preserved, and the entire story (all of the text in the linked chain) is brought in from the source document. In the target document, copied pages display text from the beginning of the story, even if the story did not start on the copied pages in the source document.

Moving a page from one document to another brings in the associated master pages from the source document as well. You cannot move pages based on a facing-page master page into a single-sided document.

Viewing Different Pages

You can view different pages by using the scroll bars to scroll up or down within the document; by using special keys on an extended keyboard; by double-clicking on the icon for a page in the Document Layout palette; or by using the Go To, Previous, Next, First, and Last commands from the Page menu.

The page number of the active page is displayed in the lower left corner of the document window.

Using the Scroll Bars

The scroll bars in the document window let you scroll vertically and horizontally—this is a standard Windows operation, described in Chapter 1. The distance the image moves when you click on the scroll bar or on an arrow varies, depending on the view you are using. The increments are smaller in enlarged views (such as 200 percent) than in reduced views (such as Fit in Window).

You can click on the scroll arrows to move the view of the page in the window or to move slowly from one page to adjacent pages. Click on either side of the scroll box in the scroll bar to move one full window per click. Notice that the page number does not change until the page is entirely out of the document window.

To move more quickly through the document, you can drag the vertical scroll box. Remember that you can see the page(s) move as you drag the scroll box if Live Scroll is checked in the Application Preferences dialog box. Otherwise, the page view does not change immediately. In either case, you can temporarily turn Live Scroll on or off (i.e., reverse the Application Preferences setting) by holding the ALT key as you drag the scroll bar.

Using the Keyboard

As mentioned in Chapter 2, you can use the following keys to move through a document:

PAGE UP	Scroll up one screen
PAGE DOWN	Scroll down one screen
CTRL+PAGE UP	Scroll to first page
CTRL+PAGE DOWN	Scroll to last page
SHIFT+PAGE UP	Scroll to top of previous page
SHIFT+PAGE DOWN	Scroll to next page

You can also use keyboard shortcuts to move through a document when the Content tool is selected and the cursor is positioned within a story that extends beyond the current screen view:

CTRL+HOME	Scroll to start of story
CTRL+END	Scroll to end of story

Using the Go To Command

You can use Page ► Go to (CTRL+J) to jump quickly to any page in the document. In the Go To Page dialog box, you can enter the user-defined page number or the absolute page sequence, which you type with a plus sign, as described earlier in this chapter for inserting pages.

In entering the user-defined page number, you must include any prefix you assigned using the Section command along with the page number. If two pages in a document have the same section and/or page numbers, including prefix, QuarkXPress goes to the first occurrence of that page number.

Using the Display Command

You can use the Page ► Display command to change from views of the document pages to views of any master page. The Display command shows a submenu that lists all of the master pages plus Document (for returning to the most recently viewed document page).

Using the Document Layout Palette

You can also turn to any master page or document page by double-clicking on the desired page icon in the Document Layout palette. Notice that the page icons show the absolute page sequence underneath each page icon, not the user-defined page number. The currently active page is labeled in the palette with italic type.

Numbering Pages and Sectioning a Document

You can set up page numbers to print on every page by creating a text box for the page number on the master page(s), as described earlier in this chapter. Here we describe how to divide a document into sections and assign the starting page number for a document or section, as well as how to create page number references within a document.

Assigning Page Numbers

Normally, QuarkXPress starts a document with page number 1. You can change the starting page number of a document by turning to its first page and using the Page ► Section command to specify a starting page number (described under the next heading). The lower left corner of the document window displays the active page number; page numbers that start a new section are followed by an asterisk (*).

Dividing a Document into Sections

You can divide a large publication into sections by creating a separate QuarkXPress document for each part of the publication. For example, you could create a separate QuarkXPress document for each chapter in a book. Chapter 12 gives some good reasons for dividing a document into parts this way.

You can also use the Section command to divide a single QuarkXPress document into any number of sections. A section is a group of sequentially numbered pages within a document. Individual sections within a document can have their own page number format and sequence. This can be useful if you are creating a document that includes a front page (with no page number), a preface (with roman page numbers i, ii, iii), and a body (with page numbers 1, 2, 3). You can also create sections with compound page numbers, such as 1-1, 1-2, 1-3, followed by 2-1, 2-2, 2-3, and so on.

To start a new section, first make sure that the page number showing in the bottom left corner of the document window is the page on which you wish the new section to start. (See also "Viewing Different Pages" earlier in this chapter.) Next choose the Page ➤ Section command to display the Section dialog box (Figure 3-17).

Figure 3-17 The Section dialog box.

In the Section dialog box, check Section Start. You can enter up to four characters in the Prefix box. This number of characters is useful if your document renumbers pages starting at number 1 for each section, such as 1-1, 1-2, 1-3, followed by 2-1, 2-2, 2-3, or APX-1, APX-2, APX-3.

Whenever you use commands that prompt you to enter a page number—such as Page ➤ Go to, Page ➤ Insert, Page ➤ Delete, and Page ➤ Move—you must enter the prefix assigned in the Section dialog box with the page number.

You can enter any starting page number in the Page Number box. Page numbers must be entered in Arabic numerals (1, 2, 3) regardless of the format you select. The Format drop-down list displays QuarkXPress's five page number format options: Numeric (1, 2, 3), Uppercase Roman (I, II, III), Lowercase Roman (i, ii, iii), Uppercase Alphabetic (A, B, C), and Lowercase Alphabetic (a, b, c).

If you choose Page ➤ Section when the active page is already set up as the start of a section, the Section Start box will already be checked and the assigned starting page number and format will show in the Prefix, Page Number, and Format boxes. You can change any of these values, or you can merge the current section with the previous section of the document, by unchecking Section Start. QuarkXPress updates the page numbers to follow the preceding section's format and sequence.

Remember that in order for page numbers to display on printed pages, you must set them up using the automatic page number characters, described under the next heading.

Referencing Page Numbers

QuarkXPress automatically numbers pages in a document and displays them in the document window, but in order to *print* the page number, you must type CTRL+2, CTRL+3, or CTRL+4 as part of a text box entry. The following table (Figure 3-18) shows the meaning of each of these entries.

Keyboard Entry	Page Number
CTRL+2	Previous Text Box Page Number
CTRL+3	Current Text Box Page Number
CTRL+4	Next Text Box Page Number

Figure 3-18 Keyboard entries for referencing page numbers.

It should be easy to remember that CTRL+3 is the entry for the current page number: The uppercase value of 3 on the keyboard is the pound sign or number sign (#), and this is the page number symbol displayed on the master pages. You make the CTRL+3 entry on a master page so that the page numbers will be positioned automatically on all document pages.

Wherever you type CTRL+2 in a text box, QuarkXPress displays the page number of the previous box in a linked chain. Similarly, wherever you type CTRL+4 in a text box, QuarkXPress displays the page number of the next box in a linked chain. If the text box containing the CTRL+2 or CTRL+4 character is not linked to any other box, the page number will reflect the links of the box immediately behind or below it.

Use CTRL+2 in references such as "Continued from page…" that appear at the top of text that jumps text from several pages earlier in the document. Use CTRL+4 with references such as "Continued on page..." that appear at the bottom of text that jumps to several pages later in the document.

It's a good idea to put jump-to text such as "Continued from page..." or "Continued on page..." in a separate, unlinked text box at the top or bottom of the linked text box that contains the story. This way, the jump-to lines will not reflow when the story is edited.

QuarkXPress automatically renumbers pages and updates all page number references within the text whenever you add, delete, or move pages within a document.

Using the QuarkXPress Library

The Library is an extremely useful feature that QuarkXPress offers in a convenient palette form that is not matched by any other page layout application. A QuarkXPress library is a file that can store any page element you can create or import into QuarkXPress. An entry can be a line, a box, a group of items, or multiple-selected items. Once items are stored in a library, they can be dragged to any document page. You can store up to 2,000 items in a library.

Libraries can be extremely useful for storing commonly used document elements. For example, you might create one library to use for all of your projects, or you might create one library for each long document. You can have more than one library open at a time, so you might create one library for each category (although this is handled easily through the library labels feature).

To store items in a library, you must first create or open a library file by selecting Utilities → Library. This command displays a Library dialog box where you type in a new file name or select from a list of files. You must type a name before you can choose the Create option. QuarkXPress normally assigns the extension .QXL to libraries. It's a good idea to follow this convention in naming new libraries, but if you don't you can type in the full name when opening the library, or ask QuarkXPress to display all file names (*.*) in the dialog box.

When you open a library, the library appears as a palette on your screen (Figure 3-19). You can drag-copy an item onto the Library palette. When the cursor changes from the Mover pointer (✥) to Library pointer (👓), release the mouse; the item will display as a thumbnail in the Library palette.

To bring items from the library onto a document page, drag the thumbnail image onto the page. When you release the mouse button, the items will appear full size on the screen. First, a full-size shadow image appears that will help you position the elements.

Commands under the Edit menu in the Library palette let you Cut, Copy, Paste, or Delete selected library entries. The Cut and Delete commands remove the item from the Library. Copy and Paste commands offer alternatives to copying library elements by dragging them with the mouse.

Figure 3-19   A library palette.

New libraries are always based on the information contained in the XPRESS.PRF file. If you place an entry in the library that does not match the XPRESS.PRF specifications for hyphenation exceptions, tracking table information, or kerning table information, the library text will be reflowed. Similarly, text items copied from a library may get reflowed in a document that does not share the same hyphenation exceptions, tracking table information, or kerning table information.

Library Labels

Don't overlook this great feature. Any item that is stored in a library can have a "label" attached to it. The Labels menu in the Library palette allows you to display All library entries, only Unlabeled entries, or selectively only those labels you want to see. You can assign the same label to more than one entry. For example, your labels might include "Pull Quotes," "House Ads," and "Picture Boxes" (with different specifications). You could opt to display only one of these categories through the Labels menu. You could also give each entry a different label, and easily find an entry by first selecting its name from the Labels menu.

Figure 3-20   The Library Entry dialog box.

To give an item in a library a label, double-click on the item to display the Library Entry dialog box (Figure 3-20). To select which entries will display, choose a label from the drop-down list at the top of the palette, or type in the label of the item you wish to display.

Changing Preferences

You have many options for setting up a document—choosing a page size, setting margins, and so on. Rather than forcing you to specify every detail from scratch, QuarkXPress begins with certain assumptions about your document, called defaults. You can change these defaults for each document as needed, or you can change the defaults *for the program* so that every new document you start will have your own customized settings.

To change defaults so that your own custom specifications will apply to every new document, start the application or close all open documents. When QuarkXPress is active but no documents are open, commands that affect the program defaults are shown in black in the menus. The commands that can be changed before you open a document include Preferences, Style Sheets, Colors, and H&J from the Edit menu; Hide/Show the various palettes from the View menu; and Auxiliary Dictionary, Hyphenation Exceptions, Library, Tracking Edit, and Kerning Edit from the Utilities menu.

The Preferences command displays a submenu of four categories of preferences: Application, General, Typographic, and Tools. Application preferences, no matter when you change them, affect the program and all files that you open. If you use the other preferences commands—General, Typographic, and Tools—with no documents open, the changes you make will be applied to all subsequently created documents. If you use these commands with a document open, your selections apply to that document only (or whatever document is active, if you have two or more documents open at once).

Setting Application Preferences

Changes made in the Application Preferences dialog box (Figure 3-21) affect all documents, including previously created documents, currently active documents, and any new documents.

Figure 3-21   The Application Preferences dialog box.

Guide Colors

If you are using a color monitor, you can change the colors in which margin guides, ruler guides, and the baseline grid display. If you are using a grayscale monitor, you can change the levels of gray. Click on the color box in front of the appropriate guides you want to change; a dialog box with a color palette is displayed (Figure 3-22). Click on the color you wish to set, then click OK.

Figure 3-22   Guide Colors can be changed in a dialog box similar to the Windows color palette.

This dialog box is similar to the standard Windows color palette displayed by the Colors utility in the Windows Control Panel—it is not the same as the QuarkXPress color palette used to assign colors to items on a page. Notice that you cannot define custom colors for the guides, unless you first define them through the Windows Control Panel.

Trap

Trapping is a rather complex concept—and a sometimes difficult practical problem in offset printing—that is described in detail in Chapter 7. Trap controls the way QuarkXPress slightly overlaps the edges between two colors when printing color separations. If you don't understand what it's all about, simply let QuarkXPress handle it through its own default settings. We explain the preferences settings here for interpretation by the educated, experienced, curious, and/or wildly experimental reader.

When the Trap value is set to Automatic, the default setting is that the trapping relationship between colors is determined by an **Absolute** value, that is, one specified in the **Auto Amount** field. If the object color is darker, it will be choked by the background color; if the object color is lighter, it will spread by the Auto Amount. **Proportional** will trap automatically using a fraction of the value in the Auto Amount field, based on the luminance of the object color and background color.

When an object color is in front of several different colors, QuarkXPress traps to the value specified in **Indeterminate**. The **OverPrint Limit** allows you to specify the shade at or above which an object color will overprint its background color. Check **Ignore White** to specify that an object color in front of several different colors does not take white into account when trapping. When **Process Trap** is checked, QuarkXPress traps process separation plates individually when a page contains process colors that touch each other. When Process Trap is unchecked, all process colors are trapped equally. These settings control the Default value for trapping shown in the Trap Specifications dialog box (Edit ➤ Colors) or in the Trap Information palette (View ➤ Show Trap Information).

Pasteboard Width

The Pasteboard Width option lets you control the width of the pasteboard—the nonprinting area to the left and right of each page or spread where you can work with or store items. The default setting is that the pasteboard is 100 percent of the page size. So, for example, if your page is letter size (8½ × 11 inches), the pasteboard will be 8½ inches wide to the left and right of the spread. You can set the pasteboard width value from 0 percent to 100 percent, but the width of pages and pasteboard combined cannot exceed 48 inches. The pasteboard is always ½ inch above and below a page or spread, and at least ½ inch of the pasteboard will surround document pages, even if you set a width percentage that would be less than ½ inch.

Registration Marks Offset

When the Registration Marks option is checked in the Print dialog box (File ➤ Print), you can specify the distance from the edge of the page at which registration marks will print. When the Registration Marks option is checked, QuarkXPress prints registration marks and crop marks. The default distance from the edge of a page at which registration marks print is 6 points, but you can use this option to change that value from 0 to 30 points in .001-point increments.

Live Scroll

When you scroll through a document using the scroll box on the scroll bars, QuarkXPress updates the screen display as you scroll if the Live Scroll option is checked. If Live Scroll is unchecked, the screen is updated only after you finish scrolling and release the mouse. The default setting turns Live Scroll off to effectively increase the speed at which you can scroll through the document.

Regardless of the setting in the Application Preferences dialog box, you can toggle to the opposite setting by using the ALT key: If Live Scroll is unchecked, you can achieve a Live Scroll by holding down the ALT key as you drag a scroll box. If Live Scroll is checked, holding down the ALT key as you scroll temporarily disables a live scroll.

Page Grabber Hand

If you want to scroll in any direction by holding down the ALT key and using the page grabber hand (☝), check the Page Grabber Hand option. If the option is not checked, you cannot scroll using the page grabber hand. The preset default is that the Page Grabber hand is checked.

Auto Library Save

Normally, QuarkXPress saves library additions and changes only when you close a library or exit the program. If you want all changes to a library saved as they are made, check Auto Library Save. Since this option can introduce delays every time you change a library, the preset default is that it is unchecked.

Low Resolution TIFF

With Low Resolution TIFF checked (the preset default), imported TIFF images are displayed at half the resolution of your monitor. If this option is unchecked, they are displayed at the full resolution of the monitor. Pictures might look better on the screen at higher resolutions, but they will take longer to display on the screen. This option has no effect on the way images print.

You can override this setting for individual pictures by holding the SHIFT key when importing a picture. If this option is checked and you want an imported image to display at full monitor resolution, hold down the SHIFT key when you click Open in the Get Picture dialog box. If this option is unchecked so that images display at high resolution, but you want an imported image to display at half resolution, hold down the SHIFT key when you click Open in the Get Picture dialog box.

256 Levels of Gray

If you want grayscale pictures to display in 256 levels of gray, check this option. If the option is unchecked, the preset default, images display in 16 levels of gray, and the screen redraw is faster. If you check this option, you must be using a monitor capable of displaying 256 levels of gray, and the image must have been scanned at 256 levels of gray.

Display DPI Value

The resolution of your monitor—pixels or dots per inch (dpi)—is determined by the manufacturer. Through QuarkXPress, you can calibrate your screen more precisely so that one inch on the monitor equals one inch on a ruler. You can enter a number in the Display DPI Value field from 36 to 300 in increments of .01 dot. To see if your screen needs calibration—and to check adjustments you have made—hold a ruler up to the screen when you have a document window open and set to Actual Size view, with on-screen rulers displayed and set to the measure on your ruler. If the screen ruler appears shorter than the physical ruler, *decrease* the Display DPI Value.

Scroll Speed

Use the Scroll Speed to set the speed at which a document scrolls when scrolling through a document using the scroll bar arrows. The faster the speed is set, the greater the distance the document moves with one click of a scroll arrow.

Setting General Preferences

Unlike Application preferences, settings in the General Preferences dialog box affect only currently active documents or newly created ones; they do not affect documents created previously. You can display the General Preferences dialog box (Figure 3-23) by choosing Edit → Preferences → General or by typing the keyboard shortcut: CTRL+Y.

Figure 3-23   The General Preferences dialog box.

Horizontal and Vertical Measure

You can set the rulers on the screen to display inches (multiples of 8 units per inch), inches decimal (multiples of 10 units per inch), picas, points, millimeters, centimeters, or ciceros. You can set the two rulers separately, so that the horizontal ruler displays picas, for instance, while the vertical ruler displays inches (common in traditional newspaper production), as shown in Figure 3-24.

Inches, picas, and points are common measurements used in the United States and other English-speaking countries. There are 12 points in a pica and 6 picas in an inch—or approximately 72 points in an inch. (The actual measure is 72.051 points per inch; you can adjust this as described under the heading "Points/Inch" which follows.) Ciceros are a French measure, with 1 cicero equivalent to approximately 4.552 millimeters.

Figure 3-24 *Different measures and how they display on rulers in actual-size view.*

QuarkXPress always shows type sizes, frame widths, and line widths in points in the Measurements palette and dialog boxes related to these elements, regardless of your selection for the ruler displays. Similarly, page width and height are usually measured in inches, the measurement QuarkXPress displays in the dialog boxes related to page size, if your selection for the ruler displays is inches, picas, or points. Page size is given in millimeters if your ruler display selection is millimeters or ciceros.

Auto Page Insertion

When you import more text into a text box than it can display, QuarkXPress automatically adds pages for the text overflow *if* all of the following are true:

- Auto Page Insertion is enabled (not set to *Off*) in the General Preferences dialog box;

- the master page specified via Auto Page Insertion has an automatic text box (indicated by the intact chain icon [▩] in the upper left corner of the master page); *and*
- the overflow is from the automatic text box or from a chain of at least two text boxes.

Normally, when there is overflow text QuarkXPress adds pages at the end of the section. A *section* is a group of pages—one chapter of a book, for example—with sequential page numbering defined by the Page ► Section command.

You can change the default for automatic page insertion in the General Preferences dialog box by choosing *Off* (to prevent QuarkXPress from adding pages automatically), or End of Story (to add new pages immediately after the last text box in the chain that overflows), or End of Document.

You can *prevent* pages from being added automatically by setting Auto Page Insert to *Off*, or by adding text to a text box that is not the automatic text box and that is not linked to any other box.

Framing

The Framing option in the General Preferences dialog box lets you specify that frame widths be added either Inside or Outside the box edge. If the frame is added inside, the dimensions of the box remain the same. If the frame is added outside, the dimensions of the box *increase* by the frame width. This setting determines the immediate effect of using the Item ► Frame command—*existing* frames in the document do not change when you change the Framing preference.

For example, if you draw a 12-pica square box and add a 1-pica wide frame using the Item ► Frame command, the effective size of the box will remain 12 picas square if the Framing option is set to Inside, or will increase to 14 picas square if the Framing option is set to Outside.

Guides

Nonprinting guides—margin guides, column guides, and ruler guides—can be set to display behind all items on the page (the preset default) or in front of them.

Item Coordinates

Normally, the horizontal ruler shows a 0 at the top left corner of each page. On facing pages or multiple-page spreads, the measurements begin again at 0 at the top left corner of each new page. The drop-down list for

Item Coordinates lets you change this so that the measurements along the ruler are continuous across the spread.

Auto Picture Import

If Auto Picture Import is on, when you open a document QuarkXPress automatically updates all imported, linked pictures that have been modified using another program (i.e., outside of QuarkXPress) since you last saved the document. If it cannot locate a picture, it displays the Missing/Modified Picture dialog box (described in Chapter 6) through which you can locate the moved or renamed file. If you set this value to On (verify), and open a file that contains modified or missing pictures, QuarkXPress will display a warning message (Figure 3-25) asking if you want to list missing or modified pictures; if you click OK, the Missing/Modified Picture dialog box listing each missing or modified picture file is displayed.

Figure 3-25   The option Auto Picture Import On (verify) causes a warning message each time you open a file containing missing or modified pictures.

If Auto Picture Import is Off, you can selectively update pictures through the Utilities → Picture Usage command, or QuarkXPress will ask you if you want to update modified pictures when you use the File → Print command.

If you use Edit → Preferences → General to change the Auto Picture Import preference On (or Off), modified pictures will be updated (or not updated) *when you next open* the active document; no changes take place immediately.

Master Page Items

As discussed earlier in this chapter, QuarkXPress offers the option of having changes made to master pages apply automatically to all document pages that have already been created based on that master page *unless you have modified those items on the document page*. The Master Page Items option in the General Preferences dialog box lets you control how applying a new master page affects document pages.

If you choose Keep Changes, when you apply a new master page, *unmodified* master page items are deleted from the document page and replaced with elements from the new master page. Master page elements that have been *modified* on the document page will remain unchanged.

If you choose Delete Changes, when you apply a new master page, both *unmodified* and *modified* master page items are deleted from the document page and replaced with the elements from the new master page.

Points/Inch

Normally, QuarkXPress converts points to inches (and vice versa) using 72 points per inch. You can change this by entering a value between 72 and 73 in .01-point increments. The true measure is 72.051 points per inch.

Ciceros/cm

QuarkXPress converts ciceros to centimeters using 2.1967 ciceros per centimeter. To change the value of ciceros to centimeters, enter any value between 2 and 3 in .0001-cicero increments.

Snap Distance

As discussed in Chapter 2, items will "snap-to" guides if Snap to Guides is checked in the View menu. The preset default is that items snap when they are moved within 6 pixels of a guide. You can change the distance at which items will snap by entering a value from 0 to 100 (pixels).

Vector Above

QuarkXPress can substitute Windows vector fonts for bitmap fonts on the screen. By default, fonts that are 72 points or larger will be vectored. You can change this value to any size between 2 and 720 points. Increasing the value will speed the time required for screen redraw.

Greek Below

QuarkXPress accelerates the speed of screen redraw by *greeking* text below a certain point size—displaying the text as a gray bar on the screen (Figure 3-26). The preset value is 7 points, but you can set this to any value from 2 to 720 points.

Figure 3-26   Greeked text.

The value you enter here determines the size below which text is greeked in Actual Size view. The value is adjusted automatically for other magnifications. For example, if you set type to be greeked below 7 points in Actual Size, then it will be greeked below 3.5 points in 200 percent view or below 14 points in 50 percent view. Greeking increases the speed at which pages are displayed on your screen, but it does not affect printing.

Greek Pictures

QuarkXPress displays inactive, imported pictures as gray boxes if Greek Pictures is checked. This is a great way to speed up screen redraw while editing a document with a lot of imported pictures. You can selectively un-greek a picture on the screen by selecting it. Picture greeking does not affect printing.

Accurate Blends

The Accurate Blends option affects how blends will display on the screen of 8-bit monitors (Figure 3-27). The preset default is that Accurate Blends is checked, so that blends display without banding. To display blends more quickly, uncheck this option. Monitors with 24-bit video displays always show blends as accurate blends, whether the option is checked or not. This option does not affect how blends print.

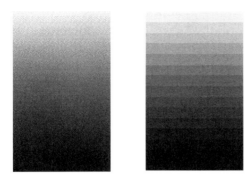

Figure 3-27   Screen display when Accurate Blends is checked (left) and unchecked (right).

Auto Constrain

Normally, you can move items anywhere on a page regardless of their relationship to other items on the page. However, if Auto Constrain is checked, items that you create within a box are constrained by that box. You cannot move constrained items out of their constraining box or scale them to be larger than the constraining box. Changes in Auto Constrain affect items that you add to the document but will not affect items previously positioned on pages.

Setting Typographic Preferences

You can display the Typographic Preferences dialog box (Figure 3-28) by choosing Edit → Preferences → Typographic or by typing the keyboard shortcut: CTRL+ALT+Y. Unlike the General Preferences settings, Typographic Preferences *do* affect how the page—specifically the type—will appear when printed.

Figure 3-28   The Typographic Preferences dialog box.

Although you can change your Preferences settings at any time, it is a good idea to set preferences that affect the way a document will print before you build the document. Otherwise, changing these preferences can result in text reflow and change the appearance of pages you have already laid out. Preference settings that can affect the appearance of the text include Superscript, Subscript, Small Caps, Superior, Baseline Grid, Auto Leading, Flex Space Width, Auto Kern, and Leading Mode from the Typographic Preferences dialog box. Entries in the Typographic Preferences dialog box are described in Chapter 5.

Setting Tool Preferences

You can display the Tool Preferences dialog box (Figure 3-29) by choosing Edit → Preferences → Tools or by double-clicking on a tool in the Tool palette. The Tool Preferences dialog box lets you modify defaults for the Zoom tool and the item creation tools.

Figure 3-29   The Tool Preferences dialog box.

View Scale

The View Scale determines the range and increment of the view changes when you click on the document window with the Zoom tool (🔍) selected. You can set the Minimum to 10 percent view or higher, the Maximum to 400 percent or lower, and the Increment to any value from 10 percent to 400 percent.

Modify, Frame, and Runaround

The Modify, Frame, and Runaround options are available when one of the item creation tools is selected in the abbreviated Tool palette displayed inside the Tools Preferences dialog box (Figure 3-30).

The Modify button displays the Text Box Specifications dialog box if the Text Box tool (A) is selected; it displays the Picture Box Specifications dialog box if one of the picture box creation tools (⊠, ⊗, ⊘, or ⊠) is selected; or it displays the Line Specifications dialog box if one of the line tools (+ or \) is selected.

Figure 3-30   Text box specifications that can be modified in the Tool Preferences dialog box.

The Frame and Runaround buttons display the Frame Specifications and Runaround Specifications dialog boxes (respectively). You can change the defaults for items created with the selected tool.

Summary

In Chapter 2 you learned how to start a new QuarkXPress document and begin adding elements to a page. In this chapter you went on to learn how to create and apply multiple master pages; add, move, and delete pages; add page numbers; and divide a document into sections. You also learned how to set QuarkXPress preferences.

Up to this point we have focused on creating and editing boxes created using QuarkXPress' item creation tools. The next few chapters describe how to edit lines and the *contents* of boxes (text and imported pictures) in QuarkXPress.

4 *Word Processing*

QuarkXPress has many of the same capabilities as a dedicated word processing program and you can input text, even long documents, directly into QuarkXPress without using a word processor. However, many people input text using a word processing program, then import the text into QuarkXPress. In doing so you can preserve not only the text, of course, but also much of the formatting, such as type specifications, tabs, and paragraph alignment. This chapter presents an overview of the process of getting text onto a page—by typing, copying, or importing—and describes some of QuarkXPress' basic formatting commands and word processing capabilities, including global search, global replace, and spell checking.

It's important to understand how text that has been formatted in a word processing program is interpreted when it is imported into QuarkXPress. By seeing what you can do in QuarkXPress and knowing what you can do using your word processor, you'll be able to make decisions about how to prepare text and whether to put more time into formatting from the beginning—during the word processing step—or later, in QuarkXPress.

Chapter 3 explained how to position text boxes on a page and link text boxes on the same page or link text boxes from one page to the next. In this chapter you learn how to get text onto a page, how to edit the *content* of the text, and how to apply basic formatting. Chapter 5 on Typography covers issues that pertain to character formatting, including leading, spacing, and special effects, such as drop caps.

Setting Up a Text Box

As mentioned in earlier chapters, you must first draw a text box using QuarkXPress' Text Box tool before you can type text or import text from a word processing program. In Chapter 2, you learned how to move, resize, and apply color to boxes. Here you will learn how to adjust three other specifications that are unique to text boxes: setting the number of columns in a text box, setting gutter width, and adjusting the text inset value (Figure 4-1).

Figure 4-1 Basic text box specifications include setting the number of columns, gutter width, and text inset.

The number of columns may be set using the Measurements palette or the Text Box Specifications dialog box (Item → Modify), but gutter width and text inset can be specified only in the Text Box Specifications dialog box. The preset defaults for all three may be changed by modifying the Text Box tool preferences (Edit → Preferences → Tools), as described in Chapter 3.

Setting Columns

QuarkXPress divides the number of columns in a text box evenly. You cannot have columns of two different widths within the same text box (unless a text inset value is specified; see below). The preset default is 1 column. The maximum number of columns in a text box is 30 columns.

Gutter Width

Gutter width is the space between columns. The preset default is .167 inches, or 1 pica. You can specify a gutter width from 3 points to 24 points in .001-point increments.

Text Inset

Text inset is the distance that text will be spaced from the four edges of a text box. The preset default is 1 point.

If you specify a text inset in a text box with three or more columns, the rightmost and leftmost columns will be 1 point narrower than all other columns in the text box, since text inset is calculated from the edges of the box, not from the columns within a text box. We highly recommend that you set the text inset to zero by changing the preferences for the text box tool (Edit ➤ Preferences ➤ Tools).

Sources of Text

There are several ways of entering text on a page in QuarkXPress. You can type text directly using QuarkXPress. Most QuarkXPress documents that are longer than one page—and many one-page documents—are composed of text that has been typed in a word processing program (or other programs that can save data as text) and *imported* into QuarkXPress, using the File ➤ Get Text command. You can also copy text from a QuarkXPress library. Or you can select the Edit ➤ Paste command to copy the contents of the Clipboard; or use the Edit ➤ Paste Special or Edit ➤ Paste Link commands to import text that you want to manage through Windows' Object Linking and Embedding (OLE) feature. You'll see the pros and cons of each of these methods under the following headings.

Typing Text

To type text on a page in QuarkXPress, first use the text Box tool to create a text box (or activate the automatic text box, as described in Chapter 2), then select the Content tool (☞) in the Tools palette. When the Content tool is selected, the blinking text insertion bar appears at the top of an empty text box or, in a text box that already contains text, wherever the insertion bar was last positioned. When the Content tool is positioned inside an active text box, the mouse pointer changes to an I-beam pointer.

You can click the I-beam pointer in the text box to set the insertion point and start typing. The procedure is:

Step 1 Create or activate a text box.

Step 2 Select the Content tool in the tool palette.

Step 3 The text insertion point blinks in the text box. (If the box already contains text, you can click anywhere in the text to reposition the text insertion point.)

Step 4 Type text in through the keyboard.

The format and position of the typed text will vary depending on where you click the I-beam to position the text insertion point. If you click the I-beam in existing text, the typed text will be inserted within the text block and will appear in the same format as the text immediately left of the insertion point.

If you click the I-beam in an empty text box, the typed text will be in the default character format or the format set up for the active text box. The default settings that are initially set up for text when you first install QuarkXPress are listed in Figure 4-2.

Font:	Helvetica 12-point
Alignment:	Left
Leading:	Auto
Tabs:	Set every half inch
Hyphenation:	Auto Hyphenation is off
Auto kerning:	Above 10 points
Spacing between paragraphs:	Zero

Figure 4-2 QuarkXPress' default settings for text.

Text typed directly into QuarkXPress will take on these default characteristics unless you specify otherwise. If you want to change the format for the next text you will type, first click the I-beam to position the text insertion point, next select the commands under the Style menu (as described later in this chapter) to format the text, then type the text. In this case, you will be setting new specifications for the current insertion point only.

To change the default settings for text, select the Edit ➤ Style Sheet command (as described later in this chapter) and change the specifications for the Normal type style sheet. The default character format is defined by the Normal style sheet.

To change the default settings for a specific text on a master page, create or select the text box, then select the commands under the Style menu (as described later in this chapter) to format the text. Document pages based on this master page will have this text box; text typed into this text box on the document pages will take on the format you define on the master page. However, it will usually be more convenient to set up a style sheet for the format that you wish to define.

Typing Symbols and Other Special Characters

Most fonts have a variety of special characters available, including ™, ®, and ©. You can access these symbols by holding the ALT key and typing a number through the numeric keypad (with NUM LOCK on). To find out what keys need to be pressed for certain characters, use the Windows Character Map accessory, described below.

Certain fonts are composed entirely of symbols and special characters, such as the Symbol font and Zapf Dingbats, both of which are built into many PostScript printers. In addition to the keystroke combinations revealed through the Character Map feature, QuarkXPress offers keyboard shortcuts for some of the most common symbols, listed in Figure 4–3.

Special Character	*Typed Entry*	*On-screen display*
Open double quote	ALT+SHIFT+[	"
Close double quote	ALT+SHIFT+]	"
Open single quote	ALT+[	'
Close single quote	ALT+]	'
Nonbreaking hyphen	CTRL+SHIFT+HYPHEN	-
Discretionary (soft) hyphen	CTRL+HYPHEN	- or invisible
Nonbreaking en dash	CTRL+=	–
Breaking em dash	CTRL+SHIFT+=	—
Nonbreaking em dash	CTRL+ALT+SHIFT+=	—
Registered	ALT+SHIFT+R	®
Copyright	ALT+SHIFT+C	©
Section	ALT+SHIFT+6	§
Paragraph	ALT+SHIFT+7	¶
Bullet	ALT+SHIFT+8	•

Figure 4-3 Typing Special Characters.

Using the Windows 3.1 Character Map Feature

The Character map accessory in Windows 3.1 is like an electronic reference card. It is handy for viewing the character set available with each installed font, including special symbols such as ™, ¶, •, ®, and ©. Most fonts include these common symbols. The Symbol font (a TrueType font that comes with Windows 3.1, and a PostScript font that is built into many PostScript printers) includes a wide range of Greek and mathematical characters. The Wingdings font (a TrueType font that comes with Windows 3.1) and the Zapf Dingbat font (a PostScript font that is built into many PostScript printers) include a wider variety of symbols such as arrows, boxes, and stars.

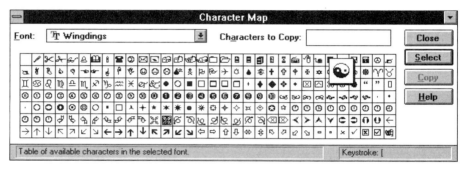

Figure 4–4   The Character Map window.

To view the character set in the Character Map window (Figure 4–4), double-click the Character Map icon in the Accessories group under the Windows Program Manager. (You can minimize the QuarkXPress application window in order to get to the Windows Program Manager.)

To view the full character set for a specific font, first choose the font from the Font drop-down list. Next, click on the desired character in the character map. The keystroke combination for the character is shown in the lower right corner of the window. You can click the Copy command key in the Character Map window to copy the character into the Windows Clipboard, then open the QuarkXPress application window and use the Paste command to insert the character in text.

In either case, you will need to set the character in the appropriate font. If the symbol you wish to use is not available in the font you are using for the rest of your text, you will need to set the symbol in a font that includes the symbol.

Typing Invisible Characters

Besides typing the normal characters you associate with text, you can insert special characters by typing the entries shown in Figure 4-5. These special characters are normally invisible on the screen and on the printed pages. You may find it useful to display the invisible characters while you are typing in QuarkXPress; these characters can be displayed by choosing View ➤ Show Invisibles.

Invisible Character	Typed Entry	Onscreen display
Space	SPACE BAR	·
Nonbreaking space	CTRL+SPACE	·
Breaking en space	CTRL+SHIFT+6	·
Nonbreaking en space	CTRL+ALT+SHIFT+6	·
Breaking flexible space	CTRL+SHIFT+5	·
Nonbreaking flexible space	CTRL+ALT+SHIFT+5	·
Breaking punctuation space	SHIFT+SPACE	·
Nonbreaking punctuation space	CTRL+SHIFT+SPACE	·
Tab	TAB	→
Right Indent Tab	SHIFT+TAB	→
New Paragraph	ENTER	¶
New Line	SHIFT+ENTER	↵
Discretionary Line Break	CTRL+ENTER	no display
Indent Here	CTRL+\	¦
New Column	KEYPAD ENTER	↓
New Box	SHIFT+KEYPAD ENTER	⇟

Figure 4-5   Typing Invisible Characters.

The New Line, Discretionary Line Break, Indent Here, New Column, and New Box characters are described later in this chapter, under "Paragraph Formatting."

Importing Text

You can select File ➤ Get Text (CTRL+E) to import text that has been typed in a word processor or to import data that has been saved as text from a spreadsheet or database program.

To import text into QuarkXPress, first create or activate a text box. Next select the Content tool; a blinking text cursor will appear automatically in a new text box, or you can position the cursor within an existing block of text. Select the File ➤ Get Text command, then find the file name from the list displayed in the Get Text dialog box. Double-click on the file name to select it, or click once and click the Open button. These steps are illustrated in Figures 4-6, 4-7, 4-8, and 4-9.

Notice that you can change directories and drives through the Get Text dialog box (File ➤ Get Text) using the same techniques you learned in Chapter 2 for the Open dialog box (File ➤ Open). The one difference is that only QuarkXPress documents are listed in the dialog box when you select the Open command, and only text files in formats for which the corresponding import/export filter is available are listed when you select the File ➤ Get Text command.

Step 1 **Create or activate a text box and select the Content tool, or position the cursor within an existing block of text with the Content tool.**

Figure 4-6   Active text box.

Step 2 **Select the File ➤ Get Text command (CTRL+E).**

Figure 4-7   Get Text command.

Chapter 4: Word Processing 155

Step 3 Find the name of the text file you want to import in the Get Text dialog box.

Figure 4-8 Get Text dialog box.

QuarkXPress recognizes all the most common text files on the PC, including RTF (Rich Text Format) documents and documents created in Microsoft Word 4.0 for DOS, Microsoft Word for Windows versions 1.0 and 2.0, Microsoft Write, WordPerfect 5.1, WordPerfect for Windows, Ami Pro 2.0, and XyWrite III Plus. If the file name you seek is not listed in the directory where it is stored, it might have an extension that QuarkXPress does not recognize as a text file. You can type the full file name in the dialog box, or ask for a list of all file types by typing *.* in the File Name area.

Check **Convert Quotes** if you want inch and foot marks (",') converted to open and close quotation marks and apostrophes ("," ,',') and double hyphens (--) converted to em dashes (—). Click on **Include Style Sheets** if you want the style sheet names and formats imported with the text from Microsoft Word, or if you want to convert XPress Tags to format text.

Step 4 Select the name by double-clicking on it. (This is a shortcut for the more obvious method: Click on the file name to select it, then click on OK.)

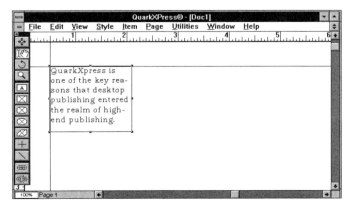

Figure 4-9 Imported text.

Long files or complex formats can take awhile to import. To take the worry out of waiting, the lower left corner of the Document window displays the percentage of the file that has been imported during the import process.

Imported text will be inserted at the text insertion point or will replace text that was selected when the Get Text command is chosen. The text will take on the width of the column in which it is imported. It will stop flowing when it reaches the bottom of the text box (if links have not been established) or flow into linked boxes and/or add new pages as needed for overflow text (as described in Chapter 2).

If the imported text has not already been formatted in a word processing program, or if QuarkXPress does not support the word processor and therefore cannot preserve the formatting, the text will take on the default format and type specifications, as specified in the Normal Style Sheet. If the text has been formatted in a word processing program that the QuarkXPress program supports, QuarkXPress will preserve some of that formatting, as described under the next heading.

Formatted Text

QuarkXPress preserves the formatting of text imported from supported word processing programs. You can format text using any supported word processor's formatting commands, or you can format text in any word processor by embedding QuarkXPress Tag codes that will be translated into formats when you import the text into QuarkXPress. See Chapter 10 for the procedure and codes for creating XPress Tags.

In order for the formatting to be preserved when text is imported into QuarkXPress, the correct filter (WORD1.XXT, WORD2.XXT, WRITEXT.XXT, or XTAGS.XXT) must be available in the XPRESS application directory.

Formatting characteristics that are usually preserved include:

- Left margin
- Left and right indents
- First-line indent
- Carriage returns
- Tabs
- Character formats (font size, style)
- Style sheets from Microsoft Word only, and only if Include Style Sheets was checked

The right margin is changed to match QuarkXPress' column width, with right margin indents preserved from some word processors.

QuarkXPress ignores specialized formatting commands, such as headers and footers or footnotes.

Tables created using Microsoft Word's Insert Table command are imported as text, with each cell separated by a tab and each row separated by a carriage return. The graphic borders of a table are not preserved.

If the fonts specified through the word processor are not loaded in your system when you import the text into QuarkXPress, a warning message appears.

Unformatted Text

Although it is usually preferable to do as much formatting as possible in the word processing program, you can also import unformatted text to QuarkXPress and format it with QuarkXPress' features. There are three common sources of unformatted text: ASCII files from any word processor, data saved in ASCII format from a spreadsheet or database program, and text that has been telecommunicated through the type of electronic mailbox or bulletin board that forces you to use ASCII text.

Initially, unformatted text will take on the default type specifications and format, or whatever format is specified for the current location of the text insertion point. It's a good idea to set up the text specifications at the insertion point before you select the Get Text command to import ASCII text. Choose specifications appropriate to the largest percentage of the imported text (not necessarily the first line of imported text: if it is a heading, for example).

Text from a Library

You can drag text from a QuarkXPress library as described in Chapter 3. Text dragged from a library will retain all of its formatting. If a style sheet was used to format the text in the library, the style sheet names will be added to the document's style sheet list when the text is dragged from the library. If the library text uses the same style sheet names as in the target document, the text will use the style sheet specification of the target document, though the library text will retain its original formatting and the style sheet will need to be reapplied.

Text in a library takes on the default typographical preferences that are stored in XPRESS.PRF. When it is copied into a document, it takes on the typographical preferences defined for that document through Edit ➤ Preferences ➤ Typographic. Differences in preference settings for auto leading, auto kerning, flex space width, and other variables will affect the appearance of the text.

Pasting Text from the Clipboard

If you have already put text into the Clipboard using the Cut or Copy command, you can select the Paste command to bring in text from the Clipboard. You can put text into the Clipboard while you are working in another program, then open the QuarkXPress document and paste the text onto the page. You can also use the Clipboard to paste from one QuarkXPress document to another, or from one part of a document to another.

A pasted text *box* will appear in the center of the screen. If you have clicked an insertion point in existing text, the box will paste at the insertion point as an anchored box and move instream with the text.

Using Object Linking and Embedding with Text

The Paste Special, Paste Link, and Links commands are designed to be used under Windows version 3.1 and higher that support Object Linking and Embedding (OLE). You can link or embed an object, including text, from another application that supports OLE into a QuarkXPress document. First, create the text in the other application, then use Paste Special or Paste Link command in QuarkXPress to import the object.

If the text is embedded using the Paste Special command, then the text remains under control of the original application. The other application is used to create the screen image and to print the object. When you double-click on the object with the Content tool, you automatically open the original application and you can edit the object. Using Paste Special, you can import text in formats not directly supported by QuarkXPress such as data from Excel version 3.0 or higher. When you edit the text through QuarkXPress, it is updated only in the QuarkXPress document—not in the source document.

If the text is linked using the Paste Links command, changes you make through QuarkXPress are made directly to the source file. Also, you can specify whether the text is updated automatically in QuarkXPress if it is changed using the original application when QuarkXPress is not active. You can specify whether the updating is done automatically or only when you request it. Update or change your link preferences through the Links command.

Selecting and Editing Text

Once text is on a page (or on the Pasteboard), you can use QuarkXPress' rich and flexible assortment of commands and tools to edit it, including the commands from the Edit menu and the Style menu, plus global search, global replace, and spell-checking features. The first step in changing any text is to position the text insertion point or select a range of text. To select portions of text within a block of text or to establish the text insertion point before typing new text, be sure the Content tool (☝) is active.

The basic methods of selecting text in QuarkXPress are similar to selecting text in any Windows application, although QuarkXPress adds additional shortcuts (Figure 4-10).

Basic Windows Techniques for Selecting Text

Certain selection techniques are common to all Windows programs, including QuarkXPress:

- Position the I-beam in a text box and click once to position the text insertion point for typing or importing new text.
- Position the I-beam beside a character, and drag the I-beam to the end of the desired selection. You can drag the I-beam in any direction—you need not follow along one line of text.
- Double-click on a word to select it.
- The HOME key jumps to the start of a line, the END key jumps to the end of the line. Holding the CTRL key while pressing HOME or END jumps to the beginning or end of the document. Holding the SHIFT key while pressing HOME or END highlights the text from the cursor location to the start or end of the line. Holding the SHIFT and CTRL keys while pressing HOME or END highlights the text from the cursor location to the start or end of the document.
- Arrow keys move the text insertion point. Holding the SHIFT key as you press the arrow key will highlight (that is, select) the text as the insertion point moves:
  - Arrow keys alone move the insertion point one character (left or right) or one line (up or down) at a time.
  - Arrow keys with the CTRL key move the insertion point one word (left or right) or one paragraph (up or down) at a time.
  - Arrow keys with the CTRL and ALT keys move the insertion point to the beginning or end of the line (left or right) or to the beginning or end of the story (up or down).

QuarkXPress Techniques for Selecting Text

QuarkXPress adds its own shortcuts for selecting text (Figure 4-10):

- Triple-click anywhere in a line of text to select it.
- Click four times anywhere in a paragraph to select it.
- Click five times anywhere in a story to select the text in the active box and the text in all boxes linked to the active box.
- If the Content tool is selected and the cursor is positioned in a text box (by positioning the I-beam pointer [I] in the text box and clicking once to position the blinking text cursor [(|)]), then the Select All command will select all of a story.

Figure 4-10   Methods of selecting text in QuarkXPress.

Highlighted text will be replaced when you begin typing from the keyboard—you need not delete it first before inserting new text.

Keyboard Shortcuts to Deleting Characters

You can delete any selected text by pressing Backspace or Delete, or by using the Cut or Delete commands. When no text is selected, you can delete characters adjacent to the cursor position using four keyboard shortcuts:

- Backspace deletes the previous character.
- Delete key deletes the next character.
- CTRL+Backspace deletes the previous word.
- CTRL+Delete deletes the next word.

Character Formatting

In Chapter 2 you learned how to control the position and size of text boxes and how to link text from one box to another. Earlier in this chapter you also learned that typed and imported, unformatted text takes on the default text specifications, or QuarkXPress retains the text formatting that was set up in the word processing program used to prepare the imported text. In the next sections you will learn how to change the attributes of individual characters and the format of paragraphs once text is on a page.

There are two ways of changing the format of text in QuarkXPress. One way—the obvious way—is to select text, then select the commands described next to change the appearance of the selected text. The second method is to apply a Style Sheet, as described later in this chapter.

If you choose the first approach, there are three ways of changing the format of text: through commands under the Style menu, through the use of keyboard shortcuts, or through the Measurements palette. In this section we discuss the basic character attributes: Font, Size, Type Style, Color, and Shade (Figure 4-11). Other Character attributes listed on the Style menu are discussed in Chapter 5.

Figure 4-11 QuarkXPress lets you apply the same character attributes found in many word processing programs.

The Style menu lets you apply attributes that are also included in the Character Attributes dialog box (CTRL+SHIFT+D) (Figure 4-12). If you need to apply several different attributes, you may find it's faster to open the Character Attributes dialog box rather than to select several commands from the menu.

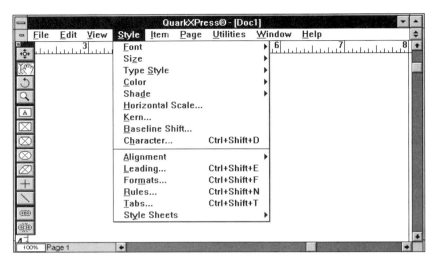

Figure 4-12   The Style menu when a text box is active.

Keyboard shortcuts, which are listed under individual headings later in this section, are available for most character attributes.

The Measurements palette (View → Measurements) can also be used to apply character attributes when a text box is selected. The right half of the palette displays various icons and drop-down lists that affect selected text (Figure 4-13).

Figure 4-13   The Measurements palette when a text box is active.

When you display the Character Attributes dialog box or any of the associated submenus, the options that apply to the current selection are checked or displayed. If the current selection includes more than one attribute of the same type—two different sizes or both bold and italic text, for example—then none of the options will be checked or displayed. Check boxes for Type Style in the Character Attributes dialog box will display in gray when more than two styles exist in selected text.

Font

Fonts are displayed in the submenu of the Style → Font command (Figure 4-14), in the drop-down list in the Measurements palette, or in a drop-down list in the Character Attributes dialog box. Only fonts available to your system are shown. See Chapter 5 for information on loading screen fonts and setting global conditions that relate to fonts.

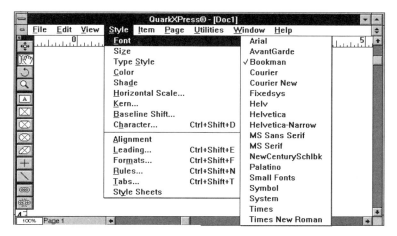

Figure 4-14   The Font list under the Style menu.

To select a font, position the pointer over one of the font lists (in the Style ➤ Font submenu, in the Measurements palette, or in the Character Attributes dialog box) and click the mouse button to view the list; then click on the desired font name.

As a shortcut, you can type the font name in the Measurements palette or the Character Attributes dialog box, or type the first character(s) of a font name. For example, you can choose Zapf Chancery by simply typing "z" in the font name area *if* that is the only font name beginning with the letter *z*. Otherwise, QuarkXPress displays the *first* font name that it finds—scrolling either forward or backward—that matches or follows the characters typed.

Size

Font sizes are displayed in the submenu of the Style ➤ Size command, in the drop-down list in the Measurements palette, and in a drop-down list in the Character Attributes dialog box. Commonly used sizes are listed, but you are not limited to the sizes listed on the submenu or in the drop-down lists; you can enter any size from 2 to 720 points in .001-point increments.

To select a size, position the pointer over one of the three submenus and click the mouse button to view the list, then click on the desired font size, or type the new size in the entry area in the Measurements palette, in the Character Attributes dialog box (CTRL+SHIFT+D), or in the Font Size dialog box (CTRL+SHIFT+\) as shown in Figure 4-15.

Figure 4-15   Press CTRL+SHIFT+\ *to display the Font Size dialog box.*

Desired Action	Keyboard Shortcut
To specify a size	CTRL+SHIFT+\
To enlarge selected type	CTRL+SHIFT+>
To enlarge selected type in 1-point increments	CTRL+ALT+SHIFT+>
To reduce selected type	CTRL+SHIFT+<
To reduce selected type in 1-point increments	CTRL+ALT+SHIFT+<

Figure 4-16   Keyboard shortcuts for changing the size of text.

You can also change the size of selected type using keyboard shortcuts (Figure 4-16): CTRL+SHIFT+> increases the size of the selected type, CTRL+SHIFT+< decreases the size. These shortcuts change the size in the following preset sequence of sizes: 7, 9, 10, 12, 14, 18, 24, 36, 48, 60, 72, 96, 120, 144, 168, and 192 points. To change the size in 1-point increments between 2 points and 720 points, press CTRL+ALT+SHIFT+> or CTRL+ALT+SHIFT+<. You can use CTRL+SHIFT+\ to quickly check the resulting size.

Type Style

The 13 styles listed in the Type Style submenu are repeated in the Measurements palette (Figure 4-17) and in the Character Attributes dialog box (CTRL+SHIFT+D). They all have keyboard equivalents.

Figure 4-17   Symbols in the Measurements palette are set in the font style they represent: ▣ = *Plain,* ▣ = *Bold,* ▣ = *Italic,* ▣ = *Outline,* ▣ = *Shadow,* ▣ = *Strikeout,* ▣ = *Underline,* ▣ = *Word Underline,* ▣ = *Small Caps,* ▣ = *All Caps,* ▣ = *Superscript,* ▣ = *Subscript,* ▣ = *Superior.*

To select a style, position the pointer over the style name on the Style ➤ Type Style submenu, click on the appropriate symbol in the Measurements palette, or click on the style name in the Character Attributes dialog box.

You can apply more than one style to selected text, but some styles are mutually exclusive, such as SMALL CAPS and ALL CAPS (FIGURE 4-18). With SMALL CAPS, lowercase characters are set as caps that are 75 percent smaller than normal for the font size. (You can change this default through Edit ➤ Preferences ➤ Typographic, as described in Chapter 5.) ALL CAPS sets all characters as normal capitalized letters, whether they were typed as caps or as lowercase letters. Other mutual exclusives include Underline and Word Underline, and Superscript and Subscript.

This text is upper and lowercase Stone Serif
THIS TEXT IS SMALL CAPS STONE SERIF
THIS TEXT IS ALL CAPS STONE SERIF

The underline style underlines spaces between words
The word underline style underlines words only

Figure 4-18   Mutually exclusive styles include Small Caps and All Caps (top), Underline and Word Underline (bottom).

The difference between Superscript and Superior characters is that Superior characters are roughly half the size of normal characters in the font size, and they are set above the baseline but never rise above cap height for the font. Superscript characters are usually set in normal size and can rise above the top of the ascent line; they also can run into text on the line above (depending on the leading and your settings through Edit ➤ Preferences ➤ Typographic).

Each style can be applied with its keyboards shortcut, listed in Figure 4-19. The shortcuts are usually obtained by pressing down the CTRL key and the SHIFT key, then pressing one other key.

Style Menu Command	Keyboard Shortcut
Bold	CTRL+SHIFT+B
Small Caps	CTRL+SHIFT+H
Italic	CTRL+SHIFT+I
All Caps	CTRL+SHIFT+K
Outline	CTRL+SHIFT+O
Plain	CTRL+SHIFT+P
Shadow	CTRL+SHIFT+S
Underline	CTRL+SHIFT+U
Word Underline	CTRL+SHIFT+W
Superscript	CTRL+SHIFT++
Subscript	CTRL+SHIFT+Hyphen
Strike Through	CTRL+SHIFT+/
Superior	CTRL+SHIFT+V

Figure 4-19 Keyboard shortcuts for applying styles to text.

Color

Color can be applied to text by choosing from the Style ➤ Color submenu, from the drop-down list in the Character Attributes dialog box, or by using the Colors palette. The colors listed are those created through the Edit ➤ Colors command.

Figure 4-20 To apply color to text using the Colors palette, click on the text icon and choose a color from the list.

To use the Colors palette to apply a color to selected text, click on the icon for text at the top of the palette, then click on a color name in the list (Figure 4-20). Or you can position the pointer over the Colors submenu on the Style menu or in the Character Attributes dialog box, and select from the list of colors.

Chapter 8 on Printing describes the basics of setting up new colors; advanced issues relating to printing color separations are discussed in Chapter 13.

Shade

You can set selected type in a shade of gray (sometimes called a "screen" or "tint") or a shade of color by choosing from the Style → Shade submenu, from the drop-down list in the Character Attributes dialog box, or by using the Colors palette (Figure 4-21).

Figure 4-21   To apply a shade to text using the Colors palette, input a percentage or choose a percentage from the list.

To indicate selected text to be shaded, position the pointer over the Shade submenu on the Style menu or in the Character Attributes dialog box, and input a percentage in increments up to .001 percent or select from the list of percentages, which lists shades in 10 percent increments.

To use the Colors palette to apply a shade percentage to selected text, select the icon for text at the top of the palette, then move to the percentage area and input a value or choose from the list.

Paragraph Formatting

A "paragraph" in QuarkXPress includes all of the text between two hard carriage returns. A hard carriage return occurs wherever you press the ENTER key while entering text. You can force text onto a new line without marking it as a new paragraph by typing the special character for a new line: SHIFT+ENTER. This and other special formatting characters are described under the heading "Special Characters" later in this section.

When you select one of the commands that affect whole paragraphs, the options you choose will apply to all of the text between hard carriage returns, regardless of how much text is actually highlighted. In other words, you need not select every word in a paragraph in order for these commands to apply to the whole paragraph in which the text insertion/selection point is positioned.

You can format paragraphs using any one of three different methods: through commands under the Style menu, using keyboard shortcuts, or through the Measurements palette. In this section we discuss those paragraph formats that QuarkXpress shares in common with many word processing programs: alignment, indents, space before or after, and tabs (Figure 4-22).

Figure 4-22 QuarkXPress lets you apply many of the paragraph formatting commands found in word processing programs.

When you display the Paragraph formats dialog box (Figure 4-22), the Alignment submenu, or any of the dialog boxes associated with tabs, the options that apply to the current selection are checked or displayed. If the current selection includes more than one format, then none of the options is checked or displayed.

Besides using the commands described under the next headings to format a paragraph, you can also format paragraphs using a style sheet (as described later in this chapter).

 As an alternative, you can copy the format of one paragraph to others in the same text chain. To copy the paragraph format from one paragraph to another, first select the paragraph you want to change, then hold down the ALT and SHIFT keys and click in the paragraph containing the format you want to copy.

Alignment

You can specify the alignment of a paragraph by selecting from a drop-down list in the Paragraph Formats dialog box (CTRL+SHIFT+F), from the

Alignment submenu, by clicking on icons in the Measurements palette (Figure 4-23), or by using keyboard shortcuts.

Figure 4-23 The Alignment icons in the Measurements palette.

The keyboard shortcuts for alignment are shown in Figure 4-24.

Style Menu Command	*Keyboard Shortcut*
Left Alignment	CTRL+SHIFT+L for Left
Centered	CTRL+SHIFT+C for Centered
Right	CTRL+SHIFT+R for Right
Justified	CTRL+SHIFT+J for Justified

Figure 4-24 Keyboard shortcuts for aligning text.

You may be accustomed to using typographical terms to describe the four alignments listed in QuarkXPress' menus:

- Left = left aligned, flush left, ragged right.
- Centered = ragged left and right.
- Right = right aligned, flush right, ragged left.
- Justified = flush left and right.

The spacing between words and characters for Left aligned, Centered, or Right aligned text is determined by the Edit → Preferences → Typographic settings for Auto Kern Above and Character Widths, and Style → Kerning settings. Spacing between characters also is determined by entries made through the Edit → H&Js command. Chapter 5 explains these typographic settings.

Indents

You can select Style → Formats (CTRL+SHIFT+F) to display the Paragraph Formats dialog box to set paragraph indentation as well as leading, spacing between paragraphs, and other formats. The Paragraph Formats dialog box includes a text ruler for the selected paragraph (Figure 4-25). You can move the dialog box to align the ruler below the selected text.

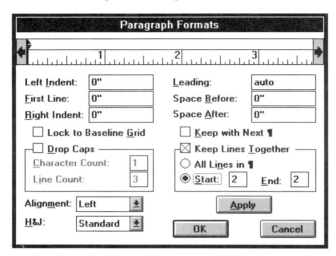

Figure 4-25   Paragraph Formats dialog box and ruler (CTRL+SHIFT+F).

You can make all entries in the text entry areas of the dialog box, or you can make changes by positioning or moving icons on the ruler. Icons that can be positioned and moved on the ruler include:
- First Line
- Left Indent
- Right Indent

You can also set left tabs by clicking on the ruler in the Paragraph Formats dialog box, but you must set other tabs and tab fill characters through Style → Tabs (CTRL+SHIFT+T), discussed later in this section. If you cannot see both ends of the ruler (i.e., the full width of the text margins) on the screen, click on the arrow to the left or the right of the ruler.

If the ruler is very small, or so large that you cannot see both margins, you can enlarge (or reduce) the view of the ruler by closing the dialog box and enlarging (or reducing) your view of the text, then choosing Style → Formats again.

The appearance of the text on the page does not change immediately as you make changes to the ruler or dialog box entries. Click on Apply to view the effects on the page, then click on OK to keep the settings or Cancel to close the dialog box without recording any of your changes.

There are three different indention settings for any paragraph: Left Indent, First Line Indent, and Right Indent. The Left and Right Indents are measured from the left and right side of a text box, less the text inset, described earlier in this chapter. The First Line Indent is measured relative to the Left Indent. To create a hanging indent, for example, you would enter some positive value for the Left Indent, then enter a negative value for the First Line Indent. Values that would force text beyond the margins or column guides are not valid entries and will result in a warning message. Figure 4-26 shows how different indention settings affect the text, and what those settings look like in the dialog box and on the text ruler.

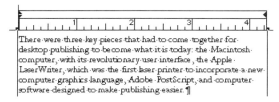

a   Flush-left paragraph with no indent.

b   Normal paragraph with first-line indent.

c   Hanging indent format positions first-line indent left of the other lines.

Figure 4-26   Paragraph indentation settings.

Space Before/Space After Paragraphs

The amount entered in the Space Before and/or Space After boxes is added to the normal spacing between lines (leading) wherever there is a new paragraph. More precisely, the value you enter for spacing between paragraphs is added wherever there is a hard carriage return in the text.

This method of defining breaks between paragraphs is more flexible than using extra carriage returns (blank lines) to add space between paragraphs. Where there are two or more hard carriage returns in a row, the spacing value will be added twice or more.

Space Before does not add space before paragraphs at the top of a text box or when the paragraph begins after an item set up to have text runaround. Space After is not added when a paragraph falls at the bottom of a text box or when it ends at an item set up to have text runaround. Select Item ▸ Modify to set the First Baseline to adjust the white space at the top of a text box.

Keep with Next Paragraph

If you check Keep with Next ¶, the selected paragraph will not be split from the next paragraph by a page break, column break, or text box border. This command can be used to prevent headings from appearing at the end of a page or column, for example, or to keep lines of a table or list together.

Keep Lines Together

Check Keep Lines Together to control widows and orphans, the line(s) of text that are separated from the rest of the paragraph by a page break, column break, or text box border. You can specify that the entire paragraph should be kept together by checking All Lines in ¶, or you can specify the number of lines at the Start and at the End of the paragraph that must be kept together.

QuarkXPress ignores the settings for Keep with Next ¶ and Keep Lines Together if by following the rules a box in a chain would be left empty. If you apply both All Lines in ¶ and Keep with Next ¶ to a range of paragraphs and QuarkXPress cannot do both, the program will keep all lines together and ignore the Keep with Next ¶ setting.

Tabs

You can select Style ▸ Tabs (CTRL+SHIFota+T) to display the Paragraph Tabs dialog box (Figure 4-27). Like the Formats dialog box, the Tabs dialog box displays a text ruler for the selected paragraph. You can move the dialog box to align the ruler below the selected paragraph. You can use the text entry areas in the dialog box or the ruler to set or change tabs and indentation settings for selected paragraphs. QuarkXPress sets default tabs every half inch on the ruler for Normal text. If you set tabs in a word processing program, then QuarkXPress' rulers will change to reflect those settings when you import the text.

Figure 4-27   Paragraph Tabs dialog box (CTRL+SHIFT+F) includes a text ruler.

You can make all entries through the dialog box, or you can make changes by positioning or moving icons on the text ruler. Up to 20 tabs may be set. Tab character icons that can be positioned and moved on the text ruler include:

- Left
- Right
- Center
- Decimal
- Comma
- Align On

plus paragraph indent markers (described earlier):

- First Line
- Left Indent
- Right Indent

To set a tab, first choose the appropriate tab character from the drop-down list, then either click on the ruler to position and move the tab, or enter a value in the Position entry area in the dialog box. The position can be entered in any measure using the abbreviations described in Chapter 1. The measure always starts with 0 at the left edge of the ruler (as defined by text inset and left indent).

Left, Right, and Center tab characters align text flush left, flush right, or centered, respectively, relative to the location of the tab character. Decimal tabs align text on a decimal point, and are used most often for aligning financial data. Comma tabs work like decimal tabs, except text is aligned on commas, which are used in place of decimal points in many countries. Align On lets you specify the character you want QuarkXPress to use for alignment.

When there is no decimal, comma, or other character in text set with the Decimal, Comma, or Align On tab characters, a numeral that precedes a nonnumeric character will be aligned with the tab. This enables correct alignment of columns text that may include numbers with parentheses or that may not contain a decimal or comma (Figure 4-28).

```
→   $|4,259.50→      100%→         $0.19↵
→     ($987.90)→      96%→         $45↵
→   12,000→            1%→        ($10.70)
```

Figure 4-28 Tabs align on a numeral preceding a nonnumeric character, or on the final numeral in text that does not contain a decimal.

You can specify any Fill Character for a selected tab. The most common fill characters (other than blank spaces) include periods (for dotted lines) and hyphens (for dashed lines), but any character can be a fill character. The fill character will be repeated from the end of the text where the tab key is pressed up to the tab mark to which the fill character is applied (Figure 4-29). To adjust the spacing between fill characters, use the Tracking command.

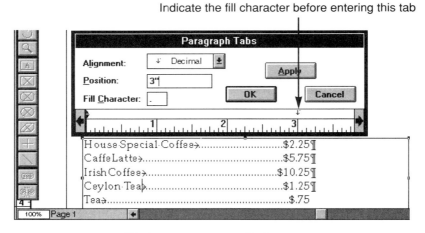

Figure 4-29 How fill characters are applied.

You can change the alignment setting for a tab by clicking on it in the ruler, then clicking on an alignment setting in the dialog box. You can move a tab by dragging it on the ruler or by clicking on it to select it, then changing the Position value. The dialog box for any selected tab shows the current position and fill character.

To delete individual tabs, simply click on the tab marker and hold down the mouse button as you drag the tab off the top or bottom of the ruler. To clear all tabs from a ruler, hold the CTRL key and click on the ruler.

You can adjust the indent markers as well as the tabs when the Tab dialog box is open. If you cannot see both ends of the ruler (i.e., the full width of the text margins), click on the arrows to the left or right of the ruler.

To copy the paragraph format, including tab settings, from one paragraph to another, first select the paragraph(s) you want to format, then position the I-beam pointer over the paragraph whose tabs you wish to copy and press ALT+SHIFT+click.

The appearance of the text on the page does not change immediately as you make changes to the ruler or Paragraph Tabs dialog box entries. Click on Apply to view the effects on the page, then click on OK to keep the settings or Cancel to close the dialog box without recording any of your changes.

Once tab stops are set on the ruler, text that already has tab characters will fall into place below each tab stop. You can add tabs within the text by positioning the I-beam as appropriate for text insertion and pressing the TAB key. Remember that you can view the tab characters on the page (→) by choosing View → Show Invisibles, as described in Chapter 2.

The Right Indent tab lets you align characters flush with the right indent. To obtain this character, press the ALT+TAB keys. Unlike other tab characters, this character must be set individually in each line; it cannot be preset on the tab ruler before typing. The Right Indent tab is useful for setting up headers or footers, where text appears on a left indent and a page number symbol needs to be flush with the right indent (Figure 4-30).

Figure 4-30   The Right Indent tab can be useful for setting up footers.

Paragraph Formatting Characters

As mentioned earlier, you can insert invisible characters using keys listed in Figure 4–3. Here we highlight a few special characters that affect paragraph position or formatting, shown in Figure 4-31.

Paragraph Formatting Character	Typed Entry	Onscreen display
New Paragraph	ENTER	¶
New Line	SHIFT+ENTER	↵
Discretionary Line Break	CTRL+ENTER	no display
Indent Here	CTRL+\	¦
New Column	KEYPAD ENTER	↓
New Box	SHIFT+KEYPAD ENTER	↡

Figure 4-31   Typing paragraph formatting characters.

Pressing the ENTER key signals a new paragraph. All of the formatting described under the next headings applies to whole paragraphs; you cannot apply different formatting to lines within a paragraph.

New Line Character

The New Line character (SHIFT+ENTER) forces a line break without signaling a new paragraph. This is useful when you are using a style sheet to format whole paragraphs that might add space before or after a hard carriage return. Space will not be added before or after the New Line character, which acts as a "soft" carriage return.

Discretionary Line Break

The Discretionary Line Break (CTRL+ENTER) character acts like a discretionary hyphen, but no hyphen is shown. Use this character to break a word at the end of a line without inserting a hyphen. This character does not signal a new paragraph.

Indent Here

The Indent Here character (CTRL+\) causes the current line of text and all subsequent lines to be indented at the location of the character (Figure 4-32). Use this special character to create hanging initial caps and other special paragraph indent effects.

```
QuarkXPress QuarkXpress is one of the key reasons that
             desktop publishing entered the realm of
             high-end publishing. Before the release of
```

Figure 4-32   Effect of the Indent Here Character.

To delete the Indent Here character, position the insertion point behind it and press the Backspace key.

New Column/New Box

You can force text to jump to the next column or the next text box in a linked chain by inserting the New Column (KEYPAD ENTER) or New Box (SHIFT+KEYPAD ENTER) characters. These characters are useful in front of headings that you always want to start at the top of a column or a page.

Working with Style Sheets

One of the most powerful yet under-utilized features of desktop publishing applications (word processing *and* page layout) is the electronic style sheet. A style sheet is simply a collection of shortcuts for applying type specifications (character attributes and paragraph formats) used throughout a document. A style sheet system lets you define the character attributes and paragraph format for each type of text element in a document, such as major headings, subheadings, captions, and body text. Once you set up a style sheet for a document, you can format the text using short keystroke commands or menu selections instead of using several commands to format each paragraph. Style sheets are applied to paragraphs, not to individual characters within a paragraph.

Character-specific formats that can be applied using style sheets include all attributes that are applied using the Font, Size, Type Style, Color, Shade, Horizontal Scale, Tracking, and Baseline Shift commands from the Style menu. Paragraph-specific formatting includes all settings that are applied using the Alignment, Leading, Formats, Rules, and Tabs commands from the Style menu. Document-wide formatting, such as setting margin guides and column widths, is handled outside of the style sheet functions.

Figure 4-33 The Style Sheets dialog box.

There are two basic steps in working with style sheets: First, you must create a style sheet; second, you must apply it to the appropriate text. New style sheets are set up using the Edit → Style Sheets command. The Style Sheets dialog box (Figure 4-33) lists all the styles in the current document. You can click on any style sheet name to view a partial list of specifications for that style sheet, displayed in the lower half of the dialog box.

Choose New to add a new style sheet name, Edit to modify the specifications for a selected style sheet name, Duplicate to create a new style sheet based on an existing style sheet name, Delete to remove a style sheet name, or Append to import the style sheet specifications from another QuarkXPress or Microsoft Word document. Style sheets can be applied using any one of several techniques, described later in this section.

The process of formatting characters and paragraphs with a style sheet can take place in either QuarkXPress or in Microsoft Word. Style sheets created in Microsoft Word can be imported along with the text into QuarkXPress by clicking Include Style Sheets in the Import Text dialog box. The proper filter (WORD1.XXT, WORD2.XXT, WRITEXT.XXT, or XTAGS.XXT) must be in the same directory as the QuarkXPress program.

Creating and Editing Style Sheets

In setting up a style sheet in QuarkXPress, the first step is to create a style sheet name—one for each different paragraph format in your document. To set up a style sheet, select Edit → Style Sheets to display the Style Sheets dialog box (Figure 4-33) and click on the New button. When you choose New, QuarkXPress displays the Edit Style Sheet dialog box (Figure 4-34), which is used for creating new style sheets or editing existing ones.

Figure 4-34   *The Edit Style Sheet dialog box.*

The Edit Style Sheet dialog box allows you to assign or change a style sheet name, assign or change the keyboard equivalent for applying the style sheet, select a style on which this style sheet will be based, and change the character attributes, paragraph format, rules, or tabs.

The Style Sheets palette allows you to access the Edit Style Sheet dialog box quickly. Double-click on a style sheet name and the Style Sheets dialog box with that style name will be displayed.

Name

You can enter a style sheet Name up to 64 characters long. This name will be displayed in the Style → Style Sheets submenu and the Style Sheets palette. A single document can include up to 127 different style sheet names. You must name every new style sheet; the OK button does not become active until text is entered in the Name entry area.

Keyboard Equivalent

You can assign a Keyboard Equivalent that you can use later to apply the style sheet instead of going through the Style → Style Sheets submenu or Style Sheets palette. When the cursor is in the Keyboard Equivalent entry area, press any of the Function keys on an extended keyboard (except F1 which is reserved for Help), or press CTRL, and/or SHIFT with any keys on the numeric keypad. Whatever keys you press when the cursor is in the Keyboard Equivalent entry area will be those you press to assign the style sheet. Avoid using the ALT key with the keypad keys, since Windows uses these keys for special characters such as bullets.

Based On

The Based On entry is a drop-down list of all the current style sheet names. If you base a style sheet on another one, then changes made to the other style sheet will also affect style sheets that are Based On it, except those attributes that were specifically altered for the new style sheet.

For example, if you create a new style sheet Based On Normal, and the only difference between Normal and the new style sheet is that the new style sheet is indented 1 inch from the left, then any changes you make to the character specifications, rules, or tabs for the Normal style sheet will also be applied to the new style sheet. But if you change the left indent for Normal style sheet, the new style sheet's left indent will not be changed.

Defining the Style Sheet

Click on Character, Formats, Rules, or Tabs to display the Character Attributes dialog box, the Paragraph Formats dialog box, the Paragraph Rules dialog box, or the Paragraph Tabs dialog box, respectively. When any of these dialog boxes is first displayed, it shows the settings of the currently selected text if you have chosen New in the Style Sheets dialog box; if you have chosen Edit, it shows the settings that apply to the selected style sheet name.

To save your entries, you must click on OK (or press ENTER) to close all dialog boxes up to the Style Sheet dialog box, then click on Save. Changes made to any style sheet are applied automatically throughout the document to all paragraphs to which that style is applied. Paragraphs that use style sheets that are Based On the changed style sheet are changed.

The Edit → Style Sheets command is always available; if you create a style sheet when no documents are open, the style sheet will be included with all subsequently created new documents. Style sheets created with a document open are saved as part of that document only.

Applying Style Sheets

To apply a format that has been defined as a style sheet, select the text to be formatted, then use any one of three techniques to apply a style sheet: Press the keyboard equivalent; select Style → Style Sheets to choose from a list of style sheet names; or select a style sheet name from the Style Sheets palette (View → Show Style Sheets), Figure 4-35. Both the Style Sheets submenu and the Style Sheets palette list the names of all the style sheets you have defined. If you have assigned keyboard equivalents, those will show next to the style sheet name.

Figure 4-35   The Style Sheets palette.

Remember, style sheets apply to whole paragraphs; they cannot be assigned to individual characters within a paragraph. You need not select an entire paragraph to which you want to apply a style; just click once so that the text insertion point is within the paragraph.

To see what style sheet has been applied to a paragraph, position the cursor in the paragraph. The applied style sheet name will be checked in the Style → Style Sheets submenu or will be selected in the Style Sheets palette. If you select a range of paragraphs that share the same style sheet, that style sheet will be checked in the Style Sheets submenu or selected in the Style Sheets palette. If the selection includes mixed style sheets, no style sheet name will be indicated.

While style sheets cannot be applied to individual characters, you can, of course, still apply "local" formatting; that is, you can format individual characters within text that has been formatted using a style sheet. For example, you can italicize a single word within text that has been formatted using a style sheet called "heading 1".

If you apply a new style sheet to a paragraph that contains local formatting—i.e., formatting of individual words or characters that differs from the style sheet format—the text in the paragraph will change according to the specifications of the new style sheet, *except* for the local formatting. To change all the text in the paragraph, you must first apply No Style from the Style Sheets submenu or the Style Sheets palette, then apply the new style sheet. When using the Style Sheets palette, you can apply No Style before applying a style sheet by holding down the ALT key as you click on the style sheet name.

If you apply style sheets in QuarkXPress to imported text and the text does not change as expected, the likely problem is that text in the word processing file was formatted without using style sheets.

Deleting Style Sheets

To delete a style sheet, click on the style sheet name in the list displayed in the Style Sheets dialog box (Edit ➤ Style Sheets), then click the Delete button. You cannot delete the Normal style sheet; it is the default format for all newly typed text and for imported ASCII text. You can change the specifications for the Normal style sheet by selecting Normal and choosing Edit in the Style Sheets dialog box.

If you delete any other style sheet name, all text that is currently formatted based on that style sheet name will retain its formatting but will be assigned a No Style identification. To change those paragraphs to another style sheet, you need to go through the document, select those paragraphs, and assign another style sheet.

Duplicating Style Sheet Specifications

Sometimes you may want to create a style sheet using several specifications from another one. In that case, the fastest way is to select the Duplicate command in the Style Sheets dialog box. Click on the style sheet name you want to duplicate, then click the Duplicate button; the Edit Style Sheets dialog box appears with "Copy of <style sheet name>" in the name entry area. You can then use the dialog box to change any of the specifications for the new style sheet.

Appending Style Sheets from Other Documents

Style sheets are a great way to ensure consistency among various documents, and you may find you want to reuse style sheets created in another document. The Append command allows you to add style sheets from another document to your active document.

If you choose Append in the Style Sheets dialog box, QuarkXPress displays the Append Style Sheets dialog box (Figure 4-36). The list in the dialog box shows QuarkXPress document and template names and Microsoft Word document names; when you select one and choose Open (or simply double-click on a document name), all of the style sheets used in that document are added to the list in the active document's style sheet list.

Figure 4-36 The Append Style Sheets dialog box.

If any of the appended style sheet names match names that are already in the current style sheet, the format for the style sheet in the active document is retained—the different format is not appended. If an appended style sheet uses the same keyboard equivalent as already applied in the current style sheet, the appended style sheet is brought in without a keyboard equivalent.

Finding and Changing Text

The Edit ➢ Find/Change command (CTRL+F) finds and changes specific words or characters, or specific text attributes in text. You can search through part of a story, a whole story, or a whole document at once. Remember, from Chapter 2, that a story is all of the text in a chain of linked text boxes.

To find or change text in a story or all the stories in a document, first select the Content tool and position the text cursor in a block of text, then select Edit ➢ Find/Change (CTRL+F) to display the Find/Change dialog box (Figure 4-37). Type in the text or select character attributes you want to find, then click the Find Next button. QuarkXPress begins the search at the text insertion point and proceeds through to the end of the text block.

If you want to begin the search from the beginning of the document, you can hold down the CTRL key and the Find Next button changes to Find First. This is more convenient than typing CTRL+ALT+↑ to jump quickly to the beginning of a story.

Figure 4-37   Find/Change dialog box.

In the Find/Change dialog box (Edit ➢ Find/Change), you type text in the Find What entry area, specify changes, if any, in the Change To entry area, and select the type of search you want:

- If **Document** is checked *and no text boxes are active when you begin the search*, QuarkXPress searches the entire document. If a text box is active, QuarkXPress searches the entire document, but only from the current text insertion point to the end of the story; text before the insertion point is not checked, unless you hold down the ALT key and click Find First.
- If **Whole Word** is checked, QuarkXPress searches for the Find What text followed by a space or punctuation mark. Otherwise, QuarkXPress finds all character strings that match the Find What entry, even when they are part of a longer word.
- If **Ignore Case** is checked, QuarkXPress finds the Find What text in all forms—with and without any capital letters. If it finds text in all

lowercase, it replaces it with the all-lowercase version of the text you typed in the Change To area. If it finds text in all uppercase, it replaces it with the all-uppercase version of the text in the Change To area. If it finds initial-cap text, it replaces it with the initial-cap version of the text in the Change To area. If it finds mixed uppercase and lowercase characters (other than initial cap only), it replaces the found word with the Change To text exactly as you typed it.

- If the **Ignore Case** option is not checked, then QuarkXPress finds only those instances of text that match the capitalization exactly as you typed it in the Find What area, and it changes that text to the text exactly as typed in the Change To area.

- If **Ignore Attributes** is checked, QuarkXPress finds the Find What text in all type styles and replaces it with the text you typed in the Change To area formatted exactly the same as the found text. For example, if it finds one version of the Find What text in 10-point Times, it replaces it with the Change To text in 10-point Times. If it finds the next instance of the Find What text in 12-point Helvetica, it replaces it with the Change To text in 12-point Helvetica.

- If the **Ignore Attributes** option is not checked, then the expanded Find/Change dialog box is displayed (as described under the next heads). QuarkXPress finds only those instances of the word that match the character attributes exactly as specified and changes them to the Change To text formatted exactly as specified.

Once you have typed the Find What and (optional) Change To text and selected the search options, you can click on **Find Next**, or hold down the ALT key and click on **Find First**. After the first instance is found, you can choose **Change, then Find** to change the word and keep searching to the next occurrence, or **Change** to change the word and pause the search. If you don't want to make a change on a particular occurrence of the text, click Find Next. QuarkXPress will move on to the next occurrence without making any changes.

If you choose **Change All**, QuarkXPress will change all found instances of the Find What text. When the search is finished, it will display a dialog box with a count of the total number of instances changed. If no instances are found, the computer will beep to signal the end of the search.

If no instances are found but you know one should have been found, make sure that you started the search at the beginning by holding down the CTRL key and clicking on Find First or that you positioned the text insertion point at the beginning of the story (CTRL+ALT+↑). Also, be sure that you have spelled the Find What text correctly and not entered any extra spaces before or after it.

If the edits cannot be handled by global changes but can be found by a global search, you can also select Find Next simply to find occurrences of text or text attributes. When an instance is found, you can click in the document window and edit the text manually, then select Find/Change (CTRL+F) again to resume the search. For example, you might type "see page xxx" throughout the draft versions of a document, then search for "xxx" and manually type in the final page number after the pages have been laid out.

It is a good idea to move the Find/Change dialog box to the bottom of the screen to maximize your view of the document window during a search. You can also make the dialog box smaller—reducing it to the search buttons only—by choosing Condense from the Control menu at the top left of the title bar (Figure 4-38). Choose Expand from the Control menu to restore full size.

Figure 4-38 Choose Condense from the Control menu at the top left corner of the window to shrink from full size to a reduced version of the Find/Change dialog box.

Find or Change Text

You can type up to 80 characters in the Find What and the Change To areas of the Find/Change dialog box. If you don't type anything in the Change To area, then the text typed in the Find What area will be deleted when found in the story or document.

You can include spaces in the Find What and Change To entry areas by using the space bar, but most other "invisible" characters that use keys such as a TAB or ENTER, require special entry. (Otherwise, the TAB key jumps you to the next entry area in the dialog box, and the ENTER or KEYPAD ENTER key starts the search.) You can search for special characters and invisible characters by typing a backslash followed by a letter that is a code for the invisible character, as shown in Figure 4-39. Notice that you cannot search for Discretionary Line Breaks or Indent Here characters.

Special Character	Find/Change Entry	Dialog Box Display
Tab	\t	\t
New Paragraph	\p	\p
New Line	\n	\n
New Column	\c	\c
New Box	\b	\b
Previous Box Page #	\2	\2
Active Box Page #	\3	\3
Next Box Page #	\4	\4
Wild Card	\?	\?
Back Slash	\\	\\

Figure 4-39 *Searching for special characters.*

When searching for special characters, it is usually best to uncheck Whole Word since special characters are usually bounded by other letters or numbers. To view invisible characters on the screen, choose View ➤ Show Invisibles.

You can type the wild card character (\?) in the Change From entry area to find words with similar but different spellings. For example, a search for "gr\?y" will find both "gray" and "grey." You cannot use wild cards in the Change To text entry area.

You can find or change spaces by typing a space in either entry area (using the space bar) but, if the space falls at the end of the entry, the program will ignore instances where the word or phrase is followed by punctuation. If you type a space on either side of the Find What entry, however, be sure to type a space in the Change To entry area as well (unless you want the replacement to eliminate the space).

Find or Change Character Attributes

You can find or change attributes such as font, size, and type style. This feature is especially handy for globally changing words that have been given special attributes within paragraphs. For example, if you are working on a review of a book titled *Never Tomorrow* and the title was set as underscored (except in some cases where the author of the review forgot to apply the underscores), you can globally change all cases to italics. You can also select Find/Change globally to change the formats of headings or captions or other standard elements within the text; however, these changes are handled more efficiently through a style sheet.

Figure 4-40   Expanded Find/Change dialog box.

To find or change attributes, uncheck Ignore Attributes to display the expanded Find/Change dialog box (Figure 4-40). The initial display shows the attributes of the active text selection (or shows grayed options if more than one attribute is represented). You can search for specific text as entered in the Text area under Find What, or uncheck Text if you want to search for attributes only.

You can check Font, Size, and/or Style to include these categories of attributes as part of the search, or uncheck them if you want to search for other characteristics only. The Font list is a drop-down list. Any Style option can be checked (so *only* text with that style will be found), unchecked (so *no* text with that style will be found), or grayed (so text *with and without* that style will be found). Simply click on each style option until the desired setting is shown.

Similarly, under Change To you can check Font, Size, and/or Style to include these categories of attributes as part of the replacement, or uncheck them if you want to replace other characteristics only. Any Style option can be checked (so all text found will be changed to that style), unchecked (so all text found will be changed to not have that style), or grayed (so found text will retain its style in that category).

The expanded Find/Change dialog box is similar to the Font Usage dialog box (Utilities ➤ Font Usage). In fact, if you want to change character attributes only and not change any text, you can use the Font Usage dialog box (Figure 4-41).

Figure 4-41   Font Usage dialog box.

The fonts shown in both the expanded Find/Change dialog box and the Font Usage dialog box include only those actually used in the document. The Change To font list includes all fonts currently loaded in the system.

Checking Spelling

QuarkXPress offers a spelling check feature that compares the words in your text against a 120,000-word dictionary. The XPRESS.DCT file is included in the same directory as the QuarkXPress program when you first install QuarkXPress, if you follow normal installation procedures. Note that it must be in this directory in order for the Check Spelling command to work. You can also create auxiliary dictionaries to add your own terms for use in spelling checks. The Utilities → Check Spelling command lets you check the spelling of a highlighted word, all the words in a story, or all the words in a document (Figure 4-42).

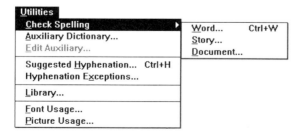

Figure 4-42   The Utilities → Check Spelling submenu.

To check spelling for any **word**, first select the word or position the insertion bar to the left of or anywhere within the word, then select Utilities → Check Spelling → Word (CTRL+W) to check the spelling of the selected word only. If more than one word is selected, QuarkXPress checks the spelling of only the first word or partial word selected.

Figure 4-43   Check Word dialog box for a word search.

QuarkXPress checks the dictionary and displays the Check Word dialog box, showing close or exact matches from the dictionary in the scrolling window, or displaying the message "No similar words found" (Figure 4-43). You can choose a replacement word by double-clicking on the word in the list (or clicking on the word once to select it, then clicking on Replace) to replace the word with a found match, or Cancel the process and leave the word unchanged.

To check spelling for any **story**, first activate a text box and select the Content tool, then select Utilities → Check Spelling → Story (CTRL+ALT+W) to check the spelling in the selected story. Remember, from Chapter 2, that a story is all of the text in a chain of linked text boxes.

After QuarkXPress checks spelling, a **Word Count** dialog box (Figure 4-44) shows how many **Total** words are in the story or document, how many **Unique** words were found (how many different words), and how many **Suspect** words are identified (words not found in the dictionary).

Figure 4-44   Word Count dialog box.

To close the dialog box, click on OK. If no suspect words were found, then the spelling check process is complete for the story. If suspect words were found, then the Check Story dialog box (Figure 4-45) is displayed when you close the Word Count dialog box.

Figure 4-45   Check Story dialog box.

The Check Story dialog box displays the first suspect word found in the text and shows how many instances of the same word were found, if more than one occurred. If you click on Lookup, QuarkXPress offers suggested alternatives (if any close matches are found in the dictionary) or displays the message "No similar words found." You can click on one of the suggested alternatives, or type the correct word in the Replace with area of the dialog box, then click on Replace (or simply press ENTER) to replace the suspect word. If the correct word is similar to the suspect word in spelling, you can click on the suspect word to enter it in the Replace with area, then make the corrections to the word and click on Replace.

To let the suspect word remain unchanged and go on to the next found suspect word, click on Skip. To let the suspect word remain unchanged, add it to the open auxiliary dictionary (see next heading), and go on to the next suspect word found, click on Keep. (An auxiliary dictionary *must* be open during the spelling check process in order for the Keep option to be available in the Check Story, Check Document, or Check Masters dialog box.) To end the spelling check process, click on Cancel.

To check spelling for a whole document, select Utilities → Check Spelling → Document. QuarkXPress starts on the first page of the currently open document and goes through all of the stories in it. The first dialog box displayed is the Word Count dialog box, showing the Total words in the document, how many Unique words were found (how many different words), and how many Suspect words are identified (words not found in the dictionary). If any Suspect words are found, click on OK to display the Check Document dialog box. The Check Document dialog box is handled exactly the same as the Check Story dialog box, described above.

You can check the spelling on Master Pages by turning to a master page in the document—the Document entry in the Check Spelling submenu changes to display **Masters**. The dialog boxes displayed to check spelling on Master Pages are the same as those displayed for checking a story or a document.

Customizing Your Own Dictionaries

You cannot change the XPress Dictionary (XPRESS.DCT file) that comes with QuarkXPress, but you can add your own terms to auxiliary dictionaries. To create a new auxiliary dictionary, choose Utilities ➤ Auxiliary Dictionary and type in a name for the new dictionary, then click the Create button. To open an existing auxiliary dictionary, choose Utilities ➤ Auxiliary Dictionary, locate the appropriate file, and select it from the dialog box (Figure 4-46).

Figure 4-46   Auxiliary Dictionary dialog box.

If you choose Utilities ➤ Auxiliary Dictionary when no document is open, the new or existing dictionary you open will be applied automatically to all new documents that you create (until you change the setting later when no document is open). If you choose the Auxiliary Dictionary command when any document is open, the new or existing dictionary you open will be applied automatically to that document whenever you open it (until you change the setting later when the document is open).

You can add terms to the open auxiliary dictionary by going through the spelling check process and using the Keep option in the dialog box, as described above. (An auxiliary dictionary *must* be open during the spelling check process in order for the Keep option to be available in the Check Story, Check Document, or Check Masters dialog box.) You can also add or delete terms in an open auxiliary dictionary by using the Utilities ➤ Edit Auxiliary command (Figure 4-47).

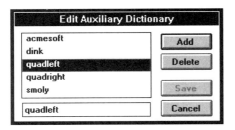

Figure 4-47   Edit Auxiliary Dictionary dialog box.

Terms in a dictionary are all stored in lowercase form—you cannot type uppercase characters in the entries. Only one auxiliary dictionary can be open at a time during a spelling check. You can select the Auxiliary Dictionary command to Close the currently open auxiliary dictionary and Open a different one.

QuarkXPress will be unable to locate a dictionary if either the dictionary or the document has been moved to a different drive or directory since the first time the dictionary was opened. The program displays a warning message whenever you select the Check Spelling command, so you can go through the Auxiliary Dictionary command to Close the missing dictionary or find and Use the relocated dictionary.

Exporting Text to Other Programs

You can export text from QuarkXPress to create text files in formats that can be opened by word processing programs and other applications, or imported to other QuarkXPress documents. Remember that you can also copy text from one QuarkXPress document to another by dragging the text box from one open Document window to another, or through the Library feature, as well as through the Edit menu's Copy, Cut, Paste, Paste Special, and Paste Link commands.

To export text, first activate a text box with the Content tool selected, or highlight a range of text to be exported. Then select File ➤ Save Text to display the Save Text dialog box (Figure 4-48).

Figure 4-48   Save Text dialog box.

Type the name of the exported text file in the **File Name** area. If you activate a text box without selecting any text within it, you must save the **Entire Story** (the text in the currently active box plus all linked text boxes). Otherwise, you have the option of saving the Entire Story or the **Selected Text** only. You can export only one story at a time.

The **Type** drop-down list lets you choose the format in which to save the exported text, including ASCII Text plus any other formats for which the import/export filter is stored in the same directory as the QuarkXPress program before you launch the program. Formatting is retained in all formats except ASCII Text. (See notes under "Importing Formatted Text," earlier in this chapter, about import/export filters, and see Chapter 14, Managing Documents, for tips on efficient file organization.)

If you save in ASCII Text format, all formatting is lost. If you save text as XPress Tags format, then the formatted text from QuarkXPress is exported as ASCII Text with embedded XPress Tags for formatting. See Chapter 10 for a description of ASCII formatting tags.

It can take several minutes to export long text files, so QuarkXPress shows the percentage complete in the lower left corner of the document window, right of the View Percent area.

Summary

In this chapter you learned that the process of importing text in QuarkXPress is relatively simple—select a text box with the Content tool and use the File ➤ Get Text command to bring in text files created in a word processing program. Select the Paste command to bring in text that was Cut or Copied from another part of the document. Use Paste Special or Paste Link to copy text from another application that supports Windows' Object Linking and Embedding feature. Select the Item tool to move text boxes from another QuarkXPress document or library. Select the Content tool to type text directly in a text box.

Build a test file using your own word processor to see how QuarkXPress handles the text when you import it on a page. Try placing the same test file under each of the options—Convert Quotes and Include Style Sheets—to see how they differ.

Once you are familiar with how QuarkXPress handles your files, you may want to do as much preparation as you can in the word processing program before importing the text in QuarkXPress, or you may use QuarkXPress only for word processing. Once the text is in QuarkXPress, you can format it directly or use style sheets. You can also find and change text or character attributes, and spell check your document. Text from QuarkXPress can be exported to file that can be opened by word processing programs. The next chapter describes QuarkXPress' rich assortment of typographical features.

5 Typography

Typography, the study and application of the aesthetics of letterforms, is an integral part of design. Designers and typographers have a unique way of describing the characteristics of text in a document, expressed in terms not only of fonts but also of leading, kerning, intercharacter spacing, and other words that may be somewhat foreign to the typical user of word processing programs. Typographic control from the desktop is one of QuarkXPress' strong points.

In this chapter you will learn how to work with QuarkXPress' typographical features, including inputting special typographic characters; working with leading, hyphenation, and justification; and kerning and tracking characters.

Whether you—as the designer or typographer—are writing out the design specifications for a document or actually using QuarkXPress to set up a template, knowing how QuarkXPress works before you make your design specifications will help.

Setting Global Conditions

Before you start working with the typographic specifications for a document, it's a good idea to set up the global conditions that will affect how type looks in a document or how type prints. The first condition that affects your typographic choices is the set of installed fonts. The fonts you want to use should be installed through Windows before you create a new QuarkXPress document.

A second source of settings that can globally change the type in a document is the set of typographic preferences set up through the Edit → Preferences → Typographic command. It is a good idea to set these preferences before you start formatting text in a document, since changes to these settings can change the way text fits on lines throughout the document.

Loading Screen Fonts

The word *font* is derived from the French word *fondre*, which means to melt or cast. It once referred to the trays of cast metal characters that printers used to compose a document. Each tray or font included all letters of the alphabet (plus special characters) for a specific typeface/style/size combination. For example, one tray held only 10-point Times italic characters, another tray held only 10-point Times bold, and so on. A font, then, was a particular typeface, style, and size combination.

More recently, however, font has been taken more loosely to mean the name of the typeface, such as Times or Helvetica. This is the meaning of the word in QuarkXPress' Style menu and Character Attributes dialog box, for instance. This definition is appropriate for the scalable computer fonts that are based on formulas, such as PostScript fonts. Each letter of the alphabet is "cast" or designed only once, to define the shape of the letter. This information is then stored as a complex curve-fitting equation. A printer that uses a programming language—such as PostScript—to create text can produce any size typeface once the shape of each character is provided.

PostScript fonts usually have two versions of each font—a screen font and a printer font. The screen font is necessary to display the fonts on the screen, and the printer fonts contain the information needed by the output device, whether it's a laser printer or a high-resolution imagesetter, to create and print the font on a page.

Most PostScript laser printers come with a basic set of fonts, including Courier, Times, and Helvetica. Many printers also include Avant Garde, Bookman, New Century Schoolbook, Symbol, Palatino, and Zapf Dingbats, along with a set of screen fonts for each. In addition, various vendors, including Adobe Systems, Bitstream, and Monotype, among others, sell additional fonts.

TrueType fonts became available with the advent of Windows 3.1. Unlike PostScript fonts, they do not require a separate screen and printer font; essentially they derive the screen image of a font from its printer font outlines, which must be present in the system file. (Some other fonts that come with or can be installed for Windows—such as the System font—are not true typographic fonts and are not commonly used in typeset documents.)

To display a font name in the QuarkXPress menus, the font must be available to your system. There are a number of different ways to load fonts, depending on what type of fonts and which version of Windows you are using. The method you use also depends on your personal preference. Refer to the manufacturer's manuals for the correct way to install fonts in your system.

On-Screen Font Vectoring

Regardless of the sizes of the screen fonts that are loaded into the System, QuarkXPress can vector Type 3 PostScript (unencrypted) screen fonts with optimal resolution for more accurate screen display. To activate screen font vectoring, select the Edit → Preferences → General to set up the Vector Above type size, as described in Chapter 3.

Using Adobe Type Manager

One of the advantages of TrueType fonts is that the characters do not appear jagged on the screen. The on-screen font vectoring feature of QuarkXPress does not work with Type 1 PostScript fonts, which are by far the most widely used fonts. But Adobe Type Manager (ATM), a software product available from most Windows software suppliers, provides a way of getting a clear screen display of PostScript fonts in all sizes—not just those sizes loaded in the System.

Typographic Preferences

The Edit → Preferences command lets you set specifications for a document globally. Two preferences that affect the appearance of the type on the *screen*—Vector Above and Greek Below—are in the General Preferences dialog box and were described in Chapter 3. These two settings do not affect how type looks when it is printed. The preferences that affect how type looks on the screen *and* prints are set through Edit → Preferences → Typographic (CTRL+ALT+Y), in the Typographic Preferences dialog box (Figure 5-1).

Figure 5-1 The Typographic Preferences dialog box.

When you specify Typographic Preferences with no document open, your specifications apply to all subsequently created documents but not to previously created ones. When you specify Typographic Preferences for an active document, your specifications apply only to that document; changes made while the document is active will change the document retroactively.

Superscript and Subscript

The **Offset** value determines how high above (or below) the normal baseline QuarkXPress places the baseline of a superscript (or subscript) character, expressed as a percentage of the *ascent height* (the height of the capital letters in the current font). **VScale**—the percentage by which the height of the superscript or subscript is reduced—is also measured as a percentage of ascent height. **HScale**—the percentage by which the width of the superscript or subscript is reduced—is measured as a percentage of normal character width (one of the internal font specifications that cannot be changed).

Small Caps

The Small Caps style (Style ➤ Type Style ➤ Small Caps) changes all noncapital letters in selected text to small capital letters. The proportion of small capitals to regular-size capital letters is determined by a setting similar to the Superscript and Subscript preferences. **VScale**—the percentage by which the height of the small-cap character is reduced—is measured as a percentage of ascent height. **HScale**—the percentage by which the width of the small-cap character is reduced—is measured as a percentage of normal character width.

Superior Characters

Superior characters are reduced in size from normal characters, with the top of the reduced character aligned with the cap height of the adjacent text. Superior characters will not affect leading, unlike Superscripted characters, which may. The size of superior characters is determined similarly to small caps: **VScale**—the percentage by which the height of the superior character is reduced—is measured as a percentage of ascent height, and **HScale**—the percentage by which the width of the superior character is reduced—is measured as a percentage of normal character width.

Baseline Grid

You can lock the baselines of text to the nonprinting baseline grid of a document. This is useful if you are producing a multicolumn document and you want the baselines of the text to align across columns—a common practice in most newspapers and magazines. To define the baseline grid, enter the **Start** value, which determines how far from the top of the page the first line of the grid is placed, and the **Increment** value, which determines the distance between the grid lines.

To lock text to the baseline grid, check Lock to Baseline Grid in the Paragraph Formats dialog box (Style ➤ Formats). To display the baseline grid, select the View ➤ Show Baseline Grid command.

Auto Leading

Normally, when you select Auto Leading for selected text, QuarkXPress sets the leading (the space between lines of text) to 120 percent of the point size of the largest font in the line. In other words, auto leading for 10-point type will be 12 points, or 10/12 specifications. (You can change the leading for selected text to a specific value other than auto by using various methods described later in this chapter.)

You can change the Auto Leading value to a different percentage, or you can enter a signed incremental value, from –1080 to 1080 points. For example, a value of +1.005 will add 1.005 points of leading above the largest point size on the line. You can enter measurements in any unit of measure, but you must add the abbreviated code for measurements other than points.

If you change the Auto Leading value in the Typographic Preferences dialog box, QuarkXPress automatically adjusts all of the text in the document that has been set to Auto Leading. Since this change can affect the entire document, it is a good idea to change the Auto Leading setting before you lay out each page with text and graphics.

Flex Space Width

The width of a flexible space, a user-modifiable space based on an en space, can be changed. Flexible width space is defined as a percentage of the normal flexible space width for any given font. The default flexible space width is 50 percent, and can be changed from 0 percent to 400 percent in .1 percent increments. A flexible space can be input by entering CTRL+SHIFT+5, or for a nonbreaking flexible space, CTRL+ALT+SHIFT+5.

Auto Kern Above

Check Auto Kern Above to specify that QuarkXPress use kerning tables built into scalable fonts, such as PostScript or TrueType fonts, to control intercharacter spacing, and specify the size above which fonts will be kerned—from 2 to 720 points. Under the kerning option, QuarkXPress removes spaces between certain character pairs using the kerning tables built into individual fonts. Since this adds time to screen redraw and during printing, some people prefer to kern only large font sizes. If you are going to use this feature, set your preferences *before* manually kerning individual letter pairs. If this option is not checked, QuarkXPress will not use any custom kerning tables, and any modifications made to tracking curves are not implemented. "Tracking and Kerning Text," later in this chapter, includes a more detailed description of the kerning customization option.

Maintain Leading

Maintain Leading affects how text is leaded following a box or line with a runaround (Figure 5-2). If Maintain Leading is turned off, the ascenders of text that follows an item with a runaround butt against the item. If Maintain Leading is turned on, the default setting, QuarkXPress adds the currently specified leading between the bottom of the item and the baseline of the line of text following.

Figure 5-2   A document with Maintain Leading on (left) and off (right).

Hyphenation Method

The hyphenation method refers to the algorithm QuarkXPress uses to hyphenate paragraphs for which Auto Hyphenation has been enabled (Edit ➛ H&Js). The default method is Enhanced. To hyphenate using the method used by versions of QuarkXPress prior to 3.1, select Standard. If you work with documents created with QuarkXPress Macintosh version 3.0, the Enhanced mode may cause the document to reflow. However, as long as all your documents are created in version 3.1 on the Macintosh or under Windows, the Enhanced mode will produce more accurate results and should remain the default.

Leading Mode

Normally, with the Leading mode set to Typesetting, QuarkXPress measures leading upward from the baseline of one line of text to the baseline of the line of text above it. If you change this to Word Processing mode, QuarkXPress will measure leading downward from the top of the font height on one line of text to the top of the font on the line below.

   The space above the first line in a text box is determined by the text inset plus the height of the ascender of the largest font in the line for both modes. You can change the distance of the first line of text, regardless of which mode you use, by changing the First Baseline setting under Item ➛ Modify. In Typesetting mode, when Absolute Leading is specified, baselines will line up across columns when different font sizes are used;

text baselines will *not* line up in Word Processing mode if different type sizes are present.

Special Typographic Characters

Typesetters have special characters that are often not available, or often not used, in word processors. Some of these characters include the use of true opening and closing quotes (",") rather than inch marks ("), an apostrophe (') rather than a foot mark ('), and an em dash (—) rather than a hyphen (-).

Figure 5-3, based on Figure 4-3 from Chapter 4, shows various special typographic characters. This table is not exhaustive; rather it lists those characters used most frequently. You can find the ASCII codes for creating these and other characters using the Windows Character Map accessory.

Special Character	*Typed Entry*	*Onscreen display*
Opening double quote	ALT+SHIFT+[	"
Closing double quote	ALT+SHIFT+]	"
Opening single quote	ALT+[	'
Closing single quote	ALT+]	'
Standard hyphen	Hyphen	-
Nonbreaking hyphen	CTRL+SHIFT+HYPHEN	-
Discretionary (soft) hyphen	CTRL+HYPHEN	- (or invisible)
Nonbreaking en dash	CTRL+=	–
Breaking em dash	CTRL+SHIFT+=	—
Nonbreaking em dash	CTRL+ALT+SHIFT+=	—
Registered	ALT+SHIFT+R	®
Copyright	ALT+SHIFT+C	©
Section	ALT+SHIFT+6	§
Paragraph	ALT+SHIFT+7	¶
Bullet	ALT+SHIFT+8	•

Figure 5-3   Special typographic characters that can be used in QuarkXPress.

It's a good idea to familiarize yourself with these basic characters that typesetters have been using for years.

Working with Leading

Leading is a measure of the distance from the base of one line of text to the base of the next line. The term *leading* rhymes with *bedding*. It originally referred to thin strips of lead that typesetters used to adjust the space between lines of metal type—the precursor of electronic or phototypesetting methods. Usually, leading is measured from the baseline of one text to the baseline of text above (unless you change the Leading mode as described earlier in this chapter). (See Figure 5-4.)

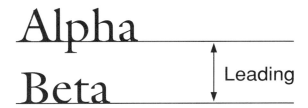

Figure 5-4   Leading is the distance from the base of one line to the base of the next.

Three different leading methods can be used in QuarkXPress: auto, absolute, and incremental. The default setting, auto, is set at 120 percent of the point size—to the nearest .001 point. Ten-point type would have 12-point leading, for example. You can specify a different default value for Auto Leading through Edit → Preferences → Typographic, described earlier in this chapter.

Absolute leading is achieved by entering an unsigned numeric value. The value entered will be applied no matter how you change the point size. If you enter a leading value of 14 for 12-point type, for instance, the leading will remain 14 when you change the type size to 10. If you enter an absolute value for leading, you may need to change the leading when you change the point size.

Incremental leading can be specified by entering a value preceded by a + or - sign. Incremental leading is based on the largest type size in a line plus or minus the value as indicated.

Because auto and incremental leading are relative to the size of text in a line, the leading will be based on the largest character in any given line. This means that uneven leading could occur within a paragraph that uses either of these methods and contains text in different sizes.

You can specify leading through the Paragraph Formats dialog box (CTRL+SHIFT+F), the Leading dialog box (CTRL+SHIFT+E), the Measurements palette, or keyboard shortcuts. Enter an absolute or incremental value, up to .001-point increments, in the leading field in the Paragraph

Formats dialog box or Measurements palette (Figure 5-5), or enter a value in the Leading dialog box.

Figure 5-5 *Using the Measurements palette, you can type in a leading value or use the scroll arrows to change the leading.*

You can change the leading by adding or subtracting a value from the current entry or by clicking on the arrows next to the leading field in the Measurements palette. Click on the arrows to change leading in 1-point increments, or hold down the ALT key and click on the arrows to change the leading in .1-point increments. You can also change leading using keyboard shortcuts:

- CTRL+SHIFT+" to increase leading 1 point.
- CTRL+SHIFT+: to decrease leading 1 point.
- CTRL+ALT+SHIFT+" to increase leading 0.1 point.
- CTRL+ALT+SHIFT+: to decrease leading 0.1 point.

Both the Measurements palette and the keyboard shortcuts can be used to adjust auto leading as well as absolute and incremental leading. When the leading is set to auto and you click on a leading arrow in the Measurements palette or use the keyboard shortcuts to change leading, the automatic value is changed to its absolute value; values are then added to or subtracted from the absolute equivalent.

Changing the leading is one way of fitting copy to a defined space. You can make fine adjustments to the leading in order to squeeze text onto a tight page, to expand text to fill an area, or to force two columns to be the same length. Even though leading can be adjusted in .001-point increments, you may not be able to detect fine changes on low-resolution printers.

Setting the First Baseline

The baseline of the first line of text in a text box can be adjusted in the Text Box Specifications dialog box (Item ➤ Modify), as shown in Figure 5-6. Enter a value in the Offset field to add more space at the top of the box than allowed by the Text Inset alone.

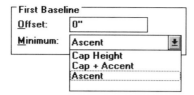

Figure 5-6   The first baseline of text in a box is set in the Text Specifications dialog box.

The Minimum drop-down list displays three choices for determining the position of the first baseline:

- Cap Height positions the first baseline based on the size of capital letters.
- Cap + Accent positions the first baseline based on the size of capital letters plus the size of accents.
- Ascent positions the first baseline based on the height of ascenders (portions of lowercase letters such as *b* and *d* that rise above letters without ascenders such as *a* and *c*).

The position of the first baseline is determined by whichever is larger, the Offset value or the selection in the Minimum drop-down list (Figure 5-7).

Figure 5-7   First baseline determined by Ascent, Cap Height, and Cap + Accent (left to right, top row) when Offset is 0. Minimum values are overridden by .5-inch Offset in bottom row.

Lock to Baseline Grid

Check Lock to Baseline Grid to lock the baselines in the selected paragraph to the baseline grid specified in the Typographic Preferences dialog box (Edit → Preferences → Typographic).

To lock text to the grid, first select the paragraph or range of paragraphs, then choose Style → Paragraph Formats to get the Paragraph Formats dialog box, and check the Lock to Baseline Grid option. Lines in a paragraph locked to the baseline grid are spaced in multiples of the grid's Increment value. The Increment value of the baseline grid should be a multiple of the leading of the text you plan to lock to the grid. For example, if the body copy throughout the document has 12-point leading, the grid Increment should be 12 points.

If the leading for the locked paragraph is *less* than the baseline grid increment, the lines will be spaced wider apart than the leading specification in order to match the grid. If the leading for the locked paragraph is *more* than the baseline grid increment, the lines will be spaced two grid lines apart. If you later change the Baseline Grid, lines in paragraphs that are locked to it will be respaced throughout the document as shown in Figure 5-8.

Figure 5-8   How the grid increment changes the space between lines in locked paragraphs.

You can display the baseline grid by selecting the View → Show Baseline Grid command.

Vertical Alignment

The space between the last line of text and the bottom of the text box is determined by the Vertical Alignment specifications in the Text Box Specifications dialog box (Item → Modify); choose Top, Centered, Bottom, or Justify. If you choose Justify, then small increments of space (up to the Inter ¶ Max) will be added between the lines and paragraphs of text to make the text fill the box (Figure 5-9).

Figure 5-9 Vertical alignment set Top (left), Centered (middle), and Justify (right).

Baseline Shift

You can shift the position of selected characters relative to the baseline by using the Style → Baseline Shift command to get the Baseline Shift dialog box (Figure 5-10), or by using Styles → Character (CTRL+SHIFT+D) to get the Character Attributes dialog box. In either case, enter a positive value to shift the baseline up, or enter a negative value to shift the baseline down.

You can also select two keyboard shortcuts: CTRL+ALT+SHIFT+) (or 0, zero) to shift up in 1-point increments, CTRL+ALT+SHIFT+((or 9) to shift down in 1-point increments.

Notice that if you do these operations *without* the ALT key, these keystrokes become the shortcuts for applying Superscript (CTRL+SHIFT+0) or Subscript (CTRL+SHIFT+9).

Figure 5-10 The Baseline Shift dialog box.

You can enter a positive or negative Baseline Shift value up to three times the font size of the selected text. For example, 10-point type can be shifted up to 30 points above or below the baseline. If you change the size of characters that have been shifted, the baseline shift is automatically adjusted proportionately.

Hyphenation and Justification

Hyphenation and justification are so interrelated that professional typesetters usually refer to them simultaneously as "H&J." Both hyphenation and justification function, each in its own way, to make text appear as even as possible—a common aesthetic goal in typesetting—and they both affect how many characters or words will fit on a line. For example, in left-aligned paragraphs, the right margin is less ragged and QuarkXPress can fit more words on a line when hyphenation is allowed than when it is not allowed (Figure 5-11).

The default setting is that hyphenation is turned off, but you can change the Standard H&J specification to Auto Hyphenation On. You can turn hyphenation on or off for selected paragraphs and make other adjustments, including how long a word must be before it is hyphenated and how many hyphens are allowed in a row. You can specify how wide the spaces between words and characters will be in justified text, and you can also build your own list of hyphenation exceptions. All of these adjustments are described later in this section.

Figure 5-11   How text changes with hyphenation and justification.
1. *Paragraph with no hyphenation shows extremely ragged right margin.*
2. *Same paragraph shows less ragged right margin when hyphenated.*
3. *Same paragraph shows wide "rivers" of white space between words and characters when justified but not hyphenated.*

Hyphenating text is a two-step process in QuarkXPress: First you must define hyphenation and justification "rules;" then you must apply those rules to paragraphs in the Paragraph Formats dialog box (Style ➤ Formats). QuarkXPress uses an algorithm to hyphenate text and also looks to hyphenation exceptions that you've defined (described later in this chapter). New H&J specifications are set up using the Edit ➤ H&Js command. The H&Js dialog box (Figure 5-12), listing all the H&Js that have been defined in the current document, is similar to the Style Sheets dialog box.

Figure 5-12   The H&Js list and dialog box.

Choose New to add a new H&J specification, Edit to modify the specifications for an existing H&J, Duplicate to create an H&J based on an existing one, Delete to remove an H&J, or Append to import H&J specifications from another QuarkXPress document.

If you select the H&J command when no documents are open, you can create or edit the sets of rules that will be applied to all subsequently created documents. If you select this command with a document open, you can edit the sets of rules that apply to that document only.

Creating and Editing H&Js

You can create and apply more than one set of H&J rules within a document—you need not use the same rules throughout one document. For example, you could apply one set of rules to all Normal body copy and apply a different set of rules to all headings. Different named sets of rules can be applied to selected paragraphs through the Style ➤ Formats command, as described later in this section.

When you choose New or Edit, QuarkXPress displays the Edit Hyphenation & Justification dialog box. This dialog box lets you set up all the specifications for how QuarkXPress will hyphenate text and how it will space justified text.

Figure 5-13 The Edit Hyphenation & Justification dialog box.

Name

The first text box in the Edit Hyphenation & Justification dialog box (Figure 5-13) lets you enter the name of a new H&J set or change the name of the set you are currently editing or duplicating. You must name new H&J specifications.

Auto Hyphenation

QuarkXPress will hyphenate if Auto Hyphenation is checked; uncheck this box to turn hyphenation off. The Auto Hyphenation area lets you specify the **Smallest Word** that will be hyphenated. For example, the word *area* might be hyphenated (a-re-a) if you allow four-letter words to be hyphenated, but it will never be hyphenated if you specify that only words of five letters or more will be hyphenated.

You can also specify the **Minimum** number of characters you want on a line **Before** a hyphen, and the **Minimum** number of characters you want on a line **After** a hyphen. For example, even if you allow four-letter words to be hyphenated, word *area* will never be hyphenated if you specify that there must be at least two letters before and two letters after a hyphen (since ar-ea is not a valid form).

You can also specify whether you want to **Break Capitalized Words**. If you want to allow the first word of a sentence to be hyphenated, you will need to check this box. If, at the same time, you do not want proper nouns hyphenated, you will have to select Utilities ➤ Hyphenation Exceptions to list them individually in the Hyphenation Exceptions dictionary.

Hyphens in a Row

The next area of the dialog box lets you specify how many Hyphens in a Row will be allowed. You can enter a number (including 0) or type the word *unlimited*. Entering the value of zero is the same as typing *unlimited*.

Hyphenation Zone

The Hyphenation Zone can be entered in any unit of measure and applies to nonjustified text only. If you enter a value of 0, QuarkXPress will break any words that start on a line and would cross the right margin if not hyphenated. You can enter a value higher than 0 to set how far in from the right margin QuarkXPress will go to hyphenate a word—the word must have an acceptable hyphenation point that falls within the zone (Figure 5-14); otherwise, the entire word will be brought to the next line.

```
Desktop pub-                    Desktop
lishing, and it's               publishing, and
associated tech-                it's associated
nologies have                   technologies
been in exis-                   have been in
tence for just                  existence for
around four                     just around four
years.                          years.
```
  Hyphenation Zone: 0"   Hyphenation Zone: .5"

Figure 5-14 Increasing the hyphenation zone increases the raggedness of the right margin.

Justification Method

Most of the entries under the Justification Method area apply to justified text only—except Optimum values, which is applied to nonjustified text as well. You can enter the Minimum (down to 0 percent between words, or –50 percent between characters), Optimum, and Maximum (up to 500 percent between words, or 100 percent between characters) Space (space between words) and Char. (space between characters) that QuarkXPress will apply in adjusting horizontal space in order to justify a line of text. Values are normally entered as percentages of the manufacturer's normal interword space for the font and size currently in use. QuarkXPress will never go below the Minimum space specified, but it will exceed the Maximum if there is no other alternative.

Flush Zone

The Flush Zone determines whether the last line of a justified paragraph will be justified. A value of zero indicates that the last line will never be justified. Otherwise, the last line of a paragraph *will* be justified if the last word falls within the Flush Zone as measured from the right indent.

Single Word Justify

If Single Word Justify is checked, any single word that falls on its own line will be justified from the left to right indent. If Single Word Justify is not checked, the word will be flush to the left margin (Figure 5-15). This option does not apply to the last line in a paragraph; the last line is controlled by the Flush Zone option.

Figure 5-15   Single Word Justify checked on (left) and unchecked (right).

Applying H&Js to Text

Once you have defined a set of rules for hyphenation and justification, you can apply those rules to selected paragraphs using Style → Formats (CTRL+SHIFT+F). The Paragraph Formats dialog box (Figure 5-16) includes a drop-down list of the H&J rule sets that you have prepared for the active document. Normally, the Standard H&J set is applied automatically to all Normal text unless you change the H&J associated with Normal through the Edit → Style Sheets command.

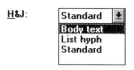

Figure 5-16   The H&J drop-down list in the Paragraph Formats dialog box.

The H&J selection can be applied as part of the style sheet specification, described in Chapter 4.

Deleting H&Js

To delete an H&J specification, click on the H&J name in the list displayed in the H&J dialog box (Edit → H&Js), then click the Delete button. When you delete an H&J specification, QuarkXPress displays a warning asking if you want to delete it (Figure 5-17). All paragraphs to which this specification has been applied will take on the specifications listed in the Standard H&J.

Figure 5-17   Deleting an H&J specification causes an alert message.

Since a different H&J will apply to the text, deleting an H&J specification may cause text reflow.

Duplicating H&J Specifications

Sometimes you may wish to duplicate an H&J specification using another H&J. The fastest way is to click on an H&J you want to use as the basis for a new one, and click Duplicate. The Edit Hyphenation & Justification dialog box will appear with "Copy of <H&J name>" in the name field. You can then use the dialog box to change any of the specifications.

Appending H&Js from Other Documents

If you want to use H&Js set up in another document, click on the Append button in the Edit H&Js dialog box. The Append H&Js dialog box displays a list of the QuarkXPress documents and templates—you can change drives or directories as you would in other dialog boxes. Choose a document by double-clicking on the name. You cannot append the H&J specifications from an open document. QuarkXPress imports all of the H&J specifications from the selected document except those that have the same names as the H&J specifications already in the list.

Suggested Hyphenation

You can see how QuarkXPress would hyphenate a selected word (or the first word to the left of the insertion bar or the first word in a selected range of text) by using Utilities → Suggested Hyphenation (CTRL+H). This is handy as a precheck before you enter a word in the Hyphenation Exceptions dictionary, or if you want manually to hyphenate a word in a paragraph that is formatted with Auto Hyphenation turned off. The Suggested Hyphenation dialog box (Figure 5-18) shows the hyphenated word.

Figure 5-18   Suggested Hyphenation dialog box.

To access this feature, the Content tool must be selected and the insertion point must be positioned within a word. You cannot make changes to the suggested syllable breaks. In addition, this command and dialog box do not make any changes to the text itself. If you want to change the way QuarkXPress hyphenates a word, you can insert your own discretionary hyphens or select Utilities → Hyphenation Exceptions, described under the next headings.

Discretionary Hyphens

You can insert discretionary hyphens within words manually by typing CTRL+hyphen. These discretionary hyphens can be inserted using some word processing programs, before the text is imported in QuarkXPress, or after the text is imported in QuarkXPress. Discretionary hyphens behave exactly the same way that automatic hyphens behave: They only appear on the screen and the printed pages when they fall at the end of a line. To prevent a word from being hyphenated, enter the word in the Hyphenation Exceptions (see next section).

Discretionary hyphens are useful for quick fixes or one-time-only exceptions, but if you want to permanently change the way QuarkXPress hyphenates a word, or turn hyphenation off entirely for selected words, you can build a dictionary of Hyphenation Exceptions, as described next.

Hyphenation Exceptions

Select Utilities ➤ Hyphenation Exceptions to display the Hyphenation Exceptions dialog box (Figure 5-19) and control the way QuarkXPress breaks a word. This command is always available. Any exceptions will be included with all subsequently created new documents.

Figure 5-19   Hyphenation Exceptions dialog box.

In the Hyphenation Exceptions dialog box, type a word in the entry area with hyphens positioned where you want QuarkXPress to break the word—or without hyphens if you never want the word hyphenated—then click on **Add**. You must enter every variant of the word (plural, gerund, and so on) separately. If you click on an entry in the list of exceptions, the word appears in the entry area where you can make changes, and the Add button changes to **Replace**. Use the **Delete** button to remove a selected word from the list. When you are finished making changes to the exceptions list, click on **Save** to keep all your changes, or click on **Cancel** to ignore all changes.

Any changes you make to the hyphenation exceptions affect all documents when you next open them—whether they are new documents or ones that existed before you changed the hyphenation exceptions.

Hyphenation Exceptions are stored within a document and in XPress Preferences (XPRESS.PRF); if they were created when no document was open, they are stored in XPress Preferences (XPRESS.PRF) only. See Chapter 14 for more information on the XPress Preferences file.

Kerning and Tracking Text

Kerning and tracking characters are other methods of aesthetically improving the spacing of text. *Kerning* refers to the spacing between two specific letters; *tracking* refers to the adjustment of white space between multiple characters and words.

When the text insertion point is positioned between two characters of text, the Style ► Kern command lets you adjust the space between the characters numerically; or you can make the same adjustment in the Measurements palette, the Character Attributes dialog box, or by using the keyboard shortcuts. The command changes to Style ► Track when a range of text is selected; as with kerning, you can make the same adjustment in the Measurements palette, the Character Attributes dialog box, or by using the keyboard shortcuts.

Values entered in these fields must be from –100 to 100, and each unit represents 1/200th (0.005) of an em space. (An em space is the equivalent of two zeros, 00, in any given font.) You can enter values in .001 increments, which means you can kern or track in increments as fine as 1/200,000th of an em (Figure 5-20).

Figure 5-20 *Examples of various kern settings between the* H *and the* e.

Entering a positive value increases the space between characters; entering a negative value tightens it. In the Measurements palette, you can also click on the arrows adjacent to the entry area to increase or decrease the value in 1-unit increments (Figure 5-21). Hold down the CTRL key and click to make changes in .1-unit increments.

Figure 5-21 *You can type a numeric value to the right of the arrows, or click on the arrows to change kerning or tracking values.*

You can use keyboard shortcuts for kerning or tracking:

- CTRL+SHIFT+{ decreases the kerning or tracking space by 1/20th of an em.
- CTRL+SHIFT+} increases the kerning or tracking space by 1/20th of an em.
- CTRL+ALT+SHIFT+{ decreases the kerning or tracking space by 1/200th (0.005) of an em.
- CTRL+ALT+SHIFT+} increases the kerning or tracking space by 1/200th (0.005) of an em.

Tracking values affect both word and character spacing, and can be useful for copy-fitting (Figure 5-22). Tracking values, unlike kerning values, can be applied as part of a style sheet.

There were three key pieces that had to come together for desktop publishing to become what it is today.	Track Amount:	0
There were three key pieces that had to come together for desktop publishing to become what it is today.	Track Amount:	-5
There were three key pieces that had to come together for desktop publishing to become what it is today.	Track Amount:	20

Figure 5-22 Examples of various track settings.

The results of entries in the Kern, Track, or Character Attributes dialog boxes are not reflected on the screen display until you close the dialog box, but entries made in the Measurements palette or by using the keyboard shortcuts are reflected immediately. For this reason, it is a good idea to perform all manual kerning through the Measurements palette or with the keyboard shortcuts, unless you are applying a specific numeric value consistently.

Since kerning and tracking adjustments are a percentage of an em of any given font, rather than a fixed size, the actual space between letters will be scaled proportionally if you change the font size of the kerned or tracked characters. For example, if you kern by 1 unit two letters that are 10 points in size, then scale them to 20 points in size, the unit they are kerned will still be 1; however, the em of a 20-point font, of which the unit is a percentage, is larger, and the unit represents a correspondingly larger space. QuarkXPress does *not* offer any way to set an absolute distance between characters, a feature common to many typesetting systems.

Editing Tracking Values

Global intercharacter spacing (tracking) values are built into QuarkXPress. You can select Utilities ➤ Tracking Edit to change the global setting for a specific font. The Utilities ➤ Tracking Edit command is available only if the KTEDIT.XXT XTension is in the same directory as the QuarkXPress program when you launch the program.

The first dialog box displayed when you select the Utilities ➤ Tracking Edit command lists all of the installed fonts (Figure 5-23).

Figure 5-23   The Tracking Edit dialog box.

To Edit a font's tracking values, double-click on the font name. QuarkXPress displays the Tracking Values chart for the selected font (Figure 5-24). Normally tracking is set to zero for all sizes—indicated by a horizontal line across the center of the chart.

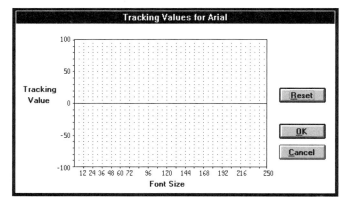

Figure 5-24   Normal Tracking Values chart.

You can specify tracking values from –100/200ths to 100/200ths of an em space for font sizes from 2 to 250 points by clicking on the line in the chart area to create new handles. Each click positions a handle and changes the direction of the line. When you click on a handle, the font size and tracking table value are shown in the upper right corner of the dialog box (Figure 5-25). You can move a handle by dragging it. You can position up to four handles in a chart.

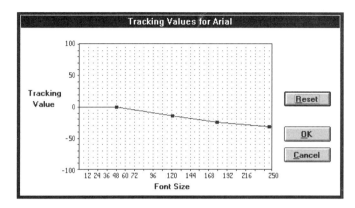

Figure 5-25   Custom Tracking Values chart.

Hold the ALT key and click on a handle to remove it. Click on Reset to revert to normal tracking (0 for all sizes), or click on Cancel to reverse any changes you have made to the current font.

When you click on OK, the new tracking values for that font are stored *temporarily*. QuarkXPress displays the Tracking Edit dialog box, and you can Edit another font's tracking values. To end the process, click on Save in the Tracking Edit dialog box—or click on Cancel to reverse all entries made to the Tracking Values.

Global Kerning Adjustments

Usually, text above 10 points in size is automatically kerned using the built-in kerning tables for the font—unless you change this setting through the Edit ► Preferences ► Typographic dialog box as described earlier in this chapter. When kerning, the spacing between characters is adjusted slightly in accordance with the values stored in a table of "kerning pairs." For example, the space between the characters *AV* should be tighter than the space between the characters *AX*. In fact, if the spacing between the different pairs is not adjusted, then it will appear to the eye that the *A* and *V* are farther apart than the *A* and *X* are. For this reason, kerned text generally looks better than text that is not kerned—especially in larger point sizes.

You can select Edit → Preferences → Typographic to change the point size above which kerning is enabled, or turn kerning off entirely for a whole document. (Your pages will redraw and print more quickly if kerning is turned off for small point sizes.)

Editing Kerning Tables

You can customize the kerning table of scalable fonts, such as PostScript or TrueType fonts, using Utilities → Kerning Table Edit. In order for this command to be available, the KTEDIT.XXT XTension must be in the same directory as the QuarkXPress program when you launch the program. The first dialog box displayed when you use this command is the Kerning Table Edit dialog box (Figure 5-26), which shows a list of all the installed fonts.

Figure 5-26   The Kerning Table Edit dialog box.

To Edit a font's kerning table, double-click on the font name/style in the list. (You must edit the kerning tables for plain, bold, italic, and bold-italic styles separately.) QuarkXPress displays the Kerning Values for the selected font (Figure 5-27). If the selected font has a kerning table, the values are displayed and you can edit them as described next. If no values are displayed in the dialog box, then no kerning table exists for that font. You can create one by entering values in the dialog box.

Chapter 5: Typography   221

Figure 5-27   Kerning Values dialog box.

The Kerning Values scroll list shows all of the pairs that have assigned kerning values. Pairs *not* on the list have an assumed kerning value of zero. To edit a value, first click on a pair in the list to select it or simply type the pair in the Pair text box. The Value field shows the currently assigned kerning value or remains blank if you typed a new pair that is not on the list. The window below the Value field shows how the pair would be spaced with the current Value setting; the display changes as you enter different numbers in the Value field. Values are entered in 200ths (0.005) of an em space, and can be between –100 and 100. A value of –20, for example, will reduce the space between letters by 1/10 of an em space.

If you have typed a new pair in the Pair field, you must click on **Add** to add it to the list. If you have selected an existing pair, the Add button changes to **Replace**. You must click on Replace in order to update the table, or you can click on **Delete** to remove a pair from the table (and thereby set the kerning value to 0). The **Reset** button restores the original kerning table set up by the font manufacturer. If Reset is grayed, you know that the original table has not been modified.

Click on Export to create an ASCII text file version of the table. This displays a directory dialog box that lets you name an exported table and specify where to store it (Figure 5-28). Click on Import to replace the entire table with values from a table that was generated using a text editor or by the Export command. The Import command displays a list of all ASCII files, but it displays a warning and does not import any files that are not in the proper format for kerning tables.

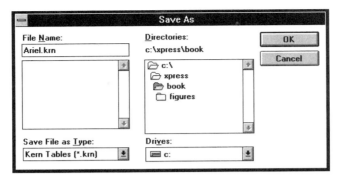

Figure 5-28 The Export dialog box.

When you click on OK, the new kerning table for that font is stored *temporarily*, QuarkXPress displays the Kerning Table Edit dialog box, and you can Edit another font's kerning table. To end the process, click on Save in the Kerning Table Edit dialog box—or click on Cancel to reverse all changes made to the kerning tables.

Changes you make to the kerning table with a document open are stored as part of the document and in the XPress Preferences file (XPRESS.PRF). Changes made when no document is open are stored in the XPress Preferences file. If you export text to a word processing format (File ➛ Save Text), kerning adjustments are lost.

Special Effects

You can create many special typographic effects, such as custom-scaled type, drop caps, and rules attached to text, which are discussed in this section. See Part II for examples of other special typographic effects.

Horizontal Scale

QuarkXPress allows you to make expanded or condensed versions of a font's normal character widths by adjusting the width of characters numerically. You can select the Style ➛ Horizontal Scale command (Figure 5-29), input a value in the Horizontal Scale entry in the Character Attributes dialog box or the Measurements palette, or use keyboard shortcuts to scale characters horizontally. Values entered in these fields represent percentages of the font's normal character widths: entries above 100 percent (up to 400 percent) make the characters wider than normal; values below 100 percent (down to the minimum 25 percent) make the characters narrower than normal.

Figure 5-29   The Horizontal Scale dialog box.

 The keyboard shortcuts for changing scale are:
- CTRL+[to condense in 5 percent increments.
- CTRL+] to expand in 5 percent increments.

Because horizontal scaling distorts a font in only one direction, overscaling can result in some character strokes being relatively thin compared to other strokes (Figure 5-30).

This is Galliard at normal width

This is Galliard EXPANDED to 140% of original width

This is Galliard CONDENSED to 75% of original width

Figure 5-30   Examples of expanded and condensed characters.

Drop Caps

A drop cap is a large initial character, or characters, in a paragraph with two or more lines of text beside it. To create a drop cap, click on Drop Caps in the Paragraph Formats dialog box (Style → Formats). In Character Count, specify the number of characters that you want to make drop caps (the first characters in the paragraph), and in Line Count give the number of lines of text that you want to fall next to the drop cap (Figure 5-31).

Figure 5-31   The Drop Cap area of the Paragraph Formats dialog box and the resulting drop cap.

QuarkXPress automatically scales the first letters of the paragraph to the size needed to match the number of lines you specified as being beside the drop cap. To enlarge or reduce the size of drop caps, highlight the drop cap characters; then choose Size from the Style menu. Enter a size value or a percentage value between 10 percent and 400 percent in .1 percent increments in the Font Size dialog box. If you enter a percentage, the drop cap characters will be scaled as a percentage of the number of lines deep you specified the characters to be.

You can change the space between the drop cap and the adjacent lines by clicking in between the drop cap and the adjacent first line of text, then applying kerning values using any one of the several methods described earlier in this chapter. All lines indented by the drop cap will move at once, based on the kerning values used.

You can specify alignment (left, right, centered, justified) in this dialog box, as described in Chapter 4 (Word Processing). Select a set of H&J rules and specify Leading (space between lines) in this dialog box, both as described earlier. Drop caps can also be specified as part of a style sheet.

Applying Rules to Text

QuarkXPress lets you specify rules—ruled lines—as part of the paragraph formatting. Thus you can create rules above and/or below a selected paragraph through numerical specifications (instead of using one of QuarkXPress' drawing tools). Those rules will move automatically with the text when the text is reflowed due to editing changes; you don't have to use the anchoring feature.

Select Style → Rules (CTRL+SHIFT+N) to display the Paragraph Rules dialog box (Figure 5-32) and set rules above and/or below a paragraph. Check Rule Above and/or Rule Below to expand the initial dialog box.

Figure 5-32 Paragraph Rules dialog box (CTRL+SHIFT+N).

A rule can be assigned a Style, Width, Color, and Shade just as in the Line Specifications dialog box, used to define lines drawn with QuarkXPress' line drawing tools.

Length

For text rules, you can also specify Length to match the line of **Text** to which the rule is attached or to match the **Indents** set up for the paragraph through the Style → Formats command. You can further adjust the length by specifying distances in the From Left and/or From Right fields, determining how the rule will be shortened (by a positive value entry) or extended (by a negative value entry) relative to the Text or Indents as specified in the Length setting.

Offset

The Offset distance specified is added between the rule and the baseline of the text below (for rules above text) or between the rule and the baseline of the text above (for rules below text). The Offset value can be an absolute measure or a percentage of the total space between paragraphs (as determined by the values entered for Space Above and Space Below in the Paragraph Formats dialog box).

If you enter an absolute offset value, the rule will be placed from the bottom of the rule to the baseline of the first line of text for rules above. For rules below, an absolute value will determine the space from the top of the rule to the baseline of the last line of text.

Values entered as percentages are determined as a percentage of the total space between paragraphs. For example, if you enter an Offset value of 20 percent, QuarkXPress will divide the total space between paragraphs so that 20 percent of the space falls between the rule and the ascent height of the tallest character in the text below (for rules above text) or between the descent of the largest character in the text above (for rules below text); 80 percent of the space will fall between the rule and the following paragraph. When the Offset is a percentage, rules are displayed between paragraphs but not above the first paragraph or below the last paragraph in a text box (Figure 5-33).

Figure 5-33   Example of a rule attached to text.

Summary

Now that you know the alternatives available for formatting text in QuarkXPress, you can create design specifications that take advantage of QuarkXPress' extensive typographic capabilities, and you can decide which method of applying the specifications will be most efficient.

The next chapter describes the basics of how to work with graphics that have been created in QuarkXPress and those created in other programs and imported into QuarkXPress.

6 *Graphics*

Text and typography represent just one aspect of design and printed communication. Graphic images also play an important role. One of the key characteristics of QuarkXPress is its ability to incorporate graphics with text on a page. QuarkXPress offers some graphic tools of its own, but you can also import graphics that were created in other programs, such as Micrografx Designer, CorelDRAW, Adobe Illustrator, Aldus FreeHand, and Aldus PhotoStyler, to name a few.

Chapter 2 presented an overview of the basic steps for working with boxes and lines created using QuarkXPress. In this chapter you learn how to further manipulate graphic shapes and lines that have been created using QuarkXPress, and how to work with graphics that have been imported from other programs.

Before you start, it's a good idea to set up the global conditions that will affect all the graphics in a document. These include options in the the Edit ➤ Preferences ➤ General and the Edit ➤ Preferences ➤ Tools commands, described in Chapter 3. Before you begin working, you may also want to start building your color palette using the Edit ➤ Colors command, as described in Chapter 7.

Broadly, there are four ways to bring graphics onto a QuarkXPress page:

- Use the Paste command to bring in a graphic from the Clipboard.
- Drag elements from another QuarkXPress document or library, which essentially copies them.
- Use QuarkXPress' own built-in graphic tools with the File ➤ Get Picture command to import graphics that were created in other programs.
- If you are running under Windows 3.1, you can use the Insert Object keyboard command (CTRL+SHIFT+I) or the Edit ➤ Paste Special or Paste Link commands to use Windows' Object Linking and Embedding (OLE) feature to embed or link graphics created in another program.

The Paste command is common to most Windows applications and was described in Chapter 1. Methods of copying elements from another QuarkXPress document or library were described in Chapter 2. In this chapter we first take a closer look at how to manipulate QuarkXPress' built-in graphic tools, then we look at how to work with graphics created in other programs using the File ➤ Get Picture command and the Insert Object keyboard command (CTRL+SHIFT+I) or the Edit ➤ Paste Special or Paste Link commands.

Working with QuarkXPress Drawing Tools

As you learned in Chapters 1 and 2, QuarkXPress' built-in graphics tools are shown as icons in the tool palette (Figure 6-1).

Figure 6-1 The drawing tools in the tool palette.

You can select the Rectangle Picture Box tool, the Rounded-corner Rectangle Picture Box tool, the Oval Picture Box tool, or the Polygon Picture Box tool to create boxes with square corners, boxes with rounded corners, circles and ovals, or polygons, respectively. You can select the Orthogonal Line tool to draw horizontal and vertical lines, and the Line tool to draw lines at any angle. Each of these items may be used as a stand-alone graphic; or the picture box items may contain graphics created in other programs.

A Review of Modifying Picture Boxes

Chapter 2 covered the basic techniques for drawing, moving, resizing, and rotating picture boxes as well as applying color to the background of a box and adding a frame to a box. You can make most basic modifications to a box with one of three methods: with the mouse and keyboard, through the Measurements or Colors palettes, or by making entries in the Picture Box Specifications dialog box (Item → Modify). This section continues to discuss the modification of picture boxes themselves, as opposed to modifying the *contents* of picture boxes, which is discussed later in this chapter.

Aside from using keyboard commands or the mouse to visually move or resize picture boxes, the Measurements palette can be one of the fastest ways to modify picture boxes numerically. Note that the entries on the left side of the Measurements palette affect the selected picture box itself, not the content of the picture box (Figure 6-2). The content—that is, a graphic—is modified through entries in the right side of the Measurements palette, discussed later in this chapter.

Figure 6-2 The left side of the Measurements palette contains entries that affect the picture box, not its content.

The Colors palette is the fastest way to apply color to box backgrounds (Figure 6-3). The palette displays a list of all colors created using the Edit → Colors command. The Colors palette is the only way to apply two-color blends to box backgrounds. See Chapter 7 for more detail on applying color blends to box backgrounds.

230   *The QuarkXPress Handbook*

Figure 6-3   The Colors palette allows you to apply color to a picture box background quickly.

The Picture Box Specifications dialog box can also be used to modify the position, size, or rotation of a box numerically. This dialog box contains the same entries for adjusting picture boxes as those found in the Measurements palette (Figure 6-4). It also contains an option to Suppress Printout of the picture box (and its content).

The Picture Box Specifications dialog box gives you options similar to the Colors palette: You can apply color and shade to the background of the picture box, but you cannot apply a two-color blend. As mentioned earlier, using the Colors palette is the only way to apply two-color blends in QuarkXPress.

Figure 6-4   Entries in the Picture Box Specifications dialog box that affect a picture box, as opposed to affecting the content only.

Picture box items can be framed and filled with any color and shade. Drawn objects initially have the default settings for line widths, styles, colors, and shades. The program starts with default values set to no frame, a white background for picture boxes, and 1-point black lines for the line creation tools. You can change the defaults by changing these settings before you draw the item, or you can change the settings after you draw the item. Review Chapter 2 for a detailed discussion of changing these defaults.

Changing the Shape of Picture Boxes

No matter what drawing tool you use to draw a picture box, you can change its shape using Item → Picture Box Shape. With this command you can change a rectangular box, oval, or polygon to any of six basic shapes: a rectangle with square corners, a rectangle with rounded corners, two concave-cornered rectangles, an oval, or a polygon.

To use this command, first select the box(es) you want to change, then choose a shape from the Picture Box Shape submenu (Figure 6-5). See Chapter 13 for examples of how unusual shapes, such as cartoon balloons, can be created by converting ovals to polygons and dragging a handle.

Figure 6-5 The Picture Box Shape submenu.

Reshaping Polygons

Once you have drawn a polygon, or changed a box to a polygon using the Item ▸ Picture Box Shape command, you can resize it by changing the size of its bounding box or reshape it by moving, adding, and deleting box handles, and by moving line segments. You can follow these procedures using either the Item tool (✥) or the Content tool (☜).

When a polygon is active and Reshape Polygon is *not* checked in the Style menu, you can adjust the size of the polygon by moving any of the eight handles displayed on the bounding box (Figure 6-6). Hold down the SHIFT key while you resize if you want to maintain the same proportions.

Figure 6-6 Adjusting a Polygon's bounding box. The bounding box is displayed when Reshape Polygon is not *checked in the Style menu.*

When a polygon is active and Reshape Polygon *is* checked in the Item menu, you can adjust the shape of the polygon by moving any of the handles displayed at the vertices of the polygon or by moving a line segment (Figure 6-7). You can move any handle or line segment by positioning the pointer over it and dragging the mouse. You can constrain the movement of a handle or a line segment to 45° lines (0°, 45°, or 90°) by holding the SHIFT key as you drag.

Figure 6-7 Adjusting a Polygon's shape. The corner handles are displayed when Reshape Polygon is checked in the Style menu.

You can add new handles by holding the CTRL key as you click the pointer anywhere on a line segment. You can delete a handle by positioning the pointer over it and holding the CTRL key as you click. A new line segment will automatically join the two vertices that were adjacent to the deleted handle. You cannot delete a handle from a three-sided polygon.

Modifying Lines

This section will expand upon the basics of drawing lines as discussed in Chapter 2. To draw horizontal and vertical lines, select the Orthogonal Line tool; to draw lines at any angle, use the Line tool. Lines drawn with the Line tool or Orthogonal Line tool show small black squares as handles at each end when they are first drawn, or when they are later made active with the Item tool. Change the length and/or angle of a line by dragging one of these corner handles, as mentioned above. Move a line to another position by dragging anywhere on the line *except* on a handle.

Actually, you need never select the Orthogonal Line tool, since you can constrain any line drawn with the diagonal Line tool to 0°, 45°, or 90° angles by holding down the SHIFT key as you draw. The SHIFT key also constrains lines to these angles when you resize them by dragging one of the handles.

 The SHIFT key will also constrain lines when changing the length of a line with the mouse. If you hold down the SHIFT key as you drag one of these handles, you will force the line to follow an angle that is a multiple of 45°, thus ensuring the line will remain straight. If you do not hold down the SHIFT key while dragging, the line may get the "jaggies."

 Normally, the tool that was selected before you select a line creation tool is automatically reselected as soon as you draw a line. If you want to draw more than one line, hold down the ALT key when you select the line tool.

Similar to picture boxes, lines can be modified using any one of several techniques, including using keyboard commands, the mouse, the Measurements palette, the Colors palette, the Style menu, or the Line Specifications dialog box (Item ➞ Modify), shown in Figure 6-8.

Figure 6-8 Line Specifications dialog box.

You can force text to runaround any line, including a transparent, or colorless line, by using the Item ▸ Runaround command (described in Chapter 2). Or, if you change Runaround to None, there is no displacement of the text behind the line and you can "see through" the line to the contents of the box below. You can also specify that a line not print, and still have it affect text runaround. See Part II for examples of using transparent or nonprinting lines to force unusual effects with text runaround, such as slanted margins.

Modifying the Position and Length of a Line

As discussed in Chapter 2, a line can be moved visually by using the mouse, or its length can be changed by moving one of the endpoint handles. To make these modifications numerically, use the Measurements palette or the Line Specifications dialog box (Item ▸ Modify).

The length, position, and angle of a line is adjusted differently in the Measurements palette and in the Line Specifications dialog box depending on the Mode selected. Choose **Endpoints** to describe a line by specifying the position of the endpoints. Choose **Left Endpoint** to describe a line by specifying the position of its left endpoint, its length, and its angle. Choose **Midpoint** to describe a line by specifying the position of its midpoint, its length, and its angle. Choose **Right Endpoint** to describe a line by specifying the position of its right endpoint, its length, and its angle (Figure 6-9).

Figure 6-9 Measurements palette shows different values for the same line with different modes selected.

The Measurements palette for lines changes depending on the Mode selected. A drop-down list lets you select the Mode for the line and the display changes depending on the Mode chosen:

- When Endpoints is chosen, X1 and Y1 show the location of the left end of the line, and X2 and Y2 show the location of the right end of the line.
- When Left Point is chosen, X1 and Y1 show the position of the left point; ∡ shows the rotated angle of the line; and L shows the length of the line.
- When Midpoint is chosen, XC and YC show the location of the midpoint of the line; ∡ shows the rotated angle of the line; and L shows the length of the line.
- When Right Point is chosen, X2 and Y2 show the position of the right point; ∡ shows the rotated angle of the line; and L shows the length of the line.

Regardless of the Mode selected, some of the entries in the Measurements palette represent the line consistently:

- W shows the width of the line.
- A drop-down list lets you select the Style for the line.
- A drop-down list lets you select the Endcaps for the line.

In entering angles of rotation, a positive value indicates a counterclockwise rotation, a negative value is measured clockwise.

Modifying Line Style

Lines drawn in QuarkXPress may be specified in any one of 11 basic styles, including as a solid line, dashed or dotted lines, and double or triple lines. Line style may be changed using the Line Specifications dialog box (Item ➤ Modify), or more efficiently by using the Style ➤ Line Style submenu

(Figure 6-10), or by choosing from the first drop-down list on the right side of the Measurements palette.

Figure 6-10   Line Style submenu.

Modifying Line Endcaps

You can specify six variations of endcaps for lines, including arrows at one or both ends, or arrows and tailfeathers. Endcaps of a line may be changed using the Line Specifications dialog box (Item → Modify), or more efficiently, by using the Style → Endcaps submenu (Figure 6-11) or by choosing from the second drop-down list on the right side of the Measurements palette.

Figure 6-11   Endcaps submenu.

Modifying Line Width

The width of a line can be set from seven common pre-set widths or can be set in any measure from 0 to 504 points in .001-point increments. You can adjust the line width by entering a value, by choosing from the drop-down list in the Line Specifications dialog box (Item → Modify) or, more efficiently, by using the Style → Width submenu (Figure 6-12), the Measurements palette, or keyboard shortcuts. To enter a custom value using the Style → Width submenu, choose Other (CTRL+SHIFT+\) to display the Width dialog box.

The Measurements palette has no drop-down list for size; values are input directly in the size field. Note that entering .25-point in the Measurements palette is the equivalent of choosing Hairline from the Style → Width submenu or the drop-down list in the Line Specifications dialog box.

Figure 6-12   Width submenu.

You can also use the following keyboard shortcuts to change the width of an active line:

- CTRL+SHIFT+< decreases line width by 1 unit at increments that follow the menu list: hairline, 1, 2, 4, 6, 8, 12 points.
- CTRL+SHIFT+> increases line width by 1 unit at the increments that follow the menu list.
- CTRL+ALT+SHIFT+< decreases line width by 1 point (from 0 to 504 points).
- CTRL+ALT+SHIFT+> increases line width by 1 point (from 0 to 504 points).

Modifying Line Color and Shade

You can make a line any Color and Shade, or specify a color of None to make a transparent line. Normally, the line color is set to 100 percent Black. Color may be applied to a line by choosing a color in the Line Specifications dialog box (Item → Modify), by choosing a color from the Colors palette, or more efficiently by using the Style → Color submenu (Figure 6-13). The colors listed are the colors that you have set up for the active palette through the Edit → Colors command.

Figure 6-13   Color submenu.

Shade may be applied to a line by choosing a pre-set percentage of shade in the Line Specifications dialog box (Item ➤ Modify), by choosing a shade from the Colors palette, or more efficiently by using the Style ➤ Shade submenu (Figure 6-14). Using any of these methods, you can also enter a custom shade value in increments of .1 percent. Chapter 7 provides a detailed discussion of creating and applying colors in QuarkXPress.

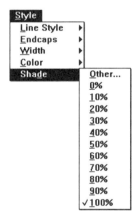

Figure 6-14   Shade submenu.

Importing Graphics from Other Sources

As discussed in Chapter 2, you can bring graphics created in other programs onto a page by drawing a picture box and selecting the File ➤ Get Picture command. You can import a graphic into any box created with QuarkXPress' four picture box tools: the Rectangle Picture Box tool, the Rounded-corner Rectangle Picture Box tool, the Oval Picture Box tool, and the Polygon Picture Box tool. The types of graphics that can be imported into QuarkXPress and some of the programs that can be used to create them are listed in Figure 6-15.

File Formats	Sources
.BMP, .DIB, .RLE (bitmap)	Windows Paint
.GIF	Compuserve
.PCX	Paintbrush
.WMF (Windows Metafile)	Windows Standard
.CGM (Computer Graphics Metafile)	Harvard Graphics
.PLT (HPGL)	AutoCAD
.PCT	Macintosh PICT
.DRW	Micrografx Designer
.CT	Scitex
.TIF (TIFF line art, grayscale)	scanning applications
.EPS (Encapsulated PostScript)	CorelDRAW, Adobe Illustrator, Aldus FreeHand

Figure 6-15 Sources of graphics that can be used in QuarkXPress.

Many programs can save or export graphics files in more than one of these formats. For example, Arts & Letters can export files in several formats, including .EPS, .CGM, .WMF, or .TIF.

Types of Graphics

One of the factors that has contributed to the success of Windows applications in the publishing industry is the consistency of graphic file formats across applications. There are really only a few basic types of file formats, each of which has its own unique characteristics.

Bitmaps

Bitmapped graphics are composed of a pattern of dots or pixels rather than stored as mathematical formulas (Figure 6-16). This type of graphic comes from a paint-type program, such as PC Paintbrush. Scanned images are also bitmapped images which can usually be saved in .PCX format, but they can also be stored at higher resolutions than allowed by most paint-type programs. (See "TIFF Files," later in this section.) Bitmap file formats supported by QuarkXPress include .BMP, .DIB, .GIF, .PCX, and .RLE.

Figure 6-16 Bitmapped images drawn using Windows Paint.

Metafiles

Metafiles are called object-oriented graphics because the lines and patterns that you see are actually stored as mathematical formulas of the objects that compose the image, (though images can also have a bitmap associated with the screen data). Because object-oriented graphics are defined mathematically, they are smooth, and create crisp line art and fill patterns (Figure 6-17). Metafile formats supported by QuarkXpress include .CGM (Computer Graphics Metafile), .DRW (Micrografx Designer's native format), .PLT (HPGL, Hewlett Packard Graphics Language for plotters), and .WMF (Windows Metafile).

QuarkXPress for Windows can also import PICT graphics created on the Macintosh (.PCT). The PICT format is the native Macintosh format. PICT graphics are object-oriented graphics that are created by some drafting programs like Claris CAD, draw-type programs such as MacDraw, and other image-editing programs such as Adobe Photoshop.

Figure 6-17 A graphic created in Arts & Letters and exported as a Computer Graphics Metafile.

PICT graphics can be copied directly onto a PC disk using a Macintosh that has the capability to read PC disks. Utilities that give the Macintosh this capability include DOS Mounter by Dayna Communications and Apple's Macintosh PC Exchange system extension.

EPS Graphics

Encapsulated PostScript files (EPS) are PostScript files that have a screen preview, so they can be viewed. EPS files are defined by the mathematical algorithms of PostScript, and print smooth, crisp lines at the resolution of the output device, which must be a PostScript printer. Encapsulated PostScript is the native format of Adobe Illustrator, but most graphics programs can create EPS files (Figure 6-18). EPS files can also be created using QuarkXPress by selecting the File → Save Page as EPS command, as discussed in the next section.

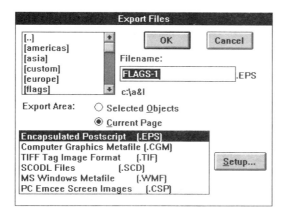

Figure 6-18 The Export dialog box from Arts & Letters—graphics must be saved as Encapsulated PostScript (EPS).

You can use certain programs on the Macintosh or other platforms to create graphics and save them in Encapsulated PostScript format, then telecommunicate that EPS file to the PC to import it in QuarkXPress.

Because EPS images can be quite large, QuarkXPress stores and displays the images in a low-resolution format rather than incorporating them in the document. The EPS file is linked to the document, however; when you print the document, QuarkXPress looks for the original EPS file on the disk in order to print at high resolution.

Save Page as EPS

To save a QuarkXPress document page as an EPS picture, choose the File → Save Page as EPS command. In the dialog box (Figure 6–19), enter the page number you want to save and a name for the picture. You can save the page as a color or black-and-white EPS picture, and you can specify the scale of the picture from 10 percent to 100 percent. You can also choose to include OPI comments or not.

Figure 6-19 Save Page as EPS dialog box and the printed EPS version of a page.

You can also create a PostScript version of the document, so that all of the printing information will be stored as a disk file instead of being sent to the printer.

TIFF Files

The Tag Image File Format (TIFF), which usually has the file extension .TIF, is a picture file format designed for use with scanners and printing programs. TIFF files are most commonly used to store continuous-tone images such as photographs. When these images are printed on a high-resolution typesetter, such as a Linotronic 330, most of the levels of gray found in the original image will appear on the page printed through QuarkXPress. When printed on a relatively low-resolution printer, such as a 300 dpi laser printer, some of the levels of gray stored in the TIFF format will be compressed (not printed). True grayscale viewing is available on 8-bit or higher color or grayscale monitors.

Because TIFF images are usually stored at 300 dpi resolution or higher, image files can be quite large—easily larger than 1 megabyte. As with EPS files, QuarkXPress stores and displays the images in a low-resolution TIFF format, rather than incorporating such large images in the document. The high-resolution version of the file is linked to the document, however; when you print the document, QuarkXPress looks for the original scan file on the disk in order to print at high resolution.

For this reason, it is a good idea to store the TIFF file in the same directory as your document. If you copy the document to another drive, copy the TIFF image too. Without that file, the image will be printed at low resolution, even on high-resolution printers. If QuarkXPress cannot find the TIFF file when you print, it prompts you to locate the file.

You can convert a TIFF picture format as you import it by using various keyboard commands:

- Holding the CTRL key when importing a TIFF grayscale picture converts it to TIFF line art.
- Holding the ALT key when importing TIFF line art converts to TIFF grayscale.
- Holding the CTRL key when importing TIFF color converts it to TIFF grayscale.

Normally, an imported TIFF image is displayed at 36 dpi on screen. You can increase the on-screen display resolution to 72 dpi by holding the SHIFT key as you import the image, or you can choose to display 256 levels of gray by setting that option in the Application Preferences dialog box (Edit ➤ Preferences ➤ Application).

Scanned Images

Graphics can also be created when images are digitized through a scanning device. These images can usually be saved in PIC format (usually for line art), in PCX or BMP format (for low-resolution bitmap images), or in TIFF format for continuous tone images, such as photographs or watercolor paintings (Figure 6-20).

Figure 6-20   A scanned image.

Importing Graphics

QuarkXPress lets you import graphics created in other programs, using a process similar to the method used for importing text files created in other programs. To import graphics, first select one of QuarkXPress' Picture box creation tools (⊠ ⊠ ⊗ ⊠) to create the picture box into which you wish to import the graphic. Next, make sure the box is active with the Content tool (🖑) selected, and choose the File ➤ Get Picture command to display the Get Picture dialog box. Find the name of the graphics file you want to import in the dialog box and double-click on the file name to import the graphic into the active picture box.

Here is a step-by-step summary of the steps required to import graphics into QuarkXPress:

Step 1   First create or select the picture box into which you want to import the graphic (Figure 6-21).

Figure 6-21   Active picture box.

Chapter 6: Graphics   245

Step 2   Select File → Get Picture to display the Get Picture dialog box (Figure 6-22).

Figure 6-22 *The Get Picture command in the File menu.*

Step 3   Next find the name of the graphics file you want to import in the dialog box (Figure 6-23). Use the scroll bars to scroll through the list names, and click the drive identification to view the graphics. If the file you wish to import is not listed, it might have been saved with an unusual extension. You can try listing all files (*.*) or entering the exact name of the file you seek.

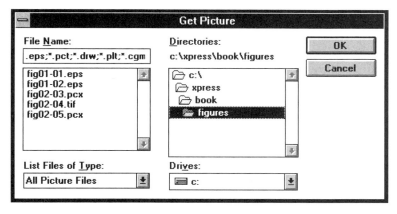

Figure 6-23 *The Get Picture dialog box.*

Step 4 Once you have found the name of the file you want to import, double-click to import the graphic. All file formats will be imported directly (except .CGM, .DRW, and .PLT files which require special XTensions and cause an additional dialog box to appear, as discussed in the next section).

Figure 6-24   An imported graphic.

The entire, unscaled picture that you import is placed in the active picture box (Figure 6-24), replacing any previous contents of the box. You may need to scale the picture to make it fit the box. Methods of scaling, cropping, and editing pictures are described later in this chapter.

The entire graphics file will be imported in QuarkXPress as a single graphic object, regardless of how large the graphic or how many different objects were in the original source file. If the graphic includes text, QuarkXPress retains the font settings made in the graphics program. You cannot change individual parts of the graphic, such as the line styles or the colors of individual elements.

Importing .CGM, .DRW, and .PLT Pictures

Certain graphics formats require special XTension files to import correctly. Computer Graphics Metafiles (.CGM) require the CGMFILTR.FLT XTension; graphics created in Micrografx Designer (.DRW) require the DRWFILTR.FLT XTension; and graphics in plotter format (.PLT) require the HPGL.FLT XTension.

As you import a graphic that has been saved in one of these formats, a dialog box appears that lets you control certain aspects of how the graphic is imported. In the case of .CGM files, the CGM Format dialog box lets you indicate how fonts and lines are converted when you import a graphic. The DRW Format dialog box lets you control the way background fills and bitmap fonts are converted when you import a graphic (Figure 6-25). The HPGL Format dialog box lets you select the size the image was saved in, and the Colors option lets you control the way plotter pen colors will print from QuarkXPress.

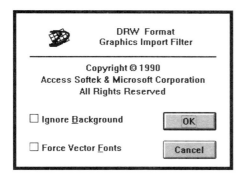

Figure 6-25 Dialog box for importing a .DRW file.

Using OLE

As discussed in Chapter 1, QuarkXPress lets you take advantage of Windows 3.1's Object Linking and Embedding (OLE). OLE allows you to embed or link objects created in other programs that can then be edited from within QuarkXPress. Double-clicking on an embedded or linked object in a QuarkXPress document launches the application the graphic was created in and lets you use the application to edit the graphic.

Before you embed or link graphics in a QuarkXPress document, it's important to understand the difference between using OLE and using QuarkXPress' Get Picture command. The Get Picture command imports a screen image of the graphic into an active text box, and links to the original graphic file, which it reads at the time the document is printed, thus producing high-resolution output of the image. The graphic can be manipulated using QuarkXPress commands such as scaling, rotating, and skewing, but the graphic itself cannot be changed. To edit the graphic, you must launch the original application in which it was created. The link between the QuarkXPress document and the graphic is maintained using the Auto Import Feature in the General Preferences dialog box or the Utilities ➤ Picture Usage command. Chapter 8 on Printing contains more information about these commands.

QuarkXPress' OLE commands—Insert Object (CTRL+SHIFT+I), Paste, Paste Special, and Paste Link—let you embed or link a graphic that can be edited by double-clicking on the graphic and thereby launching the application in which the graphic was created (assuming the graphic application is OLE-compliant). You can then make the required edits while still in the QuarkXPress document.

To embed a graphic that has been copied into the Clipboard, use the Paste command or the Paste button in the Paste Special dialog box (Edit ➤

Paste Special). To link a graphic, use the Insert Object command (CTRL +SHIFT+I), the Paste Link button in the Paste Special dialog box, or the Edit ➤ Paste Link command.

As discussed in Chapter 1, embedding graphics places a copy of a file on the page, and edits to that file do not affect the original. Editing a *linked* graphic changes the original graphics file, and also changes all occurances of that graphic in other QuarkXPress documents. To list and manage linked files, use the Edit ➤ Links command (Figure 6-26).

Figure 6-26 OLE-linked files can be listed and managed using the Edit ➤ Links command.

The Edit ➤ Links command can be used to update, cancel, or change links from one graphic file to another. Embedded graphics do not appear on this list, nor is there a command available for doing so.

Manipulating Imported Graphics

Up to this point, most of the commands described affect items created in QuarkXPress—lines and boxes—but they do not change the appearance of pictures that have been imported into QuarkXPress. The next headings describe commands and features that can be used to change the position and appearance of imported graphics within the picture box.

When you import a graphic into a QuarkXPress picture box, the graphic will be imported at 100 percent size, unless you have changed the settings for the box. The actual, as opposed to the visible, upper lefthand corner of the graphic is positioned in the upper lefthand corner of the picture box.

If the large *X* that normally appears in a blank picture box disappears after importing a graphic, but the box still appears blank, then a blank part of the picture is showing. You can use command CTRL+SHIFT+M to center the image in the picture box, or select the Content tool (with the Picture Mover pointer displayed (🖑)) to move the picture around (usually up and left) in the box. CTRL+SHIFT+F scales the picture to fit within the box, and CTRL+ALT+SHIFT+F scales the picture to fit within the box while maintaining the aspect ratio.

Scaling Imported Graphics

In Chapter 2 you learned how to move, scale, or rotate a box, without affecting the content of the box. Now you will learn how to move, scale, or rotate the *content* of a box—an imported picture. Most of these procedures can be accomplished using the Content tool and keyboard commands described under the next headings, but they can also be accomplished by making entries in the Measurements palette or through the Picture Box Specifications dialog box (Figure 6-27) that is displayed by using the Item → Modify command.

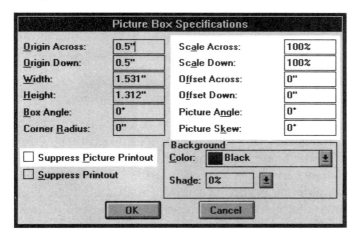

Figure 6-27   Entries that affect the content of a box in the Picture Box Specifications dialog box.

As discussed in Chapter 2, you can resize a box without affecting the content and apply these special keyboard shortcuts:

- SHIFT+click and drag to constrain boxes to square shapes (for text or rectangular graphics boxes) or circles (for oval graphics boxes).
- ALT+SHIFT+click and drag to force the box to maintain its same aspect ratio.

You can also scale the picture box *and* the picture inside it using the following keyboard/mouse combinations:

- CTRL+SHIFT+click and drag to constrain boxes to square shapes (for text or rectangular graphics boxes) or circles (for oval graphics boxes) and scale the picture.
- CTRL+ALT+SHIFT+click and drag to force the box to maintain the same aspect ratio for the box and scale the picture.
- CTRL+click and drag to resize box and the picture within it without maintaining proportions.

Four other keyboard commands scale the picture without scaling the box:

- CTRL+SHIFT+F scales the picture to fit within the box without changing the box size; this may change the aspect ratio of the picture.
- CTRL+ALT+SHIFT+F scales the picture to fit within the box without changing the box size while maintaining the aspect ratio.
- CTRL+ALT+SHIFT+< scales the picture down by 5 percent.
- CTRL+ALT+SHIFT+> scales the picture up by 5 percent.

You can also select Item → Modify to display the Picture Box Specifications dialog box and scale a picture numerically by entering percentage values in the **Scale Across** and **Scale Down** fields, or by entering percentage values in the **X percent** and **Y percent** fields of the Measurements palette. If you have previously scaled the picture, the amount by which the picture has been scaled will show in these areas. You can enter values from 10 percent up to 1000 percent. Unless the values in the two fields are equal, the picture will be distorted.

Moving a Picture Within a Box

The simplest way to move an imported picture within a picture box (without moving the box itself) is first to select the Content Tool (). When you position the pointer over an imported picture, the pointer changes to a hand () . Hold down the mouse button and drag the hand to move the picture within the box. Remember, CTRL+SHIFT+M centers a picture in a box.

As described in Chapter 2, you can select Item → Modify to display the Picture Box Specifications dialog box and specify the distance from the edge of the box by which the picture will be Offset Across and Offset Down from the left and top edges of the box. You can also move a picture by entering values in the ✥ and ✤ fields of the Measurements palette. These fields appear in the palette only when the Content Tool (☞) is active. You can also move a picture by pressing the arrow keys when the Content Tool is selected. Enter negative values to offset the picture to the left or upward from the top left corner of the box.

Rotating a Picture Within a Box

You can rotate a picture box using the Rotation tool, but to rotate the picture within the box at a different angle than the box, you must select the Item ➤ Modify command or the Measurements palette. You can rotate a picture numerically without rotating the picture box that contains it by entering an angle value (from –360 to 360 degrees) in the Picture Rotate field, or you can enter an angle value in the second ∡ field of the Measurements palette. (The first ↻ field is used to rotate the picture box.) If you have previously rotated the picture, the amount by which the picture has been rotated will show in these areas.

In entering angles of rotation in either the Picture Box Specifications dialog box or the Measurements palette, a positive value indicates a counterclockwise rotation, a negative value rotates the picture clockwise.

Skewing a Picture Within a Box

Skewing a picture within a box changes the angle of its vertical axis. Skew a picture by entering degree values (from 0 to 75) in the ∠7 field of the Measurements palette. In entering skew angles, a positive value skews the top of the picture toward the right, a negative value skews the top of the picture toward the left.

You can also select Item ➤ Modify to display the Picture Box Specifications dialog box and skew a picture numerically by entering a percentage value in the Picture Skew field. If you have previously skewed the picture, the amount by which the picture has been skewed will show in this dialog box.

Applying Color and Contrast to Pictures

Certain picture types can have color, shade, contrast, and halftone screen applied to them. This section will discuss applying color, shade, and contrast to a graphic, and the next section will detail applying halftone screens to graphics.

Color and shade can be applied to picture box frames and backgrounds as described in Chapter 2. But you can also apply color to certain kinds of pictures. The commands listed under the Style menu for pictures will be available depending on what type of picture is active when you view the menu. When a picture box containing an imported black-and-white bitmap or TIFF picture is active and the Content tool (☞) is selected, the Style menu (Figure 6-28) shows commands that let you adjust a picture's color and shade (separate from the picture *box's* background color and shade), as well as the contrast and line screen of the picture.

```
Style
Color                    ▶
Shade                    ▶
Negative              Ctrl+Shift+-
✓ Normal Contrast     Ctrl+Shift+N
  High Contrast       Ctrl+Shift+H
  Posterized          Ctrl+Shift+P
  Other Contrast...   Ctrl+Shift+C
✓ Normal Screen
  60-lpi Line Screen/0°
  30-lpi Line Screen/45°
  20-lpi Dot Screen/45°
  Other Screen...     Ctrl+Shift+S
```

Figure 6-28 Style Menu when a picture is active.

The Style menu commands cannot be applied to object-oriented PIC or EPS format pictures. The table below (Figure 6-29) summarizes the Style menu commands that can be applied to various picture formats.

Picture Type	Color	Shade	Negative	Contrast	Screen
Bitmaps, TIFFs and Metafiles					
Color	No	No	Yes	No	No
Grayscale	Yes	Yes	Yes	Yes	Yes
Line Art	Yes	Yes	Yes	No	Yes
EPS	No	No	No	No	No

Figure 6-29 Style Menu commands that can be applied to various picture formats.

Applying Color and Shade to a Picture

To apply a color to a picture, first select the picture box that contains the image, then choose a color from the Color submenu (Figure 6-30) under the Style menu. This list includes the QuarkXPress default colors plus any that you have added using the Edit → Colors command.

Figure 6-30   The Color submenu.

To apply color to a picture using the Colors palette (Figure 6-31), click on the icon for the picture box content and click on a color from the list.

Figure 6-31   You can apply color to certain types of pictures using the Colors palette.

To apply a shade using the Style menu, first select the picture box that contains the image, then choose a shade from the Shade drop-down list under the Style menu. You can choose from the listed shades in 10 percent increments, or enter any value in .1 percent-increments in the Shade dialog box by choosing Other. Apply a shade using the Colors palette by selecting a shade from the drop-down list or inputting a value in the field adjacent to the Shade drop-down list.

The color and shade that you apply will affect all areas of the image that would otherwise print as black or a shade of gray. If you specified a Color and Shade for the box background using the Item → Modify command or the Colors palette, then the box background will appear in any transparent areas of the bitmap or TIFF image.

As mentioned earlier, you cannot use Style menu commands to change the colors or shades of an imported color image, an object-oriented PIC, or EPS formats.

Applying Contrast to a Picture

Contrast is a term used to describe the relationship between the light and dark areas of an image. Contrast settings can be adjusted for imported grayscale bitmap, metafile, or TIFF images. Contrast cannot be applied to line art, color images, or EPS files.

Normal contrast is the picture's original contrast when imported into QuarkXPress (the contrast that was set up in the scanning process or in a photo retouching application). High-contrast settings make the light areas lighter and the dark areas darker. Low-contrast settings have the reverse effect, making light areas darker and dark areas lighter.

Applying Predefined Contrast Settings

In QuarkXPress you can select commands under the Style menu to choose from three predefined contrast settings (Figure 6-32) or to set your own custom contrast.

Normal contrast is, of course, the default setting. Normal contrast displays as a 45°-line in the Picture Contrast Specifications dialog box (Style → Other Contrast). This line basically indicates that the "input", or original value of an image will be "output", or printed, at the same value. For example, 5 percent grays will display 5 percent grays. The output values can be adjusted to produce alternate effects or to actually improve an image, as discussed below.

Choose Style → High Contrast (CTRL+SHIFT+H) to convert the picture to two shades of gray: solid black and white. When you select high contrast, QuarkXPress converts all shades below 30 percent black to white, and all shades above 30 percent to black. Choose Style → Posterized (CTRL+SHIFT+P) to convert the picture to six levels of gray (including black and white as two of the gray levels).

Choose Style → Other Contrast (CTRL+SHIFT+C) to display the Picture Contrast Specifications dialog box and set custom contrast, as described below. Choose Style → Normal Contrast (CTRL+SHIFT+N) to reset the picture to the original contrast at which it was imported. The contrast setting affects only the way QuarkXPress displays and prints the image, not the way the image is stored or saved.

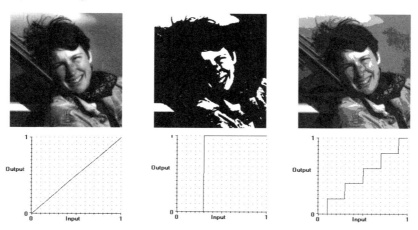

Figure 6-32 Examples of normal contrast (left), high contrast (center), and posterized (right).

Creating Negative Images

Choose Style → Negative (CTRL+SHIFT+hyphen) to create a negative of the image based on the *Normal curve* settings. This selection reverses any changes made to the contrast curves (described under the next sections) and is the same as checking the Negative field in the Contrast dialog box.

Applying Custom Contrast

Choose Style → Other Contrast (CTRL+SHIFT+C) to display the Picture Contrast Specifications dialog box (Figure 6-33). The chart in this dialog box maps the darkness percentages of the input (the original image as imported) to darkness upon output (on the screen and when printed). The best way to see how the chart works is to study how it changes under the three predefined contrast settings.

The Picture Contrast Specifications dialog box provides nine tools on the left of the box to help you adjust the contrast.

Figure 6-33   The Picture Contrast Specifications dialog box set to darken midtones in an image.

- Click on the **Hand** tool (☝) and use the hand to drag the entire curve around on the chart. Hold down the SHIFT key to constrain the movement to horizontal or vertical.
- Click on the **Pencil** tool (✎) and click anywhere on the chart to create spikes or drag any point on the chart to reshape the curve in any path.
- Click on the **Line** tool (\) and drag any point on the chart to reshape the curve in straight lines. Hold down the SHIFT key to constrain the lines to 45° angles: 0°, 45°, or 90°.
- Click on the **Posterizer** tool (↗) to create handles *in between* the 10 percent incremental marks on the curve. Click on the **Spike** tool (↗) to create handles *on* the 10 percent incremental marks on the curve. You can then move each handle in any direction.
- Click on the **Normal Contrast** tool (◢) to set the picture back to its original contrast. This is the same as choosing Style ➤ Normal Contrast.
- Click on the **High Contrast** tool (◼) to set the picture to high contrast. This is the same as choosing Style ➤ High Contrast.
- Click on the **Posterized Contrast** tool (◢) to set the picture to posterized contrast. This is the same as choosing Style ➤ Posterized.
- Click on the **Inversion** tool (↻) to rotate the curve around an imaginary line that is parallel to the X-axis and bisects the curve, thereby creating a negative of the image by changing the *current curve* settings.
- Check the **Negative** box to create a negative of the image based on the *Normal curve* settings. This is the same as choosing Style ➤ Negative.

Normally, the changes you make in the dialog box will not be reflected on the page display until you click Apply or use the keyboard shortcut CTRL+A (to view the effects and still have a chance to change or cancel them) or OK (to apply the changes). If you hold the ALT key and click Apply or use the keyboard shortcut CTRL+ALT+A, you can see the effects of the changes as you make them, but this might be a slow process if the image is very large. Click CTRL+Z while the dialog box is open to reverse the most recent change.

Defining Halftone Screens

In QuarkXPress you can import *line art* that is composed of solid black-and-white areas or *grayscale* images that are continuous-tone images (such as photographs) incorporating shades of gray as well as black and white. In traditional publishing, a photograph that has been prepared for printing is called a *halftone* rather than a grayscale image. With traditional methods, a halftone is created by photographing the artwork through a *screen* so that dots are produced, since a printing press has to simulate gray tones with dots of different sizes. See "Screen Angles" in Chapter 7 for more information on traditional halftone screens.

The term "screening" has therefore carried over to the electronic process applied through QuarkXPress. The fineness of a screen is defined in terms of lines per inch (lpi) and is as important as setting resolution when printing a high-resolution continuous-tone image.

The halftone settings in QuarkXPress let you specify the line screen (lines per inch), screen angle, and dot shape that will define the pattern of dots in the halftone that you print of grayscale TIFF images.

Applying Predefined Screen Settings

The Style menu offers four predefined settings, or you can set your own custom screen angle and line frequency. Choose 60-lpi Line Screen/0° (Figure 6–34), 30-lpi Line Screen/45° (Figure 6–35), or 20-Line Dot Screen/45° (Figure 6-36) to print the active image at one of the three most common lines per inch and angle settings. Choose Style → Other Screen (CTRL+SHIFT+S) to display the Picture Screening Specifications dialog box (Figure 6-37) and set custom line frequency and angle, as described under the next heading.

Figure 6-34   60-lpi Line Screen/0°. "Screen" lines are spaced 60 lines per inch, 0° (horizontal).

Figure 6-35   30-lpi Line Screen/45°. "Screen" lines are spaced 30 lines per inch, at 45° angle.

Figure 6-36   20-Line Dot Screen/45°. "Screen" dots are spaced 20 lines per inch, at 45° angle.

The halftone screen setting affects only the way QuarkXPress prints the image, not the way the image is displayed, stored, or saved. You can change screen settings or convert to normal screen at any time. Choose Style ➔ Normal Screen to reset the picture to the normal setting of a 45° angle, with the line frequency determined by the value entered in the

Halftone Screen field in the Printer Setup dialog box (as described in Chapter 8 on Printing).

Applying Custom Screens

Choose Style → Other Screen (CTRL+SHIFT+S) to display the Picture Screening Specifications dialog box.

Figure 6-37 The Picture Screening Specifications dialog box.

Screen

You can enter any value from 15 to 400 lines per inch in the Screen field. If you leave the Screen field blank, the default frequency defined in the Halftone Screen field in the Printer Setup dialog box will be used in printing. The normal default—60 lpi—is the most common setting for printing halftone pictures in newspapers. A 300 dpi printer cannot accurately reproduce screens finer than 75 lpi. Higher line frequencies will not display accurately on most monitors and will work best when printed on high-resolution printers and on glossy paper stocks or film.

Divide twice the number of *lines per inch* in the screen into the *dots per inch* resolution of the output device to get an idea of how many dots *wide* each line will be. On a 300 dpi printer, for example, a 60-lpi line screen will print with only five dots per black line/white line pair, leaving only two to three dots for the line width. Finer screens would be imperceptible to the human eye when printed on a 300 dpi printer. When printed at 1270 dpi, however, the same screen will print with up to 10 dots per line; you could specify up to a 130-lpi line screen and still get good results at 1270 dpi. (All of the images in preceding figures were printed at 1270 dpi on a Linotronic typesetter.)

Screen Angle

You can enter any angle between 0 and 360 in the Angle field, but the most common settings are in 15° increments. In entering angles of rotation, a positive value indicates a counterclockwise rotation, a negative value is measured clockwise.

Screen Pattern

Select Pattern to choose from five different halftone screens: Dot, Line, Ellipse, Square (Figure 6-38), or Ordered Dither. The Ordered Dither screen pattern is designed for printing grayscale images on a low-resolution laser printer, such as a 300 dpi laser printer, and should not be used when your output will be reproduced using offset lithography.

Figure 6-38   Examples of different halftone screen patterns.

Click Display Halftoning to preview the effects of the settings you have chosen. Once you have previewed the image, it is a good idea to turn this option off, since it slows down the screen display. Note that you can specify line frequencies and angles for active imported images only—shaded lines, box frames, and box backgrounds specified in QuarkXPress are always printed using the Halftone Screen field in the Printer Setup dialog box.

Summary

Now that you know the alternatives available for adding graphics to a page, you can decide whether to use QuarkXPress or another program to create various graphics, and which other applications to use. The next chapter discusses the use of color in QuarkXPress, and Chapter 8 describes printing procedures. Chapter 13 offers tips on advanced graphic techniques.

7 *Color*

One of the most exciting aspects of desktop publishing today is the ability to create high-quality color documents directly from your personal computer. Over the last several years, desktop publishing applications have made significant inroads into the world of color prepress, the process of preparing pages for printing on an offset press. There are two basic ways color can be reproduced on press: with "spot" color specifications requiring special pre-mixed inks; and through process color separation, in which color pages are broken down into four separate pieces of film representing the primary press inks (cyan, magenta, yellow and black) necessary for full color reproduction.

This has been possible due to a variety of technological advances, including capabilities offered by QuarkXPress. Since the release of QuarkXPress 3.0 on the Macintosh, QuarkXPress users have had the option of producing color separations of pages, including those containing Encapsulated PostScript (EPS) illustrations, and, with the help of other programs, pages containing continuous-tone color images (that is, color photographs). In this chapter we discuss how to create and apply colors in QuarkXPress and how to create color separations.

General Considerations

In order to take advantage of QuarkXPress' excellent capabilities for printing color separations, it's important to understand some of the basics of color printing. With desktop publishing, for the first time, designers and production staff have been given technology that allows them to directly control the entire prepress process. Whether you choose to take advantage of these capabilities is a matter of individual choice.

The computer can be part of the production of final film for printing at various levels. For example, many times pages are created in QuarkXPress and output to film, with traditional process color separations stripped in manually. However, it is becoming more practical to bring together all elements on a page, including high-resolution images, and output them directly from QuarkXPress to a PostScript imagesetter.

No matter which alternative you choose, it is imperative that you talk to your printer before preparing any job that involves printing in color. The best method will often be dictated by the economics of time or cost for a specific job.

Color Calibration

If you've worked with creating color separations on a personal computer, you know that there are many variables that come into play in getting the results you're looking for. One key challenge is calibrating the color definition on display and output devices. This allows you to achieve the most predictable results possible.

There are a variety of solutions for monitor calibration on the Macintosh, ranging from simple, no-cost solutions to hardware and software solutions that cost thousands of dollars. On the PC platform, however, there are currently only the simple solutions: some common-sense steps can help ensure consistency in the colors that appear on your monitor. For example, keep the lighting conditions stable in the room where you're working, which usually means using artificial light that has the same brightness at all times of day, or using a color swatchbook, discussed later in this chapter, to select colors. It's reasonable to expect that solutions for color calibration for both Windows and QuarkXPress will be developed in the future.

Another important calibration that needs to be made for working with color separations is the adjustment of the imagesetter that will be used to output film. It's important to adjust the gray screens printed on the imagesetter to match those used by a software program, so that, for example, a 10 percent screen really prints as 10 percent, rather then 12.5 percent. A key piece of equipment, called a densitometer, is often used by service bureaus to measure the actual screen percentages printed by an imagesetter.

Regardless of how carefully you calibrate your monitor or imagesetter, it's important to obtain a quality color proof of your work. In the simplest case, this might be a printout on a 300- or 400-dpi color printer. In the case of pages containing color photographs, a proof made from the actual film, such as a proof created on a Matchprint or Chromalin system, is necessary.

Spot Color vs. Process Color

As mentioned at the beginning of this chapter, there are generally two ways to prepare film for color printing jobs. One is to create separate plates for printing with spot colors; the other is to create separate plates for each of the four process colors—cyan, magenta, yellow, and black. Spot color separations, often used for drawn illustrations and solid-color graphics, usually involve preparing film that will be used by a printer when premixed inks will be used in the printing process. PANTONE colors are one of the most common systems for premixing inks. Film prepared for a spot color printing job includes a layer of film output for each premixed ink.

Process color, usually used for continuous-tone images, like photographs, is made up of four inks—the three subtractive primaries, yellow, cyan, and magenta, plus black—printed one on top of the other in a pattern of halftone dots. Both spot color and process color require separation of color elements, and QuarkXPress lets you specify either type of separations for any color you create.

Offset printing presses produce spot color by filling each ink well(s) of the press with one premixed color. If the press has only one ink well, the job would be run through once with one color, then the pages would be allowed to dry, the press would be cleaned and filled with a second color, and the dry pages would be run through a second time for the second color. Many print shops have presses that can print two or more colors in one run, but each individual color requires a separate plate, or color separation in any case.

On the other hand, to understand process color, think about a pointillist painting. The painting actually consists of many minute dots of paint, but the eye blends the dots into solid tones. Similarly, in four-color process printing adjacent dots of ink printed in different colors—usually cyan, magenta, yellow, and black—will be interpreted as a single color by the eye. For example, in areas where yellow and cyan are printed together the eye will perceive green.

Screen Angles

As mentioned earlier, the film that must be generated to produce plates for four-color process printing consists of a pattern of halftone dots for each color—cyan, magenta, yellow, and black. Traditional halftone screens are generated by photographing an image through a screen that actually contains dots of various sizes (Figure 7-1). Lighter areas of an image are made up of smaller dots, darker areas are created by larger dots. The spacing of the lines of dots is called the screen frequency, or screen lines per inch (lpi).

Figure 7-1 A traditional halftone screen enlarged.

If cyan, magenta, yellow, and black were printed directly on top of each other, the result would be muddy and inexact colors. So in traditional color printing, each color is printed at an angle; the combined angles, when printed together, form tiny rosettes of color, which simulate a particular hue. The algorithms for the angle of rotation necessary, called *irrational* angles, were developed by Dr. -Ing. Rudolph Hell GmbH., the parent company of Hell Graphics Systems, now Linotype-Hell Co., and all prepress systems have licensed these screen angles for use on their equipment. The traditional screen angles rotate cyan at 105°, magenta at 75°, yellow at 0° or 90°, and black at 45°.

To understand some of the potential problems of printing color separations to PostScript imagesetters, it's important to understand how PostScript devices simulate halftone screens. Imagesetters cannot physically create dots of various sizes; a pixel is either on or off. In order to create halftone dots, an imagesetter prints pixels that are grouped in cells, with each cell corresponding to a halftone dot, thus simulating the traditional halftone dot. On an imagesetter, the only line frequencies possible are those that divide evenly into the resolution of the imagesetter, since it cannot print half of a pixel. As a result, color separations printed on PostScript imagesetters cannot always accurately reproduce irrational screens. Sometimes they produce moiré patterns in color images.

Since producing irrational screens requires tremendous computational power, Adobe has licensed Linotype-Hell's *rational tangent* screening (RT screening) algorithm, which approximates the ideal values. RT screening, however, limits the variety of screen angles and frequencies that can be achieved and varies the screen frequency from plate to plate, producing unsatisfactory results, especially moirés, with some images. Most PostScript imagesetters manufactured before 1991 use RT screening. Newer imagesetters, however, are employing improved screening methods.

High Quality Screening (HQS)

The merger of Hell Graphics and the Linotype Company has led to the incorporation of some of Hell's irrational screen technology in Linotype's PostScript RIP 30 and RIP 40. High Quality Screening (HQS) algorithms approximate traditional screen angles by modifying the traditional angles only slightly (Figure 7-2). For an image set to print with a line frequency of 133 lpi, each plate printed using HQS angles varies from the traditional angles somewhat, but the variance from plate to plate is much less than RT angles.

Process Color	Traditional Angle/Screen	RT Screening Angle/Screen	HQS Screening Angle/Screen
Cyan	15°/133 lpi	18.435°/133.871 lpi	15.0037°/138.142 lpi
Magenta	75°/133 lpi	71.565°/133.871 lpi	74.9987°/138.142 lpi
Yellow	0°/133 lpi	0°/127 lpi	0°/138.545 lpi
Black	45°/133 lpi	45°/119.737 lpi	45°/138.158 lpi

Figure 7-2 Traditional irrational screening vs. RT screening vs. HQS screening.

Adobe Accurate Screens

Accurate Screens is a technology for optimizing the results of process printing that has been developed by Adobe Systems Incorporated. Accurate Screening uses a rational algorithm that attempts to eliminate the need for the heavy computational power required by irrational screening algorithms.

Accurate Screen first examines the difference between the desired screen and the achievable screen. When the program determines that the optimum screen and angle would require printing half a pixel, it builds a "supercell" and distributes the error over that supercell. For example, if a cell measuring 14.5 pixels is required, Accurate Screens builds a supercell of 29 pixels representing the same dot size that would have previously been represented by 14.5 pixels. By using memory more efficiently, more cells are possible than before.

Creating Colors

QuarkXPress lets you create colors and apply them to selected items on a page. Although color pages created in QuarkXPress can be printed directly on a color printer, most often the final document is reproduced in color by an offset printing press. Once colors are created, QuarkXPress offers the option of automatically separating colors through the Print command. QuarkXPress can print color separations of any elements that have been assigned colors through QuarkXPress commands, as well as color separations of certain types of pictures.

You can create new colors in QuarkXPress using the Edit Colors dialog box (Edit → Color). This dialog box offers similar types of options as those offered in the Edit Style Sheets dialog box or the Edit H&Js dialog box: You can add to the preset default list of colors or append colors set up in another QuarkXPress document. The preset default list of colors includes black, blue, cyan, green, magenta, red, registration, white, and yellow. Only blue, green, and red can be deleted from the default list.

If you choose Edit → Colors when no document is open, changes you make to the color palette are stored as part of the QuarkXPress program. If you choose Edit → Colors when a document is open, changes you make to the color palette are stored as part of that document only.

The first dialog box displayed when you choose Edit → Colors (Figure 7-3) shows the list of colors currently available and offers several options.

Figure 7-3   The Colors dialog box.

Click **New** to get the Colors dialog box and create a new color. Click on a color name and then click Edit (or press ENTER) to change the specifications set up for a current color, click **Duplicate** to create a new color based on an existing color, or click **Delete** to remove a color from the list. If you Edit a color, all of the elements in the document that have been assigned that color will change to reflect the new color definition. If you delete a color, black is substituted wherever that color was applied. (You cannot edit or delete the primary colors used by QuarkXPress: cyan, magenta, yellow, black, or white.)

Click **Append** to import the color palette from another QuarkXPress document. Click **Edit Trap** to change the specifications in printing traps for a selected color. Click **Save** to save any changes that you make or **Cancel** to reverse any changes you made through this dialog box or its subsidiaries, as described under the next headings.

The Edit Color Dialog Box

The Edit Color dialog box (Figure 7-4) is displayed when you choose New, Edit, or Duplicate from the Colors dialog box. You must enter a Name for a new color, or you can change the name shown in this field. The name you assign appears in the Color submenu and drop-down lists, and is listed in the Plate drop-down list in the Print dialog box if Process Separation is not checked. If you check Process Separation, the color is reproduced by printing cyan, magenta, yellow, and black plates.

Figure 7-4 The Edit Color dialog box.

You can create or edit any color using any of six color models: Hue, Saturation, and Brightness (HSB); Red, Green, and Blue (RGB); Cyan, Magenta, Yellow, and Black (CMYK); PANTONE colors; TRUMATCH colors; or FOCALTONE colors. Regardless of how a color was initially created—using the HSB, RGB, CMYK, PANTONE, TRUMATCH, or FOCALTONE system—you can switch to any other system to edit the color further. The most commonly used color models for preparing colors for separation for offset printing are CMYK, PANTONE, TRUMATCH, or FOCOLTONE. CMYK and PANTONE colors may be designated as either spot colors or process color, by turning Process Separation on or off in the Edit Colors dialog box. TRUMATCH and FOCOLTONE colors were designed to be used to designate process color printing only.

Whichever method you choose, the color you create is automatically displayed in the New area of the dialog box, and the color wheel marker, percentage entries, and scroll bars all reflect your current changes. The Old area of the dialog box shows the color as defined when you chose Edit or Duplicate on the previous dialog box. You can click on the Old color to reset all values to the original color.

If Process Separation is checked, then the color you are creating or editing is broken into the four process colors when you print separations through the File ➤ Print command. Otherwise, the color—including PANTONE colors—is separated onto a single separate color plate bearing the color's name (when separations are specified in the Print dialog box; see Chapter 8 for more information on printing).

Click OK to end the editing process, and be sure to click Save in the Colors dialog box in order to save all of the colors you create or change for this document. Once your file is set up with the desired colors and is set to produce spot or process separations properly, check Registration Marks and Make Separations in the Print dialog box (File ➤ Print). The Plate drop-down list shows all the colors in the document that were created using the Edit ➤ Colors command. If you choose to print a plate for all the colors in a document, QuarkXPress only prints plates for colors that actually have been applied to items in the document, plus the black plate for all pages.

 If the Colors palette is displayed (View ➤ Show Colors), you can access the Edit Colors dialog box quickly by holding down the CTRL key and clicking on the name of a color.

HSB Color Model

Hue, Saturation, and Brightness (HSB) is the common system for identifying the way in which artists' paints are mixed. *Hue* is the quality that gives a color its name, such as red, orange, yellow, green, blue, and violet. *Saturation* is a measure of the tint, or purity of a color. *Brightness* is a measure of the amount of light reflected from a color; black reflects almost no light and white reflects almost all light.

To create a color, enter a percentage value in the fields for Hue, Saturation, and Brightness, or use the scroll bars adjacent to each to indicate values. You can also click in the color wheel to indicate Hue and Saturation, and use the scroll bar to indicate Brightness. The color created is displayed in the dialog box. This color is a simulation only; you can expect some variation from the color displayed on the monitor and the final printed color.

RGB Color Model

Red, Green, and Blue (RGB) are the colors used to display color on computer monitors. To create a color, enter a percentage value in the fields for Red, Green, and Blue, or use the scroll bars adjacent to each to indicate values. You can also click in the color wheel to indicate color. The color created is displayed in the dialog box. This color is a simulation only; you can expect some variation from the color displayed on the monitor and the final printed color.

CMYK Color Model

When you choose the cyan, magenta, yellow, and black (CMYK) color model, QuarkXPress displays a color wheel (Figure 7-5). The wheel represents the hue and saturation, and the scroll bar represents the value, or the lightness and darkness of a color.

To create a color, first type in a name, then specify the percentages of CMYK desired by typing a value in the field adjacent to each color, or by using the scroll bars. The color you specify is displayed in the dialog box. Bear in mind this is a simulation only. You can expect some variation from the color displayed on the monitor and the final printed color. You can specify CMYK colors to print spot color or process color separations.

Figure 7-5 The Edit Colors dialog box when the CMYK color model is selected.

Color Swatchbooks

For spot color printing, you must specify precisely what color you want the offset print shop to use. There are a number of different ways of doing this. For example, you can give the printer a sample of the color you want—it can be a piece of paper, a piece of material, anything—and indicate that it be duplicated as closely as possible.

A more precise way of specifying color is to use a color matching system, such as the PANTONE Matching System (PMS). PMS ink swatchbooks can be purchased at any graphic arts supply store. Printers can usually get most of these types of inks, or they will mix the inks they have to match your swatch. You can create a color in QuarkXPress by specifying PANTONE color numbers in the Edit Colors dialog box (as described later in this section).

Even though you can see colors used on QuarkXPress pages if you have a color monitor, it is a good idea to have an ink swatchbook available for reference. Color monitors can give you only an approximation of what the final printed color will really look like. Also, you can create colors on a monochrome monitor by applying specifications shown in the swatchbook. Ink swatchbooks generally give you a sample of a wide range of different inks, printed on both coated and uncoated paper. Paper type is very important; the appearance of the ink varies a great deal depending on the type of paper on which it is printed. In general, inks appear more brilliant on coated papers, softer and duller on uncoated papers. Finally, the swatchbook is a good reference when specifying spot colors at the print shop.

PANTONE Color Model

The PANTONE MATCHING SYSTEM is one of the most widely used systems for identifying ink colors. The system is based on nine basic PANTONE colors plus black and white. When mixed in various percentages, these colors yield the more than 700 colors in the system. PANTONE colors are cataloged in a swatchbook; choosing a color from this system ensures accurate color reproduction on a press.

To select a color from the PANTONE system, either type in the full name in the Name area, or enter a number in the PANTONE No. area underneath the display of colors (Figure 7-6). You can also scroll through the display of colors and click on a color. The color you specify is displayed in the dialog box.

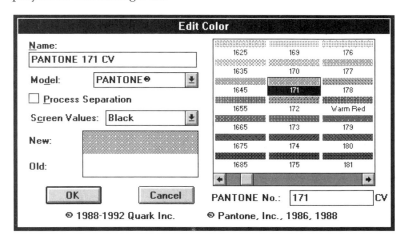

Figure 7-6 The Edit Colors dialog box when the PANTONE color model is selected.

This color is a simulation of the PANTONE color; the "CV" behind each color name indicates the color is a computer video simulation of the actual PANTONE color. Like CMYK colors, you can specify that PANTONE colors be printed as spot colors or process colors. Greatest accuracy will be achieved if you choose a spot color separation and let your printer mix the ink according to the color shown in the PANTONE swatchbook. QuarkXPress separates the PANTONE color to its process color equivalent, but some colors may vary from the original PANTONE color when finally printed by this method.

TRUMATCH Color Model

The TRUMATCH system was developed for achieving optimum results in printing process color separations using PostScript output devices. The TRUMATCH system is based on 50 different hues, with value graduations or tints of each color, totaling some 2,000 colors. It is essential to use the TRUMATCH swatchbook, called the TRUMATCH Colorfinder, when creating colors using this system, since your monitor can only approximate the color on the screen.

To select a color from the TRUMATCH system, either type in the full name in the Name area, or enter a number in the TRUMATCH No. area underneath the display of colors (Figure 7-7).

Figure 7-7 The Edit Colors dialog box when the TRUMATCH color model is selected.

You can also scroll through the display of colors and click on a color. Since the TRUMATCH colors were designed for process colors, turn on Process Separation for best results.

FOCOLTONE Color Model

Like the TRUMATCH color system, the FOCOLTONE system was created to facilitate the selection of accurate process colors. The basic 763 FOCOLTONE colors consist of combinations of cyan, magenta, yellow, and black in varying percentages from 5 to 85 percent, in 5 percent increments. Additionally, 13 variations on each color are created by eliminating one, two, or three of the process colors. For example, color #1000, a light brown, contains 15 percent cyan, 30 percent magenta, 50 percent yellow, and 25 percent black. Variation number 1, color #1001, contains 15 percent cyan, 30 percent magenta, 50 percent yellow, and 0 percent black.

To select a color from the FOCOLTONE system, either type in the full name in the Name area, or enter a number in the FOCOLTONE No. area underneath the display of colors (Figure 7-8). You can also scroll through the display of colors and click on a color. Since the FOCOLTONE colors were designed for process colors, turn on Process Separation for best results.

Figure 7-8 The Edit Colors dialog box when the FOCOLTONE color model is selected.

Appending Colors

If you click Append in the Colors dialog box (Figure 7-9), QuarkXPress displays a directory dialog box through which you can select the document containing the colors you want to append.

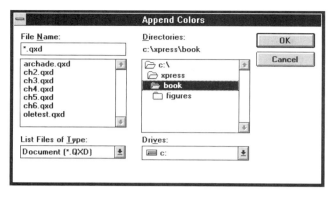

Figure 7-9   The Append colors dialog box.

Append imports all colors from the selected document except those that have the same names as colors already in the palette of the active document. You can define up to 128 colors in one palette.

The Edit Trap Dialog Box

The Edit Trap dialog box allows you to specify trapping relationships between colors in a QuarkXPress document. Trapping controls the way two colors print when they are adjacent to each other, by overprinting, knocking out, or overlapping slightly (spreading or choking).

You can also specify the Automatic trapping used by QuarkXPress in the Application Preferences dialog box (Edit ► Preferences ► Application), or you can specify trapping on an item-by-item basis using the Trap Information palette (View ► Show Trap Information). Each of these methods is discussed in detail later in this chapter.

Applying Color

QuarkXPress comes with nine preset colors that are displayed on the Style ► Color submenu and on the drop-down lists in dialog boxes. You can apply color to text or text rules through the Style ► Character and Style ► Rules commands; the Style menu lets you apply color to selected lines drawn using QuarkXPress' tools, or an imported Black-and-White bitmap picture or TIFF picture. (You cannot change the color of color pictures that have been imported into QuarkXPress, nor can you change the color of EPS files.) You can specify color for a box background through the Item ► Modify command, or for a box frame through the Item ► Frame command. The fastest way to apply color, however, is using the

Colors palette (View ► Show Colors), which lets you apply color to all of the above items (except rules in text).

Applying Color to Text, Rules, and Pictures

To apply a color to text or to an imported picture, first select the item with the Content tool (🖑) then choose the color from the Style ► Color submenu. For text, highlight the text you want to color, then select color from the Style ► Color submenu; or you can also apply color through the color drop-down list in the Character Attributes dialog box (Figure 7-10).

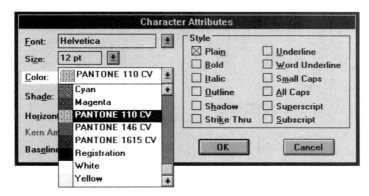

Figure 7-10   You can apply color to selected text through the Character Attributes dialog box, or make it part of a style sheet through the Edit ► Style Sheets command.

You can also apply color to text or pictures using the Colors palette (View ► Show Colors). For text, select text and click on the text icon, then click on a color in the list. For pictures, make sure the picture box is active and the Content tool is selected, then click on the icon for the content of the picture box and choose a color from the list (Figure 7-11).

Figure 7-11   The Colors palette set to apply color to text (left) and to a picture (right).

The color and shade that you apply to an imported picture using the Style → Color submenu (Figure 7-12) or the Colors palette affect all areas of the image that would otherwise print as black or a shade of gray; white areas are not affected.

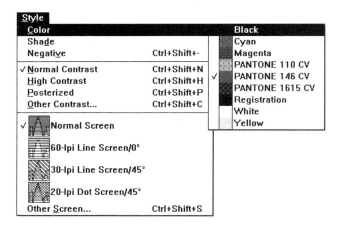

Figure 7-12   You can apply color to imported pictures through the Style → Color submenu.

To apply color to rules above or below paragraphs, select Style → Rules. You can then specify color in the Paragraph Rules dialog box (Figure 7–13).

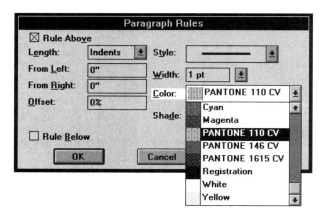

Figure 7-13   You can apply color to selected Paragraph rules through the Style → Rules command.

Applying Color to Lines and Box Backgrounds

To apply color to a line or to the background of a box drawn using QuarkXPress tools, first select the item, then select the Item → Modify command and choose a color from the Line Specifications dialog box, the Picture Box Specifications dialog box, the Text Box Specifications dialog box, or the Colors palette (Figure 7-14). To apply color to lines, you can also use the Style → Color submenu.

Figure 7-14 You can apply color to active lines through the Item → Modify command (left) or by using the Colors palette (right).

When you apply color to a box, the box background appears behind text and in the white areas of an imported bitmap or TIFF image (Figure 7-15). (Background color does not show through color TIFF or EPS images.)

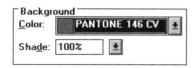

Figure 7-15 You can apply color to the background of an active picture box or an active text box through the Item → Modify command.

To apply color to the frame around a box, first select the item, then select the Item → Frame command (Figure 7-16), or use the Colors palette.

Figure 7-16 You can apply color to the frame around an active box through the Item → Frame command.

Applying Two-color Blends

QuarkXPress allows you to apply simple two-color blends to box backgrounds using the Colors palette. With a text or picture box active, select the background icon in the Colors palette, choose Linear Blend from the drop-down list, then specify the color and shades of color you wish to blend.

Step 1   With a picture or text box active, select the background icon in the Colors palette and choose Linear Blend from the drop-down list (Figure 7-17).

Figure 7-17 Select Linear Blend from the drop-down list in the Colors palette.

Step 2   Make sure the button for color #1 is selected, then choose the color and shade for the first color of the blend; click on the button for color #2 and choose the color and shade of the second color. Specify the angle of the blend (Figure 7-18).

Chapter 7: Color 279

Figure 7-18 Use the Colors palette to apply two-color blends to box backgrounds; select the color and shade of color #1 (left), then select the color and shade of color #2 (right).

Step 3   Click on the box with the Item tool selected, or deselect the box if the Content tool is selected to view the blend (Figure 7-19).

Figure 7-19   View the blend by selecting the box with the Item tool.

You can select two different colors to blend, or you can specify different shades of the same color. You can specify any angle from 0° to 360° in .001° increments.

Applying Registration "Color"

The Registration color is normally set to black, but you can change it to any color for on-screen display. You can apply the Registration color to any elements on a page. These elements then print on every separation plate—regardless of their on-screen color setting—when Make Separations is selected on the Print dialog box. You can select QuarkXPress' line tool to draw your own cut or fold marks, for instance, and print them on every plate.

Working with Trapping

If your printing job uses more than one color, but elements of different colors do not touch each other directly, then printing is fairly simple. But if elements do touch—for example, if you have yellow type in the middle of a magenta box—then these elements meet precisely, and problems can occur on the printing press. If the elements are even a hairline out of register, you will see it in the printed piece (either as a dark line where they overlap or as a white line where they don't overlap). In color printing, these registration problems are controlled with trapping, generally by causing one color to overprint another very slightly.

You can avoid trapping problems by "designing" out colors that will be problematic when printing. One common way to do this is to ensure that all the colors you use share a common process color. You could, for example, add 5 percent black to all colors, and avoid any serious trapping problems.

When you can't avoid problem colors that need to be trapped, you'll find that QuarkXPress greatly simplifies the process of setting up trapping controls. In addition to specifying trapping relationships between colors on a document-wide basis, QuarkXPress also lets you define automatic trapping and allows you to specify trapping on an item-by-item basis.

Setting Automatic Trapping

The default method that QuarkXPress uses to trap colors can be defined in the Application Preferences dialog box (Edit → Preferences → Application) shown in Figure 7-20. The default method of trapping is referred to as Automatic trapping, and it is based on the relative value (lightness or darkness) of object and background colors.

Figure 7-20 Trapping options in the Application Preferences dialog box.

In the Application Preferences dialog box, the settings that can be adjusted are as follows:

The QuarkXPress Handbook

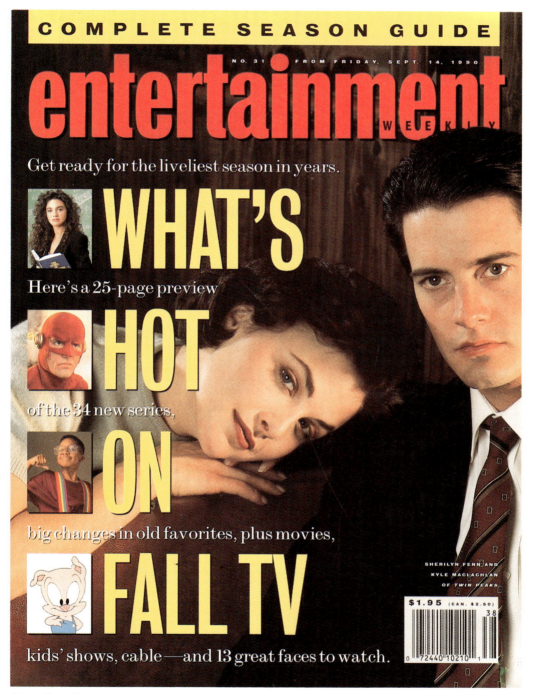

Cover from Entertainment Weekly. All photos were scanned and separated through Visionary on a Scitex system. Original size 8" x 10¾". See Chapter 15.

The QuarkXPress Handbook

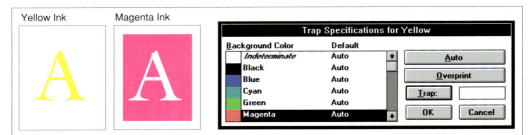

Trapping for Yellow in regards to Magenta specified as Automatic.

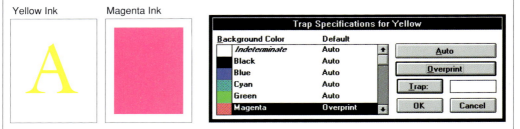

Trapping for Yellow in regards to Magenta specified as Overprint.

Trapping for Yellow in regards to Magenta specified to "choke" .75 pt.

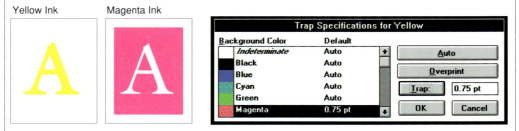

Trapping for Yellow in regards to Magenta specified to "spread" .75 pt. See Chapter 7.

The QuarkXPress Handbook

Edit Color dialog box with CMYK (top) and PANTONE (bottom) selected. See Chapter 7.

The QuarkXPress Handbook

5.08

Packaging   Colour coding

When similar products need to be both related and differentiated at the same time, follow these guidelines:

• use the same layout on the main panel of all packages to help relate them
• use different colours on each package to help differentiate them.

As shown in the examples, the colour coding may appear at the bottom of the format. Or, not shown, the different colours may appear in the graphic band with the signature reversed in white or overprinted in black.

For more information, see the following pages in the Basic standards section:

Signatures	2.03
Colour in signatures reverse use	2.18
Graphic bands	2.21
Supporting typography	2.23
Alignment	2.27

Identity standards manual for CSR Limited designed by Landor Associates. Original Size 21 cm x 29½ cm. See Chapter 15.

- **Auto Method** may be specified from a drop-down list as Absolute or Proportional. If you select Absolute, Automatic trapping occurs at the absolute value specified in the Auto Amount area. If you specify Proportional, QuarkXPress uses a fraction of the value specified in the Auto Amount based on the difference between the luminance of the object and background color. The formula used is (value of Auto Amount) × (object darkness − background darkness). If the object color is lighter than the background color, it will be spread against the background color; if it is darker, it will be choked.
- **Auto Amount** is the value used by QuarkXPress for Automatic trapping values. You can enter a value between 0 and 36 points in .001-point increments. You can also type in the word "overprint," which causes all colors to overprint their backgrounds with no trapping.
- **Indeterminate** specifies the trapping relationship between an object color item and a background consisting of more than one color. If the object color has conflicting trapping relationships with background colors—that is, if it chokes with some and spreads with others—it will trap to the value specified here.
- **Overprint Limit** specifies the shade at which a color overprints its background color. For example, if the value entered in this field is 95 percent (the preset default), and an object color was shaded 90 percent, it would not overprint, even if that was the setting defined for that color. Rather, it would knock out the color underneath with the spread or choke specified by the Auto Amount.
- If **Ignore White** is checked (the preset default), QuarkXPress will not take background items that have the color white applied into consideration when determining trapping for an object color over multiple background colors.
- **Process Trap** specifies how QuarkXPress handles trapping of process colors. When Process Trap is checked, each process plate is handled individually; for example, on the cyan plate, the darkness of cyan of an object color is compared against the darkness of cyan in the background color, and trapped accordingly. When Process Trap is unchecked, QuarkXPress traps all process colors equally using the trapping value of the object color against the background color.

Trapping Colors

Normally, QuarkXPress controls trap conditions automatically. However, if you click Edit Trap in the Colors dialog box (Edit ▸ Colors), QuarkXPress displays the Trap Specifications dialog box (Figure 7-21) through which you can control the trapping relationship between color pairs. You specify trapping in terms of the way an object color traps against its background color. Object color refers to the color applied to characters or to an item that is in front of another color, and background color is the color applied to the item that is behind another color item.

Figure 7-21 The Trap Specifications dialog box.

First, select Edit ➤ Colors; the Colors dialog box appears. In the Colors dialog box, choose the object color for which you want to specify trapping values. Click on Edit Trap to display the Trap Specifications dialog box. The scroll list displayed in the dialog box lists the trapping values specified for the the object color (shown in the dialog box title) relative to each of the colors in the Background color column. The Default column lists the trapping value specified for each background color. These values can be specified in one of three ways:

- **Automatic** lets QuarkXPress handle the trapping—the object color traps relative to the background color. Automatic utilizes the settings in the Application Preferences dialog box (Edit ➤ Preferences ➤ Application) to determine how much to spread (increase) the object color or choke (reduce) the background color. Automatic is the default setting.

- **Overprint** causes the object color to be printed without "knocking out" the background color when you are printing color separation plates—so the object color prints on top of the background color on the press. If you choose Overprint, the object color overprints the selected background color if its shade is greater than or equal to the Overprint Limit value in the Application Preferences dialog box (Edit ➤ Preferences ➤ Application).

- **Trap** value lets you enter a custom value for the trapping or overlap between the object color and the background color. You can enter a value between –36 points and +36 points, in .001-point increments. After you enter a value, click Trap to save the changes you make. A negative value chokes (reduces) the knockout area of the background color, a positive value spreads (increases) the size of the object against the background color. If you enter a value of zero, no choking or spreading occurs when the object is knocked out from the background (Figure 7-22).

Figure 7-22 Effects of different trapping specifications.

When an object is in front of more than one color, in front of certain color pictures, or if QuarkXPress is unable to identify the background color, the program checks the relationship between the object color and each of the background colors. If there is no conflict, then QuarkXPress traps to the minimum value. If there is a conflict—that is, if the object color would spread into some items and choke others—the item traps to the setting for Indeterminate color.

Trapping Items

In addition to allowing you to set trapping relationships between colors in a document, QuarkXPress allows you to set trapping relationships between individual items via the Trap Information palette (View → Show Trap Information).

First, display the Trap Information palette if it is not already displayed by selecting View → Show Trap Information. The palette shows the trapping information for the active item that has been selected. The drop-down lists allow you to control the trapping of box backgrounds, lines, text, pictures, and frames against their background color(s). The appearance of the palette changes based on the active item (Figure 7-23).

Picture 7-23 The Trap Information palette icons when a text box is selected (a), a framed text box (b), a picture box (c), a line (d).

Trapping values can be specified in one of six ways:

- Choose the **Default** setting from the drop-down list if you simply want to use the trapping values specified in the Trap Specifications dialog box. The value in the Trap Specifications dialog box is displayed to the right in the drop-down list on the palette. To obtain more information about the values, click on the question mark to the right of the value to display a window containing information. If Automatic is the setting in the Trap Specifications dialog box, trapping is determined by the settings in the Application Preferences dialog box (Edit ➤ Preferences ➤ Application).

Figure 7-24 Click on the question mark to obtain more information about Default trapping specifications.

- Choose **Overprint** if you do not want the object color to knock out or trap the background color. Choosing this option overrides the Overprint Limit value specified in the Application Preferences dialog box.
- Specifying **Knockout** causes the object color to knock out the background color with no trapping. This type of trapping is sometimes called "butt" registration.
- **Auto Amount (+)** causes the object color to spread by the amount entered in the Auto Amount area in the Application Preferences dialog box.

- **Auto Amount** (–) causes the background color to choke the object color by the amount entered in the Auto Amount area in the Application Preferences dialog box.
- **Custom** lets you set a trapping value other than that specified for Auto Amount in the Application Preferences dialog box (Figure 7-25). Enter a value from –36pt to 36pt in increments as fine as .001 point. Enter a negative value to cause the background color to choke the object color; enter a positive value to cause the object color to spread.

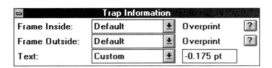

Figure 7-25 Choose Custom to specify trapping values other than the amount specified by Auto Amount in the Application Preferences dialog box.

Text always traps as the object color against the color of the background of the text box. If the text box background is specified with a color of None, and the text is positioned over another item of a single color, the text traps against the color of the item behind it.

If a transparent text box or other item is positioned over items of more than one color, the trapping relationship varies depending on the colors of the background items. If the text or other item of the object color is specified to spread against all the colors of the background items, the object color item spreads by the smallest amount specified. If the object color item is specified to be choked by all the background colors, the object color item is choked by the smallest value specified. If the object color item is specified to spread against some color and be choked by others, or if Knockout is specified, the object color item traps to the value specified for Indeterminate in the Application Preferences dialog box.

Separating Graphics Created in Other Programs

In addition to providing powerful controls for accurate separation of items created in QuarkXPress, the program also separates graphics created by other applications. In order for QuarkXPress to separate a graphic, it must be saved in a format that contains color separation information, such as Encapsulated PostScript (EPS) or color TIFF.

In EPS files, spot colors, such as PANTONE colors, are converted to their CMYK equivalents when separated through QuarkXPress. In order for these colors to separate as spot colors, you must create the color in

QuarkXPress by selecting the Edit → Colors command, and specify that color with Process Separation *off*. This causes QuarkXPress to separate each spot or PANTONE color on its own plate. In the case of colors with custom names, it's important to name the color in QuarkXPress with the exact name of the color in the graphics program, including upper- and lowercase letters and spaces.

Separating Color Photographs

QuarkXPress can, with the aid of other programs and Xtensions, provide high-quality separations of color photographic images. Pages containing color images can be output to a PostScript imagesetter or sent to a high-end system where separations can be stripped into the page digitally.

Before you can import a color photograph, it must, of course be scanned. There's an old saying about computers, "garbage in, garbage out;" this is true when it comes to scanning color images. Regardless of the sophistication of QuarkXPress and any output device, if the quality of the original scan is poor, the image will not be of high quality when finally printed on a press.

High-end drum scanners made by companies such as Linotype-Hell, Scitex, Dai Nippon Screen, and others can be used to scan images that will ultimately end up on the computer as part of a QuarkXPress page. These scanners help yield the best results. They do not merely digitize an image, but also have sophisticated controls for color correction and sharpening images.

Many of the manufacturers of high-end, traditional prepress systems have recently announced scanners that are less expensive than their top-of-the-line models and that can produce excellent results. They are still not intended to be part of an individual's desktop system; Scitex' Smart Scanner retails at around $100,000. Midrange scanners are also becoming more widely available.

Desktop scanners designed for individual use, priced at $10,000 and less, can produce acceptable results for low-quality printing, such as that found in newspapers, but generally are not considered viable sources for digitizing images for high-quality printing.

Regardless of the scanner used, it's a good idea to scan an image in at a size close to the final printed size, or slightly larger. If an image has to be made larger once it has been digitized, the software used for resizing the image essentially has to add information about the color of new pixels that are added in making the picture larger, and the final result may be a poorly reproduced image.

Another rule of thumb to use in scanning images is to scan them in at the number of pixels per inch (ppi) that is roughly equal to twice the line screen at which the image will be printed. For example, if your final page will be output at 150 lines per inch, the image should be scanned at around 300 pixels per inch.

Most high-end scanners have sharpening filters that help to further enhance the clarity of detail in an image after it's been scanned. Sharpening algorithms usually include commands for Sharp and Unsharp Masking. Unsharp Mask is a misleading name: It actually works by blurring the contrast of an image, then subtracting the blurred image from the original, thus brightening and sharpening pixels.

One of the most common ways that continuous-tone color images are output from QuarkXPress is by preparing the image for color separation using Adobe Photoshop on the Macintosh or Aldus PhotoStyler before importing the image into QuarkXPress. This technique puts the burden of the quality of the separations largely on graphics application.

Both programs give you the option of saving files in EPS format or as color TIFFs. With the information contained in these file formats, QuarkXPress can print the appropriate cyan, magenta, yellow, and black components of the continuous-tone image on the correct plate and in position.

Summary

This chapter outlined some of the basic considerations involved with printing color separations from QuarkXPress. Techniques for creating and applying colors in QuarkXPress, along with instructions for using QuarkXPress for producing color separation of pages were also presented. The next chapters cover issues related to printing QuarkXPress documents.

8 *Printing*

The ultimate goal of the production process with QuarkXPress is to print the document on a high-resolution printer. Sometimes this output becomes the distribution copy or copies. More often the output from QuarkXPress to a toner-based laser printer will be used for editing and proofing only, and the final output to a phototypesetter or imagesetter will become the "camera-ready pages" from which the document is reproduced using offset printing equipment. In this chapter you learn how to to select the printer for a document (if you are using more than one printer) and how to print a document.

You also learn about the basic techniques involved in creating and editing colors and how to apply color to the elements on a page. (Chapter 7 contains more detailed information on printing spot color and process color separations.) Finally, you learn how to handle special problems related to printing, including font limitations, linking large pictures, printing oversize pages, and printing a document from another system (other than the one on which it was created) or through a service bureau.

Differences Between Printers

Publications that have been created using QuarkXPress can be printed on certain dot-matrix printers, laser printers, and typesetters that are supported by Microsoft Windows, including (among others):

- PostScript laser printers, imagesetters, and color printers
- Hewlett Packard LaserJet (PCL) printer models
- Epson and other dot-matrix printers

It's a good idea to become familiar with the capabilities of your particular printer before designing pages for QuarkXPress. You will generally want to design with the capabilities and limitations of your final printer in mind.

Resolution

One of the key differences between printers is the resolution at which they print. Resolution is a measure of the density in which text and graphics are printed, and it is usually expressed in dots per inch (dpi). Most desktop laser printers print at 300 dpi. But some toner-based laser printers can produce higher resolutions (400 dpi, 600 dpi, and 1200 dpi). While this is considered high resolution compared to dot matrix printers, which print at 120 dots per inch, it is low resolution compared to typesetting equipment, or imagesetters, that print at 1200, 2400, 3600, or up to 5000 dpi (Figure 8-1). Some printers have a range of settings for resolution.

Printer	Resolution Settings—dpi
Dot matrix printers	72–120
Toner-based laser printers	300–1200
Linotronic 100 (imagesetter)	1270, 900, or 600
Linotronic 300 (imagesetter)	2540, 1270, or 600

Figure 8-1   Some QuarkXPress-compatible printers and their resolutions.

The higher the resolution, the smoother the appearance of the edges of text and graphics; the lower the resolution, the greater the jaggedness of the edges. The average reader may not notice jaggedness in text printed at 300 dpi, but professional designers, typesetters, and lithographers can readily see the difference between low (300 dpi) and high (1200 dpi or more) resolution.

Some of the adjustments you can make through QuarkXPress commands have no discernible effect when printed on a low-resolution printer. For example, leading can be adjusted in .001 point increments, but low-resolution printers do not print leading adjustments in such fine increments: Most laser printers, for example, can only print 1/300th of an inch (0.24 point).

Printer Fonts

Another major difference between printers is the number of fonts that are built in to the printer's ROM (read-only memory). You learned in Chapter 5 how to install *screen fonts* through the menus in QuarkXPress, but to print a document, the same fonts must also be available as *printer fonts*. Built-in printer fonts are installed by the manufacturer, and are always available for printing any document. They are always high-resolution fonts and are never jagged when printed out. Ideally, every font would be built in to the printer. Unfortunately, because fonts take up space in the printer's ROM, most printers have few or no built-in fonts.

If the printer font is not built in to the printer itself, then it must be available on your system when printing so it can be downloaded to the printer. The number of typefaces you can download at one time is limited by the amount of memory in the printer (as described later in this chapter), unless you are using fonts that are permanently downloaded to a hard disk attached to the printer. (See "Font Selection," under "Special Considerations in Printing," later in this chapter.)

Paper Size and Type

Most laser printers use ordinary paper stock; some special paper stocks are also available for these printers, including glossy paper, transparencies, waxable paper, adhesive labels, and so on. High-resolution imagesetters use rolls of photographic paper or clear film. Some color printers require thermo-sensitive papers.

The most common laser printers handle paper in letter or legal sizes. Some feeders let you load smaller sizes of paper, but you can't load paper wider than 8.5 inches. Other printer models accommodate a wider range of sizes, including letter, legal, 11" × 17", A3, A4, A5, B4, and B5. For example, the Linotronic series imagesetters are roll-fed printers that handle up to 12-inch-wide rolls, and you can print pages of any length. The Versatec Thermal Color Printer handles 8.5 × 11" or 11 × 17" paper.

Another Versatec color printer handles pages up to 42 inches wide, of any length, and can print files that have been saved in EPS format and rasterized through Adobe's Encapsulated POWERSCRIPT workstation developed by Colossal Graphics, Inc.

All printers leave a margin of white space at the edge of the paper or roll—nothing will print in this area. The page outlines in the QuarkXPress document window represent the actual edges of the paper (if page size is the same as paper size), so you need to be familiar with your printer's margin limitations and make sure that your page designs do not include text or graphics in the nonprinting area at the edges of the page. On a typical laser printer, for example, you should leave at least .33-inch margins all around the page. On a Linotronic with a 12-inch-wide roll, the maximum print width is 11.7 inches. To effectively print bleeds, you need to print to a paper size that is larger than the page size.

Color

An increasing number of color printers and slide recorders are available for electronic publishing. There are electrophotographic, ink-jet, dye-sublimation, thermal, and thermojet color printers, which offer a range of resolutions (200 dots per inch and up) and color quality. Very often, they are used to print color *comps* (design ideas) or *proofs* (to check the final page layout), but they also offer opportunities for printing short-run color publications, color overhead transparencies, and slides. While most of these printers do not currently have the resolution to effectively output type, significant advances in this area are beginning to be made with printers like the 400-dpi Canon CLC 500 color laser printer.

Meanwhile, color printers are generally impractical for making many color copies for distribution because:

- The color and typographic quality available on most color printers is not as good as offset lithography.
- Some color printers require special paper that cannot be printed on both sides (so you cannot produce two-sided color documents).
- Most color printers are extremely slow, requiring three minutes or more per full color page.

In QuarkXPress, color is most commonly used to produce color separations for printing on an offset press. The basics of issues relating to color printing are described later in this chapter; Chapter 7 offers a detailed explanation of creating and applying colors.

Printing from QuarkXPress

The first time you print a particular QuarkXPress document, you might go through three different commands or procedures: Verify that the appropriate printer has been set up through the Windows Control Panel, make additional printer-specific specifications through the Printer Setup command under QuarkXPress, and finally activate the Print command. These procedures are described under the next headings.

If you have only one printer that you always use, you will go through the Windows Control Panel to set up the printer only once. If you have more than one printer hooked up to your system, you must go through the Control Panel to select the active printer whenever you want to change from one printer to another under Windows 3.0. Under Windows 3.1, you select the default printer through the Control Panel, but you can switch from one installed printer to another through QuarkXPress' Printer Setup command. These differences are described below.

Choosing the Target Printer

In many cases you will go through the entire production sequence using the same printer for early proofs as for final masters. If you have more than one printer hooked up to your workstation, then you can select the default printer through the Printers icon and dialog box that is part of the Windows' Control Panel, either before starting a document or during production.

To do this, double-click the icon for the Program Manager under Windows (if the Program Manager window is not already open), then double-click the Main program group icon (where the Control Panel is normally available, unless you have customized your program groups), then double-click the Control Panel icon, and (finally!) double-click the Printers icon to display the Printers dialog box. The next steps differ between Windows 3.0 and Windows 3.1.

Activating a Printer Under Windows 3.0

Under Windows 3.0, only one printer can be active at a time. After double-clicking the Printers icon in the Windows' Control Panel, select the appropriate printer driver from the Installed Printers scroll list in the Printers dialog box. Click Active in the Status area of the dialog box. To select or change the port to which the printer is connected, click Configure to display the Printers-Configure dialog box, and select a port from the Ports scroll list. Click Setup to display the Printer on [Port] dialog box and choose the exact printer brand and model (or one that most closely matches the features and resident fonts of your printer) from the Printer drop-down list. This last dialog box might include other options specific to the printer you have selected, such as printer resolution. When you have completed all your dialog box entries, click OK to close each dialog box and exit the Control Panel.

If the printer driver you want is not listed in the Printers dialog box, or in the Printer on [Port} dialog box, you can add drivers that are available on your Windows installation disks (see Windows *User's Guide*).

Note that you can select a different printer type for a specific document in QuarkXPress by using the Printer Setup command, described later in this chapter. However, you cannot *print* to a specific printer under Windows 3.0 unless that printer is also the Active printer defined through the Control Panel.

Changing Printers Under Windows 3.1

Under Windows 3.1, all installed printers are automatically active. You can even install multiple printers on the same port. You can select a printer or install a new driver or change assigned printer ports under Windows 3.1 using the same procedures as just described for activating a printer under Windows 3.0. The only difference is that the Configure button under Windows 3.0 becomes the Connect button under Windows 3.1. Instead of selecting one printer to be *active*, you can select one printer as the *default* printer. The default printer will be the first one QuarkXPress chooses when you start a new document, but you can change the printer assigned to a specific document through the Printer Setup command thereby making it available for printing without going through the Control Panel.

If you often change between two types of printers on the same port—changing between a toner-based laser printer and an imagesetter, for example, or between a color printer and a black toner printer—install both printers on the same port through the Control Panel (Figure 8-2). Then, when you switch the cables hooked up to the port, change the printer specifications through the Page Setup command in QuarkXPress.

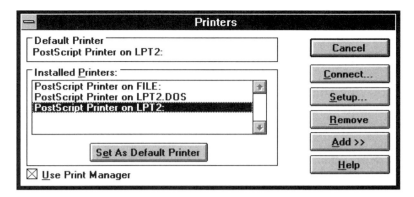

Figure 8-2 The Printers dialog box under the Windows 3.1 Control Panel.

Switching a document from a PostScript printer to a non-PostScript printer, or vice versa, may cause unexpected changes to the way in which text prints.

When printing to a PostScript printer, it's best to set the Character Widths to Fractional in the Typographic Preferences dialog box by selecting Edit ► Preferences ► Typographic; when printing to a non-PostScript printer, such as a dot-matrix printer, it's best to set Character Widths to Integral.

Adding a New Printer

Click the **Add>>** button to expand the Printers dialog box and choose from a drop-down list of printer brand names and models. The **Printer** drop-down list lets you choose from specific models of printers, corresponding to the Printer Description files that are installed through Windows. For example, for PostScript printers the list includes various models of printers manufactured by Agfa, Apple, AST, Digital, IBM, Linotronic, NEC, Olivetti, QMS, TI, Varityper, and Wang. PCL printers include various models of Hewlett-Packard printers.

The selection shown here need not match your printer type exactly, but it does affect the Paper Size list and other options in the Printer Setup dialog box. If you are printing to a device that is not included in the list, simply choose the model that is most like yours in features. If you are printing to a non-PostScript printer that has been enhanced with a PostScript board, you would choose PostScript as the printer type and select a PostScript printer model such as Apple LaserWriter Plus, rather than the actual printer model.

Printer Setup

The File ➤ Printer Setup command displays a dialog box that contains information for printing purposes only—these entries do not affect the document itself (page size, orientation, and so on). The keyboard shortcut for displaying the Printer Setup dialog box is CTRL+ALT+P (Figure 8-3). You can select File ➤ Printer Setup to change the Paper Size and Orientation, as well as other settings specific to the printer.

Under Windows 3.1, you can select any installed printer through the Printer Setup dialog box in QuarkXPress. Under Windows 3.0, you must change printers by going through the Windows Control Panel.

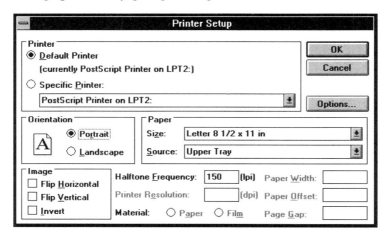

Figure 8-3   Printer Setup dialog box for a typical laser printer.

Portrait (tall) orientation is the default selection unless the Page Size defined in the New or Printer Setup dialog box is wider than 8.5 inches, in which case default orientation changes to **Landscape** (wide).

For some printers, a drop-down list for **Paper Size** lists the range of paper sizes handled. Possibilities include letter, legal, ledger, and statement, as well as European sizes, such as A3 (11.7" × 16.5"), A4 (8.3" × 11.7"), and A5 (5.8" × 8.3"). The list shown in the drop-down list corresponds to the sizes supported by the printer selected in the Printer field.

The difference between Paper Size (specified through the Printer Setup command) and Page Size (specified in the New or Document Setup dialog box) is that *page size* determines the dimensions of the pages shown on the screen display in QuarkXPress, and it is from these dimensions that margins and crop marks are measured. If the *paper size* is larger than the page size, the page will print in the upper left corner of the paper; if the paper size is smaller than the page size, the document must be printed Tiled (as described later under "The Print Command").

The **Paper Source** option is most often used when printing to laser printers. If you specify the Paper Source as Upper Tray, then the printer draws sheets of paper from the currently-loaded paper cassette. Some printers also offer a Lower Tray option. If you specify Manual Feed, the printer pauses after printing each page and looks for a sheet through the manual feed slot.

The manual feed option is sometimes used when you want to print just one or two pages on special paper, such as letterhead stationery, and you don't want to change the paper in the cassette. It is also useful when you are using special stock that does not feed smoothly from the tray (such as card stock, small paper sizes, envelopes).

When printing to a phototypesetter, you can output negative film (right-reading, emulsion-side-down page art that reads correctly when the emulsion side of the film is facing down), by checking **Flip Horizontal** and **Invert** in this dialog box, and choosing **Film** as the Material.

You can also set a **Halftone Frequency** by typing any number between 15 and 400. The halftone screen is the number of lines per inch that will define the pattern of dots in the halftone when you print grayscale and bitmap images. This setting also applies to shades—for backgrounds, frames, and text—created in QuarkXPress. The normal default, 60 lpi, is the most common setting for printing halftone pictures in newspapers. A 300 dpi printer cannot accurately reproduce screens finer than 75 lpi. The setting shown in this dialog box will apply to all such images unless you override this default for specific pictures using commands under the Style menu, as described in Chapter 6 (Graphics).

The next options are available only if you have selected a roll-fed photographic typesetter, such as the Linotronic, as the Printer (Figure 8-4). You can specify the **Printer Resolution** here in dots per inch. You should enter a resolution that is supported by the specified printer, or you can enter your own preferred resolution between 72 and 5,000. (This setting affects QuarkXPress's smoothing algorithms and does not change the settings on the imagesetter itself; but it should *match* the current setting on the imagesetter.) You can choose Paper or Film, to specify whether you are printing on opaque photographic paper or clear film.

For printers that can handle rolls of paper in different paper roll widths, you can specify the **Paper Width** here. You can also enter **Paper Offset** to shift the printing area to the right of its normal position (against the left edge of the paper). The **Page Gap** is the amount of space QuarkXPress will leave between pages on the roll-fed typesetter. When **Spreads** is checked in the Print dialog box (described later in this chapter), the value you enter in the Page Gap field is inserted between spreads, not between the pages in the spread itself.

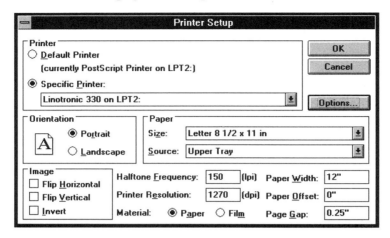

Figure 8-4   Printer Setup dialog box for a Linotronic 300.

Click the **Options** button to view and change other options in this dialog box which are specific to particular printer types. The Options dialog box varies depending on the type of printer you have selected (PostScript, PCL, dot matrix, etc.), and the list of options may change depending on the printer driver version installed with your system. The next section describes the options specific to a PostScript printer.

PostScript Printer Options

Click the Options button in the Printer Setup dialog box to view additional options available for specific printers. The Options dialog box for a PostScript printer (Figure 8-5) lets you specify whether the document will print to the printer or to a disk file as Encapsulated PostScript (described later in this chapter). Here you can also specify the print-area margins relative to the printer (this does not affect the margins specified for the document), scale the document, specify whether the header is sent with each job, and set advanced options.

Figure 8-5 The Options dialog box shows various options for PostScript printers.

A PostScript file is sent to the printer as PostScript code, including a "Header" which contains general information not specific to the document. Normally, the header is sent with each print job, but you can send the header to a disk file and download it once to the printer at the beginning of the day, then print each job without re-sending the header. We don't recommend that you change the defaults for **Header** without having some familiarity with printing PostScript, beyond that offered in this book.

You can reduce or enlarge pages by entering any **Scaling** percentage from 25 percent to 400 percent. The top left corner of each page as shown on the screen remains the top left corner of each printed page, and all enlarging or reducing is done to the right and down the page. The results of printing enlargements are easily predicted: If you scale a page to be larger than the printer paper, you will lose part of the page image from the right and bottom edges.

The results of printing reductions might not be what you'd expect. Only those elements that actually touch the page on the screen will appear on the printout. Elements that fall completely onto the Pasteboard will not be printed in a reduction. Elements that overlap both the page and the Pasteboard will be printed.

The buttons on the right of the Options dialog box let you choose other **Advanced** options applicable to the type of printer you have chosen, send the header to a disk file, or access an extensive series of Help screens.

The Print Command

Use the File → Print (CTRL+P) command throughout the production process to print both preliminary drafts and final camera-ready copies of your document. The File → Print command results in a dialog box (Figure 8-6) through which you specify the number of copies and range of pages to be printed, as well as other special options described below. The Setup button in the Print dialog box gives access to the same series of dialog boxes as described for the Printer Setup command in the previous section.

Figure 8-6   The Print command and dialog box.

It is always a good idea to save your document immediately before using the Print command.

Copies and Page Range

You can specify the number of Copies of each page that you want to print (up to 999) as well as the range of Pages (either All or starting From and going To the page numbers you specify).

The page range option is useful when you make changes that affect just a few pages, or when you want to print the finished parts of a document that is still in process. You can enter a user-defined section number, or you can enter the "absolute" location within the active document by preceding the number with a plus sign. For example, if the active document includes 10 pages beginning with page 11 and you want to print beginning with page 13, you can print From page 13 or you can print From page +3 (that is, start with the third page in this document). An absolute page sequence number represents a page's sequential location in a document, regardless of the automatic page numbers. If the document has more than one section, you must include any prefix that has been assigned as part of the page number through the Page ➤ Section command in specifying an actual page number.

Cover Page

If you are printing to a PostScript printer, you can print a Cover Page that shows the name of the document and the date and time printed. This is not counted as one of the numbered document pages. Having a cover page is handy when printing in a networked environment where several people use one printer or when printing more than one document at a time through a print spooler—it can help you separate documents printed from different locations or multiple documents printed from one location. You can specify that No cover page will be printed, or you can print it as the First Page or the Last Page.

Normal Versus Rough Output

On PostScript printers, Normal output can be changed to Rough (in which text is formatted but pictures are not printed and complex frames are simplified).

Printing Thumbnails

QuarkXPress allows you to print Thumbnails, in which each page is printed in miniature, with several pages on a sheet of paper. You can make Thumbnails larger or smaller, thus allowing more or fewer thumbnails to print per page, by entering a value in the Reduce or Enlarge field of the Printer Setup dialog box.

Printing Only Odd or Even Pages

You can print All pages, or only the Odd Pages or the Even Pages in a document. These options enable you to print two-sided copies directly on the printer—by printing all the odd-numbered pages first, putting them in the paper feed tray, and printing all the even pages. These options are also useful when you are preparing a two-sided manuscript to be reproduced on the type of copier that prompts you to insert all odd or even pages first.

Collating Pages

You can print pages Back to Front (that is, in reverse order), which has the effect of collating a single copy in the correct order when you are printing to a laser printer that feeds printed sheets out face up. If you are printing multiple copies, you can choose Collate to print one complete set of pages at a time. This means that when you go to pick up the document from the printer's tray, it will already be in the correct order for the readers. This can be handy if you want the first copy to be available for review while the other copies are printing. It definitely saves you the time it would take to sort the copies manually, but it often requires significantly longer printing time than when multiple copies are not collated. When copies are not collated, the printer processes each page once only and prints multiple copies immediately from the same drum image. For collated copies, the printer must process each page for each copy—in other words, the drum image is reprocessed for each sheet of paper printed.

Printing Spreads

If you click Spreads, facing pages or pages arranged as horizontal spreads print contiguously (if the paper size can accommodate this)—side by side with no break between pages.

Printing Blank Pages

QuarkXPress gives you the option of printing the blank pages in a document. A blank page is one that contains no printable items. Empty, unframed boxes and items to which Suppress Printout (Item ➤ Modify) has been applied are considered nonprinting items. When Blank Pages is unchecked, blank pages in the document are not printed.

Registration Marks

You can select the Registration Marks feature to automatically generate marks traditionally used to indicate where the pages would be cut when trimmed to their final size as well as registration marks for color separations. This option works when you are printing on a paper size at least one inch taller and wider than the page size specified for the document. You can also use this option when you are printing a reduced page size using the Scaling factor described later under this heading.

The registration marks can be Centered between the cut marks on each side of the document or printed Off Center so that the bottom and left registration marks are slightly off center (Figure 8-7). This is useful when you are printing color separations (described in Chapter 7).

Figure 8-7   A page printed with registration marks centered and off center.

Open Prepress Interface (OPI) Comments

This drop-down list lets you specify the way in which pictures and OPI comments are output. The Include Images option includes both high-resolution TIFF and EPS files in the output. Omit TIFF files includes comments about a TIFF file (location, size, and so on), but not the high-resolution image itself; choose this option if high-resolution images will be substituted for TIFF images on the OPI prepress device. Omit TIFF and EPS includes the OPI comments, but not the high-resolution TIFF or EPS picture.

High-end output devices that have an OPI converter use PostScript files that are downloaded. These comments have an effect only when you print a file to disk as a PostScript file. See "Making a PostScript File Version of a Document" later in this chapter.

Printing Tiled Pages

You can select the Tiling option to print large pages in pieces on smaller paper. A common application of the Tiling feature is to print out draft versions of tabloid-size (11" × 17") or larger pages on 8.5" × 11" paper. The tiled papers can be assembled into one piece for reproduction, or they can be used as proof sheets only: You can print the final version of a tabloid page directly to a typesetter's 12-inch wide roll of photosensitive paper without using the Tiling option.

In Tiling, you can select the Auto option and specify by how much you want the images on each tile to overlap (from 0 to 6 inches). Normally, the top left corner of the page becomes the first tile and is positioned at the top left corner of the paper. The right margin of the page might be wider on the paper, depending on the page size, the paper size, and the amount of overlap specified. If you want the image on the leftmost and rightmost tiles to be equal sizes, precede the overlap value with a greater-than character (>).

Once you start printing a page with Auto Tiling selected, you cannot interrupt the printing process and restart where you left off. If you stop the printing process, printing will begin again at the top left corner of the page when you restart QuarkXPress.

You can also select the Manual option and define the limits of each tile piece by moving the 0 on the ruler. For example, under the Manual Tiling option you would first print one "tile" with the zero point at the top left corner of the page, then you would move the zero point to mark the top left corner of the next tile and print again. (Remember from Chapter 2, Creating One Page, that you move the zero point by choosing Show Rulers from the View menu, positioning the pointer over the box where the two rulers intersect, and dragging the pointer to the position on the page where you want the zero point to be.) See "Oversize Documents," later in this chapter, for more information about Tiling.

Printing Color Separations

If the pages include **Color**—whether imported as part of color graphics or applied using QuarkXPress commands—you can Make Separations or Print Colors as Grays. If you Print Colors as Grays, each color is printed at a shade of gray. If the color is set to print at a shade of 100 percent, it will print lighter when this option is selected in order to distinguish it from true blacks. Lighter shades of the same color appear correspondingly lighter on the printout. Otherwise, if you are printing to a black-and-white printer and you are not printing color separations, all colors set at 100 percent shade appear black on the printout.

If you select Make Separations, QuarkXPress prints each page color plate separately, as specified in the Plates field. This option is described briefly in a discussion of the issues involved in printing color documents, later in this chapter, and in more detail in Chapter 7.

Print Status

The Print Status dialog box displays information about your job as it's printing, giving messages about the page numbers being printed. Such information is especially reassuring when a document takes a long time to send to the Print Manager, so you don't have to wonder whether it's working or not. To display an expanded Print Status dialog box with information about specific graphics as they are being processed, hold down the SHIFT key as you click the Print button in the Print dialog box (File → Print), as shown in Figure 8-8.

Figure 8-8 Hold down the SHIFT key as you click the Print button in the Print dialog box to display the Print Status dialog box.

The Print status dialog box displays the page number that is currently printing, the CMYK or spot color separation plate currently printing (if Make Separations was selected in the Print dialog box), and the path and file name of the picture that is currently printing. If you have selected the option for printing tiled pages, the number of the currently printing tile is displayed.

Stopping the Printing Process

You can stop the printing process by clicking Cancel in the Print dialog box before you start printing. Once you click OK in the Print dialog box, QuarkXPress begins preparing each page for printing, and displays a dialog box with a changing message about the current status of the printing process.

You can click Cancel in the Print Status dialog box to terminate the process while pages are printing or while they are being formatted for the Print Manager, if you have activated that resource in the Windows environment.

Turning the printer off is an emergency measure and is advisable only if you are the only person on the printer network, if the printer does not include downloaded fonts, and if the equipment allows midprocess termination (see the manual for your hardware).

Making a PostScript File Version of a Document

You can create a PostScript version of a document, so that all of the printing information is stored as a disk file instead of being sent to the printer. This is useful for printing the document from other systems without installing QuarkXPress, or for sending a document to another location (such as a service bureau) for printing.

To create a PostScript file, you must configure your printer driver to print to FILE instead of a physical port such as LPT1 or COM2. Double-click on the Printers icon in the Windows Control Panel. Choose a PostScript printer from the Installed Printers scroll list.

If you are running Windows 3.0, click Configure to display the Printers-Configure dialog box. From the Ports scroll list, choose FILE. Click Setup and specify the printer, paper source, paper size, orientation, and scaling you want. Click OK to close the Printer on [Port] dialog box. Click OK to close the Printers-Configure dialog box. Click OK to close the Printers dialog box.

If you are running Windows 3.1, click Connect to display the Connect dialog box. From the Ports scroll list, choose FILE. Click OK to close the Connect dialog box. In the Printers dialog box, click Setup to display the Printer on FILE dialog box. Specify the paper source, paper size, and orientation you want. Click Options and specify the scaling you want. Click OK to close the Options dialog box. Click OK to close the Printer on FILE dialog box. Click Close to close the Printers dialog box.

After you have configured a PostScript printer driver for output to a file, select that printer driver in Printer Setup (File menu in QuarkXPress) and specify any additional settings you want for the device to which the PostScript file will be printed. Then select Print (File menu in Quark XPress). You can print the entire document or selected pages. After you click OK in the Print dialog box, the Print to File dialog box is displayed. Enter a name for the file in the Output File Name field and click OK.

You can create a PostScript file regardless of the printer you have attached to your computer. The PostScript file contains all the files needed to output your document—the document itself, all picture files (including EPS and TIFF pictures), and all printer fonts. The PostScript file can be output to a PostScript printer only.

If you will be taking your PostScript file to a service bureau for printing, make sure the printer selected in the Printer Setup dialog box is the printer being used at the service bureau, not the printer to which you are currently connected. (Call your service bureau before taking your PostScript file and ask what settings they want under Printer Setup.)

Special Considerations in Printing

The next sections discuss some of the special considerations that can arise in printing documents, including printing master pages, font selection, imported picture types, system changes (including sending documents to a service bureau), and oversize documents.

Printing Master Pages

You can print out the master pages in a document. To print a master page, simply display that page in the document window. All the commands in the Printer Setup dialog box and in the Print dialog box are available, except From and To pages.

Font Management

Up to this point in the book we have assumed that the fonts you use are already installed on your system, as screen fonts and as printer fonts. How did they get there? What do you have to do to add a font? What if you have trouble printing a font? These questions might never concern you if you are using a system that has already been set up for you, and you always produce the same documents or use the same formats with the same tried-and-true fonts every time. However, if you get adventurous with a new document design by adding new fonts or trying new combinations of fonts, and you run into problems in printing the document, the answers to these questions can help you solve the problem.

Installing Fonts

The first step in using a font is to install the *screen* font on your system. The second step is to install the *printer* font files onto your hard disk or onto a hard disk attached to your printer. These steps might be handled for you automatically when you install a new font or a new printer, or when you install a new application that comes with fonts, such as Adobe Type Manager or Windows.

If these two conditions are met, you will be able to select the fonts through QuarkXPress. When you print the document, QuarkXPress automatically sends the fonts to the printer as needed by each page during the printing process. If you have installed the screen font but do not have the equivalent printer font, you can choose the font from the QuarkXPress menus. But, when you print the document, either the font will print as low-resolution bitmap characters (based on the screen font) or another font will be substituted.

Some service bureaus will give you their screen fonts on disk so you can use them in your documents. But the document will have to be printed by a service bureau that has the printer fonts, which are licensed only to the purchaser.

Using a Type Manager

Printer fonts are commonly distinguished as being either *scalable outline fonts* (such as PostScript and TrueType fonts) or *non-scalable bitmap fonts* (such as commonly used on Hewlett Packard PCL printers). Outline fonts can be stored as mathematical formulas for each character, or as miniature software programs that actually draw the outline of each character when executed. This means that the formula or program for the characters in the font can be stored in one file and used to generate characters of any size. Non-scalable bitmap fonts, on the other hand, must be stored as complete character sets for each size installed. They can take up a tremendous amount of disk space and memory.

To eliminate the need to install every size of a bitmap font, you can use a type manager (such as Adobe Type Manager) along with scalable fonts to generate the bitmap versions used by the printer as you print—rather than storing them on the disk. With a type manager, you can scale a font to virtually any size you want, and you can also rotate text in .001° increments. Using a type manager with scalable fonts will also reduce the amount of memory QuarkXPress needs to display and print fonts in large point sizes.

Temporarily Downloading Fonts

When using fonts that are not built in your printer, the fonts must be sent—or downloaded—to the printer prior to printing the page or document. Windows does this automatically when printing, as long as the printer fonts have been installed and listed in the WIN.INI file.

The WIN.INI file is automatically updated whenever new fonts are added through the Fonts icon in the Windows Control Panel or through Adobe Type Manager. To add fonts to the download list under Adobe Type Manager, double-click on the ATM Control Panel icon under the Windows Program Manager. The ATM Control Panel dialog box is displayed. Click Add. The Add ATM Fonts dialog box is displayed. In the Directories scroll list, double-click on "[psfonts]." Subdirectories are displayed; double-click on "[pfm]." Select all the fonts in the Available Fonts scroll list, and click Add. You can also edit your WIN.INI manually to add or remove softfonts from the list.

Before making any changes to your WIN.INI file, make a backup of it and store it in a safe place. If Windows refuses to launch using the edited WIN.INI, you can copy your original WIN.INI back into your Windows directory.

To edit your WIN.INI manually, locate the section in your WIN.INI that lists the softfonts available to your printer and port. It will be in brackets. (There may be several lists, so be sure to get the correct port.) Here is an example of a printer entry in a WIN.INI:

```
[Postscript,LPT1]
...
softfonts=2
softfont1=c:\psfonts\pfm\fub_____.pfm
softfont2=c:\psfonts\pfm\fuh_____.pfm,c:\psfonts\fuh_____.pfb
```

Softfont entries must be numbered consecutively. The total number of softfont entries must equal the number listed in the softfonts= statement. The first directory statement in the softfonts entry displays the name and location of the printer font metrics file. The second directory statement, which follows the comma, displays the name and location of the printer font file. Each font that you use in a document must contain both the printer font metric (.PFM) and, if you want to temporarily download the font to the printer with each print job, the printer font (.PFB) file listing. If your document prints in Courier, you probably do not have the PFB file listed. (If you installed screen fonts using the Fonts dialog box in the Windows Control Panel, or if you are using a version of Adobe Type Manager earlier than 2.0, you may need to add complete softfont entries that include both the PFM and PFB font files for each of your downloadable fonts.)

In the example above, softfont1 does not have the PFB entry. To temporarily download that font, you must edit the softfont entry to read as follows:

```
softfont1=c:\psfonts\pfm\fub_____.pfm,c:\psfonts\fub_____.pfb
```

If you need to add a font (Futura Bold Oblique, for example), you must add a softfont entry and update the softfonts= statement to reflect the total number of fonts in the softfonts list.

310 *The QuarkXPress Handbook*

Your edited entry for this PostScript printer entry would read as follows:

```
[Postscript,LPT1]
...
softfonts=3
softfont1=c:\psfonts\pfm\fub_____.pfm,c:\psfonts\fub_____.pfb
softfont2=c:\psfonts\pfm\fuh_____.pfm,c:\psfonts\fuh_____.pfb
softfont3=c:\psfonts\pfm\fubo____.pfm,c:\psfonts\fubo____.pfb
```

Under Windows 3.0, if you have more than 175 PostScript softfont entries, the Windows PostScript driver may become unstable.

Permanently Downloading Fonts

Each temporarily downloaded font takes up space in the printer's memory, and it is flushed out when the page or document is finished printing. As an alternative, you can download fonts to the printer before you print, using such programs as Adobe's Font Downloader, which is included with every font you buy from Adobe.

Permanently downloaded fonts do not have to be downloaded for each print job. Instead, they remain in the printer's memory as each page is printed and until the printer is turned off. You can print publications more quickly this way, but the number of fonts downloaded limits the amount of memory remaining for processing each page.

There are two primary ways to download fonts—to memory or to a font disk. Both require a font downloader utility. Several of these are available, and you should consult your dealer or a computer consultant to determine the one that is best for your needs. To download fonts to memory, you must have sufficient memory for the fonts you download plus the print job itself. To download fonts to a font disk, you must have a font disk and a printer capable of using it.

If you choose to download fonts permanently, you should delete the printer font (PFB) file entry for each softfont listing from the printer entry in your WIN.INI. Doing so will decrease the time it takes to output your document, especially if you use many fonts in a document, since the printer driver won't download those fonts for every print job.

If you have pre-downloaded any fonts at the beginning of the day, and you run into memory problems when printing pages with graphics that do not use those fonts, you can flush the fonts out of the printer's memory by turning it off.

Font Selection

Each font requires 50 to 90K of memory in printing. Bold, italic, and condensed versions of a PostScript or TrueType typeface (Futura, for example) are three separate fonts; each one takes up printer memory. If you are using bitmap fonts (i.e., not PostScript or TrueType), such as commonly used on Hewlett Packard PCL printers, then each *size* is also a separate font file that takes up printer memory. If you are having trouble printing a document that uses many fonts, and you do not have a font disk attached to your printer, try to reduce the number of fonts used in the document, or follow some of the other suggestions in this section for downloading fonts.

To see a list of the fonts used in a document, select Utilities → Font Usage. You can also globally find and change fonts through the Font Usage dialog box (Figure 8-9), described in Chapter 4.

Figure 8-9 The Font Usage dialog box.

Experiment a little with downloadable fonts before you design a large document that calls for them, and before you decide whether to download the fonts *before* you start printing or as part of the printing process.

Limiting the Number of Fonts

If you are following the rules of good design, your pages probably use a limited number of different typefaces, styles, and sizes. There are at least two reasons other than good design for limiting the number of fonts you use in a document: time and space. The more fonts you use, the more space they require in your printer's memory (if they are downloaded fonts) and the more time it takes to print each page.

Remember, as you learned in Chapter 5, a font is a particular combination of typeface and style. You need to download four different fonts in order to use the entire "family" in the Palatino typeface, for example: normal, bold, italic, and bold italic. Different typefaces and styles take up different amounts of memory, and different types of graphics make different demands on memory as well. Before you design a long document with downloadable fonts, try printing one or two sample pages with representative graphics as well as text that uses all of the fonts called for in the design.

Working with Large Picture Files

Because EPS and TIFF images can be quite large, QuarkXPress stores and displays them in a low-resolution TIFF format rather than incorporating them in the document. QuarkXPress uses the larger, high-resolution image to print the document.

If you move or change the name of the high-resolution picture file, or if you use another program to modify it, then, when you print the document, QuarkXPress displays a dialog box (Figure 8-10) that enables you to re-establish the link, to print anyway, or to cancel the print job.

Figure 8-10   Alert box prompting for response to missing or modified picture condition.

Click Yes to view a list of all missing or modified pictures. The Missing/Modified Pictures dialog box is handled the same way as the Picture Usage dialog box, described below. Click No to continue printing, using the low-resolution version of all missing pictures. Click Cancel to cancel the printing process.

If you want QuarkXPress to automatically reimport all pictures that have been modified since the document was last open, you can select Edit ▸ Preferences ▸ General to set Auto Import to On (as described in Chapter 3). Missing pictures will still result in a dialog box during the printing process.

If you want to resolve all of these issues before you print, select Utilities ▸ Picture Usage. EPS and TIFF files are listed in the Picture Usage dialog box (Figure 8-11), through which you can locate pictures for printing and determine their status. Status indicators include OK (QuarkXPress knows where the picture is and it has not been modified), modified (QuarkXPress knows where the picture is but it has been modified), and missing (QuarkXPress does not know where the picture is).

Figure 8-11 Picture Usage dialog box.

To locate a missing picture in the document, double-click on the picture name, or click once on the picture name and click Update. The Missing/Modified Picture dialog box is displayed (Figure 8-12), through which you can specify the new path to the picture or the new picture name.

Figure 8-12 The Missing/Modified Picture dialog box.

To view the picture, click once on the picture name and click Show Me. QuarkXPress scrolls through the document and displays the page with the picture on it.

Printing at High Resolutions

Because of the way information is stored for grayscale TIFF images, the amount of memory required to process the image increases the higher the resolution. For this reason, printing images takes longer at higher resolutions. You might run into memory overload or printing time-out errors when printing pages with grayscale TIFF images at high resolutions—especially the high resolutions offered by imagesetters such as the Linotronic models. You can work around these problems by printing those pages at lower resolutions.

Changing Systems and Using Service Bureaus

If you take your QuarkXPress document from one system to another, you need to take the following files with you besides the document file itself:

- All high resolution picture files (EPS, TIFF, or RIFF) used in the document.
- Printer and screen fonts used in the document (or a list of fonts, so you can check that they are installed in the other system).
- The XPRESS.PRF file (if you have customized any typographic settings that affect how the text prints).

If you will only be printing and not editing the document on the other system, you might prefer to send the document as a single Encapsulated PostScript file, as described earlier in this chapter.

In either case, whether you send all of the files related to the document or one Encapsulated PostScript file, you should always keep a backup of your files, especially when taking them from one machine or system to another.

Oversize Documents

QuarkXPress lets you specify page sizes up to 48 inches square. Unfortunately, no PostScript printers can handle paper this large. (The largest we know of is a Versatec printer that can print rasterized versions of QuarkXPress pages that have been saved as EPS files, and handles pages up to 42 inches wide, of any length.)

When you print a document with pages that are larger than the size of the paper in the printer, you must either print a reduced version of the pages or print them out in *tiled* sections.

Printing Reductions

As you learned earlier in this chapter, you can print reduced versions of pages by entering a value below 100 percent in the Reduce or Enlarge field of the Printer Setup dialog box. Some standard reductions are shown in Figure 8-13.

Original Size (inches)	Percentage reduction needed to fit on 8.5" × 11" paper:
8.5" × 11" (letter)	100%
11" × 14" (legal)	77%
11" × 17" (tabloid)	64%
15.5" × 22.5" (newspaper)	48%
34" × 44"	25%

Figure 8-13 Reduction percentages required to fit oversize proofs on an 8.5" x 11" page.

Printing Tiled Sections

The Tiling option in the Print dialog box (Figure 8-14) lets you print large pages in sections on a PostScript printer. This feature was mentioned earlier in this chapter, but we will describe it in more detail here.

```
Tiling:     ○ Off   ● Manual   ○ Auto, overlap: 3"
```

Figure 8-14 The Tiling options in the Print dialog box.

When you select Auto Tiling and specify the amount of overlap you want between tiles, QuarkXPress automatically divides the page into the number of tiles needed to print given the size of the page, the size of the paper, and the amount of overlap specified. QuarkXPress prints the tiles at the top of the page first, from left to right, and works down the page.

When you select Manual Tiling, you control the placement of the upper left corner of each tile by relocating zero point on the ruler. This is useful if you want to reprint one tile after you have printed all tiles automatically, or for printing the last few tiles of a page that was interrupted during printing.

Since moving the zero point on one page effectively moves it for all pages (if Item Coordinates is set to Page in the Edit → Preferences → General dialog box), you can print the currently specified tile for all pages in the document at once.

To help assemble tiles that are printed with the Auto option, QuarkXPress prints tile location information in the upper left corner of each tile, in the format "Page x (y, z)" where x is the page number, y is the column number, and z is the row number. QuarkXPress prints tick marks where each tile can be cut or trimmed for alignment, but if you have allowed overlap you might choose to trim tiles along column gutters or some other natural feature of the page. You do not get tick marks or tile location information when you select Manual Tiling.

Whether you select Auto or Manual Tiling, you generally need some overlap in order to achieve precise alignment between adjacent tiles when you paste them together (Figure 8-15). At minimum, the overlap needs to account for the nonprinting edges of the paper (that is, at least .5 inches on a laser printer, or at least .25 inches if you select Larger Print Area through the Print dialog box's Options for laser printers).

Figure 8- 15 Newspaper page printed in four tiles on 8.5" by 11" paper, with overlap between pages (left), then assembled into full-page layout (right).

Document Setup

Ideally, you want to be printing to a *paper* size (on the printer) that is the same or larger than the *page* size of the document (as displayed on the screen, measured by the rulers, and defined by crop marks). Otherwise, you can print tiled sections of large pages on smaller paper or film as described under the Print command in this chapter. You can select File → Document Setup (Figure 8-16) to change the page size that was originally set up for the document when it was started through File → New (CTRL+N).

You can change the page size at any time, and all of the elements on each page will keep their same position relative to the top left corner of the page. The automatic text box will change to meet the margins of the new page size *if it met the old margins*, but automatic text boxes that do not meet the page margins, and items that fall outside the automatic text box, will not be changed by the new page size, and might need to be adjusted manually on every page. QuarkXPress will not allow you to change the page to a size that would force items currently on the page to move off the page.

Figure 8-16 Document Setup dialog box.

Diagnosing Problems in Printing

The most common problem you are likely to encounter in printing is that the document—or selected pages—will not print. Specific problems might be indicated by an error message on the screen, or the printing process might literally take forever with no results. The root of this problem can be mechanical, or it may be related to the construction of the document pages.

Diagnosing Mechanical Problems

The most obvious diagnostic steps may sound silly, but they happen to be the most common causes of printing problems. Besides, these problems are equipment-based and are usually easier to solve than problems that arise from the document's construction. The symptom of the problem might simply be that the file will not print, or you might get a clue from an error message such as "Can't Print to LPT." In either case, go through the checks suggested here before you tackle it as one of the more complicated problems listed in the next sections.

Examine the front panel of the printer to determine if the "On-Line Busy" light is flashing, indicating that the printer is processing your document. Other lights on the front panel may flash to indicate a particular problem – for example, toner is low or paper is jammed. Check to see that the printer is turned on. Make sure that there is paper in the paper tray(s) and that the paper tray(s) are firmly inserted into their slots. Verify that the printer cable is firmly connected to both printer and computer. Open the Control Panel and double-click on the Printers icon. Examine the settings for your printer driver to verify that the printer driver is active and properly configured for your printer and port. If you are printing under Windows 3.0, examine the printer settings in QuarkXPress (Printer Setup and Print in the File menu), and be sure they match the Control Panel settings for the active printer. (Remember that under Windows 3.0 you must change printers through the Control Panel only, whereas under Windows 3.1 you can also change printers through QuarkXPress' Printer Setup command.)

If you are using a serial printer, examine your COM port settings. Open Control Panel and double-click on the Ports icon. Click on the icon for the COM port to which your printer is connected and click Settings. Consult the documentation that came with your printer to determine the correct settings for Baud Rate, Data Bits, Parity, Stop Bits, and Flow Control. Verify that your printer is configured using these settings. If all settings are correct, lower the baud rate until the printer prints. Baud rates should be configured identically for both printer and Windows COM port. (If you are using a parallel printer, no port configuration is required.)

If your printer is responding to the print command issued from QuarkXPress—that is, the proper light is flashing to indicate that the printer is processing your print job—it is possible that the print job is exceeding the memory capacity of your printer. This situation is more common with PostScript devices than with non-PostScript printers such as PCL, dot-matrix, and ink-jet printers.

Solving the Problem of Limited Disk Space

If you get an I/O error saying that you are out of disk space, then Print Manager is on, and you have insufficient space on your hard drive for Print Manager to write the file to disk. The obvious solutions are to add more disk space (i.e., buy a bigger drive), or delete unnecessary files from your current hard drive, or use a file compression utility to free more disk space. The simplest solution, however, is to turn the Print Manager off.

Print Manager is essentially a spooling device; when Print Manager is on, you can send your job to the printer and get back to work. Printing may take a little longer, but meanwhile you have access to your computer. When Print Manager is turned off, your computer is tied up until your job has finished printing; it is not available for other tasks. To turn it off, open Control Panel and double-click on the Printers icon. Uncheck Use Print Manager in the lower left corner of the Printers dialog box. Click OK. Unchecking this box will increase the amount of time it takes before you can use your computer again during printing.

Diagnosing Problems with Graphics in the Document

If none of the steps suggested above solve the problem in printing, or if some pages do not print or do not print completely, or if the pages print but the graphics resolution is poor, try the following tests to determine the nature of the problem.

Pages Won't Print

If the pages that fail to print contain graphics, you can verify that the graphics are the source of the problem by clicking Rough in the QuarkXPress Print dialog box when you print. When you click Rough, QuarkXPress prints boxed Xs in place of the pictures in your document. If the document prints when Rough is selected, one or more graphics files are corrupt, or the combination of graphics and QuarkXPress items exceeds the capacity of the printer memory.

You can simplify a page by removing QuarkXPress items that are not part of the page design (items obscured by other items). Documents that cannot be printed often have items obscured by other items. The more layers you have in a document, the more time and memory will be required to print the document.

If the document contains TIFF pictures, reduce the resolution of the printer and the line screen (the number of halftone lines per inch). If the document prints at the lower resolution and line screen, your printer requires additional memory to print the job at the resolution and line screen you specified.

If you are printing to a PostScript printer and you have complex EPS files, simplify them. Remove any elements in your graphics file that are completely obscured by other elements. Adjust the flatness of curves in your drawing. Flattening a curve (that is, reducing the number of points used to define the curve) can yield memory savings, but making drastic changes may compromise the quality of output. If you have blends in EPS picture files, reduce the number of steps in the blends. If you have graduated fills, consult the documentation for the program that you used to create the fills for information about simplifying them. Consult the documentation that came with your illustration package for more information about simplifying drawings without compromising design.

Be aware that a document may print to a lower-resolution laser printer but fail to print to a high-resolution imagesetter because resolution and line screen are generally much higher on imagesetters and, therefore, imagesetters require significantly more memory to print a document. As a result, documents that print successfully at low resolutions or to a PCL printer may fail to print to a PostScript imagesetter.

Graphics Print at Low Resolution

If you are outputting proofs to a PCL printer (such as a printer in the Hewlett-Packard LaserJet series) and plan to send the document to a PostScript imagesetter for final output, be aware that EPS and TIFF picture files, which require printer memory for interpretation, are not processed by PCL devices. QuarkXPress sends the low-resolution bitmaps incorporated into the document to the PCL printer, but it will send the actual EPS and TIFF picture files to the high-resolution imagesetter.

If you are printing to a PostScript printer and the graphics seem to print at a low resolution, then the link between the EPS or TIFF file and the QuarkXPress document is probably severed (that is, the picture is missing). Reestablish the link to print the high-resolution picture files. Choose Utilities → Picture Usage, click on the missing picture, and then click Update. A directory dialog box is displayed. Locate the missing picture and click OK. QuarkXPress will reestablish the path between the picture and the document. For more information about updating the links between a picture file and a QuarkXPress document, see Chapter 6.

Diagnosing Problems in Printing Colors

Color issues are discussed in Chapter 7, but here are a few color considerations that relate directly to printing.

Color Won't Print on Color Printer

QuarkXPress documents that have been set up with different colors through the QuarkXPress menus, or which contain imported color graphics, should print in color on any PostScript color printer. Be sure to specify Use Color for your printer driver. To do this, open the Control Panel and double-click on the Printers icon. Click Configure and Setup buttons in successive dialog boxes to access the Printer on [Port] dialog box. Make sure that you have selected a printer brand and model that supports color output from QuarkXPress. QuarkXPress cannot print color to non-PostScript printers.

Color Separation Plates Won't Print

You can print color separations of a QuarkXPress document to any PostScript printer or imagesetter. Make sure that you have checked Make Separations in the Print dialog box.

If you have imported TIFF and EPS pictures, make sure that the picture files are linked to the document. Choose Utilities → Picture Usage and locate the picture files in the scroll list. The Status of the picture files must be either OK or Modified. If the Status is Missing, click on the picture name in the scroll list and then click Update. Locate the picture file in the directory dialog box and click OK to relink the picture file to the document.

If the picture files are linked to the document but you do not get separation plates, make sure that TIFF picture files are in CMYK format and that EPS files contain color plate information. Not all illustration and photo retouching software can save picture files with color separation information.

Picture files not saved in a color-separated format cannot be separated by QuarkXPress. You will need to separate them before importing them into QuarkXPress.

If some but not all color plates print, then you are not printing to a PostScript printer, or you have not selected All Plates in the Print dialog box, or you have not created all colors in QuarkXPress. Choose File → Print. Choose All Plates from the Plates drop-down list. The Plates drop-down list is available only for PostScript printers. If you do not have a PostScript printer, you can print only composites.

If you are printing to a PostScript printer and have selected All Plates from the Plates drop-down list, make sure that you have specified in the document all spot colors used in imported color EPS files. You must add all spot colors used in an EPS picture to the document's list of colors available for these colors to separate properly.

Diagnosing Problems in Printing Fonts

If pages fail to print at all, it could be that the fonts require more memory or disk space than available. (These two problems were addressed in earlier sections.) This section addresses the problem that the pages print, but the fonts do not print the way you intended.

Fonts Print Smaller Than Expected

If you are printing to a PCL printer and the fonts print smaller than specified., you have probably chosen a bitmap font in a size which you have not installed. Bitmap fonts are defined by their typeface, style, and size. For example, if you want to print using 10-point Letter Gothic Italic, you must have installed an italic Letter Gothic font at 10 points. If you are printing to a PCL printer and have not installed the size you are using and, if you are not using a type manager, the font will be printed at the nearest smaller size.

If fonts print extremely small on a PostScript printer, you are probably using an old PostScript printer driver. Verify that you are using the PostScript printer driver that shipped with Windows 3.0a or later. To do so, launch File Manager and open the WINDOWS\SYSTEM directory. Choose View → File Details if file size and date are not already displayed. Locate the file named PSCRIPT.DRV. It should be dated 10/31/91 or later. If you have a version of PSCRIPT.DRV with an earlier date, call Microsoft or obtain the correct printer driver from your dealer.

Some Characters Do Not Print Correctly on a PCL printer.

Some fonts do not include special characters such as daggers, typesetter's apostrophes and quotation marks. If this is not the problem, you may not have configured your Windows printer driver correctly. Open the Control Panel and double-click on the Printers icon. Verify that you have specified the correct settings for your printer. Verify that you have chosen the correct printer brand and type. If you have a printer that is not listed, consult the documentation that came with your printer or contact the printer manufacturer to determine which printer brand and type you should choose.

If you are printing to your printer using a serial cable, your COM port settings may be incorrect. To adjust the COM port settings, open the Control Panel and double-click on the Ports icon. Click on the icon for the COM port to which your printer is connected and click settings. Consult the documentation that came with your printer to determine the correct settings for Baud Rate, Data Bits, Parity, Stop Bits, and Flow Control. If all settings are correct, lower the baud rate until the printer prints correctly. Baud rates should be configured identically for both the printer and the computer.

Fonts Print Smashed Together

On a PostScript printer, this problem may be because you have metrics files but not the printer font file for the font you want to print. When this happens, QuarkXPress substitutes another font's characters but uses the metrics for the font you specified to keep the correct line and page breaks. Install the correct printer font for the font you have chosen. Consult the documentation that came with your fonts for information about installing printer font files. If you are using Adobe Type Manager, you may need to update your softfonts list. See your ATM documentation for information.

This problem could also be due to the fact that the printer font you want to use is not listed in the WIN.INI entry for the printer you are using. Edit your WIN.INI to include the location of printer fonts.

Finally, your font files might be damaged. Replace your PostScript printer font files and printer font metrics files. Consult the documentation that came with your fonts for information about installing these files.

Fonts Look Good on Screen but Print Incorrectly

Sometimes PostScript fonts look fine on-screen, but they will not print to the PostScript printer. They print as either Courier or they are incorrectly sized or placed. Most likely, the fonts that you are using are not downloading to the printer. (See Downloading Fonts, earlier in this chapter.)

If you are running ATM and the PostScript fonts that print are not the same as the fonts on the screen, your fonts may have been remapped in the ATM.INI. ATM stores map information in the ATM.INI file. This map tells ATM which printer font metrics (PFM) files and which printer font (PFB) files to use for a specified font.

Although you can reassign font files for any font name you choose, we don't recommend it as a general practice. On a few occasions, you may want to remap your ATM.INI file. (For example, Futura Bold will print bolder from the PC than from the Macintosh. To print the same weight of Futura Bold on the PC as on the Macintosh, you can remap your Futura Bold font in your ATM.INI to Futura Medium Bold.) On other occasions, however, you may want to undo some remapping that has been done in the past and restore the original mapping.

Before making any changes to the ATM.INI file, make a backup of it and store it in a safe place. If Windows or ATM refuses to launch using the edited ATM.INI, you can copy your original ATM.INI back into your Windows directory.

Here is an example of some font mappings in the Fonts section of the ATM.INI.

```
[Fonts]
Futura=c:\psfonts\pfm\fuw_____.pfm,c:\psfonts\fuw_____.pfb
Futura,BOLD=c:\psfonts\pfm\fuh_____.pfm,c:\psfonts\fuh_____.pfb
Futura,BOLDITALIC=c:\psfonts\pfm\fuho____.pfm,c:\psfonts\fuho____.pfb
FuturaMedium,BOLD=c:\psfonts\pfm\fuh_____.pfm,c:\psfonts\fuh_____.pfb
```

In this example, Futura Bold prints as Futura Medium Bold. Note that the PFM and PFB files for Futura Medium Bold have the filenames "fuh_____", and that these files have been assigned to both Futura Medium Bold and Futura Bold. By assigning these files to the "Futura, Bold" entry, you force ATM to display and print Futura Medium Bold whenever you specify Futura Bold. If you want to change this, you must remap the Futura, BOLD entry to reference the Futura Bold metric and printer files. The modified entry appears below:

```
Futura,BOLD=c:\psfonts\pfm\fub_____.pfm,c:\psfonts\fub_____.pfb
```

Your fonts may also have been remapped in the Alias section of ATM.INI. Scroll through ATM.INI until you locate the Alias section. Beneath the [Alias] header, you might, for example, find:

```
Futura,BOLD=FuturaMedium,BOLD
```

Like the previous example, this one shows Futura Medium Bold substituted whenever Futura Bold is specified. Delete this line if you do not want the substitution.

You will need to quit, then restart windows for ATM to recognize any changes you make to ATM.INI.

You will find additional information about special mapping of fonts in the README.TXT files located on the disk of fonts you purchased. For more information about PostScript fonts and font mapping with ATM, consult your ATM User's Guide or contact Adobe Systems, Inc.

Using the Windows Error Handler

As an aid to troubleshooting, you should download the error handler built into Windows. To do so, double-click on the Printers icon in the Control Panel.

If you are running Windows 3.0, click Configure, Setup, and Options buttons in successive dialog boxes. The Options dialog box is displayed. Press ALT + E. The Error Handler dialog box is displayed. Click Printer as the destination for Error Handler. Click OK in the dialog box that asks if you want to Download Error handler immediately.

If you are running Windows 3.1, click Setup, Options, and Advanced buttons in successive dialog boxes. Then check Print PostScript Error Information in the Advanced Options dialog box.

If there is a printing problem, the error handler will print out a page with the error and offending command. You can look up the error and the offending command in a PostScript manual; or, if you are covered by a Quark Service Plan (see the Service Plan information in your Getting Started booklet), you can call a technician at Quark to determine your course of action.

If All Else Fails

If the document did not print in Rough mode and the Windows error handler didn't reveal the problem, there may be problems with the fonts (see next section) or QuarkXPress document may be damaged. In the latter case, create a new document with the same page dimensions as the existing document. View both documents in thumbnails view by choosing Thumbnails (View menu). Drag-copy the pages from the existing document to the new document. Print the new document.

Summary

In this chapter you learned how to print pages from QuarkXPress, and about special considerations in printing oversized pages or in using a service bureau to output your pages. This chapter also covered diagnosing the most common printing problems.

This chapter completes Part I of this book, a description of all the commands, tools, and features of QuarkXPress. Part II presents some of the advanced techniques that can be used in building QuarkXPress documents.

PART II

ADVANCED TECHNIQUES

9 Templates and Design

Whenever you start a new document, you must go through certain steps to set up the pages before you begin importing text and graphics from other programs. In traditional terms, you define the design specifications for the document. In QuarkXPress terms, you make selections in the New dialog box, set up guides and other elements on the master pages, define style sheets, and set other preferences and defaults before you begin adding elements to the first page. This chapter describes how to use QuarkXPress to generate design ideas and to create templates that embody the design specifications.

QuarkXPress can be used to sketch rough ideas for designs that can be reviewed with the rest of the production team or the client; however, it goes a step further than the traditional pencil sketch because it can implement the design by creating templates, including style sheets, that help ensure that all parts of a document will follow the same design specifications.

In practice, some of the steps described here might be done first on paper rather than on the computer. In fact, the designers on some teams might never actually touch the mouse. Whether you—as the designer—are simply drawing and writing out the design specifications or actually setting up the master template yourself, knowing how QuarkXPress works before you make your specifications will help.

For example, QuarkXPress generally defines a page in terms of the margins, the number of columns, and the space between columns. If you divide a text box into columns, you cannot enter the column widths directly. Your specifications must be in terms of the number of columns and space between, rather than the width of the columns themselves. This chapter shows you how to prepare your design specifications in terms of QuarkXPress' commands and capabilities.

Whenever you want to create a series of similar documents in QuarkXPress—documents with similar design specifications and page layouts—you can avoid repeating steps by initially capturing the design in a template, as described later in this chapter.

Creating Design Alternatives

You can use QuarkXPress to create a series of quick roughs of different designs for a document before deciding on the final design. The advantage of using QuarkXPress rather than pencil and ruler to sketch your ideas is threefold:

- It is easy to copy and move elements on a page as you work on a design.
- It is efficient to make copies of the first design and modify it to create alternative designs.
- It is effective to show clients crisp text and graphic elements printed on a high-resolution printer. (We use the term "client" to include managing editors, publication department managers, end-user groups, or others with whom the designer must share decisions.)

Since you import the actual text and graphics that comprise the work in final documents, you do not need to know the exact text or contents of the document in order to rough out a design idea. You can use QuarkXPress' built-in text and graphics features to create representations of the basic elements in a document. For example, you can use *dummy text* to show the position and size of text on a page, shaded boxes to show where graphics will be imported, and rules to enhance the design. Figure 9-1 shows how design ideas can be handled in QuarkXPress.

Chapter 9: Templates and Design 331

Figure 9-1   Rough page comps can be done by hand or by using QuarkXPress.

Rather than create a different QuarkXPress document to represent each design idea, you can use one design document to create many variations, as shown in Figure 9-2.

Step 1   **Create representations of all the basic design elements once and store them on the master page.**

Step 2   **Add a page for each design idea.**

Step 3   **Modify or rearrange the master page elements on each page to develop design variations.**

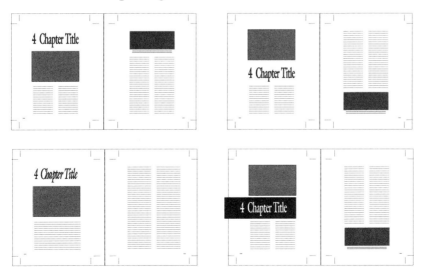

Figure 9-2   Example of variations on one design idea in a design document.

After reviewing different design ideas, the designer can translate those ideas into the specifications that will be applied in QuarkXPress and the other programs that will be used to construct the pieces of the document, such as a word processing program or graphics programs.

By printing documents as Thumbnails (File → Print), you can see several different design treatments or the overall layout for a longer document, such as a book (Figure 9-3). You can vary the number of thumbnail pages that will print on a sheet of paper by changing the percentage of enlargement or reduction in the Printer Setup dialog box (File → Printer Setup). Reduce the percentage to make each thumbnail page smaller, allowing more pages to print on each sheet of paper; enlarge the percentage to make each thumbnail page larger, with fewer pages shown on each sheet of paper.

Figure 9-3 Printing thumbnails lets you see how well a design carries throughout a document.

Create a Grid System

The best document designs are based on an underlying *grid* structure that is used to position elements throughout the document. Pages of Gutenberg's Bible show traces of the grid system he used to lay out his pages. A few decades later a book named *De Divina Proportione*, written by Fra Luca Pacioli and illustrated by Leonardo da Vinci, applied the rules of classic proportion to book design. Contemporary designers still study this masterwork and apply the same principles in new book designs. One such method of defining the margins for a book is shown in Figure 9-4.

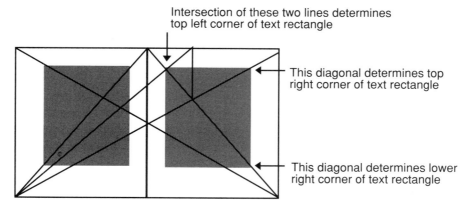

Figure 9-4   One method of determining the classic proportions for a book design.

In traditional production, a grid system is a series of vertical and horizontal lines drawn or printed in light-blue ink on the layout boards used to paste up galleys of typeset text and inked line art. The "nonrepro" blue lines are not picked up by the camera during the process of making plates for printing the final pages. The practical function of the blue lines is to help ensure that the galleys of type are laid straight on each page and that all pages have the same margins. Because every page is pasted up using the same grid of blue lines, the entire document has a fundamental consistency.

In QuarkXPress you can set up a grid of page and ruler guides on the master pages or document pages to make it easy to align elements consistently. These guides are visible on the screen but will not print. We normally think of a grid as simply the margin guides and column guides for a document. Of course, these are the basic elements of any grid system. Professional designers often use more elaborate grid systems than that, however. In QuarkXPress the grid can include up to 200 ruler guides as well as printed elements, such as rules between columns or frames around pages.

Simple grid structures that involve one, two, or three columns are relatively easy to work with, but complex grids usually offer more design possibilities. For example, a one-column grid structure can have only as much variety in the layout as can be achieved by varying the type specifications and paragraph indentations. A two-column grid structure offers the added possibility of making graphics and text expand to the full page width on selected pages if necessary or desired. A three-column grid offers at least three page variations, as shown in Figure 9-5.

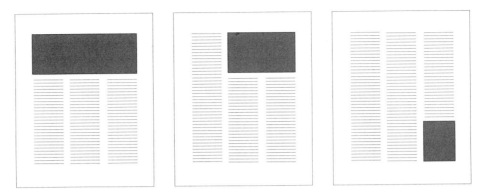

Figure 9-5   Examples of different layouts that are possible on a three-column grid.

The spacing between the columns is normally set to a default width of 0.167 inch, or 1 pica. You can make this wider if you will be dropping hairline rules between columns, but a good rule is to keep the space between columns under 2 picas.

What Is a Template?

A template is a QuarkXPress document that embodies the basic features of the design specifications (Figure 9-6). A template usually makes use of master pages, and may include some sort of grid system for laying out the pages (beginning with page size and margins), a system for applying type specifications (via style sheets or via text boxes from a Library), a source of standard symbols and graphics used in the document (stored on the Pasteboard, in a Library, or in external files to be imported), and standing items that are always printed in the same location on certain pages (such as a newsletter banner). A template is set up with all defaults tailored to match the design specifications for the document.

A template might consist of no more than a simple grid of margin guides and an automatic text box with column guides. For example, whenever you start a new document in QuarkXPress, you specify the basic parameters, such as the size of the page, the orientation of the printed image, and the text margins, before adding any text or graphics to the pages. By setting up these specifications in the template, you can be sure that all documents created from it have the same page size and orientation settings.

Figure 9-6 A template document.

A more complex template might include common text and graphic elements, such as headers and footers, headlines, rules, and other repeating symbols and graphic elements. A template can include style sheets for applying type specifications used throughout the publication. It can also incorporate productivity aids, such as guides for aligning objects across facing pages and for positioning text and graphics as well as common elements that will appear within the document in specific locations or at repeated intervals.

Once a template document is created, it can be used over and over to create a series of documents that follow the same design specifications. For instance, a long publication might have one template document that is used to create a series of sections or chapters that all follow the same design specifications. A short publication that is produced regularly—such as a newsletter—would have one template from which each issue is created.

As you learned in Chapter 2 the Save as dialog box in QuarkXPress lets you save a document as a template (Figure 9-7). A QuarkXPress template (.QXT file) differs from a document (.QXD file) in that when you use the Save command, a template always displays the Save as dialog box without a document name, so you cannot inadvertently overwrite the original.

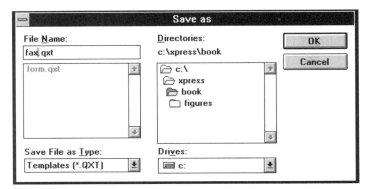

Figure 9-7 The Save as dialog box lets you save a document as a template.

You can easily distinguish between the two types of documents in the Open dialog box by choosing to display either Templates or Documents (Figure 9-8).

Figure 9-8 The Open dialog box with Templates selected.

Benefits of Using Templates

You can go through a life of publishing with QuarkXPress without using templates or knowing that they exist, but we offer the next few paragraphs in order to highlight their value and perhaps overcome that bit of inertia that pulls us to stay with old, inefficient practices. Templates can save repeated setup steps, help you to think ahead, embody a design, and enforce consistency. They can also serve as a method for working with different sets of preferences on one system.

Templates Save Repeated Setup Steps

One major benefit of using a template system is that the decisions and actions described under the next headings are executed only once during the production cycle, rather than once for every new file that will be a part of the full publication. Templates save time in large production projects by capturing a few of the steps required to set up a new document, so the same steps do not have to be repeated every time a similar document is started. You can save hours or days over the life of a project by using a template system for large or periodical publications.

It is a good idea to develop a template system for any project that will require more than one QuarkXPress document file. Books, reports, manuals, newsletters, and magazines are candidates for template systems whereby a single template is used to create a separate document file for each chapter, section, or issue. Even if the number of pages required for a document is less than the maximum allowed by QuarkXPress, there are good reasons for dividing these publications into several documents, all built from the same template. Shorter documents such as price lists, menus, ads, and brochures are candidates for template systems if you will be producing more than one document with the same or similar layout.

Templates Help You to Think Ahead!

It's a good idea to think out the design of your document before making your initial page set-up. Never sit down at your computer to produce a report or newsletter without planning ahead. The first step in thinking out a production plan is to list the design specifications that will be applied throughout a publication. Wherever possible, design specifications should be captured in the template system. Even if the design specifications are already clearly written out on paper, the QuarkXPress menus and options can provide a structure for organizing them.

Templates Let You Create Different "Default" Preferences

You can create templates that have different preference settings, and thereby work around the "tyranny" of XPRESS.PRF in defining the defaults whenever you start a new document. For this purpose, the template might have nothing set up on the master pages or any document pages, and essentially open as a new, blank document. The templates can vary any of the options available under Preferences → General, Preferences → Typographic, or Preferences → Tools. For example, you might let the default preferences (XPRESS.PRF) set the rulers to inches, and set up a special template that always opens with rulers set to picas. Or you might set up a template that had a special frame width and line width set up through Preferences → Tools.

Remember that anything you find yourself repeatedly customizing, including the Zoom tool increments, is a candidate for a template.

Templates Embody Design

Aside from the practical considerations of saving time and providing a disciplined approach to producing a document, a template system can ensure that design specifications are easy to apply. By incorporating as many of the design specifications as possible into a QuarkXPress template, the production group can better preserve the look intended by the designer.

Templates Help Enforce Consistency

It goes without saying that a good designer always applies the rule of consistency. This means that part of the designer's responsibility is to make sure that all elements have been considered, and that no one on the production team will need to invent design specifications for details that were not covered by the designer's original specifications.

In the past the designer enforced consistency by issuing lists of standards and having blue lines printed as grid guides on the final page-layout boards. In QuarkXPress you can enforce consistency by using templates and style sheets to enforce a grid system, apply type specifications, and set up specific line lengths and widths, box background colors, tab settings, paragraph alignment (flush left, justified, and so on), and indentations.

The designer also needs to specify standard spacing between figures and text as well as the spacing between headings and body copy. You can use the Item → Modify command to define the inset that will determine the distance between the contents of that box and adjacent boxes.

Creating a Template Document

The next sections describe the basic steps in creating a template document in QuarkXPress. This procedure is a very organized approach to developing a series of similar documents: Create a template that includes all of the elements that are common to all documents in the series, then use the template by adding text and graphics to create each final document in the series. Instead of creating a template per se, you might simply choose to create the first document completely, then copy that document and *delete* parts you don't need; then, add new text and graphics to create the second and subsequent similar documents.

Whichever approach you take, it is important to set up the elements described in the next sections carefully in the first document—whether it is a template or a finished document—so that subsequent documents based on it will match the design specifications. If you are careless in creating the first document, you might end up with a series of documents that all share the same *incorrect* specifications, and add hours of work in making the same corrections in every document individually.

Define the Page Size, Margins, and Columns

Whenever you open a new document you first define the page size, margins, and columns through the New dialog box (Figure 9-9). The values specified here for margins and columns will affect the first page of the document and the original Master Page A. You can change the page size at any time using the File ➤ Document Setup command. You can change the margin and column guides for any given master page by choosing Page ➤ Master Guides.

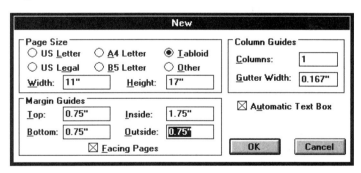

Figure 9-9   Page size and margins are set in the New dialog box when a new document is created.

Most publications use the same page size for all sections, but the orientation of the pages may vary from section to section. For instance, you might have a set of appendices that need to be printed wide to accommodate many columns of numbers in a financial report. These types of documents are easy to accommodate since QuarkXPress lets you have up to 127 different master pages.

Calculating the Width of the Automatic Text Box

In the New dialog box, you begin a new document by specifying (among other things) the width of the margins; this determines the width of the automatic text box on the first master page. The automatic text box is especially useful for longer documents, such as books or reports, since text flows into the automatic text box on a document page when a new page is inserted.

If you know the margins and the page size, as specified in the New dialog box, you can calculate the width of the automatic text box using the following formula:

Automatic text box width = (page width) – (inside margin measure + outside margin measure) – (twice the text inset)

If you know the column widths for your document, you can use the following formula to calculate the widths of a text box based on column width. You can set up columns in the New dialog box or the Master Guides dialog box (for master pages) or in the Text Box Specifications dialog box (for any text box):

Text box width = (Column width × number of columns) + (gutter width × number of gutters)

If you are more accustomed to defining page layouts in terms of the width of the text area rather than the width of the margins, you can set the width of the automatic text box *after* you close the New dialog box by making the first master page active (or whatever master page you have set up with the automatic text box), selecting the automatic text box, and using the Item ➤ Modify command to set the width of the box. This procedure changes the width of the automatic text box on all pages based on that master page, but it does not change the margin guides on the screen.

If you want the width of the automatic text box to match the margin guides, you can convert your specifications for the automatic text box width into margin widths using a variation of the previous formula:

Total space available for inside and outside margins = page width – automatic text box width

For example, if you know you want the automatic text box to be 6 inches wide on an 8.5-inch-wide page, then the total amount of space available for both the inside and the outside margins is 2.5 inches (8.5 – 6).

Remember that the actual width of the *text* in the automatic text box will be the width of the text box *minus twice the text inset value*. QuarkXPress' default text inset value is 1 point, but you may want to change this to 0 for the automatic text box by changing the text inset value for the automatic text boxes on the master pages.

If you make your calculations before starting a new document, you can enter these values directly in the New dialog box. Otherwise, you can change the margins through the File → Document Setup command or the Page → Master Guides command after you have started a document.

Select a Unit of Measure and Display Rulers

If all of your design specifications are given in the same unit of measure, you can set your preferences in the template document, then the same unit of measure will apply to all files created from the template. Use the Edit → Preferences → General command (Figure 9-10).

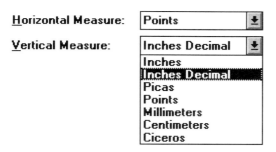

Figure 9-10 Set the preferred unit of measure in the template document in the General Preferences dialog box.

If your specifications are given in two or more different measures—inches for margins and points for type, for instance—then select that unit of measure in which you prefer to view the rulers.

You will probably use View → Display Rulers (CTRL+R) to display the rulers during the design phase in order to help lay out your grid precisely. If you leave the rulers on in the template document, they will be displayed automatically in all documents that are created from the template.

Set Up the Master Pages

We have already suggested that a different master page might be appropriate for each unique page margin specification and for each different column setting. In the previous section you saw how two master pages can be used to create four variations in facing-page layouts. In general, you should set up a different master page for each section of the document that requires different margins, columns, or page orientation (Figure 9-11).

Figure 9-11   Each section of the document that requires different margins should have a different master page.

In addition, there may be other essential differences between sections of the document that can be handled efficiently through different master pages (Figure 9-12). For example, when the overall format specifies that the headers and footers change between major sections of a document, then multiple master pages are needed.

When you display master pages in the Document Layout window (View → Show Document Layout), the name of the master page is displayed next to each icon. You can change that name by selecting and retyping the text (though the icons will still be labeled M1, M2, M3, and so on). By assigning names to master pages, you make it easy to select and apply the correct master page to document pages.

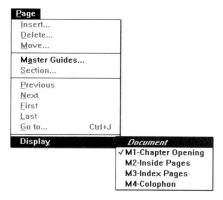

Figure 9-12   Drop-down submenu of Page → Display command shows list of master pages by letter and name.

Master Page Elements

Elements that appear on every page in the same position belong on a master page. This includes graphic elements such as a logo that appears on every page, rules between columns, frames around pages, and other design elements.

Other elements that should be included on the master page are headers and footers. The headers and footers on the master pages of the template may be set up as placeholders only: They are set up in position with the correct type specs and alignment, but the text can change for each document that is created from the template. One of the first steps in using the template, then, would be to change the text of the header and/or footer (Figure 9-13).

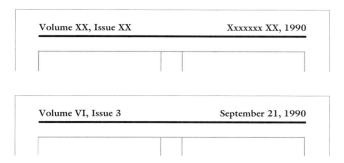

Figure 9-13   The headers and footers on the template document are placeholders only and must be updated each time the template is used.

Headers and footers have logical positions on a typical page. The most readily referenced part of any book is the outer edge of the page. Figure 9-14 shows some examples of how these four positions can be used to make page numbers and section names easy to find.

Figure 9-14 The four most easily referenced page number positions are: top left of even-numbered pages and top right of odd-numbered pages; bottom left of even-numbered pages and bottom right of odd-numbered pages.

Setting Up Multiple Master Pages

To set up multiple master pages in a document, consider how your text needs to flow throughout your document. For example, let's say you are creating a template for a book. The template file contains two master pages—one for the opening of each chapter and one for the following pages in the chapter.

The automatic text box that you specify in the New dialog box will appear on the first page of the document and on Master Page M1 (Figure 9-15). Display Master Page M1 to create the master page for the chapter opening, and format the automatic text box using Item ➤ Modify and the various commands from the Style menu.

Subsequent master pages will not have an automatic text box. To link the second master page to the first, so that text flows from one to the next, first create a second master page by choosing View ➤ Document Layout; then view master pages (Document ➤ View Master Pages). Using the Masters ➤ Insert command, insert a blank master page.

When you choose the Page → Display command, Master Page M2 will be listed. Display Master Page M2; no text boxes will appear. Draw a text box on the page (or pages, if you are using a facing-pages master page) and format the box(es).

Finally, establish a link between the text box on new master pages and Master Page M1 by clicking on the Broken Chain icon in the upper left corner of the master page; a marquee is displayed around the icon. Next, click on the text box on the master page to establish it as an automatic text box into which text will flow after it fills the automatic text box on Master Page M1.

Another method of linking master pages is to use the Masters → Insert command, and choose Master Page M1 from the list. This will cause Master Page M2 to be a duplicate of Master Page M1, including the automatic text chain. You can then modify Master Page M2 as needed.

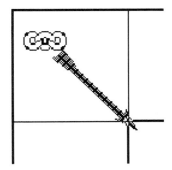

Figure 9-15 Creating an automatic text box on a master page.

Set Up Style Sheets

You can set the defaults for the normal body copy style sheet and any other standard text formats of the template document using Edit → Style Sheets as described in Chapter 5 on Typography. All documents that are created from the template will also have the same style sheets.

Identify Common Text and Graphic Elements

Most of the contents of the document will probably be imported from other programs. Some elements, however, will be repeated throughout the document. In a template, these repeated elements can be positioned on the master pages, on the Pasteboard, and on some document pages as described in this section. You can also set up a QuarkXPress library of commonly used elements to go with the template for the publication.

Library Elements

In addition to the elements that belong on the master pages, certain other elements might be repeated throughout a document in an irregular pattern. These can be created once and stored in a library (Utilities ➤ Library), for use wherever they are needed. The Library palette stores all items reduced to fit in the same size rectangle. The Library palette can be moved anywhere on the screen and can be changed to display items horizontally (Figure 9-16) by dragging a border or a corner, similarly to the way all windows under Microsoft Windows can be resized and reshaped. You can choose Maximize from the Control menu to expand the palette to fill the screen, then choose Restore from the Control menu to reduce it to its former size.

Libraries have many uses in setting up standards for a document. For example, if every story in a newsletter or magazine ends with a graphic symbol, you can store the symbol in a library and drag it onto the page whenever you reach the end of a story. Just as you created headers and footers on master pages, you can create standard dummy text blocks for pull quotes or captions within the document and store them in a library. If the document will include display ads in predetermined sizes, you can store boxes drawn to those sizes in a library. You can select multiple items on a page, such as a magazine banner made of several items, and drag them into a library as one object.

Figure 9-16   Common elements stored in a library.

You can add text boxes to the library. Any text formatting that you apply to these boxes will become the default formats when you type text in these boxes on document pages. For example, the pull quote text box in the library list shown in Figure 9-17 might be formatted with dummy text that has rules above and below, and the text box would be set up with the text inset appropriate for pull quotes. Whenever a pull quote is needed, you simply drag the pull quote text box from the library, copy or type the quote to replace the dummy text, then resize and position the box on the page.

Figure 9-17   Pull quote box from the Library file with dummy text as a placeholder for the actual text that will be typed in.

Similarly, you can format a picture box with predefined settings for frame and background. Those settings will be retained when you drag the box from the library into the document. For example, you can create an empty picture box, give it a black frame and background, and store it in the library. Then drag the black box onto a document page whenever you want to make a placeholder for a photo that will be dropped in by the print shop.

When you place an item that contains a high-resolution image into a library, QuarkXPress saves the picture file's path (the drive and directory location of the picture). When you drag the item from the library onto a page, the path information is copied onto the page as well.

Standard Elements on Document Pages

Besides the elements that are positioned on the master pages or stored in the library, certain elements may appear on the document pages in predictable locations. For example, the template for a newsletter could include the banner on page 1 (Figure 9-18). If each issue of the newsletter is always the same number of pages, you might also be able to predict the positions of the subscription information and other standing features. You can also add placeholders for the text of headlines for feature articles that start on page 1.

Figure 9-18 Newsletter templates can include standing elements on document pages.

Design Specifications for Graphics Programs

In addition to providing the specifications for the QuarkXPress document, the designer should have a good idea of the number and source of graphic elements that will go into the document and provide the correct specifications to the production team. Knowing the capabilities and limitations of the available programs, the designer is responsible for specifying the treatment of each illustration. What are the size limitations or preferences for the figures? If you are following a grid system, you will want to make each figure's width match the increments allowed by the grid: a two-column grid allows only two figure widths (one column wide or the full page width), a three-column grid allows three different figure widths, a four-column grid allows four widths, and so on.

What fonts/styles/sizes will be used in illustrations and their captions? Will the figures be enlarged or reduced during page composition? Will photographs and other special illustrations be pasted up by hand or scanned into the computer? These specifications can be written down, or the programs that will be used to create the illustrations can be used to create "figure templates" just as QuarkXPress is used to create document templates.

Special Handling of Captions

One of the characteristics of any designed document is consistency of treatment, including the treatment of labels within figures as well as the figure titles or captions. This consistency can be difficult to achieve when you are bringing figures from other programs into QuarkXPress. The designer needs to specify how captions, figure titles, and figure labels will be handled in each different program that may be the source of illustrations for the document. Will the charting program be able to match the fonts used in figures from other drawing packages? Will the figure be scaled larger or smaller after it is in QuarkXPress?

You might decide that all figure titles and captions will be entered directly in QuarkXPress to ensure consistency, but you will still need to specify the preferred font for labels that fall within the figures. Furthermore, you may need to account for changes in the size of type that result when you shrink or enlarge a figure in QuarkXPress. As you learned in Chapter 6 on Graphics, when you change the size of a graphic imported from another program, you also change the size of the type used therein. If you know that you will be shrinking a figure by 50 percent, for instance, then the illustrator might need to make the type twice as large in the drawing program as it will be in the final document.

Instructions for Working with the Template

It's important that the same steps be followed each time a template is used. You may want to provide production notes for your own reference or for others who might use the template. Such notes are especially useful if you are working in a group where work on a series of documents is shared among several people. The notes can be a simple list of steps that serve primarily as reminders, and they can be typed onto the Pasteboard. (If the word "Instructions" is typed in a large font and the template is saved in Fit in Window view, the instruction will be easy to see when the template is opened) For example:

Step 1   Open the template and immediately save it under a new name.

Step 2   Change the headers and footers on the master pages.

Step 3   Change the volume/date information on page 1, below the newsletter banner.

Step 4   Drag the Table of Contents text box from the library, and retype the new issue's contents.

Step 5   Continue placing text and graphics as specified for the current issue.

Test the Design and Template

Finally, it is a good idea to run a few sample pages of the document through the entire production process, starting with the various application programs used to create source files, including a word processing program and graphics programs, and finally using QuarkXPress. This will test all of the specifications before finalizing the design and the template. This dry run is more effective than any other review procedure in:

- flushing out any mismatches between the design specifications and the system capabilities,
- fine-tuning the template as needed, and
- identifying the detailed list of steps that should be followed for efficient production.

Unfortunately, we often skip this final test: It may seem like a luxury when working under the pressures of a short deadline. We tend to trust that our own knowledge of the system is sufficient to anticipate any problems. In fact, however, the test run can save time on a project by developing efficient procedures and thereby shortening the production cycle. Failing to anticipate major problems (such as discovering that your printer cannot handle the graphics from the sources specified in the design) can add many hours to a project.

Template File Management

Certain files should always be copied and used with any given template file, including the fonts used in the template. See Chapter 13 for a detailed discussion of this and other workgroup-related issues.

Summary

We hope the tips in this chapter have inspired you to use QuarkXPress as a design tool and to create a template for any group of documents that follow the same design specifications. The next chapters offer additional tips that can be applied to laying out individual document pages.

10 *Advanced Page Layout*

Chapters 2 and 3 described the basic steps and commands used in creating a document. This chapter goes beyond those basics, offering tips on choosing between alternative methods of storing and positioning commonly used items, aligning items on a page, changing the relationships between items, reformatting a document, and handling difficult page layouts.

Storing Commonly Used Items

Whenever you want to use the same item in several places, use one of three aids in QuarkXPress: You can put it in a QuarkXPress library, you can put a copy on the pasteboard and store it as part of the document so you can access it any time you want, or you can simply use the Copy and Paste commands to make duplicates through the Clipboard.

Using a Library

As described in Chapter 3, a library is a special QuarkXPress file for storing commonly used text and graphic items so that they can be accessed easily. Each library can contain up to 2,000 items, and you can create as many libraries as you like. A QuarkXPress library can store items in any format supported by QuarkXPress and retain the path information that is sometimes needed in printing. You can label, sort, and preview items in a library—making this a more flexible and convenient way of accessing items than simply copying from one document to another or using any of the storage methods described under the following headings.

Using the Pasteboard

The area surrounding the page in the document window serves as a pasteboard for storing text and graphics while you are working. You can use this area as an active storage area while you are building a master page or a document page, or you can use it as a permanent storage area for the document—an alternative to libraries.

To position an item on the document's pasteboard, you can drag it off a page (to remove it from a QuarkXPress page), you can paste it onto the pasteboard from another document or elsewhere in the active document, or you can use one of QuarkXPress' item creation tools to draw a box on the pasteboard and use the Get Text or Get Picture command to import other items into the box.

Items on the pasteboard remain next to the numbered page or master page where they are first positioned, so it's a good idea to store only those items that are related to individual pages. If you want to move an item from the pasteboard beside one page to another page, you can input a view percentage as low as 10 percent directly in the View Percent area in the lower left corner of the screen to reduce the page image to a smaller size, or select the Zoom tool (Q) and click with the CTRL key down to get a reduced view of many pages at once, then drag the item across several pages without using the scroll bars.

Items stored on the pasteboard are saved as part of the document. It's a good idea to keep the pasteboard clear of extraneous items to minimize the document size. Use a library to store commonly used items that appear throughout a document.

Using the Clipboard for Repeated Copies

The Clipboard, a built-in feature of Windows, is used to store selected items whenever the Cut or Copy command is used. It is common to use Cut or Copy to make copies of a selected item as part of normal editing.

It can also be efficient to use the Clipboard (rather than the pasteboard or a library) when you want to make many copies of an item and place them throughout a document. For example, let's say that you want to anchor a graphic logo within text throughout a document. For efficiency, go through the entire document pasting the graphic throughout the text from the Clipboard, as described in the next steps, rather than performing other edits on each page, then going back to a library or the pasteboard to copy the graphic again.

Step 1   In typing the text, include a text placeholder, such as the word "LOGO," wherever you want the graphic to be positioned.

Step 2   Prepare a picture box with the logo scaled to the size that will fit in the text.

Step 3   Copy the picture box into the Clipboard with the Item tool selected.

Step 4   Select the Content tool (☞) and use the I-beam pointer to position the text insertion point at the beginning of the text.

Step 5   Use the Edit → Find/Change command to locate the word LOGO. (Or scroll through the text to find all the places where you want the graphic logo.)

You cannot use the Find/Change command automatically to replace text with a graphic, so you still need to do the next step manually.

Step 6   Each time you find a place where the graphic should be anchored in the text, use the I-beam pointer to position the text insertion point or to delete the word "LOGO," then use the Paste command to insert the picture box with the logo graphic.

Repeat steps 5 and 6 until all cases of the logo have been handled, then go on with other edits in the document.

The Clipboard can hold only one selection at a time, and its contents are replaced each time you use the Cut or Copy command. Its contents are deleted when you turn the computer off. You must use the Edit → Delete command, the Item → Delete command, or the Delete or Backspace key to delete other text or graphics when you specifically do not want to replace the contents of the Clipboard. For this reason, it is better to use a library or the pasteboard for more permanent storage, as described under the previous headings.

Tips on Aligning Items

WYSIWYG (What You See Is What You Get) refers to what you see on the screen as compared with what prints out. Most desktop publishing systems and applications are not 100 percent WYSIWYG. Discrepancies occur because it is impossible to create an exact correlation between the 72 dpi screen resolution of most personal computers and the 300 dpi resolution of most laser printers or the 2540 dpi resolution of high-resolution imagesetters. Besides, the fonts displayed on the low-resolution screen are shown as bitmaps, while high-resolution printers define the letters mathematically (in PostScript code) during the printing process.

Because no system is truly WYSIWYG, it is a good idea to use QuarkXPress' built-in features and commands for aligning items on a page, rather than to rely on your eye's judgment about whether items align vertically or horizontally. The next sections summarize the alignment aids that were first introduced in Chapters 1 through 6, offering more specific tips about when and how these aids can be used.

Using Commands for Aligning Text

Always use QuarkXPress' commands for aligning text, rather than doing it visually on the screen display. For example, if you want two lines of centered text, use the Style ► Alignment ► Centered command for both lines, rather than insert space at the beginning of each line until the two lines appear to be centered. Use the Item ► Modify command to align text relative to the top of a text box, rather than insert carriage returns to drop the text in the box.

Always use the Style ► Formats command to indent paragraphs or create hanging indents, rather than using spaces or tabs to indent lines.

Always use tabs rather than spaces to align tabular columns. If, for example, you want a title on the left side of a running head and a page number on the right side, use a right tab to align the page number where you want it rather than using spaces or moving a left-aligned block to the right. These last two techniques may yield results that appear correct on the screen, but might not print out the way you'd expect.

Using the Snap to Guides

Use the "snap to" feature of QuarkXPress' margin guides, column guides, and ruler guides to align objects. The edges of boxes and lines will "snap to" a guide when brought within 6 pixels of the guide. You can change the distance at which objects "snap to" guides in the General Preferences dialog box (Edit → Preferences→ General), as described in Chapter 3. Or you can turn snap to off by toggling the View → Snap to Guides command, as described in Chapter 2.

Using Column Guides as Spacing Guides

In positioning ruler guides on document pages, you can use the automatic column guide feature to automatically divide an area on the page into equal parts, using the next steps.

Creating a Vertical Grid

The most common way to create a vertical grid is to display a master page and choose Page → Master Guides. In the Master Guides dialog box, you can enter the number of columns you want to have on the page (Figure 10-1). If an automatic text box is on the master page, the text box will be divided into columns of equal width; if there is no text box on the page, gridlines will be positioned vertically on the page but they will not affect text. The minimum gutter allowance is .042 inch, or 3 points.

You can specify vertical gridlines without a text box on the page, then draw a text box and specify a different number of columns by selecting the Item → Modify command, or by changing the number of columns for the text box in the Measurements palette.

Figure 10-1 The Master Guides dialog box lets you specify a vertical grid.

Creating a Horizontal Grid

You could create a horizontal grid on a master page by selecting Page → Master Guides and specifying the number of columns with the narrowest gutter possible (.042 inch). Then rotate the text box 90°, and drag guides from the ruler to line up with the columns in the text box (Figure 10-2). The page will then be divided equally between the top and bottom margins, and you can delete the text box.

Figure 10-2   Rotate the text box, then create a grid of equally spaced horizontal ruler guides.

Using the Space/Align Command

You can use the Item ► Space/Align command to align boxes and lines. If all the items are the same size, you can space the items apart by a specific measure between items, or you can distribute the items between the items themselves, left edges, centers, or right edges.

If the selected items are all different widths, you can make the space between items equal by setting the items to be distributed horizontally between *items*—that is, from the right edge of one item to the left edge of the adjacent item. Otherwise, the space between items will vary (Figure 10-3).

Similarly, if the selected items are all different heights, you can make the space between items equal by setting the vertical space to be measured between items—that is, from the bottom edge of one item to the top edge of the adjacent item. Otherwise, the space between items can vary.

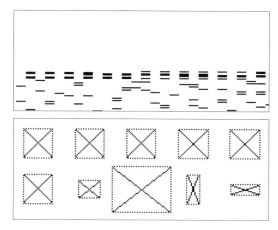

Figure 10-3 Items distributed horizontally between items (top) always have equal space between them; items distributed between centers can have different amounts of space between them (bottom).

 The Space/Align command moves all items in the group—including locked items—except the rightmost item (in horizontal movement) and the topmost item (in vertical movement).

Creating Relationships between Boxes

As you learned in Chapters 2 and 3, all text and some of the graphic items on a page are contained in boxes that are drawn using QuarkXPress' item creation tools. You can create relationships between these boxes in several ways.

- You can *link* text boxes to control a flow of text through a document.
- You can *anchor* boxes or lines within text so that they become part of the flowed text that moves when the text changes due to edits.
- You can *group* boxes or lines so that they can be multiple-selected with a single click.
- You can *constrain* a group of items to force them to remain within the boundaries of a constraining box.

The next headings offer some additional suggestions about when and how each of these relationships can be used.

Linking Boxes That Are Already Filled with Text

You can link two text boxes before they are filled with text, or you can link from a text-filled box to an *empty* text box, but you cannot link two boxes if they both already contain text. Normally, you can either import text into an automatic text box, so that a chain of linked boxes is created automatically, or link a filled text box to a series of empty boxes manually.

So what can you do when you have a series of unlinked boxes, all filled with text, and you decide you want them all to be linked? This condition might arise when you are composing a document from a series of boilerplate paragraphs that you have stored in a library, as is common in legal documents (Figure 10-4).

Figure 10-4   Legal document composed of a series of unlinked text boxes copied from a library.

You have to cut the text from each box and paste it at the end of the text in the previous box, but the obvious approach to this problem is not the most efficient.

The obvious solution is to start at the beginning—the first box in the series that you want to link. Select the Content tool (🖑), select all of the text in the *next* box in the sequence, choose Edit ➤ Cut, position the text insertion point at the end of the text in the first box, and paste. Now you can select the Linking tool (⚭) and link the first box to the (now-empty) second box. Select the Content tool (🖑) again and follow the same steps to empty the third box into the second, select the Linking tool again and link, and so on.

The less obvious solution offers one small economy in that you can stay with one tool at a time instead of switching between the Content tool and the Linking tool repeatedly:

Step 1   Start at the *end* of the series of boxes. Select the Content tool (👆), then select all of the text in the *last* box in the sequence.

Step 2   Choose Edit → Cut, position the text insertion point at the end of the text in the second-to-last box, and paste (Figure 10-5).

Figure 10-5   Text from last text box cut and pasted into second-to-last box.

Step 3   Don't link the two boxes yet. Follow the same two steps to empty the second-to-last box into the third-to-the-last box, and so on (Figure 10-6).

Figure 10-6   Text from all text boxes cut and pasted into the first box.

Step 4   When all of the text has been pasted into the first box in the series and all other boxes are empty, select the Linking tool (⚭) while holding the ALT key (to keep it selected) and link the boxes from the beginning to the end of the chain (Figure 10-7).

Figure 10-7   All text boxes linked.

In this particular example where the entire page is composed of linked text boxes only, with no graphics or other items, you could delete all the empty text boxes after step 3 and enlarge the first text box, but the steps given here will work for any type of page layout.

Linking Text Boxes on Nonconsecutive Pages

Linked text boxes need not follow on consecutive pages. This feature is especially useful for creating newspaper or magazine layouts in which an article begins on one page then jumps to another page in the document. QuarkXPress offers several ways of handling text jumps.

Method 1

If the page to which you want to link text is already part of the document, and the unlinked text box to which you want to jump the text is already in place, you can simply select the "jump from" box then select the Linking tool (⚭), click on the "jump from" box, scroll to the "jump to" page, and click the Linking pointer on the target text box.

Method 2

If the page to which you want to link text is already part of the document, and the unlinked text box to which you want to jump the text is *not* already in place, you must create the target text box before linking.

Step 1 **Scroll to the "jump to" page and create the "jump to" text box.**

Step 2 **Return to the "jump from" page, and follow the procedure under the previous heading to link the boxes.**

Depending on how far apart the two pages are, it might be quicker to create the "jump to" text box on the pasteboard next to the "jump from" page, link the two boxes, then *drag* the linked "jump to" text box to the "jump to" page (Figure 10-8). The farther apart the two pages, the less efficient it will be to drag the box down the pasteboard area.

Figure 10-8   "Jump to" text box on pasteboard at first, then moved to appropriate page.

Method 3

If you are already working at the end of the document, and you want to jump the text ahead *past pages that have not yet been inserted*, the most efficient thing to do is insert the new "jump to" page immediately after the page you are working on, and insert the other pages between these two pages later (Figure 10-9).

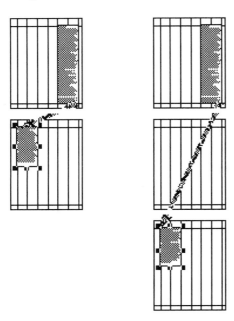

Figure 10-9 "Jump to" text box positioned on next page, with other pages to be inserted between the linked boxes later.

Working with Anchored Boxes

As you learned in Chapter 3, you can anchor a box within text. Anchored boxes can be either text boxes or picture boxes. You may find it useful to anchor an illustration to a figure caption, for example (Figure 10-10). Anchored items will flow with the text—and change position on the page if the text changes due to edits.

Figure 10-10 Anchored box contains an illustration related to a figure caption.

Anchored text boxes can be useful for anchoring pull quotes within an article (Figure 10-11). Another example of how you might use an anchored text box is to achieve a layout where single-column text is followed by two-column text; you could anchor a text box containing the two-column text within the single-column text box.

Figure 10-11   Anchored text box containing a pull quote.

You can indent any paragraph using the Style ➤ Formats command, or you can hang an anchored box to the left of indented text by entering an Indent Here character (⌘-\) following the anchored box (Figure 10-12). Lines are indented from the position of the Indent Here character.

Figure 10-12   Anchored picture box followed by Indent Here character.

Working with Constrained Boxes

As you learned in Chapter 3, you can constrain boxes within other boxes. Here we present some examples of when or why you would want to constrain or not constrain boxes.

 Never group or constrain items that you want to anchor in text—grouped or constrained items cannot be anchored. If you attempt to anchor grouped items, a warning dialog will appear that says "The items currently on the Clipboard can't be anchored in text."

Do group and constrain a selection of items that together compose a table or figure, such as the one shown in Figure 10-13.

Figure 10-13   Tabular data composed as a constrained group. The vertical line cannot be drawn outside of the constrained group.

If you are working on a document with Auto Constrain set to off in the General Preferences dialog box, you can constrain specific items in the document by first grouping them, then choosing Item → Constrain.

Tricky Page Designs

Even though you might be familiar with all of QuarkXPress' commands and tools, some page designs present challenges. Here are some tips for handling complex page layouts as well as simple problems that we have seen encountered by those who are new to document production.

Double-Sided Documents

QuarkXPress automatically handles most of the "tricky" issues in producing double-sided documents, but be aware of the points mentioned in the following sections.

Include Blank Pages

In preparing a document for double-sided printing, be sure to account for and print every page — including blank "left" pages that will be needed to force new sections or chapters to start on a right page (Figure 10-14). Having a numbered sheet for every page of the document will help in printing or copying the document. If you do not number blank pages, but want them to print so they are collated within other pages, be sure the Print Blank pages option is checked on in the Print dialog box.

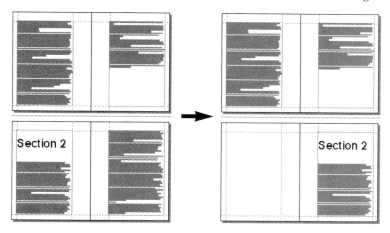

Figure 10-14   Blank page inserted to force new section onto a right-facing page.

Inserting an Odd Number of Pages

If you need to insert pages between existing pages in a document set up with Facing Pages, QuarkXPress will automatically shift the pages. If you add an even number of pages, of course, all left and right pages remain as left and right pages. If, however, you insert an odd number of pages, right pages must become left pages and vice versa. QuarkXPress will automatically "shuffle" the pages so that they take on the specifications of the appropriate left or right master.

Changing the First Page of a File

If you need to change the starting page number of a document (set up with Facing Pages) from an even-numbered page to an odd-numbered page, you can simply change the starting page number in the Section dialog box and QuarkXPress will shift the pages to the correct left and right master pages. However, to change an odd-numbered page to an even-numbered page, you need to follow certain steps to ensure that pages will shuffle correctly—so that pages formerly printed as right pages will shift to print on the left and vice versa.

For example, let's assume that you've set up a document as the second chapter of a report, beginning on an odd-numbered page, number 35 (set up in the Section dialog box by selecting Page ➤ Section). If you change the first page of the document to an even-numbered page, 36, only the first page shifts to a left page. The steps described next will shift all pages.

Figure 10-15   The first page of the file is set up as page 35 (Page ➤ Section) and needs to be changed to page 36.

Step 1   Insert a new document page BEFORE the first page of the file (Figure 10-16).

Chapter 10: Advanced Page Layout   367

Figure 10-16   The Document Layout palette after inserting a new page before the first page of a file.

Step 2   **Double-click on the Page 2 icon. Choose the Page ➤ Section command. The Section dialog box will appear; change the starting page number to 36. The pages in the document take on the format of the new, correct master pages. (Figure 10-17).**

Figure 10-17   Change the starting page number to 36.

Step 3 Delete the blank first page. View the renumbered document pages (Figure 10-18).

Figure 10-18   The document pages are renumbered with the correct master pages.

Creating Spreads

QuarkXPress lets you create multiple-page spreads, with the option of creating items that span the gutter between facing pages. Any pair of facing pages in a two-sided document is considered a spread, but you can also create spreads of more than two facing pages for multifold brochures or documents with fold-out pages

To create two-page or facing-page spreads (as is common in documents that will be printed double-sided), choose Facing Pages in the New dialog box or in the Document Setup dialog box, as explained in Chapter 2.

To create a multiple-page spread of any number of pages—or to create a facing-page fold-out panel in a single-sided document—choose the Document → Insert command in the Document Layout palette and insert the appropriate type of master page. Figure 10-19 shows various alternatives.

Chapter 10: Advanced Page Layout   369

Figure 10-19   Normal double-sided document with a fold-out panel (left) and fold-out panel in a single-sided document (right).

Bleeding Text or Graphics

Items that run off one or more edges of a page onto another page are said to "bleed" off the page. Any text or graphic item can bleed off a page. A bleed is a commonly used effect that makes a layout more dynamic by giving the reader's eye a fluid line that does not end on the page (Figure 10-20).

Figure 10-20   Image "bleeds" off left side of page.

Always print registration marks when printing pages with bleeds. When you print a document with Registration Marks selected in the Print dialog box, QuarkXPress increases the print area by .25 inches around document pages to accommodate items that bleed into the pasteboard area. To print bleeds effectively, you need to print on paper that is larger than the document page size.

All printers leave a margin of white space at the edge of the paper or roll—nothing will print in this area. The page outlines in the QuarkXPress document window represent the actual edges of the paper (if page size is the same as paper size); therefore, you need to be familiar with your printer's margin limitations and make sure that your page designs do not include text or graphics in the nonprinting area at the edges of the page. You can determine the limits of the print margins on your printer by printing out a page that is covered by a solid black box.

Figure 10-21 shows an image that bleeds across two letter-size pages. The inside margins may be lost in the nonprinting edges of the paper, particularly if you are using a laser printer that does not handle ledger-size paper.

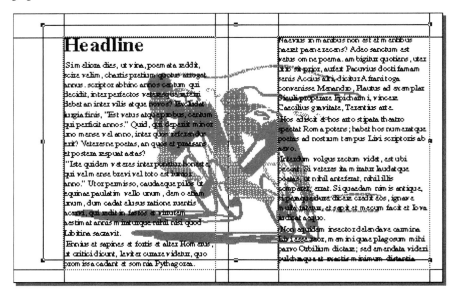

Figure 10-21   Image "bleeds" across two pages.

Controlling Text Runaround

As you learned in Chapter 3, you can make text flow around a box or line created with one of QuarkXPress' item creation tools by positioning the item on top of a text box and using Item ➤ Runaround to set runaround to a value other than None.

If you specify a runaround in the Runaround dialog box, you can enter the distance between the runaround text and the top, left, bottom, and right edges of a box. You cannot, however, specify text outset distances for lines. Here are some additional tips on how this feature can be used.

When you flow a single column of text around an item, the text will flow only on the side with the widest text area between the item and the edge of the text box (Figure 10-22).

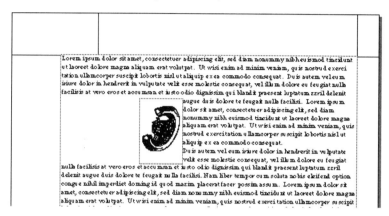

Figure 10-22   Runaround set to Item for box inside a one-column text box.

You can make a line or box any color and shade, or specify a color of none or a shade of 0 percent to make a transparent line or box. You can force text to runaround a transparent item by using the Item ➤ Runaround command to specify Item mode (Figure 10-23). You can also use the Item ➤ Modify command to suppress printout of the item and still have it affect text runaround.

Figure 10-23   Slanted margin forced by a transparent line.

Auto and Manual Image Runaround

If you have a picture box filled with an imported picture and you use Item ► Runaround to set the Mode to Auto Image, QuarkXPress automatically runs text around the picture in the active picture box. This is the type of runaround produced with graphics in QuarkXPress 2.12.

If you set the Mode to Manual Image, QuarkXPress creates an *editable* runaround polygon around the picture in the active picture box (Figure 10-24). You can modify a runaround polygon by adding, removing, or repositioning handles and by repositioning segments, as described in Chapter 6. You can specify the Text Outset for Manual Image mode just as you can for Auto Image mode.

Figure 10-24 A runaround polygon created automatically around an imported image.

You can also select Invert to run the text *inside* a picture's manual image polygon. See Chapter 12 for tips on how to use this feature to flow text inside a shape.

You can use a picture to create a runaround polygon, then delete the picture but keep the polygon. Doing so is handy when you want to use a for-position-only scan of an image to create text wrap, so the lithographer can strip in the photographic halftone of the image manually. You would use the for-position-only scan to create the polygon, and keep it on the page for draft printouts and for a sample to show the printer how to scale and crop the stripped-in halftone. The scan could then be deleted from the final camera-ready pages that you print.

Another time-saving trick if you are paying a print shop to strip in halftones and you want to use a for-position-only scan to help shape text runaround is to scan an *outline* of the photographic image instead of scanning the image itself. The outline scan will scan more quickly, take up less disk space, redraw more quickly on the screen, and print more quickly for draft versions.

You can disable screen redraw and save time in editing a runaround polygon by holding down the space bar as you edit. Release the space bar to redraw the screen and reflow text.

Creating Forms

You can use all of the alignment techniques described earlier in this chapter to create forms easily in QuarkXPress. Here we outline the steps used to create the sample form shown in Figure 10-31. You can adapt these steps to your specific needs, since the exact sequence of steps and the commands you use will vary depending on the content and design of the form you are creating. It's a good idea to start with some idea of what the final form will look like, even though you can, of course, add, delete, or rearrange fields in the process of creating the form in QuarkXPress.

Step 1   **Sketch the form and list the fields on a piece of paper before you start.**

Step 2   **In QuarkXPress, select the Text Box creation tool (A) and create separate boxes for each distinct area on the form.**

Some forms require only one text box; others might add one or two text boxes *on top of* the full-page text box; others might be composed of separate *adjacent* text boxes (Figure 10-25).

Figure 10-25   Some forms require only one text box (left); others might add one or two text boxes on top of the full-page text box (center); others might be composed of separate adjacent text boxes (right).

Step 3 Type and format the text in each text box (Figure 10-26). Set tabs to position text across a line.

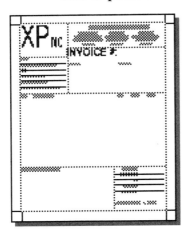

Figure 10-26   Form with text typed into boxes.

You can use flush-right tabs with underscore characters as leaders to create lines under fields that will be filled in (Figure 10-27).

Figure 10-27   Tabs with underscore characters as leaders created the two sets of entry fields in this box.

You can use Style ➤ Rules to create lines above and below fields that extend the width of the box margins (Figure 10-28).

Figure 10-28   The lines in this box are created using Style ➤ Rules.

Chapter 10: Advanced Page Layout 375

Step 4 Add frames around text boxes as appropriate (Figure 10-29).

Figure 10-29 Four of the seven text boxes in this form have 1-point black frames.

Step 5 Select the Orthogonal Line creation tool (+) to add lines that were not created using tab leaders or rules that are part of the text. Use Item → Step and Repeat to duplicate a series of lines at equal intervals (Figure 10-30).

Figure 10-30 The Step and Repeat command was used to create this series of parallel lines.

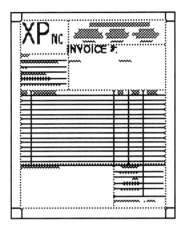

Figure 10-31   The final form.

Creating Forms for Typewriters

In creating a form that will be filled in using a typewriter, follow all the same steps as just outlined, but set the distance between lines on the form to equal a multiple of the distance between lines when typed on the typewriter.

You can determine this distance by typing a few lines on a blank sheet of paper at the intended setting—usually double-spaced or space and a half. Measure the distance between lines, and use this distance—or some multiple of it—as the leading value (in setting lines of text) or as the vertical offset value in using the Step and Repeat command.

If the form consists of more than one text box, set the Baseline Grid at the typewriter's interline spacing value, and make sure the text in each boxed form is locked to the baseline grid.

If you will be adding horizontal lines with the Orthogonal Line creation tool (+), create horizontal ruler guides across the page at intervals that match the typewriter's interline spacing value, and use these guides in creating the first line, before using Step and Repeat to duplicate the line.

Summary

This chapter provided information on the pros and cons of various ways to store items—using a library, the pasteboard, or a scrapbook. We also provided tips on aligning items, linking text boxes, and anchoring boxes in text. Finally, we offered guidance for working with tricky page layouts, including creating spreads and bleeds, and tips for creating forms.

The next chapter discusses how to work with text from databases or mainframe computers.

11 Working with Text from Databases and XPress Tags

Database publishing encompasses many kinds of documents, from financial reports to membership directories. The text, or data, which is generated by spreadsheets and databases often has the unique characteristic of containing commas or tabs to separate information. Another characteristic of text from a database is that it is often published in a repetitive format.

While publishing databases offers a unique set of challenges, another category of text that also has special characteristics is text created using text editors on mainframe computers, which often have little or no formatting capabilities. It would be nice if the entire computing world enjoyed the many benefits of using personal computers, but since the reality is that they don't, it may be useful to know how to work with text you get from another type of computer. Especially bothersome can be the fact that sometimes unwanted characters, such as paragraph returns at the end of every line, are embedded in the text.

This chapter offers tips on how to work globally with invisible characters as an aid to both database publishing and in "cleaning up" text telecommunicated from other computers. This chapter also covers XPress

Tags, special codes for formatting text that can be input in any ASCII text file and are recognized in QuarkXPress.

Finding and Changing Special Characters

As you learned in Chapter 4, QuarkXPress has a Find/Change command for searching and globally replacing words, phrases, or character attributes in text. You can search for special characters and hidden characters by holding down the ⌘ key and typing the key that you would normally use to insert the special character in the text, as shown in Figure 11-1.

Special Character	Find/Change Entry	Dialog Box Display
Space	Space	
Tab	\t	\t
New Paragraph	\p	\p
New Line	\n	\n
New Column	\c	\c
New Box	\b	\b
Wild Card	\?	\?

Figure 11-1 Searching for special characters.

The space, tab, and new paragraph characters are search parameters in the common conversions of imported ASCII text, described under the next headings.

Be sure to include spaces in the Change To entry area if you type them in the Find What entry area. You need not type a space before and after a word in the Change To entry area—if you check Whole Words, QuarkXPress will find the word when it is framed by spaces or followed by punctuation.

Eliminating Unwanted Paragraph Breaks

Text can be telecommunicated from one computer to another, either directly or through a mailbox facility. Mailbox transfers are convenient because the sender and receiver can access them at any time—you need not coordinate having a person available at each end of the phone lines at the same time. It is preferable to use a mailbox or transfer software that lets you preserve any formatting that was done, but most electronic mail

Chapter 11: Working with Text from Databases and XPress Tags 381

services force you to transfer text in ASCII format (text only with no formatting).

If the transfer or conversion method forces paragraph returns (also called hard carriage returns) at the end of every line, it is a good idea to insert at least two carriage returns after every paragraph or intended line break in the text *before it is transferred (Figure 11-2)*. You can quickly reformat this type of file in QuarkXPress without referring to a printed version of the text to find paragraph breaks, following the steps described next.

```
It·has·been·said·that·there·are·two·aspects·of·education,·both·¶
necessary..One·regards·the·individual·human·mind·as·a·vessel,·¶
of·varying·capacity,·into·which·is·to·be·poured·as·much·as·it·will·¶
hold·of·the·knowledge·and·experience·by·which·human·society·¶
lives·and·moves..This·is·the·Martha·of·education—and·we·shall·¶
have·plenty·of·these·tasks·to·perform..¶
¶
But·the·Mary·regards·the·human·mind·more·as·a·fire·that·has·to·¶
be·set·alight·and·blown·with·the·divine·afflatus..That·also·we·take·¶
·as·our·ambition.¶
¶
                                                       Lord·Crowther
```

Figure 11-2   Telecommunicated text sometimes has unwanted returns at the end of every line.

Step 1 Globally change all double carriage returns (which appear only at the end of each paragraph) to some unique character string that is not found elsewhere in the text, such as "xyz" (Figure 11-3).

Figure 11-3   Type \p in the Find/Change dialog box, which represents a carriage return.

Step 2 Globally change all single carriage returns to nothing or to a space (if the line-break returns replaced spaces in the conversion process), as in (Figure 11-4).

Figure 11-4 Find/Change dialog box shows a space as nothing.

Step 3 Globally change all occurrences of "xyz" to single carriage returns (Figure 11-5).

Figure 11-5 Change unique characters back to a paragraph return.

After following these steps, the file appears as you'd normally expect it to—with no paragraph returns *except* those at the end of each paragraph (Figure 11-6).

Figure 11-6 Text in QuarkXPress after global changes.

Converting Data Files to Tabular Format

If the text fields exported from a spreadsheet or database are separated by the tab character, then you can set tabs in QuarkXPress and the data should fall into tabbed columns. However, if the program used commas or some other delimiter, you will need to convert these to tabs before the data can be arranged in columns.

Sometimes text-only files exported from a spreadsheet or database include quotation marks around fields that happened to use the field delimiter as part of the data. In either case, you can use QuarkXPress' Find/Change command globally to convert the field delimiters to tabs.

Step 1 Export the data from the spreadsheet or database in ASCII text format, then use the Get Text command to import it into QuarkXPress (Figure 11-7).

```
Kay,Atherton,Medi-Calls,"248 Texas Street, #9",San Francisco,CA,94107,626-8343
Hector,"Barrera, Jr.",Azteca,1521 Manor Drive,San Pablo,CA,94949,415/233-9239
David,Jewett,"CJS, Inc.",1920 Francisco,Berkeley,CA,94709,415/548-4762
Grace,Moore,TechArt,400 Pacific Avenue,San Francisco,CA,94133,415/362-1110
```

Figure 11-7   Text as originally imported.

Step 2 To distinguish between a comma used as a delimiter and a comma that is part of a field entry, globally change all incidences of comma-space to some unique character string that is not found elsewhere in the text, such as "xyz" (Figure 11-8).

Figure 11-8   The Find/Change dialog box.

In order for the global searches suggested here to work, we have to assume that a comma that is part of a field entry will always be followed by a space, whereas a comma that is a delimiter will usually be followed by the contents of the next field or by another comma (if the field is empty). If a field entry in the spreadsheet or database actually starts with a space, then the delimiter in front of that field will not be converted to a tab with the searches suggested here. You should check the results of these replacements after you have set tab stops to format the text correctly.

Step 3 Globally change all commas to tabs (Figure 11-9).

Figure 11-9   Type \t in the Find/Change dialog box, which represents a tab.

Step 4 Globally change all quotation marks to nothing. Examine your file to confirm whether these are actually inch or feet marks or true opening and closing quotation marks (Figure 11-10).

Figure 11-10   Change quotation marks to nothing.

Step 5 Globally change all occurrences of "xyz" to comma-space (Figure 11-11).

Figure 11-11   Change the unique characters back to comma-space.

Step 6 Select all of the data and choose Style ➤ Formats. With the Paragraph Format dialog box displayed, set tab stops on the text ruler (Figure 11-12).

Figure 11-12   Text falls into place when tab stops are set in QuarkXPress.

In step 6, you can define a style sheet for the data lines and set tabs through the style sheet.

Converting Data Files to Nontabular Formats

Sometimes you will want to convert data from a spreadsheet or database to nontabular formats. A common example of this is converting a data file of names and addresses to a directory listing format.

One approach is to use the mail-merge feature of your word processing application to create a formatted text file directly from the data file. The alternative is to start the formatting processing in the spreadsheet or database, then finish the formatting in QuarkXPress using the Find/Change command. This second approach is described here.

Assume that the spreadsheet or database lists the entries for each record in the following order (Figure 11-13):

first name
last name
company
street address
city
state
zip code
phone number

What you want to end up with is a directory listing format:

first name last name
company
street address
city, state zip code
phone number

If you simply export the data in its current format, you will end up with commas or tabs between every field, and it will be nearly impossible to use global changes to change the format appropriately. You can save a lot of time and trouble by making a few changes to the data *before* you export it.

	A	B	C	D	E	F	G	H	I	J
1	First	Last	Company	Address	City	ST	Zip	Phone		
2	Kay	Atherton	Medi-Calls	248 Texas Street, #9	San Francisco	CA	94107	626-8343		
3	Hector	Barrera, Jr.	Azteca	1521 Manor Drive	San Pablo	CA	94949	415/233-9239		
4	David	Jewett	CJS, Inc.	1920 Francisco	Berkeley	CA	94709	415/548-4762		
5	Grace	Moore	TechArt	400 Pacific Avenue	San Francisco	CA	94133	415/362-1110		
6										

Figure 11-13   Data in a spreadsheet format.

Step 1   Insert unique search codes between certain fields in the data:

- Insert "xyz" in a new column or field between the first name field and the last name. This will be changed to a space in step 4.
- Insert the same code, "xyz", between the state field and the zip code.
- Insert a different code, such as "zzz", between the city field and the state. This will be changed to a comma in step 5.

In a spreadsheet, you can insert columns between fields and fill the columns with the search codes as shown in Figure 11-14. In a database, you could make the search codes part of the "report format" and output the data to disk as a report.

	A	B	C	D	E	F	G	H	I	J	K	L
1	First	xyz	Last	Company	Address	City	zzz	ST	xyz	Zip	Phone	
2	Kay	xyz	Atherton	Medi-Calls	248 Texas Street, #9	San Francisco	zzz	CA	xyz	94107	626-8343	
3	Hector	xyz	Barrera, Jr.	Azteca	1521 Manor Drive	San Pablo	zzz	CA	xyz	94949	415/233-9239	
4	David	xyz	Jewett	CJS, Inc.	1920 Francisco	Berkeley	zzz	CA	xyz	94709	415/548-4762	
5	Grace	xyz	Moore	TechArt	400 Pacific Avenue	San Francisco	zzz	CA	xyz	94133	415/362-1110	

Figure 11-14   Data file with unique search codes entered between selected fields.

Step 2   Export the data from the spreadsheet or database as text and import it into QuarkXPress. Here we assume that the fields are separated by tabs in the export process (Figure 11-15). (See "Converting Data Files to Tabular Format," earlier in this chapter.)

Figure 11-15   Data file when exported from the spreadsheet or database as text and imported into QuarkXPress.

Step 3   Globally change all carriage returns to double carriage returns (Figure 11-16).

Figure 11-16   Type \p in the Find/Change dialog box, which represents a carriage return.

Step 4   Globally change all occurrences of Tab-xyz-Tab to spaces (Figure 11-17).

Figure 11-17   Type \t in the Find/Change dialog box, which represents a tab.

Step 5   Globally change all occurrences of Tab-zzz-Tab to comma-space (Figure 11-18).

Figure 11-18   Find/Change dialog box.

Step 6   Globally change all remaining occurrences of Tab to Carriage Return (Paragraph Break), as in Figure 11-19.

Figure 11-19   Find/Change dialog box shows tabs as \t and carriage returns as \p.

Step 7   If the spreadsheet or database added quotation marks around fields that contained a comma, globally change the quotation marks to nothing (strip them out). Examine your file to confirm whether these are actually inch or feet marks or true opening and closing quotation marks (Figure 11-20).

Figure 11-20   Final text format.

Embedding Format Codes in Data Files

Sometimes you will want to convert data from a spreadsheet or database to nontabular formats where some fields have different character formats. A common example of this is converting a data file of names and addresses to a directory, similar to the previous example.

As you have seen earlier, you can use global searches to reformat data imported from a spreadsheet or database file. You can use the same techniques to embed QuarkXPress tag codes, discussed later in this chapter.

For example, let's say you want to convert the same data file of names and addresses to a directory listing format as described under the previous heading, but you want the different fields to have different character formats, such as:

first name last name
company
street address
city, state, zip code
phone number

You can use the mail-merge feature of your word processing application to create a formatted text file directly from the data file, or format the text in QuarkXPress using the Find/Change command as described here.

Step 1 Insert unique search codes between certain fields in the data. This is the same as Step 1 in the previous example, with the addition of inserting a unique code between last name and company, and between company and address (Figure 11-21):

- Insert "xyz" between the first name field and the last name.
- Insert "xyz" between the state field and the zip code.
- Insert "xxx" between the last name and the company.
- Insert "yyy" between the company and the address.
- Insert "zzz" between the city field and the state.

	A	B	C	D	E	F	G	H	I	J	K	L
1	First	xyz	Last		Company	Address	City	zzz	ST	xyz	Zip	Phone
2	Kay	xyz	Atherton		Medi-Calls	248 Texas Street, #9	San Francisco	zzz	CA	xyz	94107	626-8343
3	Hector	xyz	Barrera, Jr.		Azteca	1521 Manor Drive	San Pablo	zzz	CA	xyz	94949	415/233-9239
4	David	xyz	Jewett		CJS, Inc.	1920 Francisco	Berkeley	zzz	CA	xyz	94709	415/548-4762
5	Grace	xyz	Moore		TechArt	400 Pacific Avenue	San Francisco	zzz	CA	xyz	94133	415/362-1110

Figure 11-21 Data file with unique search codes entered between selected fields.

You can insert these codes using techniques described in step 1 under the previous heading.

Step 2   Export the data as text from the spreadsheet or database and import it into QuarkXPress as described under the previous heading (Figure 11-22).

```
First→    xyz→    Last→    xxx→    Company→      yyy→    Address→City→
zzz→      ST→     xyz→     Zip→    Phone¶
Kay→      xyz→    Atherton→xxx→    Medi-Calls→   yyy→    "248 Texas
Street, #9"→      San Francisco→   zzz→    CA→   xyz→    94107→ 626-
8343¶
Hector→   xyz→    "Barrera, Jr."→  xxx→    Azteca→ yyy→   1521 Manor
Drive→    San Pablo→       zzz→    CA→     xyz→   94949→ 415/233-9239¶
David→    xyz→    Jewett→  xxx→    "CJS, Inc."→  yyy→    1920 Francisco→
Berkeley→zzz→     CA→      xyz→    94709→  415/548-4762¶
Grace→    xyz→    Moore→   xxx→    TechArt→yyy→   400 Pacific Avenue→
San Francisco→    zzz→     CA→     xyz→    94133→ 415/362-1110
```

Figure 11-22   Data file when exported as text from the spreadsheet or database and imported into QuarkXPress.

(Opening the text in a word processing application and performing these global changes *before* importing the text into QuarkXPress is preferable; doing so eliminates step 10 in this sequence.)

Step 3   Globally change all carriage returns to double carriage returns and the formatting code <B> (a QuarkXPress Tag that will make the name bold), as shown in Figure 11-23.

Figure 11-23   Change single paragraph returns to double paragraph returns followed by the code for bold.

Step 4   Globally change all occurrences of Tab-xxx-Tab to <B>return<I> to turn bold off after the name, and start the company on a new line in italics (Figure 11-24).

Chapter 11: Working with Text from Databases and XPress Tags   391

Figure 11-24   Find/Change dialog box shows tabs as \t.

Step 5 Globally change all occurrences of Tab-yyy-Tab to <I>return to turn italics off and start the address on a new line (Figure 11-25).

Figure 11-25   Find/Change dialog box.

Step 6 Globally change all occurrences of Tab-zzz-Tab to comma-space (Figure 11-26).

Figure 11-26   Find/Change dialog box shows tabs as \t.

Step 7 Globally change all occurrences of Tab-xyz-Tab to spaces (Figure 11-27).

Figure 11-27   Find/Change dialog box shows tabs as \t.

Step 8   Globally change all remaining occurrences of Tab to Carriage Return (Paragraph Break) (Figure 11-28).

Figure 11-28   Convert remaining tabs to paragraph returns.

Step 9   If the spreadsheet or database added quotation marks around fields that contained a comma, globally change the quotation marks to nothing (strip them out). Examine your file to confirm whether these are actually inch or foot marks or true opening and closing quotation marks (Figure 11-29).

If the above changes were done in a word processing application, the database text is ready to be imported into QuarkXPress (step 11). If you performed these steps in QuarkXPress, you'll need to export the text and reimport it, as described in step 10, so that the XPress tags will be converted to the correct formatting.

<B>Kay Atherton<B>
<I>Medi-Calls<I>
248 Texas Street, #9
San Francisco, CA 94107
415/626-8343

<B>Hector Barrera, Jr.<B>
<I>Azteca<I>
1521 Manor Drive
San Pablo, CA 94949
415/233-9239

<B>David Jewett<B>
<I>CJS, Inc.<I>
1920 Francisco
Berkeley, CA 94709
415/548-4762

<B>Grace Moore<B>
<I>TechArt<I>
400 Pacific Avenue
San Francisco, CA 94133
415/362-1110

Figure 11-29 Text format after global changes.

Step 10 If you performed these searches in QuarkXPress, then you need to save the text to disk in ASCII format (Figure 11-30).

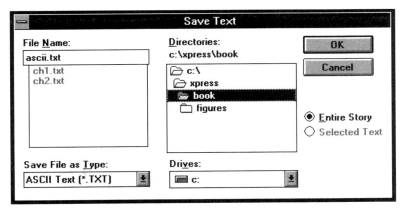

Figure 11-30 Save Text dialog box.

Step 11 Import the exported text and the embedded codes will be translated into the final formatting automatically (Figure 10-31).

Kay Atherton
Medi-Calls
248 Texas Street, #9
San Francisco, CA 94107
415/626-8343

Hector Barrera, Jr.
Azteca
1521 Manor Drive
San Pablo, CA 94949
415/233-9239

David Jewett
CJS, Inc.
1920 Francisco
Berkeley, CA 94709
415/548-4762

Grace Moore
TechArt
400 Pacific Avenue
San Francisco, CA 94133
415/362-1110

Figure 11-31   Final text format.

Using Wild Cards in Searches

You can use the wild card (\?) to search for words that have been typed with different spellings. For example, if you wanted to change all occurrences of the word gray to shaded, and if the word gray also appeared as grey in some places in the text, you could search for gr\?y (Figure 11-32). (The backslash before the question mark is what appears in the dialog box when you type the wild card code, \?.)

Figure 11-32   Changing all occurrences of gray or grey to shaded.

This procedure works because gray and grey are the only English words that fit the format gr\?y—griy, groy, and gruy are not valid words. You should use Find Next, Change, then Find rather than Change All so you can skip occurrences such as "Gray Line Tours," and manually change occurrences such as "shades of gray."

Inserting XPress Tags in ASCII Text

QuarkXPress lets you insert "tags" into any ASCII text so that the text will be formatted automatically when imported into a QuarkXPress document. This can be handy if you are preparing text using a word processor that is not directly supported by one of QuarkXPress' application-specific import filters—such as text from a dedicated word processing system or a mainframe text editor. XPress tags are also useful in preparing text in a spreadsheet or database format, as described later in this chapter.

The following table shows codes that you can type to format ASCII text. The initial attributes for text imported will be the same as the attributes where the insertion point is located when the File ➤ Get Text command is used. Current attributes remain in effect until they are explicitly changed by an embedded code.

You must check Include Style Sheets in the Get Text dialog box when importing, and the XPress Tags filter must be in the QuarkXPress program directory, or the XPress tags will come in as ASCII text. You cannot import text through two filters at the same time: XPress Tags inserted in formatted text imported from Microsoft Word, for instance, will not be interpreted as formatting codes. You must save coded text in ASCII format:

Character Attributes

Description	Start Code	End Code
Plain	<P>	<P> or <$>
Bold	<B>	<B> or <$>
Italic	<I>	<I> or <$>
Outline	<O>	<O> or <$>
Shadow	<S>	<S> or <$>
Underline	<U>	<U> or <$>
Word Underline	<W>	<W> or <$>
Strikethrough	</>	</> or <$>
All Caps	<K>	<K> or <$>
Small Caps	<H>	<H> or <$>
Superscript	<+>	<+> or <$>

Subscript	<->	<-> or <$>
Superior	<V>	<V> or <$>
Current style sheet	<$>	

These codes can be combined within brackets. For example, you can type <BI> to set text to bold and italic.

In the next codes, italicized text indicates variables that you enter and *ddd.dd* represents any two-place decimal number. Names of fonts must always be framed in quotation marks.

Description	Start Code	End Code
Change font	<f"*font name*">	<f$>
Change size	<z*ddd.dd*>	<z$>
Shift Baseline	<b*ddd.dd*>	<b$>
Change shade %	<s*ddd.dd*>	<s$>
Scale horizontally %	<h*ddd.dd*>	<h$>
Kern @ *d*/200ths em	<k*ddd.dd*>	<k$>
Track @ *d*/200ths em	<t*ddd.dd*>	<t$>
Change color	<c"*color name*">	<c$>

You can enter abbreviations for primary colors:

Cyan	<cC>
Magenta	<cM>
Yellow	<cY>
Black	<cK>
White	<cW>

Paragraph Attributes

Description	Start Code
Align Left	<*L>
Center	<*C>
Align Right	<*R>
Justify	<*J>
Normal Style sheet	@$:
No style sheet	@:
Change style sheet	@*style sheet*:
Define new style sheet	@*style sheet=definition*

In the next codes, if you omit a parameter in a string, you must still include the comma that follows that parameter. Missing parameters will be set to match the current style sheet settings.

Description	Start Code	End Code
Set tabs	<*t(*dd.dd,T."character"*)>	<*t$>

with *ddd.dd* = tab position, *T* = tab type (L,R,C,D), and *"character"* = the leader character, framed in quotation marks.

Set paragraph format	<*p(*left indent,first line indent, right indent, leading,space before, space after, G/baseline grid*)>	<*p$>

where all values are entered in the form *ddd.dd* except the baseline grid.

Hyphenation & Justification	<*h"*hyphenation name*">	<*h$>
Rule above	<*ra(*rule width,line style ID, "color name",line shade, left indent* or T*line length, right indent, rule position* or %*percentage)>	<*ra$>

where *rule width* and *right indent* are entered in points in the format *ddd.dd*;

the *line style ID* is entered as *d* (counted by position down on the menu);

the *color name* can be entered as an abbreviation for one of the primary colors: C, M, Y, K, or W;

the *line shade* is entered as a percentage in the format *ddd.dd*;

the *left indent* can be entered in points in the format *ddd.dd* or the entry can be the *length of the line* if preceded by a T (T*ddd.dd*);

and the *rule position* can be entered in points or as a percentage if followed by a % (*ddd.dd*%).

Rule below	<*rb(*ddd.dd,d,"color name", ddd.dd,ddd.dd, ddd.dd,ddd.dd)>	<*rb$>

where the parameters are as described for Rule Above.

Drop cap	<*d(*d,d)>	<*d$>

where the parameters are character count, line count.

Keep with next	<*kn1>	<*kn$> or <*kn0>

where kn$ = use current style sheet, kn0 = do not keep with next.

Keep together	<*kt(A)> or <*kt(*d,d)>	<*kt$>

where the A = all lines or *d,d* = start line, end line.

The current style sheet remains in effect until a new style sheet or no style sheet is applied using one of the @ codes shown in the table. Applying a new style sheet overrides all previous formatting codes.

In defining a style sheet, you can follow @*style sheet*= with any of the codes shown in the table. Style sheet names cannot include the special characters :, =, or @.

Style sheet names must be defined in the QuarkXPress document or in the ASCII file as an XPress tag code (using @*style sheet*=, as shown in the next table) before the text is imported. Colors and H&J names must be defined in the QuarkXPress document before the text that references them is imported. If a color is not found, Black will be used. If an H&J is not found, the default H&J is used.

Figures 11-33 and 11-34 show an example of text with XPress tags before and after being imported into QuarkXPress.

```
@DropCapParagraphStyle=<*L*h"Standard"*kn0*kt0*ra0*rb0*d(1,3)*p(0,0,0,0,0,0,
g)*t(0,0," "):
Ps100t0h100z12k0b0c"Black"f"Times">
@DropCapParagraphStyle:<*L*h"Standard"*kn0*kt0*ra0*rb0*d(1,3)*p(0,0,0,0,0,0,
g)*t(0,0," "):
Ps100t0h100z12k0b0c"Black"f"Times">Si meliora dies, ut vina, poemata reddit,
scire velim, chartis pretium quotus arroget annus. scriptor abhinc annos cen-
tum qui decidit, inter perfectos veteresque referri debet an inter vilis
atque novos? Excludat iurgia finis, "Est vetus atque probus, cent<P>um qui
perficit annos." Quid, qui deperiit minor uno mense vel anno, inter quos ref-
erendus erit? Veteresne poetas, an quos et praesens et postera respuat aetas?
@BodyCopyStyle=<*L*h"Standard"*kn0*kt0*ra0*rb0*d0*p(0,12,0,0,0,0,g)*t(0,0,"
"):
Ps100t0h100z12k0b0c"Black"f"Times">
@BodyCopyStyle:<P>"Iste quidem veteres inter ponetur honeste, qui vel mense
brevi vel toto est iunior anno." Utor permisso, caudaeque pilos ut equinae
paulatim vello unum, demo etiam unum, dum cadat elusus ratione ruentis
acervi, qui redit in fastos et virtutem aestimat ann<P>is miraturque nihil
nisi quod Libitina sacravit.
<P>Ennius et sapines et fortis et alter Homerus, ut critici dicunt, leviter
curare videtur, quo promissa cadant et somnia Pythagorea. Naevius in manibus
non est et mentibus haeret paene recens? Adeo sanctum est vetus omne poema.
ambigitur quotiens, uter utro <P>sit prior, aufert Pacuvius docti famam senis
Accius alti, dicitur Afrani toga convenisse Menandro, Plautus ad exemplar
Siculi properare Epicharmi, vincere Caecilius gravitate, Terentius arte.
@FloatingSubStyle=<*L*h"Standard"*kn0*kt0*ra(24,0,"Blue",100,T0,0,-
4.97)*rb0*d0*p(0,0,0,0,12,0,g)*t(12,0," ",93,0," ",0,0," "):
PBs50t0h100z18k0b0c"Yellow"f"Times">
@FloatingSubStyle:          Subhead
@BodyCopyStyle:<P>Hos ediscit et hos arto stipata theatro spectat Roma
potens; habet hos numeratque poetas ad nostrum tempus Livi scriptoris ab
aevo.
<P>Interdum volgus rectum videt, est ubi peccat. Si veteres ita miratur lau-
datque poetas, ut nihil anteferat, nihil illis comparet, errat. Si quaedam
nimis antique, si peraque dure dicere credit eos, ignave multa fatetur, et
sapit et mecum facit et Iova iudic<P>at aequo.
<P>Non equidem insector delendave carmina Livi esse reor, memini quae plago-
sum mihi parvo Orbilium dictare; sed emendata videri pulchraque et exactis
minimum distantia miror. Inter quae verbum emicuit si forte decorum, et si
versus paulo concinnior unus et al<P>ter, iniuste totum ducit venditque poe-
ma.
```

Figure 11-33   ASCII text with XPress tags.

Figure 11-34 ASCII text with XPress tags after being imported into QuarkXPress.

Page Number Characters

Description	Code
Previous box's page	<\2>
Current box's page	<\3>
Next box's page	<\4>

Insert Special Characters

Description	Code
Paragraph Break	<\n>
Discretionary New Line	<\d>
Indent here	<\i>
New column	<\c>
New box	<\b>
Discretionary hyphen	<\h>
Standard space	<\ → or <\! → for nonbreaking character
Figure space	<\f> or <\!f> for nonbreaking character
Punctuation space	<\p> or <\!p> for nonbreaking character
1/4 em space	<\4> or <\!4> for nonbreaking character
Hyphen	<\-> or <\!-> for nonbreaking character

Since @, <, and \ characters have a special meaning as XPress tag codes, you must use codes to enter these characters if you want them to print as part of the text:

Symbol	Code
@	<\@>
<	<\<>
\	<\\>

Summary

This chapter offered tips on how to work with text from databases and mainframe computers, including how to use the Find/Change command to remove unwanted characters or to insert formatting codes. We also discussed how to insert XPress tags into ASCII text so that text will format automatically when imported into QuarkXPress. The next chapter offers special tips and techniques for using QuarkXPress' powerful typographic capabilities.

12 *Tips on Typography*

Many people fear that desktop publishing is partly responsible for causing typography to become a lost art. Desktop publishing makes it so easy to print type that looks good at first glance that many computer users with no design training have missed some of the traditional education regarding type aesthetics. Although this book does not aim at bridging the gap, we begin this chapter with some advice about type which should be considered when designing a document in QuarkXPress: the need for style sheets, factors to take into account in adjusting leading, and information on adjusting word and character spacing.

The chapter continues with some tips on how to create special typographic effects, including special drop caps, reverse type, and setting type within a shape.

Designing Type Specifications

If you are coming from a traditional typesetting background, you are probably familiar with most of the design guidelines offered in this section. On the other hand, if you are coming from an office environment in which all documents were previously printed on a letter-quality printer, then you may find the comparatively wide range of fonts offered by

QuarkXPress rather confusing. There are two ways of approaching the type specifications for a document.

The fastest way to acquire a sense of design and develop type specifications is to study and imitate published works that are similar in structure to your document. Match your design specifications as closely as possible to the published documents; in other words, select fonts that are similar to those used for headings, body copy, and captions in the published document. You need not match the typefaces exactly, but try to substitute typefaces that are in the same category (serif or sans serif, roman, italic, or bold, and so on).

Second, study the underlying principles that designers and typographers follow. Some of these guidelines are listed here, but few documents can follow all of these guidelines without making exceptions to the rules. A good designer knows when and how to break the rules.

Match the Type Specifications to the System Capabilities

The first step in the process of creating type specifications is to list the different fonts *available* for use in your design specifications. The second step is to list the fonts that you will *use* in a particular document.

One factor in determining the number of fonts is the number of text elements used in the document. Elements that can require differentiation include:

- Chapter openings, section openings, or feature article headlines
- Different levels of headings or headlines
- Body copy
- Figure captions
- Labels within figures
- Footnotes
- Special sections such as sidebars, summaries, tables, and the like

The type specification process, then, involves merging the two lists: a list of the fonts that are available, or that you wish to use, and a list of the different type elements within the document.

The design specifications should also include instructions for paragraph alignment (left, right, justified, centered) and spacing between paragraphs—for the body copy, the captions, and the figure titles.

Use Only One or Two Typefaces

Many designers mix two different fonts (or typefaces, in the traditional world of type) at most. For example, it's common to see a sans serif face, such as Helvetica or Avant Garde, used for headlines and a serif face, such as Times or Palatino, used for the body copy. Use variations in size and style to distinguish between different elements.

Documents that incorporate many changing formats—such as magazines and newsletters—might use more than four fonts throughout the document, though each page, feature, or ad uses only one or two. Just as graphics are too often used simply because they are available, so are fonts—simply because they're there. Too many fonts make the page confusing and uninviting.

Use Larger Point Sizes for Longer Text Line Lengths

There is a good reason why the text in magazines is run two and often three columns. It is very difficult for the eye to follow text, especially in small point sizes, from one edge to the other of an 8.5-inch-wide page.

If you must use a small point size to fit more text on a page, be sure to break the page into at least two columns. Even regular text—12 point—is easier to read if it runs in columns no wider than 4 to 5 inches. One rule of thumb is that optimum line length is between 45 and 60 characters per line.

Above all, the text should be easy to read. If the copy doesn't fit the space allotted, think about editing out some of the text rather than reducing the point size or the space between lines.

Don't Use Underscores

Use italics rather than underscores within body copy. (Underscored text was a convention developed for use in documents printed on typewriters or letter-quality printers.)

Use All Caps Judiciously

Capitalize whole words as a deliberate design strategy, rather than as a method for showing emphasis or differentiating heading levels. Use variations in size rather than all-caps text to differentiate headings. One common exception to this rule occurs when the list of available fonts is too limited to accommodate all heading levels; in this case, all caps can be used to distinguish between two heading levels that are otherwise the same font.

Differentiate Figure Captions from Body Text

Here we use the term "caption" to mean the descriptive lines of text that run below, beside, or above a photo or illustration. Some layout artists use the term "cutline" instead, reserving "caption" (or lead-in or catchline or kicker) to describe only the boldface words that lead in to the rest of the descriptive text. Whatever you call it, the caption is usually differentiated from the rest of the text by boldface, italics, or a different typeface altogether.

Besides specifying the font to be used in captions, you should also specify the positioning of the caption text. The most natural position is below the illustration or photo, extending the same width as the graphic. Other variations include indenting 1 pica or more on each side or centering the catchline above justified text. Some variations are shown in Figure 12-1.

Figure 12-1 Variations in placing captions.

Tips on Using Style Sheets

The basic procedures for creating and applying style sheets were given in Chapter 4. Here specific tips and examples relating to style sheets follow a brief commentary on why style sheets are so useful. The advantages of using style sheets are similar to those outlined for using templates, described in Chapter 9.

Benefits of Using Style Sheets

Within one document or between documents, whether the production is executed by one person or many, style sheets are tremendous productivity tools. They reduce the number of steps required to format text, simplify the formatting process, embody "design," and enforce consistency. In addition, style sheets let you change your design easily.

Style Sheets Reduce the Number of Steps

The process of creating a new set of style sheets for the first time might require, let's say, 40 individual steps, whereas the process of applying each style sheet requires only two steps. This savings is one of the first benefits of using style sheets. You can save hours or days over the life of a project by using style sheets.

Fast operators might complain that it takes too long to set up style sheets—that they can format a document just as fast without one. Although it may be faster to format each paragraph independently for short documents and simple formats, there are other advantages of style sheets to consider.

Style Sheets Simplify the Formatting Process

If a document has many different paragraph formats, and some are fairly complicated, then style sheets can simplify the formatting process by reducing the number of variables that you have to remember or look up. Was the leading 13 point or 14? Does the paragraph need extra space above or below? And what were the tab settings for a five-column table?

Even if the type specifications are already clearly written on paper, it is a good idea to translate a designer's specifications into the commands you will use in QuarkXPress. When "captured" in style sheets, the list of commands is reduced to a simple list of style sheet names, and the process of marking up copy for formatting is simplified to writing the name of the style sheet assigned to each paragraph.

Style Sheets Embody Design and Enforce Consistency

Aside from the practical considerations of reducing steps and simplifying the process of formatting a document, a style sheet system can ensure that design specifications are correctly and consistently applied. By incorporating as many of the design specifications as possible into style sheets, the production group can better preserve the look intended by the designer.

Furthermore, once a set of style sheets is created, it can be used in many files that follow the same design specifications. For instance, a book or long proposal might be divided into several text files and worked on by several different editors. Once the style sheet set is created, it can be applied to each section or chapter—you don't have to re-create the style sheets for each new file.

A short document that is produced on a regular basis—such as a newsletter—would have one set of style sheets with which each issue is created. If you have ever worked on a newsletter only once a month or once a quarter, you know how hard it is to remember elaborate type specifications from one issue to the next. If the production team changes from month to month, the process of learning elaborate type specifications can add hours to each issue. With a style sheet system, a list of style sheet names is automatically displayed in a submenu in QuarkXPress and is easy to apply.

Style Sheets Let You Change Your Mind

In addition to ensuring consistency, style sheets offer a tremendous amount of flexibility in *changing* the design of a document. Have you ever gone through a long document meticulously formatting each paragraph, then decided that you really want a different paragraph indent, or all the body text to be on 13 point leading instead of 12? The change would be a nightmare without a style sheet. If you had used a style sheet from the beginning, you would be able to change the font or paragraph formats for any element globally simply by changing the specifications for the style sheet. You could change the formatting of all the level-1 headings, for instance, by changing the style sheet attributes only.

This capability can be useful over the lifetime of a magazine that you want to modify to suit changing tastes in type, but it is especially handy during the initial design stages for a new document. You can test different design ideas by changing the specifications for each style sheet name and quickly print out the variations for review by your team or your client.

You can also make slight modifications in the spacing assigned for headings or body text to make the text for a newsletter fit exactly four pages, for instance. (See "Adjusting Text Spacing" later in this chapter.)

Tips for Creating and Applying Style Sheets

If you use style sheets, the following tips can help you save time in developing and applying them.

Specify the Normal Style Sheet First

When you are setting up style sheets, make the settings for Normal text in QuarkXPress match the specifications for your document's body text. Most documents tend to be primarily one set of specifications for the body text, with variations on that specification for headings, captions, tables, and the like.

Create a New Set of Style Sheets in an Unformatted Document

In applying style sheets to paragraphs in a document that has not yet been formatted, define the style for Normal text, then proceed through the document by moving to successive paragraphs and apply the style for heads, and so on.

If the paragraph format is a new one that you have not yet defined as a style sheet, you can create the style sheet by first formatting the text as needed. When you select Edit ➤ Style Sheets, and click New, the definition of the style will be that of the selected text. Simply name the style and Save it. Then use the keyboard shortcut or the Style ➤ Style Sheets submenu to apply it to subsequent paragraphs.

Assign and Use Keyboard Equivalents

You can assign a keyboard equivalent that you can later use to assign the style sheet instead of going through the Style ➤ Style Sheets submenu. Press any keys on the numeric keyboard, along with CTRL, and SHIFT, or any of the 12 function keys (except F1, which is reserved for Help) on an extended keyboard. Avoid using the Alt key with the keypad keys because Windows uses ALT with digits to specify special characters such as bullets and accented characters. The keys you press when the cursor is in the Keyboard Equivalent entry area become the keyboard shortcut for assigning the style sheet.

Even though you are limited to using function keys and numeric keys on the numeric keypad, you can assign numbers in an organized way. For example, you could let the numbers correspond to headings levels:

- Heading level 1 would be assigned keypad 1 alone or in combination with the CTRL or SHIFT keys. (Remember that F1 is reserved for Help.)
- Heading level 2 would be assigned keypad 2 or the same combination with the CTRL or SHIFT keys as used for heading 1.
- Normal text, figure captions, and other nonnumeric style sheets could use numeric or function keys that start above the highest number used by the headings.

Organize the Style Sheet Names

You can enter a style sheet name up to 64 characters long. The style sheet names will be displayed in the Style ➤ Style Sheets submenu in alphabetical order. It's a good idea to decide on the naming conventions you will use for style sheet names so you can locate style sheets in the list easily and know what they mean.

One helpful guideline is to name the different categories of text elements in such a way that they appear in a logically grouped order when you view them alphabetically. For example, in the system shown in Figure 12-2, all the headings begin with the word "head" in the style sheet name, and all the list formats begin with the word "list."

Figure 12-2 Logically grouped style sheet names, with keyboard equivalents displayed after style sheet name.

Another approach is to include the type specifications in the style sheet names. Figure 12-3 shows style sheet names that include font, size, and other information about the style sheet specification.

Figure 12-3 Type Specifications included in style sheet names.

As a learning aid, QuarkXPress displays the keyboard equivalents in the style sheet submenu and in the Style Sheets palette. This way, you can use the keyboard equivalents when you remember them, or choose from the submenu while viewing a reminder of the keyboard equivalent that you might remember the next time. The numeric keypad is represented by the letters "KP", the ALT key by the letters "Alt", the SHIFT key by "Shift", and the CTRL key by "Ctrl." Remember, however, the best key to use in combination with others is the Shift key to avoid interfering with Windows and QuarkXPress keyboard shortcuts that use the CTRL and ALT keys.

Formatting Headings with a Style Sheet

A number of conventions in formatting headings can and should be captured in the style sheet specifications:

- Use Edit ► Style Sheets to display the Paragraph Formats dialog box and add Space Above and Space Below each heading level, rather than using leading or carriage returns to force the space around a heading. This way, you will achieve normal line spacing for headings that run more than one line long.
- Use Edit ► Style Sheets to display the Paragraph Formats dialog box and set all headings to Keep with Next ¶ and Keep Lines Together. This way, a multi-line heading will never be broken across two pages or columns or separated from the first paragraph that follows it.
- Normally, headings are not hyphenated or justified. If you have not changed the Standard H&J, which is preset with hyphenation turned off, you need not apply any other H&J. If you have changed the Standard H&J to include hyphenation, use Edit ► H&Js to create an H&J file with hyphenation turned off, then apply the new H&J to the appropriate style sheets by changing the paragraph formats under Edit ► Style Sheets (Figure 12-4).

Figure 12-4 Example of the Paragraph Formats dialog box for a heading.

- Often, headings are kerned or tracked for tighter spacing than normal body copy. Use Edit ► Style Sheets to display the Character Attributes dialog box and activate tracking for each heading style sheet, and manually kern letters in individual headings as needed.

  Another way to adjust the spacing between characters in headings is to use the Edit ► H&Js command to set optimum character and word spacing in a special H&J specification for headings, then use Edit → Style Sheets to display the Paragraph Formats dialog box and select the special H&J specifications for the heading style sheets.

Adjusting Text Spacing

Text spacing may need to be adjusted for two reasons. One is aesthetic: The spacing between lines or letters might be adjusted to be typographically pleasing. The other is to fit a certain amount of text into a given amount of space. Adjusting spacing for this purpose is called *copyfitting*.

Adjusting the Leading (Line Spacing)

Whether you initially use QuarkXpress' Auto Leading feature or specify the exact leading (spacing between lines) yourself, you can always make fine adjustments in the leading in order to improve the appearance of text or to fit copy into a defined space. You can specify leading in increments of .001 point in the Paragraph Formats dialog box. You can change the leading for the entire document, for specific style sheets, for selected text, or for selected pages to make copy fit.

In adjusting the leading, be consistent: Change the leading on all of the body copy rather than on individual paragraphs. If you do not want to change the leading for an entire article or document, change it for facing pages and keep the leading the same across columns on a single page (Figure 12-5).

A powerful idea communicates some of its strength to him who challenges it.
    Marcel Proust
	A powerful idea communicates some of its strength to him who challenges it.
	    Marcel Proust
		A powerful idea communicates some of its strength to him who challenges it.
		    Marcel Proust
			A powerful idea communicates some of its strength to him who challenges it.
			    Marcel Proust

Figure 12-5 12-point Times with leading of 12, 14, 15, and Auto.

Changing the leading is a common and preferred method of fitting copy once the design specifications are finalized—rather than changing the specifications for typeface, size, or style.

Hyphenation and Justification

Hyphenated text can take up less space than text that is not hyphenated. Furthermore, justified text can take up less space than text that is not justified (Figure 12-6).

I don't know Who—or what—put the question. I don't even know when it was put. I don't even remember answering. But at some moment I did answer *Yes* to Someone—or Something—and from that hour I was certain that existence is meaningful and that, therefore, my life in self-surrender, had a goal.

Dag Hammaraskjöld

I don't know Who—or what—put the question. I don't even know when it was put. I don't even remember answering. But at some moment I did answer *Yes* to Someone—or Something—and from that hour I was certain that existence is meaningful and that, therefore, my life in self-surrender, had a goal.

Dag Hammaraskjöld

Figure 12-6 Justified text can require less space than text that is not justified.

QuarkXPress' preset default is that text is not hyphenated automatically unless you use the Edit → H&J command to create a new H&J specification with hyphenation, or change the definition of the Standard H&J specification. The dialog box lets you turn Auto Hyphenation on or off and specify how many hyphens in a row will be allowed. You can enter a number including 0, or type the word "unlimited."

In entering the number of hyphens allowed in a row, a value of 0 has the same effect as "unlimited." It does *not* mean that no hyphens are allowed.

Hyphenation On for Justified Text, Off for Headings

Justified text usually calls for hyphenation, especially when the columns are narrow. Justified text that is not hyphenated tends to have more "rivers"—wide areas of white space within the text caused by forced spacing between words.

Normally, body copy is hyphenated but headings are not. For this reason, most documents need two H&J files: the Standard file that comes with QuarkXPress and is initially set up with hyphenation off, and one that you create that turns hyphenation on.

Adjusting the Hyphenation Zone

The Hyphenation Zone in the Edit → Hyphenation and Justification dialog box applies to non-justified text only. If you enter a value of 0, QuarkXPress will break any words that start on a line but would cross the right margin if not hyphenated. You can enter a value higher than 0 to limit how far in from the right margin QuarkXPress will go to hyphenate a word—the previous word must end *before* the hyphenation zone and an acceptable hyphenation point must fall within the zone.

In hyphenating unjustified text, QuarkXPress follows this sequence of steps:

1. If a word cannot be hyphenated within the hyphenation zone, carry it to the next line (that is, do not hyphenate).
2. Otherwise, hyphenate.

In other words, you can control the minimum line length of unjustified text through this setting. The larger the hyphenation zone, the more ragged the right margin will appear (Figure 12-7).

Hyphenation zone = zero
...the usual modern collection. Wilson Steer, water in watercolour; Matthew Smith, victim of the crime in slaughtercolour; Utrillo, whitewashed wall in mortarcolour; Matisse, odalisque in scortacolour; Picasso, spatchcock horse in tortacolour...Rouault, perishing Saint in thoughtacolour; Epstein, Leah waiting for Jacob in squawtacolour.
                                    Joyce Cary

Hyphenation zone = 1 inch
...the usual modern collection. Wilson Steer, water in watercolour; Matthew Smith, victim of the crime in slaughtercolour; Utrillo, whitewashed wall in mortarcolour; Matisse, odalisque in scortacolour; Picasso, spatchcock horse in tortacolour...Rouault, perishing Saint in thoughtacolour; Epstein, Leah waiting for Jacob in squawtacolour.
                                    Joyce Cary

Figure 12-7 A wide hyphenation zone results in a more ragged look and can increase the number of lines.

When hyphenation is turned off, the text can appear very ragged. Hyphenation is not only for justified text!

Adjusting the Number of Hyphens Allowed in a Row

The Edit Hyphenation & Justification dialog box also lets you specify how many hyphens in a row will be allowed. However, changing this setting is unlikely to change the amount of space taken up by the copy unless the text invites heavy hyphenation (that is, it is characterized by short line lengths and a lot of long words).

Adjusting Word and Character Spacing

When text is not justified, the amount of space between words and characters is determined by the font and by kerning tables. Justified text, on the other hand, is achieved by adding or subtracting infinitesimal increments of space between characters and words. The Edit → H&Js (Hyphenation & Justification) command lets you control the amount of space added or deleted between words and characters as part of the justification process.

Most publishers are likely to accept QuarkXpress' defaults for these settings rather than change them. You can change the settings to force copy to fit a given space, however, and you might want to change these settings as a deliberate design strategy to achieve a custom look in certain documents.

The entries under the Justification Method area of the Edit Hyphenation & Justification dialog box (Figure 12-8) apply to justified text only. The Optimum value only will be applied to nonjustified text. You can enter the Minimum (down to 0 percent between words, or −50 percent between characters), Optimum, and Maximum (up to 500 percent between words, or 100 percent between characters) space between words (Space) and space between characters (Char) that QuarkXPress will apply in adjusting horizontal space in order to justify a line of text. Values are normally entered as percentages of normal word space for space between words and as percentages of an en space between characters.

Figure 12-8 Justification method in the H&J Specifications dialog box (Edit → H&Js) lets you adjust word and character spacing.

QuarkXPress will start with the desired space between each word on the line, and expand or condense from there up to the limits specified as minimum and maximum for justified text. If condensing the space between words cannot make the line fit within the margins, QuarkXPress will hyphenate (if hyphenation is turned on, which it usually should be for justified text). If hyphenating and adjusting the space between words is not enough to make the line hit the margin, the space between letters will be adjusted (Figure 12-9).

Word Spacing Minimum: 80%	Word Spacing Minimum: 100%	Word Spacing Minimum: 120%
He can be called a remarkable man who stands out from those around him by the resourcefulness of his mind, and who knows how to be restrained in the manifestations which proceed from his nature, at the same time conducting himself justly and tolerantly towards the weaknesses of others. George Gurdjieff	He can be called a remarkable man who stands out from those around him by the resourcefulness of his mind, and who knows how to be restrained in the manifestations which proceed from his nature, at the same time conducting himself justly and tolerantly towards the weaknesses of others. George Gurdjieff	He can be called a remarkable man who stands out from those around him by the resourcefulness of his mind, and who knows how to be restrained in the manifestations which proceed from his nature, at the same time conducting himself justly and tolerantly towards the weaknesses of others. George Gurdjieff

Figure 12-9 Same paragraph justified with different spacing allowances.

Remember, for text that is not justified, the spacing set as Optimum will be used throughout.

If you think you can improve the appearance of your document by making the spacing between words smaller, consider the tradeoffs: With a wide allowance for spacing between words and letters, the "rivers" of white space may seem wide in justified text, but fewer words will be hyphenated. Text with a narrow allowance for space between characters and words is likely to have a high number of words hyphenated.

Special Typographic Effects

The next headings describe special effects that might be difficult to achieve using conventional typesetting technologies but are easy with QuarkXPress.

Making Drop Caps and Variations

QuarkXPress lets you create drop caps and other special effects for letters that start a paragraph. The automatic drop cap feature lets you set a large cap against two or more lines of text. The next headings describe this and other methods of setting large initial caps at the beginning of a paragraph.

Automatic Drop Caps

You can create automatic drop caps by clicking on the Drop Caps check box in the Paragraph Formats dialog box.

Step 1 Select the Content tool (🖑) and position the text insertion point in the paragraph, then choose Style ➤ Formats to display the Paragraph Formats dialog box.

Step 2 Click on the Drop Caps check box and enter the Character Count (number of drop cap letters at the start of the paragraph) and Line Count (number of lines of text to run beside the drop caps).

Step 3 Click on OK to close the dialog box and apply the drop cap specifications, or click on Apply to view the effects of the specifications before you accept them (Figure 12-10).

Figure 12-10 Paragraph Formats dialog box with Drop Caps selected and resulting drop cap.

QuarkXPress automatically adjusts the height of the first letter(s) of the paragraph to match the height of the number of lines specified in the dialog box. If the single initial drop cap is a lowercase letter, it will be adjusted to the full height of the lines specified as the line count; if the character count is greater than one and the drop caps include upper- and lowercase letters, the drop caps will retain appropriate relationships between the sizes of uppercase and lowercase letters. The maximum number of lines deep you can specify is eight. If you need to run the drop cap more than eight lines deep, try creating a separate text box with the drop cap in it, instead of using the automatic drop caps command.

Manually Sized Drop Caps

You can change the size of the automatic drop cap (Figure 12-11) by selecting it and changing the value via the Measurements palette, the Character Formats dialog box, or the keyboard shortcuts (CTRL+> and CTRL+<).

Figure 12-11 Drop caps can be sized manually after they have been created through the Paragraph Formats dialog box.

Notice that the Measurements palette and the Character Formats dialog box show the size of the drop cap as a percentage. You can enter a different percentage, but you *cannot* enter an absolute value by including the unit of measure as you can for normal characters. You can make other adjustments to a drop cap character, including changes to the style, horizontal scaling, color and shade.

Large Initial Caps

The automatic drop caps feature creates large initial caps automatically, but it forces you to set the line count to at least two lines. If you want a large initial cap followed by only one line of text, you can scale the first character(s) of a paragraph manually using the Style ➤ Size command, the Style ➤ Character command, the CTRL+SHIFT+> keyboard shortcut, or through the Measurements palette. If you have specified auto leading for the paragraph, the enlarged letters will affect the spacing between the first and second lines (Figure 12-12). Use absolute leading instead.

You can use Style ➤ Leading, Style ➤ Formats or the Measurements palette to change the leading manually. The Paragraph Formats dialog box displayed by the Style> Formats command offers the flexibility of viewing the effects of your leading entry (through the Apply button) before closing the dialog box. You can specify font size in inches for a large cap by typing an inch mark (") after the number in the size entry area.

Figure 12-12 Use absolute leading for large initial caps to avoid uneven line spacing in the paragraph.

Creating Shadow Type

You can use shaded type to create your own custom shadow type.

Step 1   Type the text you want in a text box.

Step 2   Select Item ➤ Duplicate to create a second box. Select Item ➤ Modify to make the top box transparent (Background set to 0 percent), and set the text runaround (Item Runaround) to None.

Step 3   Offset the position of the two boxes slightly so the bottom type appears behind the top layer of type.

Step 4   Select the text in the top box and use Style ➤ Shade and/or Style ➤ Color to make the shade and/or color different from the text in the bottom box (Figure 12-13).

Figure 12-13 Two text boxes overlapped create custom shadow type.

Reversing Type on a Black Background

Reversed type, or dropout type, is the name applied to white type on a dark background. To create reversed type, you can use white or lightly shaded text (Style ► Shade and Style ► Color) on any dark background color or shade in the text box (Item ► Modify), as shown in Figure 12-14.

Figure 12-14 Reverse type in a box with a dark background.

You can also create a line of reversed type on a dark background by using the Rules command. This is the preferred method of reversing elements that might be repeated throughout text that is not otherwise reversed—such as reversed headings with normal body copy. This method can be applied through a style sheet, making it easy to change the specifications globally.

Figure 12-15 Reverse type on a dark ruled line.

Step 1 Apply a rule to white text (or text of any shade or color) by highlighting the text and selecting the Rules command from the Style menu.

Step 2 Choose the color, shade, length, and width (up to 503 points) of rule desired; then input a *negative* value in the Offset entry area. Since the default unit for Offset is in percent when you first open the dialog box, and you cannot enter a negative percentage here, you must enter a unit of measure after you type in a negative value. The rule must be a different color or shade from the text, and there must be a carriage return above (or below) the text in order for a rule above (or below) to appear (Figure 12-16).

Figure 12-16 Rules dialog box for reversing type on a background.

Rotating Text Boxes in a Symmetrical Circular Pattern

Here's a simple technique for rotating text in a symmetrical, circular pattern:

Step 1 Type the *longest* text label in a text box, adjust the character attributes, paragraph format, and size of the box to fit the space allowed.

Step 2 Select Item ➤ Duplicate to make as many copies of the text box as there are elements in the circular design.

Step 3 To determine how many degrees to rotate each element, divide 360° by the number of elements to get the first angle of rotation.

Step 4 Let the first element remain horizontal (no rotation), but use the Measurements palette or the Item ➤ Modify command to enter degrees of rotation and rotate the second element (Figure 12-17).

Figure 12-17 First of five elements remains horizontal, second element is rotated 72° (360/5).

Step 5 Increase each consecutive element's rotation by the amount of the first rotation (Figure 12-18).

Figure 12-18 Third element is rotated 144° (72°+72°), fourth is rotated 216° (144°+72°), and fifth is rotated 288° (216°+72°).

Step 6 Arrange the elements in a symmetrical, circular pattern and edit the text in each text box (Figure 12-19).

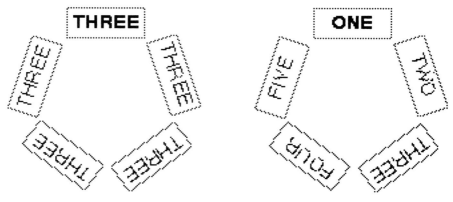

Figure 12-19 Final format.

Text Inside a Shape

QuarkXPress gives you the ability to format type inside a shape, including irregular shapes. No single command achieves this effect; rather you perform a series of steps to create both a picture and a text box. To flow text inside a shape:

Step 1   Create a text box, and type in or import the text you want flowed into a shape.

Step 2   Create a picture box (you can use any shape picture box, but the rectangle or polygon picture box works best). To create a runaround polygon, import a graphic, then choose Item → Runaround; use the drop-down list, select Manual Image, and click the Invert check box. In this case, the runaround polygon will be in the shape of the graphic (Figure 12-20).

Figure 12-20   The Runaround dialog box set up for flowing text inside a shape.

Step 3   With the editing tool selected, delete the graphic by pressing the Delete key (Figure 12-21).

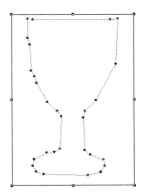

Figure 12-21   Runaround Polygon remains in a Picture Box after graphic is deleted.

Step 4 Make sure the picture box is on top of the text box (select **Item → Bring to Front**); when the space inside the polygon wrap is larger than the space available in the text box, the text will flow inside the runaround polygon shape (Figure 12-22).

Lorem ipsum dolor sit amet, consectetuer adipiscing elit, sed diam nonummy nibh euismod tincidunt ut laoreet dolore magna aliquam erat volutpat. Ut wisi enim ad minim veniam, quis nostrud exerci tation ullamcorper suscipit lobortis nisl ut aliquip ex ea commodo consequat. Duis et al autem vel eum iriure dolor in hendrerit in vulputate velit le volut esse molestie consequat, vel illum dolore eu feugiat nulla facilisis at verot et

Figure 12-22 Text flows inside the shape.

You can move the handles on the runaround polygon anywhere within the picture box. You can add handles to the runaround polygon by holding down the CTRL key as you click on the polygon. To remove handles, hold down the CTRL key as you click on a handle. To prevent screen redraw while you are adjusting the shape, hold down the space bar. When you release it, the screen will redraw.

Summary

This chapter offered tips and suggestions for creating design specifications for type and for using QuarkXPress tools and commands to achieve special typographic effects. The next chapter offers a range of ideas for using special graphic techniques in QuarkXPress.

13 Special Graphic Techniques

In this chapter we present some special techniques related to graphics. The basic issues of creating and importing graphics in QuarkXPress were covered in Chapter 6 on Graphics. Special techniques presented here include how to create special effects, such as drop shadows and custom rules, and how to draw perfect polygons (pentagons, hexagons, and the like). You will also learn how to create common graphic elements, such as bar charts and organization charts, using QuarkXPress' tools.

Working with Graphics

QuarkXPress is not a drawing package; it can in no way approach the capabilities of such programs as CorelDRAW or Aldus FreeHand, one or both of which should probably be part of your electronic "toolbox."

However, you should become familiar with the graphics tools that QuarkXPress does have to offer, because these built-in tools have much more capability than you might think. Thoroughly understanding how the picture box and line tools work will also make it easier for you to handle imported graphics, and will help you keep QuarkXPress' full design potential in mind.

Using Two Sets of Defaults for Picture Boxes

If you always want the same inset, border, or background for your picture boxes, you can use Edit ⇢ Preferences ⇢ Tools, as described in Chapter 3, to change the defaults for the item tools. Sometimes, however, you might want two sets of defaults. For example, you might repeatedly add picture boxes for imported graphics plus black-background boxes as placeholders for photographic halftones that will be stripped in at the print shop.

With normal defaults, you would need to use Item ⇢ Modify to set the background shade to 100 percent black every time you draw a box that is a placeholder for a photograph. The following method can save you from repeatedly opening the Picture Box Specifications dialog box, and save time in producing a document with a lot of placeholders:

Step 1   Use Edit ⇢ Preferences ⇢ Tools to set the defaults for a rectangular box to match what you want for boxes that will hold imported pictures.

Step 2   Use Edit ⇢ Preferences ⇢ Tools to set the defaults for the Rounded-corner Rectangle Picture Box tool (⊠) to match what you want for boxes that will serve as placeholders for photographs. Set the Corner Radius to 0 (to make the Rounded-corner Rectangle Picture Box tool draw rectangles as the default), and set the background to 100 percent black (Figure 13-1).

Figure 13-1 Picture Box Specifications dialog box set up for black-box placeholders shows corner radius is set to 0 for the Rounded-corner Rectangle Picture Box tool.

Now every time you use the Rectangle Picture Box tool (⊠), you will draw a box with the default specifications for imported pictures, and every time you use the Rounded-corner Rectangle Picture Box tool (⊠), you will draw a black box as a placeholder for a halftone to be stripped in later (Figure 13-2).

Figure 13-2 Rectangles drawn with the Rectangle Picture Box tool (left) and with the Rounded-Corner Picture Box tool (right).

You can use variations on this tip to create any two sets of specifications. The key is that you are actually turning the Rounded-corner Rectangle Picture Box tool into a Rectangle Picture Box tool by setting the corner radius to zero.

Creating Drop Shadows

The simplest method of creating a three-dimensional effect is to create a "shadow" of a box by placing a copy of the box behind it, offset slightly and assigned a dark fill pattern. The effect is commonly referred to as a drop shadow. This technique is frequently used to add dimension or visual interest to conceptual illustrations, such as bar charts and organization charts. You can add special effects to any page using this technique on boxes or lines.

Step 1   Draw a box with one of QuarkXPress' item tools. Use the Text Box tool (A) if you will be filling the drop-shadowed box with text (Figure 13-3). Use one of the picture box tools if you will be filling the box with an imported picture. Or use one of the line tools if you want to create a drop-shadowed line.

Figure 13-3 Box drawn with the Text Box tool.

Step 2 Use Item ► Modify to assign a 100 percent black fill or any shade or color other than white or transparent (0 percent) (Figure 13-4).

Figure 13-4 Box Specifications dialog box.

Step 3 Use Item ► Duplicate to create a second box, and position the copy on top of the first box, offset slightly. Or make the second box a picture box, since picture boxes store less information in them than text boxes.

Step 4 Use Item ► Modify to assign a 100 percent white fill (or any shade or color other than what you used on the first box).

Step 5 Use Item ► Frame to assign a frame to the top box (Figure 13-5).

Figure 13-5 Frame Specifications dialog box.

Step 6 ►ill the top box with text or graphics (Figure 6).

Figure 13-6 Finished drop shadow box.

Step 7 If you want to make duplicates of the drop-shadowed box, select both boxes and group them (Figure 13-7).

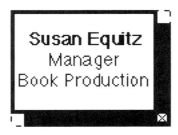

Figure 13-7 Grouped boxes show boundary box when selected.

Layering Lines for Special Effects

Sometimes you might want to draw lines that appear to have a center that is different from the the outer edge of the line—such as a white line with black edges. QuarkXPress offers several line styles with this effect. However, what if you want specific control over the width of each part of the line, or you want the center to be shaded instead of white? You can align copies of straight lines next to each other, but here is a simpler method.

Step 1 First, draw the line and set the color and width. Figure 13-8 shows a black line, 5 points wide.

Figure 13-8 A wide black line.

Step 2 Select Item ➤ Duplicate to create a second on top of the first, slightly offset. Position the second line on top of the first (you don't have to position it precisely). Set the second line's attributes — Figure 13-9 shows a white, 3-point line. (The second line must be thinner than the first.)

Step 3 Select both lines and use the Space/Align command to align the centers horizontally and vertically (if you want the outer edges to appear equal), then use the Group command to keep them together when you move them.

Figure 13-9 A wide black line overlaid by a thinner white line.

You can use this technique to create lines composed of several shades or colors, or experiment with more complex lines composed of three or more layers. If the second line is dashed, you can create the look used in maps to represent roads or railways (Figure 13-10).

Figure 13-10 More variations of layered lines.

Drawing Polygons

Equal-sided polygons—such as 3-, 5-, 6-, or 8-sided boxes—are difficult to draw visually on the screen with the Polygon Picture Box tool (⊠). Here are two techniques that will help you draw polygons with equal sides. Use the first technique to create polygons with an even number of sides; use the second technique to create polygons with an odd number of sides.

Creating Polygons with an Even Number of Sides

Step 1   Select the Orthogonal Line tool (+) and draw a straight line.

Step 2   Select Item → Duplicate to make as many copies of the line as needed. If the polygon is to have an even number of sides, you want the number of lines to total half the number of sides (Figure 13-11).

Figure 13-11 For a six-sided polygon, you want to create three identical lines.

Step 3   Select the lines one by one and rotate them in multiples of the number of degrees yielded by the formula:

> 360° divided by the number of lines

For a six-sided figure, create three lines. Because 360° divided by 3 equals 120°, rotate the first line 0°, rotate the second line 120°, and rotate the third line 240° (Figure 13-12).

Figure 13-12 Three lines rotated in multiples of 120° for a six-sided polygon.

Step 4 Select all of the lines and use the Item → Space/Align command to align the centers vertically and horizontally (Figure 13-13).

Figure 13-13 Space/Align dialog box.

Step 5 Select the Polygon Picture Box tool (⊠) and draw a polygon by clicking on the end points of the lines (Figure 13-14).

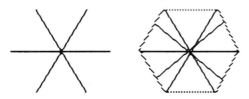

Figure 13-14 Three rotated and aligned lines create six end points. Use end points as guides in creating the polygon with the Polygon picture box tool.

Step 6   Delete the three lines that you used as guides.

Figure 13-15   The final six-sided polygon.

Creating Polygons with an Odd Number of Sides

Step 1   Select the Orthogonal Line tool (+) to draw a straight line.

Step 2   Make as many copies of the line as needed. If the polygon is to have an odd number of sides, you want the total number of lines to equal the number of sides (Figure 13-16).

———————   ———————   ———————   ———————   ———————

Figure 13-16   For a five-sided polygon, you want to create five identical lines.

Step 3   Select the lines one by one and rotate them in multiples of the number of degrees yielded by the formula:

360° divided by the number of lines

For a five-sided figure, create five lines. Because 360° divided by 5 equals 72°, rotate the lines at 0°, 72°, 144°, 216°, and 288° (Figure 13-17).

Figure 13-17   Five lines rotated in multiples of 72° for a five-sided polygon.

Step 4   Select all of the lines and use the Item → Space/Align command to align the centers vertically and horizontally.

Step 5   Select the Polygon Picture Box tool (⊠) and draw a polygon by clicking on the end points of the lines, *skipping every other point* (Figure 13-18).

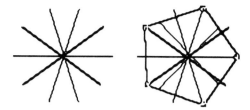

Figure 13-18 Five rotated and aligned lines create 10 end points. Skip every other point in drawing the polygon.

Step 6 **Delete the five lines that you used as guides (Figure 13-19).**

Figure 13-19 The final five-sided polygon.

Drawing Cartoon Balloons and Other Special Shapes

Unusual shapes, such as cartoon balloons, can be created by converting ovals to polygons and dragging a handle. Here are the steps in creating a cartoon balloon.

Step 1 **Select the Oval Picture Box tool (⊗) and draw an ellipse (Figure 13-20).**

Figure 13-20 An ellipse created with the Oval Picture Box tool.

Step 2 **Choose Item ➤ Picture Box Shape and select the polygon from the drop-down list.**

Step 3 Choose Item ▸ Reshape Polygon to display handles all around the ellipse (Figure 13-21).

Figure 13-21 Handles display all around the ellipse when you choose Reshape Polygon.

Step 4 Drag one of the handles to create a pointed extension from the ellipse (Figure 13-22).

Figure 13-22 Drag a handle to create a pointed extension.

Step 5 Select the Text Box tool (▣) and create a text box on top of the balloon. Use the Style ▸ Alignment command to center the text horizontally and the Item ▸ Modify command to set the background to None and to center the text vertically (Figure 13-23).

Figure 13-23 Text added in a text box.

You can use this technique to create other shapes that can stand alone as graphic design elements on a page or that can be used to crop imported pictures in unusual ways or force unusual text wraps (Figure 13-24).

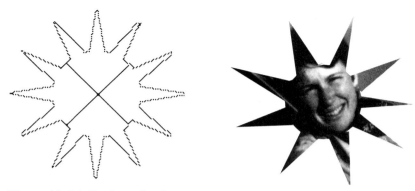

Figure 13-24 Reshaped polygon creates unusual crop.

 When creating anchored picture boxes, regardless of the shape of the box you copy into the Clipboard, the picture box will become a rectangular picture box; it will not maintain its original shape.

Creating Business Graphics with QuarkXPress

Using QuarkXPress' built-in graphics tools, you can build simple bar charts, organization charts, and other basic diagrams.

Creating Bar Charts

Bar charts are very common business graphics. You can generate bar charts by using a charting or spreadsheet application and then import the chart into QuarkXPress to create a business proposal or report. If you don't have a charting package, or if your artists don't want to learn how to use a spreadsheet package simply to generate bar charts, you can use the technique described here to generate roughly accurate bar charts using QuarkXPress.

Step 1 Select the Orthogonal Line tool (+) and draw a horizontal line the width you want for the bar chart. Draw a vertical line the height you want for the chart. Draw a short horizontal tick mark near the bottom of the vertical axis.

Step 2   Select the Text Box tool (🅰) and create a text box to the left of the tick mark, making it wide enough to hold the longest tick mark label. Type the longest label in the box (you will change the labels later), use the Style menu commands to choose the Font and Size you want, and set Alignment to Right (Figure 13-25).

Figure 13-25 Two axes and the first tick mark on the vertical axis are created with the Orthogonal Line tool. Text box initially shows the longest label.

Step 3   Select the Item tool (✥) and select both the tick mark and the text box. Optionally, you can group these items.

Step 4   Use the Step and Repeat command to make as many copies of the tick mark and text box as you want along the vertical axis (Figure 13-26).

Figure 13-26 Step and Repeat dialog box.

In the Step and Repeat dialog box (Figure 13-26), the repeat count is one less than the number of tick marks you want on the vertical axis (since you have already created one). The Horizontal Offset should be specified as 0. The Vertical Offset is the distance between tick marks, which you can calculate by dividing the number of tick marks into the length of the vertical axis (Figure 13-27).

Chapter 13: Special Graphic Techniques 435

Figure 13-27 Chart shows labels on vertical axis.

Step 5 Edit each text label for the tick marks.

Step 6 Select the Rectangle Picture Box tool (⊠) and create a rectangle the width of one bar. Position it on the horizontal axis near the origin of the two axes (Figure 13-28).

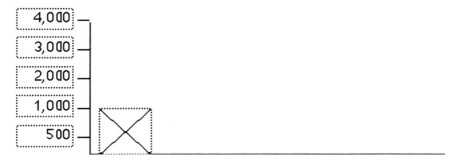

Figure 13-28 Chart shows a bar of the desired width, set to any height, in the first position.

The width you choose should be based on the length of the horizontal axis of the chart and the number of bars. For example, if the axis is 6 inches and your chart has 5 bars, you might make each bar 1 inch wide and distribute the extra inch for the space between bars. This first bar can be any height—you will adjust the height of each bar later.

Step 7 Use the Step and Repeat command to make as many copies of this basic unit as you need bars and arrange them along the horizontal axis (Figure 13-29).

436   *The QuarkXPress Handbook*

Figure 13-29 Step and Repeat dialog box.

In the Step and Repeat dialog box (Figure 13-29), the repeat count is one less than the number of bars in the chart (since you have already created one bar). The Horizontal Offset is the distance between bars. Make it equal to the bar width if you want the bars to touch each other, wider if you want space between them (Figure 13-30).

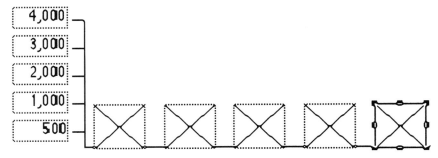

Figure 13-30 Duplicated boxes.

Step 8   Select the Item tool (✥) and scale each bar vertically by dragging the handle at the center of the top of the box up or down to align with the appropriate value along the vertical axis (Figure 13-31).

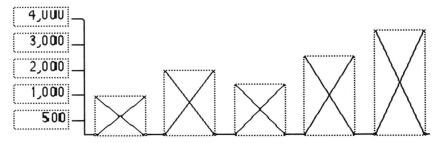

Figure 13-31 Scaled boxes.

Step 9 To add text boxes to label each bar in the chart, you can create one text box that runs the length of the horizontal axis and set tabs to position each label (Figure 13-32).

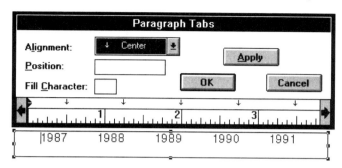

Figure 13-32 Set tabs in text box that runs below bars.

If you create each bar using the Text Box tool (△) in step 6, you can type text labels directly into each bar. Use the Style ➤ Alignment command to align the text Left, Right, or Centered in the bar. Use the Item ➤ Modify command to set the Vertical Alignment of the text to the top, center, or bottom of the bar (Figure 13-33).

Figure 13-33 Bars created with the Text Box tool can contain labels.

Step 10 Finish the chart by adding a title and caption. You can use the techniques described in steps 6 to 8 to create a second set of bars that overlay the first. You can set different background colors or shades for the two sets of boxes, and add a legend to differentiate the two sets (Figure 13-34).

Figure 13-34 Chart with second set of bars and a legend.

Using the Space/Align Command

Chapter 2 described the basic features of the Space/Align command. Here we offer a few more tips about using that command to align objects when at least one item is already positioned such that you do not want the Space/Align command to move it.

Normally, when you use the Space/Align command to align objects horizontally, the item in the leftmost position of the group will remain in place and items to the right of it will be moved to meet the specifications in the Space/Align dialog box. Similarly, when aligning objects vertically, the item in the topmost position of the group will remain in place and items below it will be moved.

If you have already positioned an item on the page and you do not want to move it, you can use the Lock command to prevent inadvertent movements with the Item tool. However, the Lock command does not prevent an item from being moved through a dialog box entry. The Space/Align command will cause *locked* items to move if they are not in the leftmost position for a horizontal move or the topmost position for a vertical move.

When aligning a group of items relative to one item that you do not want moved, position all other items to the right of the fixed item when moving along the horizontal and below the fixed item when moving along the vertical.

For example, if you have created a bar chart using QuarkXPress' tools and you want to align text labels below each bar, you can use the Space/Align command:

Chapter 13: Special Graphic Techniques   439

Step 1   Create the bar chart (as described earlier in this chapter)
         (Figure 13-35).

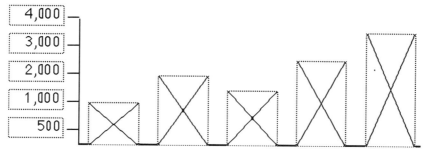

Figure 13-35 Bar chart before labels are added to bars.

Step 2   Type the first bar's labels in a text box and position it any-
         where to the right of and below the first bar. Use the
         Style → Alignment command to center the text in the box
         (Figure 13-36).

Figure 13-36 Label positioned to the right of the first bar.

Step 3   Use the Space/Align command to center the label 3 picas
         below the bar (Figure 13-37).

*Figure 13-37 Space/Align dialog box shows Horizontal spacing set to 0, with
Centers aligned. Vertical spacing is set to 2 picas with Bottom Edges aligned.*

If you want to center the label *above* the bar, you can use the Space/Align command to align the centers horizontally, but you must select the Item tool (✥) to drag the label into position above the bar. You cannot use the Space/Align command to position the label above the bar without starting with the label above the bar, in which case the Space/Align command would move the bar.

See "Creating Bar Charts" for a full description of creating this chart and alternatives for labeling the bars.

Organization Charts

Organization charts are a very common form of business graphic. Here is a technique for quickly producing an organization chart in QuarkXPress. We assume that you have already sketched the chart roughly on paper before you start building it in QuarkXPress.

Step 1 Select the Text Box tool (🅐) and create a small text box of the most common size to be used in the chart.

Make this text box large enough to fit any entry in the chart by typing the text of the longest name and title or department that will appear in the organization chart, and using commands in the Style menu to set up the type specifications that you will use throughout the chart. Then scale the text box so it is just large enough to fit each line of the entry.

Step 2 Use the Item → Modify command to make the box opaque (not transparent). Use the Item → Frame command to add a visible border around the box and special effects (such as rotation or skewing). Drop shadows can be added later, if desired (Figure 13-38).

Figure 13-38 Longest name, title, and department are typed in the first box.

This item will be the basic unit used throughout the chart. The text typed in this first box need not reflect reality—the person's name you type need not hold that title or be in that department.

Step 3 Working in Fit in Window view (CTRL+0), make as many copies of this basic item as you need to fill the chart. Drag the copies into roughly the positions they would take to fit on the page (Figure 13-39).

Figure 13-39 Initial layout can be rough.

Step 4 Select the items in each column or along each vertical division or department line in the chart and use the Space/Align command to align them precisely with Horizontal spacing set to 0, aligning the centers, and even Vertical spacing set to any amount larger than the height of each box (Figure 13-40).

Figure 13-40 Space/Align dialog box and results.

Select and align each column of boxes in the chart using the same vertical spacing.

Step 5   Optionally, you can add drop shadows to all the boxes by selecting all the text boxes in the chart: Use the Item ▸ Duplicate command to copy them. Use the Item ▸ Modify command to give the copies a dark background. Use the Group command to group them. Move them into position slightly offset from the first set of boxes. Use the Item ▸ Send to Back command to send the shadows behind the chart (Figure 13-41).

Figure 13-41 Chart items with drop shadows.

Step 6   Select the Orthogonal Line tool (✛) and draw lines to mark the chart organization (Figure 13-42).

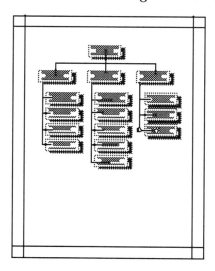

Figure 13-42 Chart items with lines overlaid.

Step 7 Group all of the lines and use the Item → Send to Back command to send them behind the text boxes.

Step 8 Finally, return to Actual Size view and edit the text in each box to reflect the appropriate name and affiliations (Figure 13-43).

Figure 13-43 Edit text in boxes in Actual Size view.

Summary

This chapter included specific tips about using QuarkXPress commands and features for special graphic effects. The next chapter discusses workgroups.

14 *Managing Documents*

More than almost any other business or activity, publishing is ruled by deadlines: you can't send June's news out in July. When the publication is part of a larger product package, it is likely that the marketing or distribution group will want the documents finished as soon as the product is ready for shipment. One way or another, the publication department is always pushed to complete everything as quickly as possible. Tips in this chapter will help you organize your projects so that they run as smoothly as possible—whether you are the only one in the production group or you are running a large department in a networked workgroup environment. Even if you are in no hurry to use QuarkXPress to create your own self-published *History of the Universe As I See It*, you'll find the tips in this chapter helpful in organizing your disk files and managing precious resources such as disk storage space and memory.

Organizing Your Disk Files

It's a good idea to organize your disk files before you start building a document in QuarkXPress. A few basic guidelines can save a lot of trouble in the long run, especially if the document you are building is very large or uses a lot of different source files.

If two or more people are involved in the production process, the disk organization and file-naming conventions should be determined by the production manager and announced to the production crew. File organization and naming conventions might be incorporated into a list of project standards, offering guidelines for moving or renaming files as they progress through the production process.

If possible, assemble all source files—the text and picture files as well as the QuarkXPress libraries, templates, and document files—onto one primary hard drive. This can be your internal hard disk if your computer will be the primary workstation for page layout activities, or it can be a file server if you are on a network and several people will be involved in the final document production. It could be a separate hard disk or a removable hard disk if you will need to carry the files from one station to another.

The key directories containing files that affect each document include the QuarkXPress program directory, the Windows directory, and the project directory.

The QuarkXPress Program Directory

The QuarkXPress program directory, usually named XPRESS (Figure 14-1), is where the QuarkXPress program (XPRESS.EXE) is stored. The directory can have any name as assigned during the installation process but, whatever directory contains the QuarkXPress program, several other files must be present for the program to be fully functional. The most essential file is XPress Preferences (XPRESS.PRF), which if it is missing from the program directory is recreated automatically whenever you start QuarkXPress. XPress Dictionary (XPRESS.DCT) is used for spell checking. XPress Help (XPRESS.HLP) needs to be available if you want access to on-line help through QuarkXPress. Both of these files are used optionally.

Chapter 14: Managing Documents 447

Figure 14-1 Contents of the QuarkXPress Program directory.

If you want to edit kerning or tracking tables, you must have the Kern/Track Editor Xtension(KTEDIT.XXT) in the program directory. Your program folder may also contain QuarkXPress import/export filters that you will need for the Get Text and Save Text commands. Each of these is described under the next headings.

XPress Preferences File: XPRESS.PRF

The XPress Preferences file, XPRESS.PRF, contains:

- the Preference settings that will apply to any new document, including any changes you have made to the defaults by using the commands available when QuarkXPress is active but no document is open, or by using the Preferences ➤ Application command at any time (as described in Chapter 3),
- the default style sheets, colors, and H&Js,
- hyphenation exceptions (if exceptions have been specified for any document),
- kerning table values (if you have edited any kerning tables), and
- tracking edit values.

If you make changes to any of these items when no document is open, or by using the Preferences ➤ Application command at any time, they are stored in the XPRESS.PRF file. If you change settings when a document is open, the information is saved in the document file only (except settings available through the Preferences → Application command).

If a document is opened on a different system containing different settings from those in the XPRESS.PRF file, or if the XPRESS.PRF file has changed since the document was last saved, the preferences that were in effect when the document was last saved will remain in effect.

Import/Export Filter Files

In order for the formatting from word processing applications to be preserved when text is imported into QuarkXPress, and in order to import some graphic file formats, the specific import/export filter files must be available in the QuarkXPress program directory. These are normally copied into that directory automatically during the installation process. File formats that require filters include Computer Graphics Metafiles (CGMFILTR.FLT), Micrografx Designer files (DRWFILTR.FLT), Hewlett Packard plotter graphics (HPGL.FLT), Microsoft Word for Windows versions 1.0 and 2.0 (WORD1.XXT and WORD2.XXT), Windows Write (WRITEXXT), WordPerfect for Windows, Ami Pro 2.0, XyWrite III Plus, and ASCII text that has been coded with XPress Tags (XTAGS.XXT).

Because storing import/export filters in the same directory as the QuarkXPress program consumes 20–30 kilobytes of memory when you run QuarkXPress, it is a good idea to store only those filters you need into the XPress Program directory. Move unused filters into a subdirectory.

The Windows Directory

The primary file in the Windows directory that affects the printing capabilities of QuarkXPress (as well as all other applications) is WIN.INI. This file contains information about what printers are attached to each port and what fonts are installed, including information about where the fonts reside on the hard disk. Fonts that come with Windows can usually be found in the System directory within the Windows directory, but you can install additional fonts wherever you like. When you install them through Windows, the WIN.INI file is automatically updated with information about where to find the font information. (Chapter 4 describes in detail how to install screen fonts; Chapter 8 describes how to install printer fonts.)

You can view WIN.INI by opening it using the Windows Notepad or any word processing application, or by placing it in QuarkXPress as a text file. You can also edit it as a text file to change the information—but we don't recommend that you do this unless you know what you are doing, which would require information not provided in this book. For advanced

Windows users who have experience modifying WIN.INI, or if you have read the appropriate sections of the manuals that come with Windows, you can heed the next tip.

 The WIN.INI file is automatically updated whenever you install a new Windows application, a new font, or a new printer. Microsoft recommends that you never let the WIN.INI file grow larger than 32K. If you do, Windows and other applications might have trouble updating the file. It's unlikely that new applications or printers will add much to the file, but you might run into trouble if you install a lot of fonts. If you want to make WIN.INI smaller, open the file using any text editor and look for duplicate information. For example, when you install a new application, new settings might be added to the file automatically. When you install newer versions of the same application, those same settings might be added again. Delete this duplicate information. Similarly, you can delete information about fonts that you never use, unused printer device driver settings, and unused application settings.

 Normally, the information in WIN.INI is read into memory whenever you start Windows. To re-read this information into memory after you update WIN.INI, you can close Windows and restart it—but this would mean closing all the open applications. You can get Windows to re-read your WIN.INI file, and implement any changes you have made, by simply opening any of the Control Panel dialog boxes, then clicking OK to close it—you need not make any entries in the dialog box. (Remember that the Control Panel is an icon in the Windows Main program group in the Program Manager window, and you open a dialog box by double-clicking any icon in the Control Panel window.)

When you install QuarkXPress, it automatically creates a file named QUARK.INI in the Windows directory, which tells Windows where the QuarkXPress program is stored, the size and location of the QuarkXPress application window when you start the program, and other technical information. Like WIN.INI, QUARK.INI can be edited if you know what you are doing, but there is no need to be concerned about this file or its contents.

Windows comes with a built-in ability to handle commonly used printers without requiring anything special from the software that runs under Windows. Drivers that you installed through the Windows installation process are normally stored in the System directory within the Windows directory, but QuarkXPress comes with a PostScript driver (PSCRIPT.DRV) that can be found in the QuarkXPress program directory. When you use File → Printer and click the Options button, the Printer drop-down list in the Printer Options dialog box lets you choose from specific models of printers, corresponding to the list you installed through Windows Setup. If you are printing to a PostScript device that is not included in the list by name, simply choose PostScript printer.

The Publication Directory

Before beginning the page layout process in an electronic publishing project, it is a good idea to set up a single directory on the hard disk for each document or publication, and move all of the text and graphic files into that directory. This is a good way to organize your files, and it is especially helpful to organize this way *before* you start importing linked graphics into a QuarkXPress document. Since QuarkXPress "remembers" where the linked graphics came from originally, you will have to re-link the files through QuarkXPress if you move the graphics after building the document (as explained in Chapter 6).

If there are very many files involved, then divide the main document directory into subdirectories. Some publishers like to keep text sources in one directory and graphics elements in another. Another way of dividing the files is to put the text and graphics files related to a single chapter together in a directory, so you end up with one directory per chapter (Figure 14-2).

The publication-specific directory can also include a subdirectory of the fonts used in the publication. This can be where you originally install fonts to be used in that publication only, or copies of fonts that are in the Windows directory or in your general font directory. If you keep a set in the publication directory, it will be easy to remember to take copies with you when you move the publication to another system to be printed.

Figure 14-2 Two sample project directories.

File-Naming Standards

No matter how you organize your files, it is a good idea to develop logical naming conventions for them. Decide on the naming conventions you will use for all new files created during the project. The first goal is to be able to find documents easily and know what they contain. One helpful guideline is to name the different parts of the document consistently, so they appear sequentially when you view them alphabetically. For example, a chapter document might be named Chap01.QXD or CH01.QXD or 01.QXD (Figure 14-3), but you don't want a set of documents related to one book to use different naming standards—Chapter1, Chap02, CH3, 04, and so on.

If you are *really* organized, you will apply naming conventions to *all* files in the project—text, graphics, and final page layouts. The file name extension is usually an indication of the file type, such as template, library, or text.

Chapter Numbers Only	Include Project ID	Different Versions/Editions
CH01.QXD	QXW01.QXD	Q01a.QXD
CH01.TXT	QXW01.TXT	Q01a.TXT
		Q01b.QXD
CH01-01.TIF	QXW01-01.TIF	Q01-01a.TIF
CH02.QXD	QXW02.QXD	Q02a.QXD
CH02.TXT	QXW02.TXT	Q02a.TXT
		Q02b.QXD

Figure 14-3 File-naming systems.

Moving Files

If you move your QuarkXPress document from one system to another, you need to take the following additional files besides the document file itself:

- All linked picture files (EPS, TIFF, and RIFF) used in the document.
- Screen fonts *and* printer fonts used in the document (or a list of fonts, so you can check that they are installed on the other system or on the hard disk drive connected to the printer). If the screen fonts are not available, the text might be reflowed when you open the document. If the printer fonts are not available, the printer might substitute other fonts when printing.

Backup Procedures

Keep a backup version of all files and back up changed files regularly. The backup system might simply be a collection of floppy disks. If you are using scanned images or very complicated illustrations, some files will probably be too big to fit on a floppy, so you will need to have a second hard disk (or a removable hard disk) in addition to the primary working hard disk.

Optimum File Size

A QuarkXPress document can be up to 2,000 pages or two gigabytes long (whichever limit is reached first), but it is more efficient to work with smaller files; long files have slower response time when redrawing pages or making text edits that carry over to subsequent pages. It's a good idea to divide a long document into individual files—divided by sections or chapters—because it is faster to work with smaller files.

If you want to be able to back your documents up onto floppy disks for storage and for transport, another important consideration in deciding how many pages a single file should have is the predicted size of the final document in bytes. You might want to keep your files under 1.2MB for high-density 5.25-inch drives, or under 1.44MB for high-density 3.5-inch drives, and less for lower-density drives.

Build your files efficiently. Clear the Pasteboard area when you are finished using the elements on it, or when you save the final version of the document.

Organizing Libraries

QuarkXPress' library feature can be a tremendous production tool if the libraries are organized efficiently. Even though a library can contain up to 2,000 elements, it is a good idea to limit the number and keep the library file under 1.2 or 1.44MB so you can copy it onto a diskette and easily move it to other systems if you are working in a geographically dispersed group.

One organization method is to create one library for each client, department, or periodical. This is a good way of distinguishing between libraries when you work on a wide variety of publications that have different design specifications and different standard graphics.

It's a good idea to assign labels to the elements in a library, using well-thought-out naming standards (since you can sort labels alphabetically, or selectively display entries with the same label, as described in Chapter 3).

Workgroup Scenario

Up to this point we have presented some general rules and guidelines for organizing disk files in a large project. The next sections present a scenario of how these ideas might be applied in workgroups.

A networked workgroup is a group of personal computers, each with its own local hard disk, hooked up to a common file server through which they can share files. Network software through which personal computers can share files include NetWare, VINES, Lan Manager, and LANtastic (as mentioned in the introduction to this book). Many large publications around the world have replaced their dedicated publishing systems with personal computers and QuarkXPress. Many use commercially available or custom QuarkXTensions to use QuarkXPress in conjunction with dedicated publishing systems.

For example, Cybernetic Systems Inc. offers an editorial management system that links to Macintosh and PC applications and features its own relational SQL database running on a VAX or Sun server. Ideal for demanding, fast-paced newspaper environments, inital costs start around $500,000. At a more modest level, Quark, Inc. has announced its own workgroup products, CopyDesk and Dispatch soon to be available for both the Macintosh and Windows. CopyDesk is an editing program that can be used in conjunction with QuarkXPress, and includes document management features. Dispatch is a server-based XTension that provides management and tracking capabilities for a variety of applications, including, but not limited to, QuarkXPress. Other products currently available for the Macintosh environment include Publication Administrator (North Atlantic Publishing Systems, Inc.), P.Ink Press (P.Ink America), Double Helix (Helix Technologies), WriteOn (Publication Technologies, Inc.), and Page Director and Ad Director (Managing Editor Software). We expect to see many of these products released for the Windows environment in 1993.

The File Server

The file server in a network is a computer with a hard disk. Depending on the size of the hard disk, the file server stores the following types of files.

- The master files for the project. This includes everything described under the "Publication Directory" section earlier in this chapter. Some projects might be so large that the file server's entire hard disk is devoted to the project files.
- Other files shared among workstations, such as clip art and QuarkXPress Libraries that are not project-specific.
- Printer fonts and screen fonts must be stored on the file server if printing will be spooled through the server. If printing is not spooled through the server, then each workstation must have the printer and screen fonts. In a production environment that uses many fonts, the ideal is to keep *all* printer and screen fonts on the file server and let local workstations copy only those fonts that are in use on active projects.

Quark and many other software manufacturers require that you purchase a separate software package for each workstation if you want more than one person at a time to work with the application. QuarkXPress is network-sensitive; when you start the program from any station on a network, QuarkXPress checks to see that a program with the same serial number is not already running on another station.

Individual Workstations

Individual workstations in a network often have the following types of files stored on their local hard disks.

- The project files currently in progress on that workstation. These files are copied from the file server, worked on at the local workstation, then copied back to the file server (see "Backup Procedures" described under the next section).
- Printer fonts and screen fonts that are in use on active projects.
- Applications and desk accessories that are commonly or currently used. Each station that uses QuarkXPress will also have copies of other QuarkXPress files as described earlier in this chapter.

If your workgroup shares one room, or if the project is well managed and there is good communication between group members, you should not need to take extra precautions that two people might start working on copies of the same file at once. If procedures are followed correctly and a project coordinator monitors the status of each file as work progresses, it is unlikely that someone will start working on a file that is not that file's latest version.

However, if the group is widely dispersed in a building, if recommended procedures aren't followed, if the project is too large and the pace is too fast, if chaos reigns, then accidents can happen. By far the most efficient method of tracking the master copy of a document is through the careful attention of a project coordinator. The coordinator can use one of the publication management products that will soon be available for the Windows environment, mentioned earlier in this chapter, or simply maintain and post a log of each document's status, such as the one shown in Figure 14–4.

Disk File Name	Master File Start date	WIP Station ID	Date	Back to Master Date	Station #ID	WIP Date
CH01	4/1	SV	4/3	4/5	DB	4/8
CH02	4/1	SV	4/6	4/8		
CH03	4/1					

Figure 14-4 Example of a log of disk files.

Backup Procedures

The master files—or the most recently printed files that are still works-in-progress—are stored on the file server. When a file is to be modified, it is copied to a local workstation. Under this system, the file server is the backup for whatever files are actively being worked on at local workstations. When the work is finished, the file is copied from the local workstation back to the file server.

If the work in progress on each workstation is going to require more than a day to complete, then you might want each workstation to copy its works in progress back to the file server at the end of each day, to serve as interim backups. Be sure to maintain a copy of the most recently *printed* version of the documents; do not copy the work-in-progress files over the most recently printed "master" file on the file server. Instead, copy the interim versions into a separate directory.

When the entire project is finished, copy all files from the file server onto diskettes or removable hard disks for storage. It is a good idea to keep copies of all disk files at least until the final document has been mass-produced and distributed. You can erase the disk files later if storage space is limited. If you are producing a newsletter or a magazine, for example, you can erase the disk files after each issue is printed.

At the end of each project, it is a good idea to collect parts of the document that can be re-used and store them as part of the template or a QuarkXPress library for use in later documents.

Memory and System Resource Management

QuarkXPress does not actually operate on its own, but rather operates in the context of your particular hardware configuration. Normally, the memory usage in your computer is automatically controlled by DOS, Windows, your memory manager, and the applications you are running. Information that is stored in memory is always available immediately, but because memory space is limited, bits of information are constantly being put into memory, then replaced by new information as needed. The process of getting new information from the hard disk and moving it into memory takes milliseconds of time—primarily disk access time. When the milliseconds add up to noticeable delays while we are working, we are likely to want to add more memory to the system.

If you have already installed as much memory as your system can handle, or if you don't want to spend the time and money to add more memory, then you can participate in the memory management process by knowing what takes up memory and how to make the best use of it.

One part of memory—exactly 128K—is used for what are called Windows' "system resources." Sometimes you might run into a problem starting a new application because the part of memory reserved for Windows' system resources is all used, even though there is plenty of free memory left for running the application. The last sections of this chapter offer some tips on how to make the most of your memory and usage of system resources.

You can see how much free space is available for memory and for system resources by choosing the About Program Manager command from the Help menu of the Program Manager.

You can get access to "virtual" memory—and have access to even more RAM than you have installed on your system—by setting up a permanent swap file on your hard disk. See the Windows documentation for more information about this option.

The Program Manager at Startup

Each open application under Windows uses up some part of the system resources, as well as part of the larger memory area. In most cases, when you close an application it frees up those parts of the system resources it was using. The one exception is the Program Manager. Because the Program Manager is always running (to close it is to exit Windows), it never frees or recycles system resources once they have been allocated.

Each open window uses some system resources, and each icon within each open window uses some resources. If, when you start Windows, the Program Manager opens with only one window open—the Program Manager application window—it will start out using fewer resources than if one or more additional windows are opened within it at startup. The Program Manager window will also require more system resources the more icons it shows. Similarly, each window opened under the program manager will require more or less system resources depending on the number of icons in the window.

Closing the windows under Program Manager once they have been opened does not free system resources. The best way to minimize the initial bite of system resources is to Close all the windows under Program Manager, then exit Windows and check Save Changes in the Exit Windows dialog box. When you restart Windows, you will be using the least possible amount of system resources. Thereafter, when you exit Windows, be sure that Save Changes is *not* checked.

If you are always using the same application(s) under Windows, such as QuarkXPress and one graphics application, put the icons for those applications in one group window and start Windows with that window only open, using the procedure in the previous paragraph for saving changes to the Program Manager for future startups. You can create a new group icon by choosing File ➤ New from the Program Manager menu and clicking Program Group. With a group window open, you can add an application icon by choosing File → New from the Program Manager menu and clicking Program Item.

You can have icons for the same application stored in more than one program group. Windows provides several program groups arranged by type of application, and a program group called QuarkXPress can be created during the installation process. You can keep or delete these groups and create your own. For example, you can create a different program group for each project. The Newsletter program group might include the icon for the template (news.qxt) that would start QuarkXPress and open the template in one double-click. The same program group might include an icon for a graphics application, and for a mailing list of all newsletter subscribers.

Delete icons for applications that you never use. Remember that you can start any application using the Run command from the File menu under the Program Manager, or by finding and double-clicking the application under the File Manager. You delete an icon by clicking on it once to select it, then choosing File → Delete.

If you always use the same application(s), under Windows 3.1 you can add icons to the Startup program group under the Program manager. Whatever icons are in that folder will automatically start when you start Windows. Under Windows 3.0, you had to add lines to the WIN.INI file that will automatically launch the application when you start Windows; this still works under Windows 3.1. To launch QuarkXPress, for example, you type a line in WIN.INI with Run= or Load= followed by the directory path to the program:

    Run=c:\xpress\xpress.exe

In either case, you would not need to open a window under the Program Manager to start the most common application.

There is no right or wrong way to set up the Program Manager, but there are an infinite number of possibilities. We've mentioned a few here. Whatever approach works for you, simply remember that one goal is to make the best use of precious space for system resources.

Open Applications

One of the great things about working under Windows is that you can have several different applications running at once, and might even have several different document windows open under each application. The problem is that memory is used by each open window on the screen. This includes windows that show documents and palettes, such as the Measurements palette and the Colors palette.

Remember that you can free system resources by closing *applications*, but you do not free resources by simply closing windows and palettes that are not in use. Once you open a palette or a document window in QuarkXPress, the system resources used by that window will remain allocated until you close QuarkXPress. When you have two or more applications running at the same time, make sure it's because you routinely go back and forth between the two, not just because Windows allows you to run multiple applications.

Reboot to Recover Memory

In spite of all the tricks you might use to conserve or release memory, you still can run into problems that cannot be controlled. The most common problem is that even when you quit an application, not all of the memory or resources it was using will be released. This can be due to the application itself not releasing memory, or it can happen that after running many different applications the memory contains a lot of small (and therefore unusable) fragments.

You can rebuild Windows' system resources space by closing and restarting Windows. To clear the larger memory area, you need to reboot your system. This is more likely to happen if you leave your computer on 24 hours a day, but it can happen to anyone who uses a lot of different applications. Remember this as a possible solution whenever you run into the "Insufficient memory" message.

Of course, you can ignore all of the suggestions in these last sections if you have no problems with memory, system resources, or system speed!

Summary

In this chapter you learned how to manage your projects through QuarkXPress, through Windows, and through a network. The tips offered here are not necessary for using QuarkXPress, but are essential for handling large projects with tight deadlines. Ultimately, the advice in this chapter can do more to improve productivity than any of the design or production techniques presented earlier.

This chapter marks the end of our good advice and recommendations as the authors. The next chapter—the last chapter in the book—gathers additional tips from other sources by describing four projects that were produced using QuarkXPress and have been published. You can learn a lot by seeing how other professionals work!

15 *Case Studies*

This chapter presents a number of case studies of companies that are using QuarkXPress to design and produce various products, some of which you see and use every day.

All of these case studies involve documents that were produced using QuarkXPress on the Macintosh, since this book was written before QuarkXPress for Windows was released. However, the value of these profiles is to look at the overall process of QuarkXPress in a publishing environment. We hope that they will help you think about your own publishing environment in a more objective and creative way. You will see that many of the supporting applications used on the Macintosh—such as Microsoft Word and Aldus FreeHand—are also available in the Windows environment. Besides, many of us will be using QuarkXPress on *both* platforms—the Macintosh and MS-DOS/Windows—and moving documents between the two environments.

First, we look at the use of QuarkXPress at a magazine, *Entertainment Weekly*. Next, we'll see how a small advertising agency in Denver, Croce Advertising, uses QuarkXPress as an integral part of its business. Then, we'll follow the design and production of a blister card package for *Hot Wheels* toy cars by toy manufacturing giant Mattel. Finally, we describe one of the many corporate identity manuals that Landor Associates created using QuarkXPress.

The following case studies explain and illustrate characteristics of documents that present their own special design and production problems and practices.

Magazine: Entertainment Weekly

Entertainment Weekly is one of Time Inc.'s internationally recognized family of magazines. Of Time Inc.'s magazine publications, which include *TIME*, *People*, and *Sports Illustrated*, *Entertainment Weekly* was the first general interest publication to be produced completely from the desktop (Figure 15-1). (See color plate.)

Figure 15-1 A cover for Entertainment Weekly *in QuarkXPress—the scan is for position only.*

Description

Entertainment Weekly is a standard magazine format, bound and trimmed to 8-by-10.75 inches. Basic grid structures within its pages include 4-column, 3-column, 2-column, and 2-column plus a column for captioned photos (Figure 15-2).

Figure 15-2 Basic grid structures are each created in documents used as templates.

Software

- QuarkXPress
- Microsoft Word
- Aldus FreeHand
- Adobe Illustrator
- Letraset ColorStudio (image editing software)
- Adobe, Bitstream, Monotype, and custom-made fonts

Equipment

Entertainment Weekly started its operation with complete systems for the entire staff, including:

- 70 Macintosh IIcx models with 80MB hard disks
- 14 LaserWriter II NTX printers
- 1 QMS Colorscript 100 printer
- 2 QMS PS-2200 Laser printers (handles tabloid-size paper)
- 2 Linotronic 300 with PostScript RIP 3
- Sharp color scanner (for opaque color)
- Nikon color scanner (for 35 mm slides)
- Apple Scanner
- 3Com Network

The total cost of *Entertainment Weekly's* system, including software and training, was approximately $1.3 million.

Production Steps and Tricks

Entertainment Weekly, as its name suggests, is published on a weekly basis. Briefly, steps in the design and production of each issue are as follows.

1. The text of articles can be written before or after a layout design is finished. Style Sheets are applied to the copy in Microsoft Word and in QuarkXPress (Figure 15-3).

Figure 15-3 A typical set of style sheets set up for the magazine.

2. Editing to fit is done in QuarkXPress, using a template file with several different master pages (Figure 15-4).

Figure 15-4 A standard document used for a regularly appearing section in the magazine.

3. Graphics are scanned in at 72 dpi and are used, in all cases, for position only. Virtually none of the final artwork, including line art, is actually produced on the computer.
4. Final proofs are generated on the Linotronic 300s.
5. Once completed, the QuarkXPress files are sent to an engraver, where the artwork is removed, and the files are printed to disk as PostScript files (holding the keys CTRL+F while printing causes any Macintosh file to be printed to disk as a PostScript file). The PostScript files are then run through a Scitex VIP (Visionary Interpreter of PostScript) RIP. Photographs are scanned in high resolution on a Scitex system and electronically merged with text from the QuarkXPress files.

Several interesting aspects involving this procedure. Surface. First of all, it works! Every week, *Entertainment Weekly* appears on newsstands around the country. Also, the system used offers design director Michael Grossman far more flexibility in modifying the design than traditional systems might.

At least ten pages of the magazine are closed daily in order to meet the weekly deadline for printing. The following section describes just two of the many issues that arise in the successful design and production of a weekly magazine.

File Management

Since QuarkXPress does not offer the type of file management and copy-routing tools offered by high-end publishing systems, *Entertainment Weekly* had to come up with a manual system of its own.

For each story in the magazine, there is a manila file folder (the type you can buy in a stationery store); only the person who has that folder is allowed to change the file. *Entertainment Weekly* calls this manual system "conch control" (Figure 15-5). (The name comes from the William Golding novel *Lord of the Flies*, in which a conch shell is used to establish protocol at meetings; only the person holding the conch shell can speak.)

Future plans include installation of P.INK Press, a publishing system that includes an SQL dataserver and a text editor front end to QuarkXPress.

Figure 15-5 A typical spread created in QuarkXPress.

Brochure by Croce Advertising

Croce Advertising, Inc., established in 1983 by Diane Croce, is a full-service marketing, advertising, and public relations firm headquartered in Denver, Colorado. Its range of services includes providing market research, direct mail campaigns, packaging, and corporate communications.

The works of Croce Advertising have been awarded several Alfie awards as well as many honors by various design and marketing associations, including the Society for Marketing Professionals, Financial Institutions Marketing Association (FIMA), and the Art Directors Club of Denver.

Croce Advertising uses QuarkXPress to produce brochures, ads, and presentations for many of its clients. In this case study we examine a sales brochure produced by Croce Advertising for a client in the financial industry, Alexander Management Capital Group (Figure 15-6).

Figure 15-6 Sales brochure for Alexander Management Capital Group.

This brochure is published in 8.5-by-11-inch format, which is convenient for mailing in standard business envelopes. However, it incorporates several design elements that require special handling—a luxury that is easily affordable when the document is short. Generally speaking, this is one of the characteristics of brochures, regardless of their size, that distinguishes them from longer documents: The importance of design as a major tool in creating an impact on the audience takes precedence over the goals of "convenience" or "efficiency" that can discourage certain design choices for longer documents.

Description

The brochure uses the same basic grid throughout, with one master page layout and a simple style sheet. The master page includes two text boxes, one for page-wide headings and one for two-column body copy. Text on each page is typed directly into the text boxes set up in QuarkXPress and edited to fit the space allowed. The Automatic Text Box option is turned off, and the text boxes are not linked on the master pages (Figure 15-7).

Figure 15-7 Master page elements for brochure by Croce Advertising.

Two text boxes on the master page are required in order to be able to position one-column headings over two-column body copy.

Croce Advertising reuses various parts of this piece. For example, the cover icons are now stored in a library and appear on all of Alexander Capital Management Group's publications. Also, the format of this brochure has been set up as a template and used for other types of documents designed for the same client.

Software

- QuarkXPress
- Adobe Illustrator
- Aldus Persuasion
- Microsoft Excel
- OmniPage scanning software

Equipment

- 1 Macintosh IIci with 80 MB hard disk
- 1 LaserWriter II NTX laser printer
- Hewlett Packard Scanjet Plus

Production Steps and Tricks

Briefly, the steps in the design and production of the brochure are as follows:

1. A QuarkXPress file was created with the default page for this document.
2. The logo for Alexander Capital Management Group in the upper lefthand corner of each page was scanned in and used for position only—it and the one or two color photos were stripped in by the printing company.
3. The pie chart–type icon in the upper lefthand corner was created in Adobe Illustrator, as were all the charts and graphs in this brochure.
4. All word processing was done in QuarkXPress, and a simple style sheet, with three different styles, was used. Other variations in text formats are handled as *No Style* and formatted through the Style menu commands. The length of the two-column text box from the master page was adjusted on each page to force the two columns to be equal length.
5. First proofs were printed on a LaserWriter printer for black-and-white proofs. Once the client reviewed the pages and changes were made, final proofs were printed on a QMS color printer.
6. The file was printed to film on a Linotronic 300 as spot color separations. The printing company said the separations were among the best they had ever seen (Figure 15-8).

470   The QuarkXPress Handbook

Figure 15-8   Colors set up for the brochure.

Croce is one of many companies in the advertising and marketing industries around the world that has made QuarkXPress an integral part of their business.

Packaging by Mattel Toys

Mattel Toys, well known by children and adults around the world, uses QuarkXPress extensively to create a number of packages for their toys. This case study focuses on the Hot Wheels Package, which is a blister card designed by Luis Solorzano, as shown in Figure 15-9 (see description below).

Figure 15-9   Blister card for Hot Wheels.

Description

A blister card is a standard form of packaging in which the product is mounted on a cardboard backing and shrink-wrapped. In Figure 15-10, the white boxes indicate where the Hot Wheels cars are positioned.

Software

- QuarkXPress
- Adobe Illustrator
- Aldus FreeHand

Equipment

- 50 Macintosh CPUs
- 15 Mac IIfx with 19-inch color monitors
- 5 Mac IIci
- 20 Mac SEs
- 1 QMS ColorScript printer
- 1 VT 600 B&W laser printer
- 3 LaserWriter laser printers
- 1 Howtek Scanmaster (for color transparencies)
- 1 Datacopy Flatbed 300 dpi grayscale scanner
- AppleShare file server running on LocalTalk
- Adobe fonts

Production Steps and Tricks

Following are the steps in design and production of the Hot Wheels Package, which are similar to those applied to other package designs by Mattel.

1. The art director prepares a rough comp by hand using markers and other traditional tools.
2. The exact specs for the size of the box are received from engineering.
3. The text that will go on the box is prepared by copywriters and stored on the file server.
4. Graphic production people review the specifications with the art director.
5. Special logos and artwork are done using Illustrator. If type on a path is required, FreeHand is used.

6. The basic XPress file is created and the the text is brought in off the file server.

Figure 15-10 Graphic elements are brought together in QuarkXPress.

7. Proofs are created on the QMS and approved by the marketing department and art director, including color adjustments.

NOTE: Illustrator creates default line screens of 65. By using Quark's print dialog box to change the screens to 85, colors are smoother on the QMS. If there are graduated colors, banding still occurs on the QMS proof, but it is significantly reduced when the color separations are printed on a high-resolution imagesetter.

8. Final color separations are printed on film on a Linotronic 300; the printing company strips in color photographs. Alternatively, Mattel sometimes uses a Solotaire transparency maker at a service bureau that creates 16-bit color 4×5-inch transparencies of the full-color pages. Then the printing company makes color separations from these. These transparencies are better than film from the Linotronic imagesetter because Mattel uses printers from around the world and each printing company can make separations optimized for its printing presses (especially overseas).

Corporate Identity Manual by Landor Associates

Landor Associates, founded by Walter Landor in 1941, is one of the largest corporate identity consulting firms in the world, with offices located in 15 countries. Headquartered in San Francisco, the company has regional headquarters in New York, Tokyo, Hong Kong, Mexico City, and London. Landor Associates has developed the corporate identity programs for companies such as General Electric, Hilton International, and Japan Airlines. It developed the brand identity for many of the products we see or use every day, including Coca-Cola, Marlboro Cigarettes (and other Phillip Morris products), Del Monte, and Pillsbury. Landor has also developed retail identities for companies such as Shell Oil, Chase Manhattan Bank, and Nissan Motors.

The CSR identity project and its accompanying manual, the subject of this case study, was created in the San Francisco office as part of a project done by Landor Associates for the CSR Corporation of Australia (Figure 15-11). CSR hired Landor Associates to completely revamp the conglomerate's entire corporate look.

Figure 15-11 A page from the CSR Corporate Identity Manual.

Description

The CSR Corporate Identity manual was designed for the Australian standard A4 page size (8.268 by 11.693 inches), with final pages punched with four holes and inserted in a standard A4 binder (see color plate). Final pages were printed on a six-color press to accommodate full-color illustrations and photographs as well as a gray spot color ink printed as the solid background color for each page (instead of using a gray *shade* to produce a similar effect). The manual uses the same basic grid throughout, with three different master page layouts (Figure 15-12).

Figure 15-12 One of three different master pages used in the CSR Corporate Identity Manual.

Software

The company uses a wide variety of software packages, with the nature of each project dictating the specific software. Software used in this manual includes:

- Microsoft Word
- Adobe Illustrator
- Smart Art
- QuarkXPress

Equipment

Companywide, Landor Associates has over 300 Macintosh CPUs; each regional headquarters office has both color scanners and printers, so any job can literally be moved around the world. The San Francisco office is not only the company headquarters, but also the company's R & D center. The San Francisco office has approximately the following equipment configuration:

- 140 Macintosh CPUs
- 15 LaserWriter II NTX printers
- 7 QMS ColorScript 100 printers
- 5 color scanners
- Novell network

Production Steps and Tricks

Following are the steps in design and production of the CSR Corporate Identity Manual.

1. The initial presentations of logo and other identity elements were created by hand. Once the client had agreed on a general direction, however, the entire project was done electronically. The first part of the project involved presenting to the client how the new identity would be handled on specific products, such as packaging, stationery, vehicles, 35 mm slides, and so on. These exhibits were prepared for the client using Adobe Illustrator.

2. As the exhibits became finalized, production on the identity manual itself was begun. Text for the manual was written in Microsoft Word.

3. In QuarkXPress, a template file with different master pages was created. Each page was set up as an 11×17-inch page, providing room to create bleeds, crop marks, and registration marks outside the A4 (8.268-by-11.693 inches) trim size of the page.

4. The Microsoft Word text was flowed into QuarkXPress, where styles were applied. The massive collection of Illustrator files that had been used for the exhibits was assembled and named using a convention of the page number followed by the position of the page (for example, 3.5/1 or 3.5/2). This naming convention was possible because of the design of the manual, which had all graphics running essentially in a column down the left side of each page (Figure 15-13).

```
□ p.5.02.eps
□ p.5.03.eps
□ p.5.03a.eps
□ p.5.04.eps
□ p.5.05.eps
□ p.5.06.eps
□ p.5.07.eps
□ p.5.08.eps
□ Tab pointer
```

Figure 15-13 Filenaming convention for graphics files.

5. Once the manual was approved by the client, the project coordinator took the disk files to Australia, where the final film was generated using the Macintosh (except for full-color photographs, which were generated on a Scitex system) and the printing was done.

Summary

The list of publications that use QuarkXPress is a long one, and we've looked at just a few. Many national publications as well as smaller, regional magazines and newspapers are finding that desktop publishing is not merely a fad, but is, in fact, the most efficient way to get the job done. Cost effectiveness and the ability to meet tight deadlines are only two of the reasons these publications are changing to desktop systems.

Appendix: Summary of Keyboard Shortcuts

Throughout this book we have offered a number of tips and shortcuts that will help you use QuarkXPress more efficiently. In this appendix, we list keyboard shortcuts for common actions other than menu commands. Feel free to photocopy these pages and distribute them to other QuarkXPress users in your office.

For Use with Items

Moving Active Items (Item tool ✥ selected)

Left in 1-point increments	←
Left in .1-point increments	ALT+←
Right in 1-point increments	→
Right in .1-point increments	ALT+→
Up in 1-point increments	↑
Up in .1-point increments	ALT+↑
Down in 1-point increments	↓
Down in .1-point increments	ALT+↓

Moving Items (Item tool not selected)

Moving Items	
With no constraints	CTRL+drag item
With horizontal/vertical constraints	CTRL+SHIFT+drag item

Creating, Resizing, and Rotating Items

Constrain box to square, oval to circle, and item rotation and line angle to 0°/45°/90°	SHIFT+drag

Activating hidden items

Activate item	CTRL+ALT+click where items overlap

Modifying Line Width

Increase line width	
Preset range	CTRL+SHIFT+>
1-point increments	CTRL+ALT+SHIFT+>
Decrease line width	
Preset range	CTRL+<
1-point increments	CTRL+SHIFT+<

Opening Item Specifications Dialog Boxes

Open dialog box	Double-click on item when Item tool ✥ is selected

For Use with Text

Moving the Text Insertion Point

Move to	
Previous Character	←
Next Character	→
Previous line	↑
Next line	↓
Previous Word	CTRL+←
Next word	CTRL+→
Previous paragraph	CTRL+↑
Next paragraph	CTRL+↓
Start of line	CTRL+ALT+← or HOME
End of line	CTRL+ALT+→ or END
Start of story	CTRL+ALT+↑ or CTRL+HOME
End of story	CTRL+ALT+↓ or CTRL+END

Highlighting Characters

To highlight	
Previous character	SHIFT+←
Next character	SHIFT+→
Previous line	SHIFT+↑
Next line	SHIFT+↓
Previous word	CTRL+SHIFT+←
Next word	CTRL+SHIFT+→
Previous paragraph	CTRL+SHIFT+↑
Next paragraph	CTRL+SHIFT+↓
Start of line	SHIFT+HOME or CTRL+ALT+SHIFT+←
End of line	SHIFT+END or CTRL+ALT+SHIFT+→
Start of story	CTRL+ALT+SHIFT+↑ or CTRL+SHIFT+HOME
End of story	CTRL+ALT+SHIFT+↓ or CTRL+SHIFT+END

Clicking the Mouse to Highlight Characters

Position insertion point	One click
Highlight the word	Two clicks
Highlight the line	Three clicks
Highlight the paragraph	Four clicks
Highlight all of the current story	Five clicks

To Enter One Font Character

Symbol font character	CTRL+SHIFT+Q
Zapf Dingbats font character	CTRL+SHIFT+Z

Modifying Font Size

Increase font size	
Preset range	CTRL+SHIFT+>
In 1-point increments	CTRL+ALT+SHIFT+>
Decreasing font size	
Preset range	CTRL+SHIFT+<
In 1-point increments	CTRL+ALT+SHIFT+<

Modifying Horizontal Scaling

Increase in 5% increments	CTRL+]
Decrease in 5% increments	CTRL+[

Modifying Kerning/Tracking

Increase Kern/Track amount	
In $\frac{1}{20}$-em increments	CTRL+SHIFT+}
In $\frac{1}{200}$-em increments	CTRL+ALT+SHIFT+}
Decrease Kern/Track amount	
In $\frac{1}{20}$-em increments	CTRL+SHIFT+{
In $\frac{1}{200}$-em increments	CTRL+ALT+SHIFT+{

Modifying Baseline Shift

Move up in 1-point increments	CTRL+ALT+SHIFT+)
Move down in 1-point increments	CTRL+ALT+SHIFT+(

Modifying Leading

Increase leading	
In 1-point increments	CTRL+SHIFT+"
In ⅒-point increments	CTRL+ALT+SHIFT+"
Decrease leading	
In 1-point increments	CTRL+SHIFT+:
In ⅒-point increments	CTRL+ALT+SHIFT+:

Copying Paragraph Formats

Copy formats to selection	ALT+SHIFT+click on target paragraph

Removing All Tabs from Selected Paragraph

Remove all tabs	CTRL+click on tab ruler

Deleting Characters

Delete	
Previous character	BACK SPACE
Next character	DELETE
Previous word	CTRL+BACK SPACE
Next word	CTRL+DELETE
Highlighted characters	DELETE or BACK SPACE

For Use with Pictures

Moving the Picture in an Active Picture Box

Left in 1-point increments	←
Left in .1-point increments	ALT+←
Right in 1-point increments	→
Right in .1-point increments	ALT+→
Up in 1-point increments	↑
Up in .1-point increments	ALT+↑
Down in 1-point increments	↓
Down in .1-point increments	ALT+↓

Scaling Pictures

In 5% increments	
Increase	CTRL+ALT+SHIFT+>
Decrease	CTRL+ALT+SHIFT+<

Resizing Picture Boxes and Pictures

Constrain* box shape	SHIFT+drag any handle
Maintain aspect ratio of box	ALT+SHIFT+drag any handle
Scale box and picture	CTRL+drag any handle
Scale picture and constrain* box shape	CTRL+SHIFT+drag any handle

Scale picture and
  maintain aspect ratio
  of box and picture
	CTRL+ALT+SHIFT+drag any handle

(*Constrain rectangle to square and oval to circle.)

Centering and Fitting Pictures

Center	CTRL+SHIFT+M
Fit exactly to a box	CTRL+SHIFT+F
Fit to a box (maintaining aspect ratio)	CTRL+ALT+SHIFT+F

For Use with Runaround Polygons

Create a handle	CTRL+click on line segment
Delete a handle	CTRL+click on handle
Constrain line or handle movement to 0°/45°/90°	SHIFT+drag any handle
Temporarily suspend text reflow	Hold down SPACE BAR while modifying runaround polygon
Delete runaround polygon	CTRL+SHIFT+click on runaround polygon

Controlling Picture Resolution

Import picture at half monitor dpi (when Low Resolution TIFF is unchecked)	Hold down SHIFT when importing picture
Import picture at full monitor dpi (when Low Resolution TIFF is checked)	Hold down SHIFT when importing picture

For Use in Dialog Boxes

OK (or bordered button)	↵ ENTER or KEYPAD ENTER
Cancel	ESCAPE
Apply	CTRL+A
Yes	Y
No	N
Highlight next control	TAB
Highlight previous control	SHIFT+TAB
Highlight word containing text insertion bar	Double-click
Cut (for fields only)	SHIFT+DELETE
Copy (for fields only)	CTRL+INSERT
Paste (for fields only)	SHIFT+INSERT

For Use with Palettes

Tool Palette

Display palette/select next tool	CTRL+TAB
Display palette/select previous tool	CTRL+SHIFT+TAB
Keep a tool selected	ALT+click on tool
Open Tool Preferences dialog box	Double-click on item creation or Zoom tool

Measurements Palette

Display palette/ highlight first field	CTRL+ALT+M
Highlight next field	TAB
Highlight previous field	SHIFT+TAB
Highlight word containing text insertion bar	Double-click
Exit/Apply	↵ ENTER or KEYPAD ENTER
Revert to original value in current field	ALT+BACK SPACE

Document Layout Palette

Open Section dialog box	Click on "Page #" area (displayed under a highlighted document page icon)
Insert multiple pages	CTRL+choose an entry from the Insert menu

Style Sheets Palette

Open Style Sheets dialog box	CTRL+click on style sheet name
Apply No Style, then style sheet	SHIFT+click on style sheet name

Colors Palette

Open Colors dialog box	CTRL+click on color name

Inputting Special Characters

Formatting

Indent here	CTRL+\
Discretionary new line	CTRL+↵ ENTER
New paragraph	↵ ENTER
New line	SHIFT+↵ ENTER
New column	KEYPAD ENTER
New box	SHIFT+KEYPAD ENTER
Right-indent tab	SHIFT+TAB

Hyphens and Dashes

Breaking standard hyphen	hyphen
Nonbreaking standard hyphen	CTRL+SHIFT+hyphen
Discretionary (soft) hyphen	CTRL+hyphen
Nonbreaking en dash	CTRL+=
Breaking em dash	CTRL+SHIFT+=
Nonbreaking em dash	CTRL+ALT+SHIFT+=

Page Numbering

Page number	
Of the previous text box	CTRL+2
Of the current text box	CTRL+3
Of the next text box	CTRL+4

Spaces

Breaking standard space	SPACE
Nonbreaking standard space	CTRL+SPACE
Breaking en space	CTRL+SHIFT+6
Nonbreaking en space	CTRL+ALT+SHIFT+6
Breaking flexible space	CTRL+SHIFT+5
Nonbreaking flexible space	CTRL+ALT+SHIFT+5
Breaking punctuation space	SHIFT+SPACE
Nonbreaking punctuation space	CTRL+SHIFT+SPACE

Typesetting

Open double quote	"	ALT+SHIFT+[
Close double quote	"	ALT+SHIFT+]
Open single quote	'	ALT+[
Close single quote	'	ALT+]
Registered	®	ALT+SHIFT+R
Copyright	©	ALT+SHIFT+C
Section	§	ALT+SHIFT+6
Paragraph	¶	ALT+SHIFT+7
Bullet	•	ALT+SHIFT+8

For Document Display and Scrolling

Switching to Different Views

Any view to Actual Size	Right mouse button click
Actual size to Fit in Window	Right mouse button click
Any view to 200%	CTRL+right mouse button click
200% to Actual Size	CTRL+right mouse button click

Temporary Zoom Mode

Zoom in	SHIFT+right mouse button click or drag
Zoom out	CTRL+SHIFT+right mouse button click or drag

Scrolling

Scroll document with Page Grabber Hand (when Page Grabber Hand is checked)	ALT+drag
Live scroll of document (when Live Scroll is unchecked)	ALT+drag scroll box
Disable live scroll of document (when Live Scroll is checked)	ALT+drag scroll box
Scroll to start of document	CTRL+HOME
Scroll to end of document	CTRL+END
Scroll up one screen	PAGE UP
Scroll down one screen	PAGE DOWN
Scroll to first page	CTRL+PAGE UP
Scroll to last page	CTRL+PAGE DOWN
Scroll to previous page	SHIFT+PAGE UP
Scroll to next page	SHIFT+PAGE DOWN

Deleting Ruler Guides

Delete ruler guides	ALT+click on ruler

Index

A

About QuarkXPress command, 53–54
absolute leading, 203
absolute page sequence, 121–122
Accurate Blends option, 142
Accurate Screens, Adobe, 265–266
Actual Size command, 67
Adobe Accurate Screens, 265–266
Adobe Photoshop, 240
   color separating in QuarkXPress, 285–287
Adobe Photostyler, color separating, 285–287
Adobe Type Manager (ATM), 197, 308
advertising, 467–470
Align On tab characters, 174
aligning items, 95
   in a bar chart, 438–440
   in organization charts, 440–443
   Space/Align command and dialog box, 356–357
   tips, 354–357
alignment, paragraph, 169–170
   vertical, 207
all caps, 403
Ami Pro, 157
anchored items, 36, 99–101, 362–363
Anchored Picture Specifications dialog box, 100
Anchored Text Specifications dialog box, 100
angle, box, 78–79
apostrophes, converting , 156
Append Colors dialog box, 273–274
Append H&Js dialog box, 213
Append Style Sheets dialog box, 182–183
Application Preferences dialog box, 132–137, 285
   trapping, 280–281
applications, running multiple, 458–459
ascent height, 198
   relative to baseline, 204–205
ASCII text import, 157–158
   from databases and mainframes, 379–400
   tag codes, 84, 395–400
ATM—see Adobe Type Manager
Auto Constrain option, 103, 143
auto hyphenation, 210
auto image, text runaround mode, 91–92
Auto Kern Above preferences, 200
auto leading formula, 199
Auto Library Save option, 136
Auto Page Insertion, 85, 95–99, 120–122, 138–139
Auto Picture Import option, 140
automatic runaround, 370–373
automatic text box, 36, 97, 113–115
   creating, 115
   multiple master pages, 344–345

automatic text box, con't
  removing, 115
  width calculation, 340
Automatic Text Box, 57–58, 63–64, 71–72
  adding pages, 120–122
  page size changes, 60
Automatic Text chain, 97
automatic trapping, 280–281
Auxiliary Dictionary dialog box, 191–192

B

back slash, search, 186
background color, 253–254, 281–283
Backspace key, 86–87, 102–103
backup procedures, 452
  workgroups, 455–456
backward, moving in layers, 94
balloons, cartooning, 431–433
banding, on screen, 142
bar charts, 433–440
based on style sheet, 180
baseline, first, 204–205
baseline grid, 199, 206–207
  viewing, 69–70
baseline of superscript/subscript, 198
Baseline Shift command and dialog box, 207
  anchored items, 99–100
  keyboard shortcuts, 207
binding edge, 62
bitmap graphics, 86, 239
black boxes, 424–425
blank pages, 45, 364–368
  printing, 302
bleed, 62–63, 369–370
blending colors, 278–279
  on screen display, 142
blister card, 470–472
blue lines, 333
border—see frame
bounding box, polygon, 232–233
boxes, 35–36
  anchoring, 99–101, 362–363
  angle, 78–79
  background color, 274–279
  color, 80–81
  constraining, 103, 364
  creating, 71–72
  deleting, 86–87
  drop shadows, 425–427
  frame, 81–82
  height, 76–78
  jump text, 176–177
  modifying, 229–231
  origin (position), 76–78

boxes, con't
  relationships between, 357–364
  shape, 231
  width, 76–78
Bring Forward command, 94
Bring to Front command, 94
brochure, 467–470
business graphics, 433–443

C

cap height, and baseline, 204–205
captions, figures, 348–349, 404
cartoon balloons, 431–433
cases studies, 461–476
centimeters, 44–45
chain icon, 115
chain of text, 36, 95–99
Character Attributes dialog box, 162, 167–168
  baseline shift, 207
character attributes, finding/changing, 187–188
character formatting, 161–168
  default, 150
  drop caps, 223–224
  keyboard shortcuts, 477–482
  style sheets, 37–38, 178–183
  tags, 395–396
  widths, 222–223
Character Map accessory, 152, 202
character set, 152
  symbols and invisibles, 151–153
character spacing, 412–414
  formula, 200
characters, viewing invisible, 69–70
charts, 433–443
check box, 26–27
Check Document dialog box, 191
Check Spelling command, 188–192
Check Story dialog box, 190
Check Word dialog box, 189
chokes, 282–283
Chromalin, 263
ciceros, 44–45, 138
ciceros/inch formula, changing, 141
Clear command, 86–87, 102–103
Clipboard, 30, 86–87
  as productivity tool, 352–353
  text, 158
CMYK color model, 268–271
collating pages, 301–302
color, 80–81, 261–287
  applying, 274–279
  applying to pictures, 251–257
  background, 253–254
  blends, 278–279
  calibration, on monitor, 262–263

color, con't
  comps, 292
  creating, 266–274
  deleting, 267
  display on monitor, 262–263
  duplicating, 267
  frame, 82
  graphics, 240–244
  guides, 133–134
  images, contrast, 254
  lines, 237–238
  model, 263, 268–273
  photographs, separating, 285–287
  picture import, 86
  printers, 290–292
  printing problems, 320–321
  proof, 263
  registration, 279
  separating graphics, 285–287
  separations, printing, 304
  spot vs. process, 263
  swatch books, 270–271
  text, 166–167
  trapping, 280–287
Color submenu, 274–279
  pictures, 253–254
  text, 166–167
colors as grays, printing, 304
Colors command and dialog box, 266–274
  alternatives, 46–47
  shortcut, 46–47
  trap information, 47–48
Colors palette, 46–47, 166–167, 274–279
  default, 447
  edit colors, 269
  importing, 273–274
column break, forced, 153, 176–177
column break, search, 186
column guides, 36–37, 39–40, 57–58, 60–62
  as spacing guides, 355
  changing, 62
  in a template, 339
  master page, 113–114
  space between, 60
  viewing, 69–70
columns in a text box, 148–149
  number per box, 61
comma tabs, 174
comps, color, 292
computer basics, 23–53
constrain, automatic, 143
Constrain command, 103
constrained boxes, 36, 364
constraint attribute, removing, 103

Content tool, 41–42, 71–72
  and text, 149–153
  Select All, 72–74
continued text, page number, 129–130
contrast, applying to pictures, 251–257
  color images, 254–257
  custom, 254–257
Control menu, 26–27, 30
Control Panel, printers, 293–295
Convert Quotes, importing text, 84, 156
converting imported text formats, 380–382
copies, printing multiple, 300–301
copies, using Clipboard, 352–353
Copy command, 30
CopyDesk, 454
copying (duplicating) items, 92–93
copying pages between documents, 125
copying paragraph formats, 175
copying style sheets, 182
corporate identity, 473–476
cover page, printing, 301
Croce Advertising, 467–470
custom dictionary, 191–192
Cut command, 30, 86–87, 102–103

D
dashed lines, 235–236
data files, converting to tabbed formats, 382–389
database import, 157–158, 379–400
database publishing, 379–400
default text format, 150
default type specifications, 157–158
defaults, changing, 132–145
Delete Changes (applying master pages), 119–120, 140–141
Delete command, 86–87, 102–103
Delete key, 86–87, 102–103
Delete Pages command and dialog box, 123
deleting a color, 267
deleting automatic text box, 115
deleting H&Js, 213
deleting items, 86–87, 102–103
  anchored items, 101
  from a group, 102–103
deleting style sheets, 182
densitometer, 263
design alternatives, 330–334
design specifications, 329–350
  graphics, 348–349
  typography tips, 401–422
dialog box entries, 28–29
dictionary, spelling, 188–192, 446

dictionary, spelling, con't
    custom, 191–192
directory listings, from database, 382–389
discretionary hyphen, 202, 214
discretionary line break, 153, 176–177
    search, 186
disk file management, 445–459
disk file organization, 56
disk location, changing, 106
disk space limitations, 319–320
Dispatch, 454
display DPI, 137
Display Page command, 113
display resolution, TIFF, 243
document creation, 55–108
document, double sided, 364–368
document file organization, 56
document format, changing, 106
Document Layout palette, 45–46, 111–120
    moving pages, 124
document management, 445–459
document name, changing, 106
document pages, 34–35
    applying master pages, 117–120
Document Setup command and dialog box, 58–59, 62–63, 316–317
document sections, 127–130
document vs. template, 38, 64–65
document window, 39–40
    closing, 107
document, predefined, 64–65
document, saving, 104–107
dot screen, 257–260
dots per inch, on screen, 137
dots per inch, line screen, 259
dotted lines, 235–236
double–sided document, 62–63, 364–368
    page insertion, 120–122
downloading fonts, 308–310
DPI—see dots per inch
drawing tools, 41, 43, 228–238
drivers, printer, 448–449
drop caps, 223–224, 414–417
drop shadows, boxes, 425–427
drop shadows, text, 417
dummy text, 346
duplicate color, 267
Duplicate command, 93
duplicating items, 92–93

E

edit colors, from Colors palette, 269
Edit menu, 30, 49

Edit menu, con't
    Clear, 86–87, 102–103
    Colors, 266–274
        alternative, 46–47
        trap information, 47–48
    Cut, 86–87, 102–103
    Find/Change, 183–188
    H&Js, 209–212
    Links, 247–248
    Paste, 86–87
    Paste Special, 247–248
    Preferences>General, 137–143
        font vectoring option, 197
    Preferences>Tools, 144–145
    Preferences>Typographic, 143–144, 197–202
        kerning, 219–222
    Select All, 72–74
    Style Sheets, 178–183
        shortcut, 46
    Undo, 86–87
Edit Trap dialog box, 47–48, 273–274
editing items, 80–82
editing master pages, 113–117
editing text, 147–193
editing tools, 41–42
em dash, 202
embedding, 31–32
emulsion, in printing, 297
en dash, nonbreaking, 202
en space, 202
en space, half, 202
en space, nonbreaking, 202
Encapsulated PostScript (EPS) graphics, 86, 241–242, 303
    version of a page, 242
endcaps, 236
endpoints, 234–235
enlargements, printing, 298–299
Entertainment Weekly, 461–466
EPS—see Encapsulated PostScript
equipment, 15–19
Error Handler, 325
examples of documents, 461–476
Excel, 159
export filters, 448
export kerning table, 220–222
export text, 192–193

F

facing pages, 39–40, 57–58, 62–63
    master pages, 111
figure titles or captions, 348–349, 404
file format, changing, 106
file formats, imported graphics, 238–248

file location, changing, 106
file management, 350, 445–459, 466
File Manager, 33
File menu, 48–49
    Document Setup, 58– 59 , 62–63, 316–317
    Get Picture, 85–86, 238–260, 244–246
    Get Text, 83–85, 153–158, 379–400
    New, 56–64
    Open, 64–65
    Print, 300–305
    Printer Setup, 296–299
    Quit, 107
    Revert to Saved, 106
    Save, 104–106
    Save as, 106
    Save Page As EPS, 242
    Save Text, 192–193
file name, 450–452
    changing, 106
file organization, 56
file server, 453–456
file size, graphics, 312–314
file size, optimum, 452–453
files, moving, 452
fill character, tabs, 175
film, printing on, 297
filters, import/export, 157, 448
    graphics, 246
Find/Change command and dialog box, 183–188
    expanded, 187–188
finding and changing special characters, 380–388
finding text, using wild cards, 394–395
first baseline, 204–205
Fit in Window, 67
flex space width, 200
flip printed image, 297
flush zone, justification, 212
FOCOLTONE colors, 268, 273
fold–out panels, 368–370
Font command, 163–164
font list, 163–164
font management, 307–312
font selection, 311
font size, 163–164
    keyboard shortcuts, 164–165
Font Usage, 311
font vectoring, 141, 197
fonts, 163–164
    downloading, 308–310
    in WIN.INI, 309–310
    installing, 307–308
    loading, 196–197
    number of, 311–312

fonts, con't
    printer, 291
    printing problems, 321–325
footers, 62–63, 116, 343–344
format codes in data files, 389–394
format, copying, 175
format, default, 150
format, style sheets, 178–183
formatted text import, 157
formatting characters, 161–168
formatting codes, ASCII tags, 157
formatting headings, 409
formatting paragraphs, 168–183
formatting text with tag codes, 395–397
formatting text, style sheets, 37–38
forms, 373–376
forward, moving in layers, 94
fraction slash, 202
frame color, 82, 274–279
frame definitions, XPress Preferences, 447
frame preferences, 145
Frame Specifications dialog box, 81–82
frames, in drop shadows, 425–427
framing options, 139

G

gap between pages, 297
General Preferences dialog box, 137–143
    font vectoring option, 197
Get Picture command, 85–86, 238–260
Get Text command, 153–158, 379–400
global search/change text, 183–188
    special characters, 380–388
grabber hand, 136
graphic techniques, advanced, 423–443
graphic, text runaround, 91–92
graphics, 227–260
    anchoring, 99–101
    applications, 15
    applying color, 274–279
    business, 433–443
    captions and labels, 348–349, 404
    color and contrast, 251–257
    color separating, 285–287
    deleting, 86–87
    design specification, 348–349
    drop shadows, 425–427
    file formats, 238–248
    greeked on screen, 142
    import filters, 246
    importing, 85–86, 238–260
    large files, 312–314
    manipulating imported, 248–260
    moving within a box, 248–251

graphics, con't
  problems printing, 319–321
  resolution, on screen display, 136, 243
  rotating, 251
  scaling imported, 249–250
  screens, 257–260
  skewing, 251
  sources of, 228
  tools, 228–238
graphics—see picture
grayscale, 86
grayscale graphics, 243
grayscale viewing, 243–244
Greek Below point size, 141–142
greeked pictures, 142
greeked text, 141–142
grid system, design, 332–334
grid, baseline, 199, 206–207
grid, horizontal, 355–356
grid, vertical, 355
grid, viewing, 69–70
group Measurements palette, 101–102
group specifications, 102
  size and position, 76–78
grouping items, 101–103
  constraining, 103
  deleting items, 102–103
guides, 36–37, 39–40, 57–58
  colors, 133–134
  column, 61
  display options, 139
  in grid design, 333
  margin, 62
  ruler, 89–90
  snap distance, 141
  snap to effect, 37–38, 355–356
  viewing, 69–70
gutter width, 57–58, 60
  in text box, 148–149

H

H&J—see hyphenation and justification
hairline, 236–237
halftone frequency, 297
halftone screen, 264–266
halftone screens, 257–260
hand, page grabber, 136
handles, 75
handles, anchored items, 99
handles, displaying, 72–74
hanging indent, 171–172
headers, 62–63, 116, 343–344
headings, kerning and tracking, 409
headings, style sheets, 409
height, box, 76–78
Hell Graphics, 265

Help file, 446
Help menu, 53–54
Hide—see Show/Hide
hiding palettes, 70
high contrast, 254–257
high quality screening (HQS), 265
Home key, 126
Horizontal Scale command and dialog box, 222–223
horizontal grid, creating, 355–356
horizontal measure, 138
horizontal ruler guides, 89–90
horizontal scaling, keyboard shortcuts, 223
horizontal scaling, text, 222–223
HSB color model, 268–269
hyphen character, 202
  discretionary, 202, 214
  nonbreaking, 202
hyphenation algorithm, 201
hyphenation and justification, 208–215, 411–412
  applying H&Js, 212
  deleting H&Js, 213
  duplicating H&Js, 213
  H&J pop-up menu, 213
  H&J set name, 210
    XPress Preferences, 447
  H&Js command and dialog box, 209–212
  merging two sets, 213
Hyphenation Exceptions command and dialog box, 215
hyphenation method preferences, 201
hyphenation rules, 211
hyphenation zone, 211, 411–412
hyphenation, automatic, 210
hyphenation, suggested, 214
hyphenation, tips for on vs. off, 411
hyphenations exceptions, XPress Preferences, 447
hyphens in a row, 211, 412

I

illustrations, 227–260
  design specifications, 348–349
illustrations—see graphics, pictures
image runaround, 91–92, 370–373
imagesetters, 290–292, 312–314
import kerning table, 220–222
import/export filters, 157, 448
imported file formats, 238–248
imported graphics, manipulating, 248–260
imported pictures, automatic update, 140
importing colors, 273–274

importing formatted text, 157
importing graphics, 85–86, 238–260
importing spreadsheets and databases, 157–158
importing style sheets, 156
importing tables, 157
importing text, 83–86, 153–158
  from database or mainframe, 379–400
  telecommunicated text, 380–382
  unformatted text, 157
inches, 44–45, 138
Include Style Sheets option, imported text, 84, 156
incremental leading, 203
Indent Here character, 153, 176–177
  search, 186
indent tab, 176
indentation, 170–172
initial caps, large, 416
Insert Pages command and dialog box, 121–122
  in double–sided documents, 364–368
Insert Object command (CTRL+SHIFT+I), 31–32, 247–248
inset, text box, 148–149
inside margins, 62–63
installing QuarkXPress, 32
inversion tool, contrast, 256
Invert option, text runaround, 91–92
invert image, in printing, 297
invisible characters, typing, 176–177, 153
  searching for, 186
  tab characters, 174
  viewing, 69–70
item creation tools, 35–36, 41, 43, 71–72, 228–238
  preferences, 144–145
Item menu, 51
  Bring Forward, 94
  Bring to Front, 94
  Constrain, 103
  Delete, 86–87, 102–103
  Duplicate, 93
  Lock, 104
  Modify, color, 81
  Modify, moving and sizing items, 76–78
  Picture Box Shape, 231
  Runaround, 91–92, 370–373
    lines, 234
  Send Backward, 94
  Send to Back, 94
  Space Align, 95, 356–357
  Step and Repeat, 93
item rotation, 78–79

item shade, 80–81
Item tool, 41–42
  Select All, 72–74
items, 35–36
  aligning, 95
  changing appearance, 80–82
  color, 80–81
  color trapping, 283–285
  constrained, 364
  constraining, 103
  coordinates, 139
  deleting, 86–87
  duplicating, 92–93
  hidden layers, 94
  layering, 94
  moving, 74–78
  relationships between, 36, 95–104, 357–364
  resizing, 74–78
  selecting, 72–74

J

jump text, 360–362
jump–to page number, 129–130
justification, hyphenation and, 208–215, 411–412
  justified text, 169–170
  method, 211
  flush zone, 212
  last line of paragraph, 212
  single word, 212

K

Keep Changes (applying master pages), 119–120, 140–141
keep with next paragraph, 173
Kern/Track Editor, 218–219
  file, 447
kerning, 215–222
  default, 200
  global adjustments, 219–222
  headings, 409
  keyboard shortcuts, 217
  table import/export, 220–222
  table values, XPress Preferences, 447
  tables, 200
Kerning Table Edit command and dialog box, 219–222
Kerning Values dialog box, 218–219
keyboard entries for page numbers, 129–130
keyboard equivalent, style sheet, 180–182, 407
keyboard shortcuts, 25–26, 477–482
  alignment, 169–170
  baseline shift, 207

keyboard shortcuts, con't
    change line width, 236–237
    font size, 164–165
    horizontal scaling, 223
    kerning, 217
    leading, 204
    scaling graphics, 249–250
    selecting text, 160–161
    tracking, 217
    turning pages, 126
    type style, 166
keyboard, extended, turning pages, 126
knock out, 281–284

L

labels within figures, 348–349
Lan Manager, 453
Landor Associates, 473–476
LANtastic, 453
layers, 94
leading, 203–208, 410
    absolute, 203
    dialog box, 203
    formula, 199
    incremental, 203
    keyboard shortcuts, 204
    mode preferences, 201
    runaround text, 200
left page icon, 120–122
levels of gray, on screen display, 136
Library Entry dialog box, 131–132
Library palette, 130–132, 346–347
Library, QuarkXPress, 31, 130–132, 351–352
    auto save option, 136
    elements, 346–347
    labels, 131–132
    organizing, 453
    text from, 158
line break, text, 153, 176–177
    keep lines together, 173
    removing, 380–382
    search, 186
line mode, 234–235
line per inch, screen, 259
line screen, 257–260
line spacing, 203–208, 410
    auto leading formula, 199
Line Specifications dialog box, 234
    defaults, 145
    size and position, 76–78
Line Style submenu, 235–236
Line tool, 41, 43, 72
lines (graphics), 35–36
    anchoring, 99–101
    color 80–81, 237–238, 274–279
    constraining, 103

lines (graphics), con't
    creating, 72
    deleting, 86–87
    endcaps, 236
    in a form, 373–376
    layered, 427–428
    modifying, 233–238
    special effects, 427–428
    style, 235–236
    text rules, 224–225
    transparent, 237–238
        and runaround, 371
    width, 236–237
        keyboard shortcuts, 236–237
linked text boxes, 31–32, 36, 95–99
    jump pages, 360–362
    Linking tool, 41, 43, 95–99, 115
    text–filled, 358–360
    viewing links, 98
Links command, 247–248
Linotype–Hell Company, 265
list box, 26–27
list, drop–down, 26–27
live scroll option, 135
location, using rulers, 88–90
Lock command, 104
lock to baseline grid, 206–207
Low Resolution TIFF option, 136

M

Macintosh, 23
magazines, 461–466
Maintain Leading option, runaround text, 200
Make Separations options, 304
managing documents, 445–459
manual runaround, 370–373
manuals, 473–476
margin guides, 36–37, 39–40, 57–58, 62–63
    in template, 339
    master page, 113–114
    viewing, 69–70
margin, runaround polygon shape, 421–422
margin, slanted, 371
master column guides, 61
Master Guides command and dialog box, 58, 113–114
Master Page Items preferences, 140–141
master pages, 34–35, 109–120
    applying to changed pages, 119–120
    applying to document page, 117–120
    column guides, 113–114
    creating, 111–120
    deleting, 123
    editing, 113–117

master pages, con't
    elements, 109–120, 341–345
    in template, 341–345
    margins, 113–114
    multiple, 344–345
    naming, 112
    printing, 307
Matchprint, 263
Mattel Toys, 470–472
maximize (window) button, 26–27
measure, horizontal and vertical units, 138
measurement system, 44–45
    abbreviations, 44–45
Measurements palette, 43–45
    alignment, 169–170
    anchored items, 101
    character formatting, 162–163
    color, 81
    group, 101–102
    moving items, 75–76
    sizing items, 75–76
measurements, entering, 44–45
memory (RAM), 104
memory management, 456–459
menus, 24–25, 48–54
    Control, 30
    Edit, 30, 49
    File, 48–49
    Help, 53–54
    Item, 51
    Page, 46, 51
    Style, 50
    Utilities, 52
    View, 50, 65–70
    Windows, 52
menus—see individual command names
merging color sets, 273–274
metafiles, graphics, 240
    filters, 246
Microsoft Word, 157
    style sheet import, 179
millimeters, 44–45
minimize (window) button, 26–27
Missing/Modified Picture dialog box, 140, 312–314
Modify command, color, 81
    moving items, 76–78
    sizing items, 76–78
monitor DPI, 137
monitor, color display, 262–263
mouse, moving items, 75
    sizing items, 75
Move Pages command and dialog box, 124
moving a picture in a box, 248–251

moving items, 74–78
    anchored items, 101
moving cursor, keyboard shortcuts, 477–482
moving files, 452
moving pages, 123–125
MS–DOS, 24
multiple–item select, 72–74
multiple–page spread, 368–370

N

naming files, 450–452
    changing names, 106
naming master pages, 112
naming style sheets, 407–408
negative film, printing, 297
negative images, 254–257
NetWare, 453
networks, 453–456
New command and dialog box, 56–64
new box character, 153
new column character, 153
new line character, 153
new paragraph character, 153
nonprinting elements, 69–70

O

Object Linking and Embedding (OLE), 31–32
    Excel, 159
    graphics, 247–248
object–oriented graphics, 240
off–screen draw, 136
offset, registration marks, 135
OLE—see Object Linking and Embedding
on–line help, 53–54
Open command and dialog box, 64–65
Open Prepress Interface (OPI) comments, 303
OPI comments, 303
option button, 26–27
options, printer, 298–299
organization charts, 440–443
orientation, paper, 296
Origin Across, 76–78
Origin Down, 76–78
origin, rulers, 88
Orthogonal Line tool, 41, 43, 72
outside margins, 62–63
Oval Picture Box tool, 41, 43, 71–72
overflow text, 84, 95–99
overprint limit, 134–135
overprint, color, 281–284
oversized documents, 314–315

P

packaging, 470–472
page breaks, keep with next paragraph, 173
page designs, tricks, 364–376
Page Down key, 126
page gap, in printing on rolls, 297
page grabber hand, 136
page icons, Document Layout palette, 45
page insert, in double-sided documents, 364–368
page insertion, automatic, 85, 138–139
page layout, advanced techniques, 351–377
page margins, master, 113–114
Page menu, 46, 51
  Delete, 123
  Display, 113
  Insert, 121–122
  Master Guides, 58, 113–114
  Move, 124
  Section, 127–130
page number, 39–40, 116
  characters, tag codes, 399
  current, 125–127
  Document Layout palette, 45
  displaying, 129–130
  format, sections, 127–130
  prefix, 127–130
  references, search, 186
  referencing, 129–130
  starting page in double-sided document, 364–368
page numbering, 127–130
page range, printing, 300–301
page size, 57–60
  changing, 59–60
  in template, 339
  oversized documents, 314–315
page view percentage, 39–40, 65–70
page, applying master pages, 117–120
page, saving as EPS, 242
Page Up key, 126
pages, document, 34–35
  adding, 120–122
  blank, 45, 364–368
  copying between documents, 125
  deleting, 123
  facing, 62–63
  master, 34–35, 109–120
  moving, 123–125
  spreads, 368–370
  turning, 46, 125–127
  view on screen, 65–70
paint graphics, 86, 239

palettes, 39–48
  Colors, 46–47, 166–167, 274–279
  displaying, 70
  Document Layout, 45–46, 111–120
  Measurements, 43–45, 75–76
    anchored items, 101
    character formatting, 162–163
    color, 81
  Style Sheets, 46
  Trap Information, 47–48, 283–285
PANTONE colors, 268, 271–272
paper edge, on screen, 39–40
paper offset, 297
paper orientation, 296
paper roll, printing, 297
paper size, 59, 291–292, 296
paper type, 291–292
paper source, 297
paper width, 297
paragraph attributes, tags, 396–398
paragraph breaks, 153
  keep with next, 173
  search, 186
paragraph format, copying, 175
Paragraph Formats command and dialog box, 168–173, 202–208
  drop caps, 223–224
  hyphenation, 212
  leading, 203–207
paragraph formatting, 168–183
  indentation, 170–172
  keyboard shortcuts, 477–482
  ruled lines, 224–225
  spacing, 172
  style sheets, 37–38, 178–183
paragraph returns, removing extra, 380–382
Paragraph Rules dialog box, 224–225
paragraph, new, 176–177
Paragraph Tabs dialog box, 173–176
Paste command, 30, 86–87
Paste Link, 31–32, 247–248
Paste Special, 31–32, 247–248
Pasteboard, 48, 352
  width, changing, 135
pasted text box, 158
pasting text, 158
percentage page view, 39–40, 65–70, 144
percentage screen, 81
photo placeholders, 424–425
Photoshop, 240
picas, 44–45, 138
PICT format (from Macintosh), 86, 240–241
Picture Box Shape submenu, 231

Picture Box Specifications dialog box, 230, 249
   defaults, 145
   size and position, 76–78
pictures boxes, 35–36
   creating, 71–72
   creating two defaults, 424–425
   modifying, 229–231
   tools, 41, 43
Picture Contrast Specifications dialog box, 254–257
picture import, 85–86, 238–260
   automatic, 140
Picture Mover pointer, 248–249
Picture Screening Specifications dialog box, 259
Picture Usage dialog box, 312–314
pictures, 227–260
   advanced techniques, 423–443
   applying color, 274–279
   color and contrast, 251–257
   greeked on screen, 142
   large files, 312–314
   manipulating imported, 248–260
   moving within a box, 250–251
   rotating, 251
   skewing, 251
pictures—see graphics
Plates, printing, 304
points, 44–45, 138
Points/Inch formula, changing, 141
Polygon Picture Box tool, 41, 43, 71–72
   text runaround, 91–92
   drawing tips, 428–431
   reshaping, 232–233
   special effects, 431–433
position of items, 74–78
position, using rulers, 88–90
posterization, 254–257
posterizer tool, 256
PostScript fonts, 307–308
   loading, 196–197
PostScript graphics, color separating, 285–287
PostScript printer options, 298–299
PostScript version of document, 306
Preferences, Application, 132–137
preferences, automatic, 143–144
preferences, changing, 132–145
Preferences file (XPress Preferences), 447–448
Preferences, General, 137–143
   font vectoring option, 197
Preferences, Tools, 144–145
Preferences, Typographic, 143–144, 197–202
   kerning, 219–222

preview, pictures, 85–86
print area, 316
Print command and dialog box, 300–305
Print Status dialog box, 304–305
Printer Description Files, 448–449, 295
printer drivers, 448–449
   adding, 295
printer fonts, 291, 307–308
printer information, 448–449
printer options, 298–299
printer resolution, 297
printer type, choosing, 295
printer, Control panel, 293–295
printer, target, 293–295
Printer Setup command, 296–299
Printer Type pop-up menu list, 448–449
printers, differences, 290–292
printing, 289–325
   blank pages, 302
   graphics, suppressing, 230
   master pages, 307
   problems, diagnosing, 317–325
   reductions or enlargements, 298–299, 314–315
   resolution, 290–291
   roughs, 301
   spreads, 302
   thumbnails, 301
   tiled pages, 303–304, 315–316
printing, high resolution, 312–314
printing, stopping, 305
process color, 263
process trap, 134–135, 281
Program Manager, 456–459
program directory, 446–448
program icon, 32
program version, 53–54
project directory, 450–452
proofs, color, 263, 292
publication directory, 450–452

Q

QuarkXPress library—see library
QuarkXPress program directory, 446–448
QuarkXPress tag codes, 156, 389–394
QuarkXPress, Macintosh version, 23
Quit command, 107
quotation marks, 202
   converting imported, 84, 156

R

RAM (memory), 104
rational tangent screening, 265

rectangle tools, 41, 43
Rectangular Picture Box tool, 41, 43, 71–72
reductions, printing, 298–299, 314–315
registration color, 279
registration marks, 59, 302
   offset, 135
   and bleeds, 369–370
relationships between items, 95–104
repeat count, in duplicating, 93
resizing items, 74–78
resolution, printer, 297
resolution, printing, 290–291, 312–314, 320
resolution, TIFF display, 136, 243
resource management, 456–459
reverse type, 418–419
Revert to Saved command, 106
RGB color model, 268–269
rotating items, 78–79
rotating pictures, 251
rotating text, 419–420
Rotation tool, 41–42, 78–79
rough designs, 330–334
rough output, 301
roughs, 329–350
Rounded–corner Rectangle Picture Box tool, 41, 43, 71–72
ruled lines, paragraph attribute, 224–225
   special effects, 427–428
ruler guides, 36–37, 89–90
   viewing, 69–70
ruler, text, 170–176
rulers, 88–90
   displaying, 69–70
   in template, 341
   origin, 88
   setting zero point, 139
   units of measure, 138
rules, anchoring, 99–101
rules, applying color, 274–279
Runaround command and dialog box, 91–92
   Invert option, 91–92
   mode, 91–92
   preferences, 145
runaround polygon, 91–92, 370–373
   text inside, 421–422
runaround text, 91–92, 370–373
   leading, 200
runaround, lines, 234
running header/footer—see header, footer

S

Save command and dialog box, 104–106
Save Text command and dialog box, 192–193
save page as EPS, 242
saving documents, 104–107
saving templates, 335–336
scaling imported graphics, 249–250
   keyboard shortcuts, 249–250
   scale across, 249
   scale down, 249
scaling percentage, printing, 298–299
scanned images, 243
   color separating, 285–287
scanning applications, 243–244
Scitex VIP, 465
screen angle, 260
   color separations, 264–266
screen display of fonts, 141–142
screen display, levels of gray, 136
screen DPI, 137
screen draw method, 136
screen fonts, 307–308
   loading, 196–197
screen pattern, 260
screen percentage, text, 167–168
screen percentages, 81
screen resolution, TIFF, 243
screen settings, pre–defined, 257–260
   custom, 259
screens, halftones, 257–260, 264–266
scroll bars, 26–27, 65–70
   turning pages, 126
scroll speed, 137
scroll, live, 135
search, global, 183–188
   special characters, 380–388
   wild cards, 394–395
Section command and dialog box, 127–130
Select All command, 72–74
selecting items, 72–74
   multiple items, 72–74
   one item, 72–73
   through layers, 94
selecting text, 159–161
Send Backward command, 94
Send to Back command, 94
separations, printing, 304–305
serial number, QuarkXPress, 53–54
service bureaus, using, 314
shade (color), 80–81
   frame, 82
   lines, 237–238
   text, 167–168

Shade submenu, text, 167–168
shadow type, 417
shortcuts—see keyboard shortcuts
Show/Hide Baseline Grid, 69–70, 199, 206
Show/Hide Colors, 46–47, 70
Show/Hide Document Layout Palette, 45–46, 70, 111–120
Show/Hide Guides, 69–70
Show/Hide Invisibles, 69–70, 176
Show/Hide Measurements, 70
Show/Hide Rulers, 69–70, 88–89
Show/Hide Style Sheets, 70
Show/Hide Tools, 40–45, 70
Show/Hide Trap Information, 47–48, 70, 283–285
single–sided document, 62–63
   master page, 111
   page insertion, 120–122
Size command, 164–165
size (window) buttons, 26–27
size of file, optimum, 452–453
size of items, 74–78
size, font, 163–164
size, graphics files, 312–314
size, paper, 291–292
   vs. page, 296
sizing items, 74–78
skewing pictures, 251
slanted margin, 371
slash fractions, 202
slide recorders, 292
small caps preferences, 198
Snap to Guides command, 90
snap distance, changing, 141
snap–to effect, 36–37, 90
snap–to guides, 355–356
space before/after paragraphs, 172
space character, 153
space, flexible, 200
Space/Align command and dialog box, 95, 356–357
   bar chart, 438–440
spacing adjustments in text, 410–414
spacing—see kerning, tracking, leading, justification, paragraph spacing
special characters, typing, 151–153
   finding and changing, 380–388
   invisibles, 176–177
   searching for, 186
   tabs, 174
   tag codes, 399–400
   typographic, 202
special effects, typographic, 222–225, 414–422
special typographic characters, 202

spelling check, 188–192
spot color, 263
spreads, 39–40, 62–63, 121, 368–370
spreads, printing, 297, 302
spreadsheet data import, 157–158
starting a new document, 55–108
starting QuarkXPress, 32–33
Step and Repeat command and dialog box, 93
   bar chart, 436
story, text, 95–99
style, frame, 82
Style menu, 50
   color, 81
   lines, 234
   pictures, 251–257
Style menu (text), 162
   Baseline Shift, 207
      anchored items, 99–100
   Character, color, 274–279
   Color, 274–279
      text, 166–167
   Font, 163–164
   Formats, hyphenation, 212
   High Contrast, 254–257
   Horizontal Scale, 222–223
   Kern, 216–217
   Negative, 255
   Normal Contrast, 254–257
   Paragraph Formats, 202–208
   Posterized, 254–257
   Rules, 224–225
      color, 274–279
   Shade submenu, text, 167–168
   Size, 164–165
   Tabs, 173–176
   Track, 216–217
   Type Style, 165–166
      Small Caps, 198
   Character, baseline shift, 207
style sheets, 37–38, 178–183
   applying, 181–183
   based on style, 180
   benefits, 404–406
   creating and editing, 179–181
   default, 447
   defining, 180
   deleting, 182
   duplicating, 182
   for headings, 409
   importing, 84, 156, 179
   in template, 345
   keyboard equivalent, 180–182, 407
   merging two sets, 182–183
   names, 180, 407–408
   tips, 404–410

Style Sheets command and dialog box, 178–183
  alternative, 46
Style Sheets palette, 46, 181–182
  opens Edit Style Sheets dialog box, 179
style, type, 165–166
subscript preferences, 198
Suggested Hyphenation command and dialog box, 214
superior characters, 165–166
  preferences, 199
superscript, 165–166
  preferences, 198
Suppress Printout, pictures, 230
swatch books, color, 270–271
Symbol font, 152
symbols, 152, 202
  typing, 151–153
system requirements, 4
system resources, 456–459

T

tab character, 153
  icons, 174
  search, 186
  viewing, 176
tab fill character, 175
tables, imported from Microsoft Word, 157
tabloid sizes, 303–304
Tabs command, 173–176
tabs, 173–176
tabular columns, alignment, 354
tabular format, converting data files, 382–389
tag codes, 84, 156–157, 389–394
  listed, 395–397
Tagged Image File Format—see TIFF
target printer, 293–295
telecommunicated text import, 157–158, 380–382
templates, 38, 64–65
  benefits, 336–338
  creating, 338–350
  design, 329–350
  instructions, 349
  repeated items, 345–348
  saving, 104–107, 335–336
text, baseline, 204–207
text box jump character, 153
Text Box Specifications dialog box
  defaults, 145
  baseline, 204–205
  size and position, 76–78
Text Box tool, 41, 43, 71–72, 148–149

text boxes, 35–36
  anchoring, 99–101
  automatic, 63–64, 97, 113–115
  creating and formatting, 148–149
  jumps, 360–362
  linking, 95–99
  linking filled boxes, 358–360
  new box character, 176–177
  page number, 129–130
  pasting, 158
  width calculation, 340
text chain, 36, 95–99
text color, 166–167
text, deleting, 86–87
text entry in dialog box, 26–27
text export, 192–193
text, finding/changing, 183–188
text format,
  alignment, 169–170
  alignment tips, 354
  applying color, 274–279
  ASCII tag codes, 84
  character format, 161–168
  default, 150, 157–158
  font, 163–164
  horizontal scaling, 222–223
  indentation, 170–172
  inset, 82, 148–149
  inside a shape, 372, 421–422
  keep lines together, 173
  kerning, 215–222
  leading, 203–208
  paragraph formatting, 168–183
  spacing, adjusting, 410–414
  special effects, 414–422
  style sheets, 178–183
  tag codes, 395–397
  tracking, 215–222
  vertical alignment, 207
  white on black, 418–419
text, greeking on screen, 141–142
text import, 83–85, 153–158
  formatted, 157
  from databases and mainframes, 379–400
  from library, 158
  unformatted, 157–158
text overflow, 84, 95–99
text, pasting, 158
text, rotating, 419–420
text ruler, 170–176
text rules, 224–225
text runaround, 91–92, 370–373
  inside a polygon, 421–422
  Invert option, 91–92
  lines, 234

text selection shortcuts, 160–161
text, selecting and editing, 159–161
text, sources of, 149–159
text, typing, 149–153
text, typography, 195–226
text, word processing, 147–193
text wrap, around items, 91–92
thumbnail preview, pictures, 85–86
Thumbnails view, 67
   alternative, 46
   moving pages, 123
thumbnails, printing, 301
   design ideas, 332
TIFF graphics, 86, 303
   conversions, 243
   display option, 136
   files, 243–244
   format, 243
   image, contrast, 254–257
Tiling option, 59, 303–304, 315–316
tint, text, 167–168
title bar, 26–27
Tool palette, 40–45
tools, 35–36
   drawing tools, 41, 43, 228–238
   editing tools, 41–42
   item creation tools, 71–72
   linking tools, 95–99
   Rotation tool, 78–79
   selecting, 41
   Zoom tool, 65–70
Tools Preferences dialog box, 144–145
tracking, 215–222
   keyboard shortcuts, 217
Tracking Edit command and dialog box, 218–219
tracking edit values, XPress Preferences, 447
tracking headings, 409
Tracking Values chart, 218–219
   editing, 218–219
Trap Information palette, 47–48, 283–285
Trap Specifications dialog box, 134–135, 281–283
trapping specifications, 47–48
   colors, 280–287
   controls, 273–274
   preferences, 134–135
   trap value, 134–135, 282–285
troubleshooting printing problems, 317–325
TrueType fonts, 197
TRUMATCH colors, 268, 272
turning pages, 125–127
Type 1 PostScript fonts, 197

Type 3 PostScript fonts, 197
type managers, 308
type specifications, 161–168, 195–226
   default, 157–158
   style sheets, 37–38, 178–183
   tips, 401–422
type style, 165–166
   reverse (white), 418–419
   shadow effect, 417
Type Style submenu, 165–166
   keyboard shortcuts, 166
   Small Caps, 198
type, printing problems, 321–325
typewriters, forms for, 373–376
type—see fonts
typing invisible characters, 153
typing symbols, 151–153
typing text, 149–153
typographic effects, 414–422
Typographic Preferences dialog box, 143–144, 197–202
   kerning, 219–222
typographic special effects, 222–225
typography, 195–226
   special characters, 202
   tips, 401–422

U

underscores, 403
Undo command, 86–87
unit of measure, 44–45
   in template, 341
   rulers, 89
Unlinking tool, 41, 43, 95–99, 115
Unlock command, 104
Utilities menu, 52
   Auxiliary Dictionary, 191–192
   Check Spelling, 188–192
   Font Usage, 311
   Hyphenation Exceptions, 215
   Kerning Table Edit, 219–222
   Library, 130–132, 346–347
   Picture Usage, 312–314
   Suggested Hyphenation, 214
   Tracking Edit, 218–219

V

Vector Above point size, 141
version, QuarkXPress, 53–54
vertical alignment, text, 207
vertical grid, creating, 355
vertical measure, 138
vertical ruler guides, 89–90
View menu, 50, 65–70
   Actual Size, 67

Fit in Window, 67
Show/Hide Baseline Grid, 69–70, 199, 206
Show/Hide Colors, 46–47, 70
Show/Hide Document Layout Palette, 45–46, 70, 111–120
Show/Hide Guides, 69–70
Show/Hide Invisibles, 69–70, 176
Show/Hide Measurements, 70
Show/Hide Rulers, 69–70, 88–89
Show/Hide Style Sheets, 70
Show/Hide Tools, 40–45
Show/Hide Trap Information, 47–48, 70, 283–285
Snap to Guides, 90
Thumbnails, 67
View Percent, 39–40, 65–70, 144
viewing grayscale images, 243–244
viewing links, 98
viewing pages on screen, 65–70
viewing tab characters, 176
VINES, 453
virgule (fraction slash), 202
Visionary, 465

W

width, box, 76–78
width, flex space, 200
width, frame, 82
wild cards in search, 186, 394–395
WIN.INI, fonts, 309–310
window size buttons, 26–27
Window, Fit in, 67
windows, 26–27, 39–40
   closing, 107
Windows applications, 14–15
Windows Control Panel, printers, 293–295
Windows Directory, 448–449
Windows environment, 23–53
Windows Error Handler, 325
Windows menu, 52
Windows metafile graphics, 240
Windows Program Manager, 456–459
Windows text selection, 160
Windows versions, 24
Word—see Microsoft
Word Count dialog box, 190
Word Perfect, 157
word processing, 147–193
word processing applications, 14
word spacing, 412–414
workgroups, 453–456

X

XPress Dictionary, 188–192, 446
XPress Help file, 446
XPress Preferences file, 215, 447–448
XPress tags, 156–157, 389–394
   filter, 395
   list, 395–397
XyWrite, 157

Z

Zapf Dingbats, 152
zero point, changing, 139
zero point, in tiling, 315–316
zero point, rulers, 88
Zoom tool, 41–42, 65–70
   preferences, 144